A commentary on the first fifteen, and part of the sixteenth articles of the Church of England. By William Nicholls, D.D.

William Nicholls

A commentary on the first fifteen, and part of the sixteenth articles of the Church of England. By William Nicholls, D.D.
Nicholls, William
ESTCID: T056126
Reproduction from British Library

London : printed in the year, 1712.
[2],98p. ; 2°

Gale ECCO Print Editions

Relive history with *Eighteenth Century Collections Online*, now available in print for the independent historian and collector. This series includes the most significant English-language and foreign-language works printed in Great Britain during the eighteenth century, and is organized in seven different subject areas including literature and language; medicine, science, and technology; and religion and philosophy. The collection also includes thousands of important works from the Americas.

The eighteenth century has been called "The Age of Enlightenment." It was a period of rapid advance in print culture and publishing, in world exploration, and in the rapid growth of science and technology – all of which had a profound impact on the political and cultural landscape. At the end of the century the American Revolution, French Revolution and Industrial Revolution, perhaps three of the most significant events in modern history, set in motion developments that eventually dominated world political, economic, and social life.

In a groundbreaking effort, Gale initiated a revolution of its own: digitization of epic proportions to preserve these invaluable works in the largest online archive of its kind. Contributions from major world libraries constitute over 175,000 original printed works. Scanned images of the actual pages, rather than transcriptions, recreate the works ***as they first appeared.***

Now for the first time, these high-quality digital scans of original works are available via print-on-demand, making them readily accessible to libraries, students, independent scholars, and readers of all ages.

For our initial release we have created seven robust collections to form one the world's most comprehensive catalogs of 18th century works.

Initial Gale ECCO Print Editions collections include:

History and Geography
Rich in titles on English life and social history, this collection spans the world as it was known to eighteenth-century historians and explorers. Titles include a wealth of travel accounts and diaries, histories of nations from throughout the world, and maps and charts of a world that was still being discovered. Students of the War of American Independence will find fascinating accounts from the British side of conflict.

Social Science

Delve into what it was like to live during the eighteenth century by reading the first-hand accounts of everyday people, including city dwellers and farmers, businessmen and bankers, artisans and merchants, artists and their patrons, politicians and their constituents. Original texts make the American, French, and Industrial revolutions vividly contemporary.

Medicine, Science and Technology

Medical theory and practice of the 1700s developed rapidly, as is evidenced by the extensive collection, which includes descriptions of diseases, their conditions, and treatments. Books on science and technology, agriculture, military technology, natural philosophy, even cookbooks, are all contained here.

Literature and Language

Western literary study flows out of eighteenth-century works by Alexander Pope, Daniel Defoe, Henry Fielding, Frances Burney, Denis Diderot, Johann Gottfried Herder, Johann Wolfgang von Goethe, and others. Experience the birth of the modern novel, or compare the development of language using dictionaries and grammar discourses.

Religion and Philosophy

The Age of Enlightenment profoundly enriched religious and philosophical understanding and continues to influence present-day thinking. Works collected here include masterpieces by David Hume, Immanuel Kant, and Jean-Jacques Rousseau, as well as religious sermons and moral debates on the issues of the day, such as the slave trade. The Age of Reason saw conflict between Protestantism and Catholicism transformed into one between faith and logic -- a debate that continues in the twenty-first century.

Law and Reference

This collection reveals the history of English common law and Empire law in a vastly changing world of British expansion. Dominating the legal field is the *Commentaries of the Law of England* by Sir William Blackstone, which first appeared in 1765. Reference works such as almanacs and catalogues continue to educate us by revealing the day-to-day workings of society.

Fine Arts

The eighteenth-century fascination with Greek and Roman antiquity followed the systematic excavation of the ruins at Pompeii and Herculaneum in southern Italy; and after 1750 a neoclassical style dominated all artistic fields. The titles here trace developments in mostly English-language works on painting, sculpture, architecture, music, theater, and other disciplines. Instructional works on musical instruments, catalogs of art objects, comic operas, and more are also included.

The BiblioLife Network

This project was made possible in part by the BiblioLife Network (BLN), a project aimed at addressing some of the huge challenges facing book preservationists around the world. The BLN includes libraries, library networks, archives, subject matter experts, online communities and library service providers. We believe every book ever published should be available as a high-quality print reproduction; printed on-demand anywhere in the world. This insures the ongoing accessibility of the content and helps generate sustainable revenue for the libraries and organizations that work to preserve these important materials.

The following book is in the "public domain" and represents an authentic reproduction of the text as printed by the original publisher. While we have attempted to accurately maintain the integrity of the original work, there are sometimes problems with the original work or the micro-film from which the books were digitized. This can result in minor errors in reproduction. Possible imperfections include missing and blurred pages, poor pictures, markings and other reproduction issues beyond our control. Because this work is culturally important, we have made it available as part of our commitment to protecting, preserving, and promoting the world's literature.

GUIDE TO FOLD-OUTS MAPS and OVERSIZED IMAGES

The book you are reading was digitized from microfilm captured over the past thirty to forty years. Years after the creation of the original microfilm, the book was converted to digital files and made available in an online database.

In an online database, page images do not need to conform to the size restrictions found in a printed book. When converting these images back into a printed bound book, the page sizes are standardized in ways that maintain the detail of the original. For large images, such as fold-out maps, the original page image is split into two or more pages

Guidelines used to determine how to split the page image follows:

- Some images are split vertically; large images require vertical and horizontal splits.
- For horizontal splits, the content is split left to right.
- For vertical splits, the content is split from top to bottom.
- For both vertical and horizontal splits, the image is processed from top left to bottom right.

A COMMENTARY

On the First Fifteen, and Part of the Sixteenth

ARTICLES

OF THE

CHURCH of *ENGLAND.*

By *WILLIAM NICHOLLS*, D. D.

LONDON:
Printed in the YEAR MDCCXII.

A COMMENTARY on the ARTICLES OF THE CHURCH of *ENGLAND*.

King Edward *the VIth's* ARTICLES

* *Articles agreed upon by the Bishops, and other Learned and good Men in the*

The ARTICLES

Articles whereupon it was agreed by the Archbishops and Byshops of both Provinces, and the whole Cleargie, in

ARTICULI

Articuli de quibus convenit inter Archiepiscopos & Episcopos, utriusq; Provinciæ, & Clerum universum in Synodo Londini, Anno

* *Articles agreed upon by the Bishops and other Learned and good Men in the Convocation held at* London *in the Year* 1552.] It is become a Controversy whether these Articles of King *Edward* were really drawn up in Convocation, as the Title seems to import, or only by Archbishop *Cranmer* and *Ridley*, and this Title put to them, to make them pass the more current. The former Opinion is maintained by Dr *Heylin* and Dr *Atterbury*, the latter by Bishop *Burnet*. The Bishop's Arguments for his Opinion, are these. (1.) The Corruptions of the Church of *Rome*, condemn'd by these Articles, were so *Beneficial to the whole Body of the Clergy, that without a Miracle they could not be agreed to by a Major part*, i. e. of the Convocation. Introd. to the Expos. on 29 Art. (2.) That there was the like Art used in setting forth *Ponnet*'s Catechism, and for this he vouches the Acknowledgement of *Philpot*, and Archbishop *Cranmer* himself. For thus *Philpot* speaks, *Concerning the Article of the Catechism, I think you are deceived in the Title of the Catechism, in that it beareth the Title of the Synod of* London, *last before this, although many of them which were then present, were never made privy thereof in setting it forth, for that this House had granted the Authority unto certain Persons to be appointed by the King's Majesty*, &c. *Fox* Vol. III. p. 20. But the Bishop of *Sarum* is willing to allow *Philpot*'s Evidence, but not his Reason upon it, saying, *That* Philpot *alledged this, being prest with an Objection, to which he had no other Answer ready, he knew there was such a Commission, and therefore he fancied he had prepared these Books*. To this he adds the Testimony of Archbishop *Cranmer*, concerning the said Catechism, in his Examination before the Convocation in *Oxford*, where *Weston* the Prolocutor objected to him in these Words. West. *Also you have set forth a Catechism in the Name of the Synod in* London, *and yet there be Fifty which Witnessing that they were of the number of the Convocation, never heard one word of this Catechism*. Cran. *I was ignorant of the setting to of that Title, and as soon as I had knowledge thereof, I did not like it. Therefore when I complained thereof to the Council, it was answered me by them, that the Book was so intituled, because it was set forth in the time of Convocation*. Fox Vol. III. p. 80. The Bishop of *Sarum* cites the further Testimony of Archbishop *Cranmer*, in the Interrogatories put to him, in order to his final Censure. Inter. *Item, That the said* Thomas Cranmer, &c. *did compile, and caused to be set abroad diverse Books*. Answ. *As for the Catechism, the Book of Articles, with the other Book against* Winchester, *he granted the same to be his doings*. Fox Vol. III. p. 656. These Proofs the Bishop thinks so strong, *that they decide the Point, so that it will admit of no more Debate*, Vid. Bp. Sar. Reflections on the Rights of Convocation.

Dr *Atterbury* on the other side contends, that these Articles were passed either by the whole Body of the Convocation, or by a Committee. As to the Bishop's Argument, that the major Part of the Synod could not have agreed to them without a Miracle, he answers, *That the Acts of another Synod, ten Years afterwards, assure us such a Miracle was done*. And for this he cites a Copy of the Acts of the Convocation, 1562, written in a Hand of *the time*, and taken from the Registers of that Convocation soon after it sate, giving an Account of the Proceedings of every Day. And in the 19th of *January* are these words. *Et* (Prolocutor) *ulterius proposuit quod Articuli in Synodo Londinensi tempore nuper Regis Edwardi sexti editi, traditi sint quibusdam aliis viris ex cœtu dicti Domus Inferioris, ad hoc etiam electis, ut eos diligenter perspiciant, examinent & considerent, ac prout iis visum fuerit, corrigant & reforment*. *And the Prolocutor further proposed, that the Articles set forth by the Synod of* London, *in the time of* Edward *VI.* &c. *Att. Rights*, &c. p. 379. This Journal, the Bishop says, *deserves no Credit, but is a plain Forgery*, but he does not tell us against whom the Charge is laid, nor upon what Reasons it is grounded.

Dr *Heylin* is of an Opinion not different from that of Dr *Atterbury*, and says, 'That it may be concluded, 'that the Convocation had devolved their Power on some 'grand Committee, sufficiently Authoriz'd to Debate, Con'clude and Publish what they had concluded in the name of 'the rest. And being so impower'd to that end and purpose, 'the Articles by them concluded and agreed upon, may war'rantably be affirm'd to be the Acts and Products of the 'Convocation, confirm'd and establish'd for such by the 'King's Authority, as appears further by the Title, *viz.* '*Regia Authoritate editi*, and for this quotes the foremen'tion'd words of *Philpot*, *That the said House had granted the* '*Authority to make Ecclesiastical Laws*, &c. spoken with 'relation to the Catechism. This he says may be also the 'Case of the Book of Articles, which may be truly and 'justly said to be the work of the Convocation tho' ma'ny Members of it never saw the same. Adding, 'Had

last Convocation held at London, *in the*

the Convocation holden at London, *in the Year of our Lorde God* 1562, *according*

1562 *secundum computationem Ecclesiæ Anglicanæ, ad tollendam O-*

it been otherwise, King *Edward*, a most Pious and Religious Prince, must needs be looked on as a wicked and lewd Impostor, in putting such a horrible Cheat upon all his Subjects, by fathering these Articles on the Convocation, which begat them not, nor ever gave consent to them. And yet it is not altogether improbable, but that these Articles being Debated and Agreed upon by the said Committee, might also pass the Vote of the whole Convocation, tho' we find nothing in the Acts thereof, which either have been lost, or were never Registred. Besides it is to be observed that the Church of *England*, for the first five Years of Queen *Elizabeth*, retained these Articles, and none other, as the publick Tenets of the Church, in point of Doctrine, which certainly she never had done, had they been commended to her by less Authority than a Convocation'.

To give my Opinion freely concerning these opposite Sentiments, I think the latter is the most Charitable, and the most Reasonable. For the Rules of our Religion forbid us to tax any one with a Crime, especially to load none as a Forgery, without such evident Proof and Notoriety of Fact, as is next to Demonstration. Which Rules bind yet closer, when the Persons accused demand, not only Respect and Gratitude from us, but the exposing their Imperfections strikes at our Religion, and gives occasion to our common Enemies to Blaspheme. With Submission to his Lordship, I think it was a little too severe to tax Dr *Atterbury*, or the Writer of the MSS he quotes, with Forgery, but to Charge such a shuffling Trick upon a pious Prince and his Ministry, to whom we owe the Benefits of our Reformation, and upon the most Eminent of the Protestant Clergy, many of which laid down their Lives for our common Religion, is a Degree of Incaution, which one would not have expected from his Lordship's Prudence and Moderation. Nor do I think that his Lordships Reasonings *have so decided this Point, that it will admit of no more Debate*. I am humbly of Opinion, that some things have drop'd from his Lordship's Pen in this Point, which have happened to perplex it more than it was before. What Dr *Atterbury* advanced, in Proof of the regular passing these Articles in King *Edward*'s Reign, from the Journal he cited, has brought to light an Authority which had lain unobserv'd before, and deserv'd a further Consideration, than to throw it off by saying, *it is a plain Forgery*. For the words which he cites are not only found in the Transcript he made use of, but in the very Original Acts themselves, as I find them published by Dr *Gibson* in his *Synodus Anglicana*, p. 192. without the variation of a Letter or Syllable. So that the Evidence produced by Dr. *Atterbury* still stands good, notwithstanding his Lordship's Impeachment, and we have the Authority of the Convocation of 1562, to prove that the first Edition of the Articles were in *Synodo Londinensi tempore super Regis Edwardi Sexti edita*, the plain English of which is, that they were either passed in Convocation at *London*, or at least drawn up by order of Convocation. But supposing the Trick had been play'd, which his Lordship suggests, would Queen *Elizabeth*'s Convocation have ventur'd to have overhal'd this Matter again, ten Years after, and have vindicated a Fraud, which was notorious to all the Popish Bishops and Clergy, who being turned out of their Preferments, would never have spared them, could they have had such an Advantage against them? If the Convocation of 1562 had been conscious, of any such indirect Practice of the Protestant Clergy in King *Edward*'s time, they would have pass'd the whole matter over in silence, they would have composed a New Set of Articles themselves, without any Relation had to the old Book, and not have gone about to have vindicated a Fraud, which must tend only to their own Disgrace, and this too when there was no occasion for it, and they might as well have gone on upon their work, without it.

Neither do I think that Archdeacon *Philpot*'s Evidence, in this Point is so little weight as his Lordship is pleased to allow it, and that he only *alledged it as, being pressed with an Objection to which he had no other Answer ready*. There is nothing in all Mr *Philpot*'s Character, which can make us suspect him to have given a prevaricating or insincere Answer, on account of the hardest Objection that he could be pressed with. He was a Gentleman by Extraction, and a Man of good Sense, that he wanted neither Honesty nor Courage, is plain from his dying for his Religion, and therefore we may be sure, he would never solemnly attest any thing to be true, which he was not certain of the Truth of. But I do not find that *Philpot* was pressed by any thing relating to the Articles, or that he was pressed by any thing else. The Convocation meeting the first of Queen *Mary*, *Octob.* 20, 1553, Resolved upon two Points. First, *That Christ was natural present in the Sacrament of the Altar*. Secondly, *That the Catechism set forth in the last of King Edward, was not of that House' Agreement set forth*, and immediately fell to Subscribing to the Truth of these two Propositions. This was indeed hot headed work, to Resolve and Subscribe, without either Proof or Debate. Therefore Mr Archdeacon *Philpot* voluntarily stood up in his place, and told them, that this Catechism was set forth by the Committee for Ecclesiastical Laws. *And in this Point he thought the Setters-forth thereof nothing to have slandered the House, as they by their Subjects, one set about to perswade the World, fact they had been Synodal authority, unto them committed on the high Spirit always thought convenient and* [illegible]. Fox Vol. II. p. 20. But still all this is with relation to the Catechism, and not to the Articles. The Articles indeed and the Catechism were printed together in 1553, but in the Title of the Book they are clearly distinguished from each other. *Catechismus Brevis, Christianæ Disciplinæ summam continens, omnibus Ludi Magistris Authoritate Regia commendatus. Huic Catechismo adjuncti sunt Articuli, &c.* Lond. cum Privileg. Serenissi. Regis A. D. MDLIII. Here, you may see that Archbishop *Cranmer* took care, in the *Latin* Edition of the Catechism, that it should be attributed only to the Royal Authority, and not to that of Convocation. Upon the whole it seems not improbable, that the Articles should have passed the whole House, or at least that they were more publickly treated of in the Committee for Ecclesiastical Laws, than the Catechism. For the Popish Convocation never ventures to arraign the Articles, but always the Catechism, as appears before in the Citation out of *Cranmer*'s Tryal, *We have set forth a Catechism*, &c. Therefore to be sure the Articles had some clearer Authority of the Synod than the Catechism, for since the Articles must needs grieve them more, they being forced by the King's Injunction to subscribe to them, yet, notwithstanding this, they have nothing to say against these hated Articles, but are forced to wreck all their Spleen against a poor Catechism.

As to Archbishop *Cranmer*'s complaining to the Council of the false Title, this likewise relates to the Catechism, for there is not a word of the Articles in all that Relation in *Fox*.

As to Archbishop *Cranmer*'s making Answer, *That as for the Catechism, the Book of Articles with the other Book against* Winchester, *he grants them to be his doings*, we may say that this does not hinder, but that the Convocation might have a hand in some of them likewise. The Archbishop might call them *his doings*, because he first proposed them to the Convocation, or, when regularly passed the Convocation, they might be attributed to him who was President thereof, as all our Provincial Constitutions bear the Name of the Archbishops who presided in the Convocations, wherein the Canons were made. And in this Sense *Constitutiones Peckam, Islep, Arundel*, &c. are *the doings* of those several Archbishops.

This was such sufficient Proof of these Articles being, some way or other, passed in Convocation, as served to silence all Objections of the Papists, as satisfy'd the Convocation of 1562, held ten Years afterwards, and settled this Matter so as hardly any one ever since has ventured to Dispute it. The first Man that ever seem'd to question it, was *Fuller* in his Church-History, who in his trifling way says, *the Lower Convocation is entituled the Parent of the Articles of Religion*, and speaking of the Committee of Convocation before-mentioned, says, *the Convocation* (it seems *passed over their Power*, and that he *should be thankful to him who should produce the Original Instrument*, ridiculing, in his awkward way, the receiv'd Opinion of their being passed in Convocation, which he says, the King could not *trust*, they having *in the fan Rank of Protestant Profession, the rotten Core of Romish Superstition*. *Fuller*'s *Church History*, p. 420.

Dr *Heylin*, in his *Examen Historicum*, takes the trifling Man to task, shewing, That this was an impudent Arraignment of the King and Council, *That the King had no reason to have any such Jealousy at that time, of the major Part of the Clergy, but that he might trust them with Power to meddle with matters of Religion*. (*which is the only Argument which our Author bringeth against those Articles.*) *This Convocation being holden in the sixth Year of his Reign, when most of the Episcopal Sees,*

Year 1552, to root out the Discord of Opinions, and Establish | *to the Computation of the Church of* Englande, *for the avoyding of the* † *Diver-* | *pinionum dissensionem, & consensum in vera Religione firmandum Editi Authoritate fe-*

Sees and Pe n h I C hurches were filled with Men agreeable to h Desires, and ge aly conformable to the Form of Worship, th b, I e r 'aolish a And in Answer to hi Argument from the silence of the Acts, he says, *The Truth is, th t the Acts of Convocation during this King's whole Reign, and th fi s Year o Queen* Mary, *are very imperfect and ne t, most of t em being lost, a d amongst others, t of this present Yea , and yet one might conclude as strongly, th t my Mither died Childless because my Christning t t the P sh R g'ster, as that the Convocation of this Te r n s h n, b c se the Acts and Articles of t ere not entred in th Jo nal Book* Dean Hist p 122, 123 This perfectly stop'd F ller's Mouth, who in his Reply can say nothing to it Now since this was of force to confute the Author of the Objection, it had deserved some Consideration from those who have been Retailers of his Argument vid P.

† *Diversities of Opinions*] These Articles could no be designed to oblige all Perso is who are to Subscribe to them, that they should agree in every Point of Theology, which is controverted among Divines, that being a thing impossible, for Men will necessarily disagree in many of these things, according to the different Degrees of their Learning, and the several Courses of their Studies but that they should so far agree as to own their Satisfaction in those Points, which are expresly determined by plain words, in these Articles So that any Person who believes the Popish Doctrines of Purgatory, Transubstantiation, Invocation of Saints, &c cannot sincerely Subscribe to these Articles, which do expresly condemn those Doctrines And this is the Reason of this Expression, *for avoiding Diversity of Opinions, and for establishing Consent touching true Religion* For it would have been a great Blemish to our Reformation, to have a Minister in one Church preaching up the Doctrine of the Mass, and another against it, one Writing for the Worship of the Blessed Virgin, and another the direct contrary But, as for those Theological Points, which do not affect the main of Religion, which seldom of te themselves to be handled in Popular Discourses, and not being in these Articles expresly determined, the Clergy are as much at liberty, to entertain different Opinions from each other concerning them, as they were before

But then considerable Caution must be used herein, and Men must not indulge fanciful Glosses, and wiredraw the Words in the Articles to unreasonable Senses, to reconcile them to their particular Opinions I do not know that we have any Authentick Rule besides the general Laws of Interpretation to govern us in this matter, unless we will allow that in King *James* the Ist's Declaration to be one, (tho' I believe the Force of it did not, nor was design'd to extend beyond his time,) *That no Man thereafter should put his own S se or Comment to be the meaning of the Article but should take it in the Literal and Grammatical Sense* From this the Learned Bishop B er draws this Inference, *That an Article being conceived in such general words, that it can admit of different Literal and Grammatical Senses, even when the Senses are plainly contrary to each other, both Sides may Subscribe the Article with a good Conscience, and without any Equivocation* Introduct to h Exposition on the Thirty Nine Art p 6 These words have been the occasion of a great deal of Discourse and Controversy, and tho' possibly his Lordship may have in some Particulars extended his own Rule too far, yet I cannot but own, that upon the main this Rule holds true And tho' I am no ways concerned to vindicate the Bishop, yet this Assertion of his having been sometimes attack'd, I think, without due caution, I will venture to say something in Justification of that and add some further Rules, for the Explication of the Articles 1 It is very probable, that some of these Articles were purposely drawn up in general Terms, for the Satisfaction of Persons, who had different Sentiments, in some particular Points And this I think can be no doubt to any one who reads over the Names of those, who Compiled and first Subscribed to these Articles Some of them learn'd their Divinity from the Fathers, without any Relation had to the Doctrines of Modern Divines, some went upon the foot of *Luther*'s and *Melancthon*'s Doctrine, others that had been Exiles at *Geneva* were perfectly wedded to *Calvin*'s Divinity, and perhaps not a little to his Form of Church Discipline. Some were for a real, tho' undeterminable Presence in the Eucharist, whilst others thought Christ's Body was only there by Figure, or Representation Now can any one say that these several Persons held no diversity of Opinions or can any one think, that they would agree to the passing these Articles, but that they thought they *were in some respects general enough, but they might Subscribe them with a good Conscience, and without Equivocation* Now take this either with relation to King *Edward*'s or Queen *Elizabeth*'s Articles we shall find that the Drawers up of them were men of very different Opinions not only before, but after their Subscription to the Articles For the Truth of this I appeal either to the Writings of several of these Divines themselves, or to the Collections made out of them by *Montague* and *Prin*, *Heylin*, Bishop *Cosins*, &c But for the present, this may suffice *Dorman* wrote his Book against our Reformation not long after Queen *Elizabeth*'s Articles were published, wherein he says, that our Divines were not agreed about the Doctrine of the Real Presence, that *Cox*, *P* and *Rowl* for the Real Presence, and *G* d *London* against it, that Archbishop *P rker* being in the mean, maintained a third Opinion His Book was answered by Dr *Nowel*, who does not altogether deny the Charge, but will not allow it to amount to a Schism, as he taxes it in our Church He only says 'These were small 'matters in Comparison however he called them by the 'Name of Schism, and that they little troubled the State 'of the Church, whilst he named one as diverse from another 'in Opinion in one Point, and falsely surnamed one another 'to be a *Lutheran*' He disallows indeed the Imputation against the Archbishop, but owns the difference between the other two, reckoning it to be but a small matter Vid. Stripe's *Annals of Queen* Elizabeth, p 297 And if we consider *Tilbet*'s Petition against the Predestinarian Doctrine, and the qualifying Clauses then added, *both chosen in Christ out of Mankind*, and the leaving out the words *that the Decree of Predestination be unto us unknown*, and making the Sentence run, *Furthermore we must receive God's Promises in such wise, as they be generally set forth to us in Holy Scripture, and in our doings, that Will of God is to be followed, which we have expressly declared unto us in the Word of God* This does clearly shew, that it was the design of the Compilers of these Articles, to oblige the Subscribers only to some general Agreement, and not to force them all to consent to any one Particularity of Opinion And truly this is the Judgment of the most Learned and Zealous Defenders of our Church Men never taxed with any Laxity Latitude of Opinions, at least with Disfavour to the Church King *Charles* the Ist, I think, is an unexceptionable Authority in this Point, who in his Declaration published with the Articles 1630 says, *If even in these curious Points, in which the present Differences lie, most Men of all sorts take the Articles of the Church of* England *for them, then may be inferred, what the Right Reverend Bishop of* Chester *hath said, This rather gives Testimony of the great Wisdom and Moderation of the Church, which in Points doubtful and controverted, hath propounded only that which no Sober Man can make matter of Doubt, or Subject of Controversy* And again, *In these curious and unhappy Differences, which have for so many hundred Years in different Times and Places exercis'd the Church of Christ, we Will that all further curious search be laid aside, and these Disputes shut up in God's Promises, as they be generally set forth to us in Holy Scriptures*, and the general Meaning of *the Articles of the Church of* England Archbishop *Laud* says, *The Church of* England *never declared, that every one of her Articles are Fundamentals in the Faith, for it is one thing to say, no one of them is Superstitious or Erroneous, and quite another to say, every one of them is Fundamental* Laud against *Fisher*, § 14 Bishop *Bramhall* declares his Opinion on in this Point thus, *If it were not for this Disciplinarian Humour, which will admit no Latitude in Religion, but makes each Nicety a Fundamental, and every private Opinion an Article of Faith which prefers particular Errors before general Truths I doubt not but that all reformed Churches would easily be reconciled, Wherefore in such Points wherein men hold diversly of n Men (salva fidei compage) I would not take any Man's Liberty from him, and humbly beseech all Men that they would not take mine from me* Bramhall's *Fair Warning* Bishop *Sanderson*, among

Some Articles purposely drawn up in general Terms.

Some of the Compilers of them of different Opinions.

That this was designed, the Opinion of the most Eminent Persons of our Church

the Agreement of true Religion *Published by the King's Authority*	*sities of Opinions, and for the Stablishing of consent touching true Religion. Put foorth by the Queens Authoritie.*	*Serenissimæ Reginæ Londini, apud Johannem Day, 1571* Titulus Artic. Ed VI Lat Articuli de quibus in Synodo Londinensi, A D 1552 ad tollendam Opinionum dissentionem & consensum veræ Religionis firmandum, inter Episcopos & alios eruditos Viros convenerat Regia authoritate in lucem Editi Excusum Londini apud Reginaldum Wolfium Regiæ Majestatis in Latinis Typographum A D M D L III

among his Directions for Peace, lays down this for one, *That particular Churches would be as tender as may be in giving their Definitions and Determinations, especially where there may be admitted* a Latitude of Dissenting, *without prejudice done either to the Substance of the Catholick Faith, or to the Tranquility of the Church, or to the Salvation of the Dissenter* Sand Pax Ecclesiæ Bishop *Sparrow* was as great a Lover of our Constitution as any one, and yet declares for a greater Liberty of Opinion, than most have done *In Controversies about Doctrines, wherein the Church has received no such clear Determination of either part from Christ and his Apostles, she hath Power to declare her own Sense in the Controversy, and to determine which part shall be received and profest for Truth by her Members, and that too under Ecclesiastical Penalty and Censure which they are accordingly bound to submit to, not as an infallible Verity, but as a probable Truth, and rest in her Determination, till it be made plain by as great or a greater Authority, that this her Determination is an Error, and if it shall appear to any of the Members to be an Error, or if they shall* think *it to be so by the weight of such Reasons as are privately suggested to them, yet they are still obliged to Silence and Peace, where the Decision of a particular Church is against the Doctrine of the Universal, not to profess in this case against the Churches Determination, because the professing such a controverted Truth is not necessary, but the Preservation of the Peace and Unity of the Church is* *Sparrow*'s Pref to his Collection Dr *Heylin* was never taxed for want of regard to the Constitution of the Church, and yet he expresses himself thus *Their* (i e the Compilers of the Articles) *Moderation was not less visible, in not stuffing the Book of Articles with all Conclusions Theological*, in which a Latitude of Judgment *was to be allow'd as far as might be with Peace and Charity As they omitted many whole Articles, and qualified the Expressions of some others, in King* Edward's Book, *so they were very sparing in Defining any thing, which was merely matter of Modality.* Hist of Queen *Elizabeth*, p 159 He yet declares himself more expresly in this Point elsewhere *The Articles of the Protestant Church, in the Infancy thereof*, were drawn up in general Terms, *foreseeing that Posterity would grow up to fill the same, meaning that these holy Men did prudently discover, that Differences in Judgment would unavoidably happen in the Church, and were loth to unchurch any, and drive them off from an Ecclesiastical Communion for petty Differences, which made them Pen the Articles* in comprehensive words, to take in all who differing *in Branches meet in the Root of the same Religion* Heyl Hist Quinquart P. 2 c 8

The meaning of Subscription ex animo

But I know not how it has come to pass, that the Bishop of *Sarum* has made his own Rule less defensible, by a Proof which he has brought from the Form of Subscription in the 36th Canon, *I Subscribe willingly and* ex animo, *&c* which words, his Lordship says, seem to *declare a Man's own Opinion, and not a bare Consent to an Article of Peace, or an Engagement to Silence and Submission* I am not altogether different from his Lordship's Judgment in this matter, but I am not so well satisfy'd with the Reason he grounds it upon For *ex animo* in that Place does not signify *according to my Opinion*, or *as I am firmly believe*, but *readily*, or *heartily* For this Form of Subscription is not a Form for Subscription to the Thirty Nine Articles, but to the Three Articles contained in that Canon, which are not so much Articles of Opinion as of Consent, and the Subscription to them declares, not what the Subscriber believes, but what he readily Consents to, for when the Subscriber by the Second Article promises, that he *will use the Book of Common-Prayer*, how can he be said to Subscribe to this, as his Opinion? He Subscribes to this Clause *ex animo*, because he *heartily* consents to use this Book But besides, his Lordship is under some little Mistake to think, that *ex animo* does signify, according to a Man's Judgment or Opinion For, as far as I am able to observe, *ex animo* never signifies so in the *Latin* Tongue, unless joined with the words *dicere*, *loqui*, &c *Equidem dicam ex animo quod sentio* Tull C Lib III signifies, *I truly will speak as I think* And so perhaps in a like Sense, *ex animo credere* Cic ad Att But when it is joined to words of *willing*, *wishing*, *loving*, &c. it then signifies *readily*, or *heartily* So *amare ex animo*, *to love one heartily* Cic ad Q Fratrem *Ex animo commendare*, to *recommend one heartily*, Cic ad Att So *ex animo miser*, says the Man in *Plautus*, *I am as miserable, as a Man could wish* Plaut. Trinum *Tibi bene ex animo volo* *I heartily wish your welfare* Teren Heaut *Ille, quem beneficio adjungas, ex animo facit*, *When you have obliged any one he will comply with your desires readily* Ter Adelph So that by the same Analogy the words *willingly* and *ex animo* being joined together, *ex animo* must in this Form of Subscription signify *readily* This may not be improper to be observed, for the misunderstanding of this Expression, in the Subscription Form, may occasion some unreasonable Scruples in conscientious Men, and keep some of the best Men from entring into Holy Orders

Articles to be explained in a Grammatical Sense

2 The Subscriber ought to Assent to each Article, taken in the Literal and Grammatical Sense For if People were allowed to make far-fetch'd Interpretations of any Article, to take words in an unusual Meaning, to add or diminish, to supply Words to be understood, to take Emphatical Words for Expletives, that have no Signification, one might by such Method make every thing out of any thing, and explain the Bible into the *Alcoran* But whereas the Civilians have divided the Grammatical Sense into two kinds, the *Sensus Grammaticalis ab origine*, and the *Sensus Grammaticalis Popularis* Grot de Jure Bell Lib II c 16 the latter only is to be allow'd in the Interpretation of any Law or Writing For to take Words in their first Original Signification, which by length of time they have much varied from, may carry them off to a Sense very different from what they were intended Therefore the Expressions must be taken, in the plain common Sense they are generally used in, or were used in at the time of the making such Law, or Writing.

There may be more Grammatical Senses

3 But then, as the Bishop of *Sarum* observes, there may several Grammatical Senses, sometimes very fairly, be put upon Expressions His Lordship instances in the third Article of Christ's Descent into Hell, which Persons may Subscribe to, who by Hell either understand the Place of Torments, the Grave, or State of separate Souls This is so clear a Case that I cannot imagine, why any one should find fault with his Lordship, upon this Account, for did not King *Edward*'s Articles determine it to a Local Hell, *his Soul being separate from his Body remained with the Spirits*, &c And was not this Clause struck out in Queen *Elizabeth*'s Articles? Now can any one think that all the Subscribers to King *Edward*'s Book did, at one instant, change their Opinions? or if they had, would not the Article have been drawn up more express than it is? The Truth of the matter is, Archbishop *Parker*, and those who drew up the New Edition of the Articles in 1562, struck out the latter Clause, which seemed a little to Countenance a Popish Doctrine, leaving the former part to stand, which being set down in general words, Persons might understand, according to their own Opinion, either one way or other, and so the matter passed over quietly, which otherways might have occasioned a Dispute

But not contrary to the known Sense of the Composers

4 For rightly understanding the Sense of an Article, besides the Governing our selves by the Grammatical Sense of the words, the Sense of the Compilers of them is to be highly regarded, a Law being to be Interpreted according to the Mind of the Legislator So that if the Compilers of the Articles have expressed themselves obscurely in any place, that is to be explained by what we find to have been their avowed Opinions, or by some other Place of their Writings or Authentick Books, where they have expressed themselves clearly For instance, in the Twenty Third Article, if it be doubted, what is meant by these words, *those we ought to judge lawfully called and sent, who have*

King Edward *VI. Articles*

ART I *Of Faith*

There is but one living and true God, ever-

ARTICLE I.

Of Faith in the Holy Trinity.

There is but [a] one [b] living and [c] true * God, [d] Ever-

ARTIC Lat.

ARTICULUS I

Unus est vivus & verus Deus, æternus,

be called and chosen to this work by Men who have publick Authority given them in the Congregation to call and send Ministers Is the Authority of the Church, or the Authority of the State to be understood? Are those that have Authority to send Ministers, to be Bishops, or mere Presbyters? If a number of *Erastians* or Presbyterians had drawn up these Articles, these general Words might have been interpreted to their Sense, but when they were drawn up by Bishops who well understood the Antient Fathers and Canons of the Church, and who themselves drew up the Forms of Ordination, where all Ordinations are enjoined to be performed by a Bishop, there can no doubt be made what they meant by *publick Authority*, for neither by the Laws of the Church or by the Laws of the Realm any publick Authority is granted to any other than Bishops, to ordain, *to call, or send Ministers into the Lord's Vineyard*

A liberty left for different Interpretations, when drawn up in general Terms

5 But what if in some Points the Minds of the Legislators be various, but however for Peace sake they agree in some Proposition which designedly they express in general Terms, that those of each Side may agree to? That this is frequently Matter of Fact, no one can be ignorant, who reads either the Antient or the Modern Councils Why, in such case, those that are obliged by the Laws have as much Liberty, for difference of Interpretation, as the Legislators themselves And if any of these Articles do plainly appear to be so, as perhaps one or two of them may, they are to be understood only as Articles of Peace or Communion, and Divines of different Judgments may conscientiously Subscribe to them

In case of Repugnancy, the most pious side to be taken

6 Another good Rule for Interpretation laid down by the Civil Law is, that if any Part of a Law shall seem contrary to another, that Part shall prevail, *Quæ causas habet, aut magis honestas aut magis utiles, Which shall be most conducing to Piety or the common Good* Now in the XVIIth Article there does appear to be the same sort of Repugnancy The former part of it is drawn up so, as very much countenances the Systematical or particular Predestination, i e God's Determination of every Man's final Doom from all Eternity The latter part positively asserts the Predestination as 'tis delivered in Scripture, which denotes only a Call to the Gospel Now whereas the latter Sense seems more to conduce to the Honour of God, to the Advancement of Piety, and to the Quiet of Mens Consciences, I ought to close with that rather than with the former

What is last said must preponderate

7 Another Rule which the Civilians in alike case lay down is *Quod postremo dictum est vincat The Obligation lies in that which is last said* Therefore, to instance again in the XVIIth Article Tho' the former part thereof did as much countenance the rigid Predestinarian Doctrine, as is pretended, yet the latter part, *we must receive God's Promises in such wise, as they be generally set forth to us in Holy Scripture*, must direct our Judgment in this matter, it being designed to qualify what had been said before, so that I am not obliged to own any manner of *Predestination, Decree* or *Purpose*, but what is *set forth in Scripture*

Original of the Word GOD

* *God*] The use of the word *God*, to signify the supreme Being, seems to be of vast Antiquity in our Northern Nations, which the *Romans* having turned into *Latin*, took the Deity designed by it to be a particular Local *Numen Asserius*, in the Life of King *Alfred*, makes him and his *Saxon* Predecessors to be descended from *Geada, quem Pagani pro Deo venerabantur*, whom the *Pagans Worshipped for a God* And the Poet *Sedulius*, a *North-Britain*, who lived in the time of *Theodosius* the Younger, speaks of the same as a particular Deity of the *Britains*, and other *Northern* Nations

> *Cum sua gentiles studeant figmenta Poetæ,*
> *Grandisonis pompare modis, tragicoque boatu*
> *Ridiculove* GEDÆ —

> Whilst Gentile Bards study their feigned Gods
> With pompous Verse to praise, with Tragick cry
> To GLAD odd-shapen Idol —

But it does not appear, that the *Saxons* by their GEAD meant any thing else than the other *Germans* did by their WOD, or WODEN, for the G and W are reciprocally used in *German* and *Gaulish* words, as *Galls, Walls, Wilhelm, Guilelm* So that in all probability, the *Northern* Nations (tho' they had several other Deities afterwards, as *Friga, Seater*, &c) yet in the most Antient Times they worshipped GEAD or WOD, as their Supreme Deity, from which we have derived to us our *English* Word GOD And the Name seems to be given from the Adjective *Good*, formerly **goad** or **gude** drawn from the most principal Attribute of God, his Goodness For not only in ours, but in other Languages, the Name of God is taken from some Attribute of the Divine Nature The *Hebrew* Name is particularly remarkable above any others, because it is drawn from the very Original Nature and Essence of the Deity, or at least from his first great Attribute, his *Self-existence* For *Jehovah* is but a Participle or the Verb *Haiah, fuit*, and denotes by way of Eminence the Being, or the Who is, or as *Moses* expresses it in the first Person, the *I AM, Maim More Nevo* c 63 In like manner the *Greek* Θεὸς is derived, ἀπὸ τοῦ θεᾶσθαι from Seeing, being a Name given to the Deity from his Providence.

Having thus spoken of the word *God*, we must now consider what is meant or signified by it As it is impossible to give an adequate Definition of *God*, so we cannot but acknowledge that all Men, who either own a God, or deny such a Being, do grant that the common Notion which Men have thereof, is, That he is a *Being of infinite Perfection, the Cause of all other Beings, and on which they do depend for their Conservation and Government* And therefore both Heathen and Christian Philosophers do take in the complex Notion of all or these Ideas, or some of the principal of them, whenever they describe the Deity or Supreme Being *Thales* calls him πρεσβύτατον τῶν ὄντων The oldest *of all Beings*, Laert in vit *Plato* calls him the Θεὸν δημιουργήσαντα πάντα θνητὰ καὶ ὄντα The God that *made all things that are born and die*, Plat Soph He elsewhere describes him by a Proverbial Speech in use among the *Greeks* ὁ μὲν δὴ Θεὸς ὥσπερ καὶ ὁ παλαιὸς λόγος, ἀρχήν τε καὶ τελευτὴν καὶ μέσα τῶν ὄντων ἁπάντων ἔχων *For God, according to the antient Adage, has in his Power the beginning, the end and the middle of all things*, Plat de Leg Lib 4 He elsewhere calls God the ὄντως ὂν the *really Being* the αὐτὸ ὂν the Being it self, *Plat de Leg. Aristotle* says αἴτιον πᾶσιν καὶ ἀρχή That *he is the Cause and Beginning of all things*, Met Lib. 1 c 2 *Theophrastus* calls him, Θεία πάντων ἀρχὴ, δι' ἧς ἅπαντα καὶ ἔστι καὶ διαμένει *The Divine Principle by which all things are, and are preserved*, Theoph Metap Cap 1 In like manner the ancient Christian Writers *Deus plena & perfecta divinitatis*

What is meant by the Word GOD

n tatis est nomen the *word God denotes a full and perfect Divinity*, Hil. de Trin Lib 11 And thus St *Austin*, *Sic intelligamus Deum quantum possumus, sine qualitate bonum, sine quantitate magnum, sine indigentiâ Creatorem, sine situ presentem, sine habitu omnia continentem, sine loco ubiq, totum, sine tempore sempiternum, sine sui ulla mutatione mutabilia facientem, & nihil patientem* *Let us understand God as much as we are able, good without Quality, and great without Quantity, a Creator without Want, present without Sight, containing all Things without Habit, being all every where without Place, eternal without Time, making things Changeable without Change of himself, and suffering nothing* Aug de Trin Lib 5 From hence it appears that the generality of Men have fixt and settled Notions of the Nature of the Deity And therefore *Sallustius* the Philosopher says very well Κοιναὶ δὲ εἰσιν ἔννοιαι, ὅσας [illegible] ἄνθρωποι ὀρθῶς ἐρωτηθέντες ὁμολογήσωσι· οἷον ὅτι θεὸς ἀγαθὸς, ὅτι ἀπαθὴς, ὅτι ἀτρεπτος *There are some common Notions, which all Men being asked will agree in, viz that God is good, impassible, and unchangeable* Sallust de Dii & Mundo, C I He does not mean any innate Notions and Propositions, in a true and proper manner inscrib'd upon the Mind, (for that is a Modern Fancy of the Schools) but some general Notions which all Men have of the Deity which they readily assent to whenever any Discourse is had of the Divine Being, all or most of which they join together to frame the Idea of it

The Arguments which have forced the Assent of all Men, in the several Ages of the World, for the Acknowledgment of such a Being, are these

I Argument for the BEING of a God, from the Necessity of a first Cause

The first is drawn from the Causality of things For we cannot assign any thing but which was caused by another and that by a third, the third by a fourth which had its Existence before all of them, 'till we come up to some first Cause which had no beginning and no Cause of it For if it has any Cause, it is not the first Cause, but another prior Cause must be sought for neither can it be a Cause to it self, for that implies many Contradictions, as its not being at all, and yet being a Cause, as being before it self as a *Producer*, and yet as not being till afterwards as the *Produced* or as supposing the greatest Contradiction of all, that nothing which has no Causality can produce something Therefore there must be one first Cause, which never was produced, and this is what we call GOD This is the Reasoning of that great Master of Reason, *Aristotle*, ὅτι ἀρχή τις [illegible] ἄπειρα τὰ αἴτια τῶν ὄντων *There must be one first Principle, the Causes of Things not being infinite* Arist Met. Lib II c 2 This Argument is so admirably strong and cogent, that *Proclus* grudges the *Aristotelians* the Honour of it, and says it was spoiled by them, by their admitting too much of Fortune in the Production of things Μόνος δὲ ὁ Πλάτων τοῖς Πυθαγορείοις ἑπόμενος [illegible] αἰτίας [illegible] ὀρθῶς [illegible] [illegible] [illegible] [illegible] [illegible] [illegible] [illegible] ἀλλ' [illegible] *For* Plato *alone following the* Pythagoreans, *says, that all things were made by a certain first Cause, setting a God and a Providence over all things that are made For tho' there be many things that are of a diverse Nature, and therefore are from many Causes, of which some have a different Effect, yet there is one Cause which collects these Efficients into* [illegible] Procl 2 in Tim

II Argument, from the Direction of all things to a proper End

The Second great Argument for the Being of a God, is drawn from the Direction of all things to a proper End Now whereas we find that every part of Nature, which we are capable of observing, is suited to some very wise end and purpose which it could not be if it had its Being from Chance or Necessity, therefore we must conclude, that there was some wise Orderer of these things, which so excellently adapted them to these several purposes This Argument will have the utmost force of Demonstration, if we take a view of the several works of Nature, which are so suited to their particular Ends that they serve for, that better means cannot possibly be contrived Can any thing be better contrived than the Air for Breathing, or the Sun for conveying Light and Heat? Or will any say that they were not made for these ends? But not to go further than the frame of our own Bodies, the Natural Philosophers have shewn the wise Ends, for which the several Parts thereof are fashioned Our Skin is contrived (as *Aristotle says*) [illegible] τῆς φυλακῆς τῆς συνεχείας, *to be Case to inclose the several Parts within* Arist. de part An Lib I c. 8 That [illegible] [illegible] *Unless the Veins were distinct and close all along from their beginning, they could not contain the Blood*, ib cap 9 That the Tongue is particularly figured πρὸς τὴν τῶν χυμῶν αἴσθησιν, *for tasting the Food*, and especially in Man is made tender and broad, πρὸς τὴν τῶν γραμμάτων διάρθρωσιν, *for framing the articulate Sound of Words*, ibid Lib II c 7. That the Teeth are ἐπὶ τὴν τῆς τροφῆς ἐργασίαν, *for the Business of chewing the Food*, ibid Lib III c I in some Animals βοηθείας χάριν, *instead of Weapons for their Security*, ibid That the Foreteeth are made [illegible] [illegible], *sharp to divide or chop off the Food* which is to be taken into the Mouth That the Cheek teeth are made πλατεῖς, ἵνα λεαίνωσι *broad to grind the Food* after it is taken in, ibid To omit innumerable other Arguments drawn from the use of the other Parts of the Body, by the *Physiologists* and *Anatomists* Now since these things were all contriv'd, and adapted to their respective Ends by some wise and powerful Being, this can be no other than what we call God

III Argument, from the beautiful Construction of the Universe

Another Argument is drawn from the admirable Beauty of the Construction of the Universe, the excellent Subordination and Harmony of its Parts, all contributing to the Well being and Regularity of the whole, which being a System of such a surprizing Art and Wisdom, could not be framed but by such a Wise and All powerful Being as we call God Divines and Philosophers have filled their Books with Instances, which illustrate and inforce this Argument *Cicero* forms this Argument thus, *Si est aliquid in rerum natura*, &c *If there be any thing in Nature, which the Mind of Man, which human Reason, Force and Power cannot do, there is certainly something which does it greater than Man But the heavenly Bodies and indefinite Order of their Revolutions, could not be caused by Man There is therefore something by which they are done greater than Man And what shall I call this but God?* —An vero si domum magnam, &c *If you behold a great and a fine House, tho' you do not see the Master of it, you cannot be brought to think, that this was built by Mice and Weesels. And shall not you seem mad to imagine, that this gallant Ornament of the Universe, that this so great a variety and beauty of the heavenly Bodies, the Power and Greatness of the Seas and the Earth, is only a House for you Men, and not rather the Building and Seat of the Immortal Gods?* Cic de Nat Deor Lib II *Sextus Empiricus* urges the same Argument, with great Beauty and Strength thus Ὥσπερ [illegible] [illegible] τῆς Τρωικῆς, &c *If any one sitting on the Top of the Trojan Mount* Ida, *shall see the Army of the* Greeks *marching over the Plain with great Beauty and Order, first the Horsemen and Chariots, and then the Foot, will not he immediately think, that there was some Person who marshalled them into this Order, and who having Command over the Soldiers disposed them so Beautifully, as suppose* Nestor *or some other of the Heroes, who knew,*

Κοσμῆσαι ἵππους τε καὶ ἀνέρας ἀσπιδιώτας,

To range the Horses and the shielded Men?

In like manner if any one who has any Knowledge of maritime Affairs, shall see at a distance a Ship sailing with a brisk Gale, all her Sails expanded, he will conclude, that there is a Pilot who directs her, and carries her to the designed Port So they who look up to Heaven, and take a view of the Sun δρόμους [illegible] (the Psalmist's very Expression) *like an Athletick running his* Stadium *from East to West, together with the well-measured Dances of the Stars, will they not look out for some Author of all this beautiful Order, not thinking that it come to pass by Chance, but that it was contrived by some better and immortal Being, which is God?* Sext Emp contr. Dogm

IV Argument, from the Consent of all Nations

Another Argument for the Being of a God, is drawn from the Consent of all Nations *Tully* says, *Inter omnes omnium gentium sententia constat omnibus enim innatum est, & in animo quasi insculptum, esse Deos* *This is a Truth which is manifest from the Opinion of all Men for it is an innate Principle, and as it were ingraven in the Mind, that there is a Deity* Cic de Nat Deor Lib. II And *Seneca*, *Nulla gens usquam est adeo contra leges moresq; projecta, ut non aliquos Deos credat* *There is no Nation so devoid of Laws and Morals, as not to believe there are no Gods* And thus *Maximus Tyrius*, Ἕνα ἴδοις ἂν ἐν πάσῃ γῇ ὁμόφωνον νόμον καὶ λόγον, ὅτι Θεὸς εἷς ἐῖς παντων πατηρ ϗ βασιλεύς And afterwards, ταῦτα ο Ἕλλην λεγει ϗ ο Βαρβαρ☉, &c *You may observe one uniform Law and Reasoning all the World over, that there is one God, the Father and King of all —— This is acknowledged both by* Greek *and* Barbarian, *&c.* Max Tyr Diss 1 This is very good Evidence of the Reality of a Supreme Being, and whether we ground it upon Tradition, or universal Principles of reasoning, it is a better Foundation to rest upon, than the fanciful Speculations of some particular private Persons, who are more liable to be mistaken, than the most learned and wise Men of all Nations, and all Ages of the World, and who probably could not have all fallen into the uniform Opinion of a Divine Creator and Governor of the World, unless he had been pleased some time or other in the early Ages of the World to have revealed it to them, which they readily at first embraced, and afterwards tenaciously adhered to, finding it so highly agreeable to their Reason It avails little to say, that there may be a stupid Clan or two of barbarous People, who have very little of these Notices For the Observation of such Peoples Practices and Opinions may not have been exactly enough made by those Traders who have made these Reports, for want of their Language, and by reason of their short and imperfect Conversation with them Or however, were the Observation true, the contrary Opinion of a few stupid People, who are almost degenerated into beasts, is but a sorry Pretence to set up against the Judgment of so many civilized Nations, in so many successive Ages of the World, confirmed by the Reason of so many wise and learned Men who have been educated in them

V *Argument, from the Checks of Conscience*

Another Argument for the Being of a God, is drawn from the Checks of Conscience in wicked Men, after the Commission of any great Sin *Conscientia* (says *Tully*) *est gravis pondus* *Conscience is a heavy weight* Cic de Nat Deor Lib III 'Tis an excellent saying of *Menander*,

> Ὁ συνιτορ ιν αὐτῶ τικαι ἢ δεωσυ[illegible]
> Ἡ συ εσις αὐτὸν δειλότατον [illegible] ποιε
>
> *For, tho' the Criminal be ne'er so bold,*
> *Conscience will make him fear——*

To the like purpose *Isocrates* Μηδὲν ἀπορρήτῳ ποιήσῃς μηδ' ὧν ποιῇς μηδὲ τοιαῦτα, μηδ' ἐπιχείρει πολλάκις πράξαι ὥστε ὅτι περὶ τὰ ἀπόρρητα τῶν πραττομένων ἀναγκαῖον ἐστὶ πολλοὺς φόβους γίνεσθαι *Let not any one hide what he unlawfully does, or possesses, or designs to do, knowing that such Secrets must produce a great many Fears* Isocr in Nicoc Now since all Men are in fear of an Avenger of secret Actions, it follows that they stand in awe of a God, whose All-searching Eye they cannot shun, and whose Justice they are lyable to, tho' their Craft, or Subtilty, or Power, has set them out of the reach of human Cognisance

VI *Argument, from the Eternity of Ideas and Truth*

There is another Argument drawn from the Maxims of the Platonick Philosophy, which may have its weight with speculative Genius's And that is this Since the Ideas of things are different from the things themselves, and had a Being before the things were, namely, in the Mind of him that formed them and since there are a number of Relations and Correspondencies, which they bear to one another, which are Eternally true, as for instance, there never was a time in which it would not have been true to have said, *A Man is a Rational Animal*, That *the outward Angle of a Triangle is equal to the two internal Opposite*, Therefore there must of necessity be a Mind to which these Ideas must from all Eternity have existed in, and in which these Eternal Truths must have been lodged For thus *Alcinous* the Platonick argues Ἐι γὰρ μην ο κόσμ☉ μη [illegible] τοιοῦτος εστιν, ὀ μονον εκ τινὸς εστι γεγονὸς, ἀλλὰ ϗ ὑπό τινος, ϗ ὀ μόνον τουτο, ἀλλὰ ϗ πρὸς τι τὸ δὲ πρὸς ὃ γέγονε, τι α ἀλλο γεγονεν ἢ ἰδεα *If the World be not by Chance, it is made not only out of something, but by some one And not only so, but is made after somewhat But that somewhat after which it is made, what can it be but the Idea of it?*

Of the divine Attributes in general

a *One*] The Articles not only affirm the Being of a God, but also declare the several Attributes, which belong to him Which Attributes are not distinct Beings really different from the Divine Essence, but different Excellencies, Properties, or ways of Operation, by which the Divine Nature is pleased to display itself to us These Attributes some of the antient Hereticks, as the *Eunomians*, were wont so to confound with the very Divine Essence, as not to allow them to be distinguished from it, even by the Mind or Understanding Others, as the *Anomeans*, made them Parts and branches of the Divine Nature, out of which the Deity was as it were compounded, as of integral or constituent Parts. To both which the Orthodox Writers of the Church with good Reason opposed themselves For thus St *Cyril*, Τὰ τοινυν ϗ οσα προσεῖναι λεγεται τω Θεω, [illegible] παντες, ἴσαι αυτῶ ϗ ουσια [illegible] τῆ ουσια συμβεβηκότα μεχει μονης [illegible] [illegible] ὀ [illegible] εν ἀυτω, [illegible] τὴν καθ' εαυτὴν λεγει ἐπὶ θεῶ [illegible] τοῖς [illegible] αὐτὸ [illegible] καὶ εαυτῆς μείζονα [illegible] ποιουμενοι [illegible] [illegible] καταγελῶντες αυτων *All things which are in God, and which are predicated of God, do not signifie his very Essence therefore, that we call them a sort of Accidents, because they are distinguishable by the Mind as such For human Nature cannot say any thing greater of the Divine Nature, than it is in its self However in speaking thereof, we use our own common ways of Expression, thereby making a faint Representation of greater things as those who describe the Circle of the Heavens [illegible]* Cyr Thes[illegible] 31 And *Gregory Nyssene*, [illegible] the blasphemous Consequences of the *Anomean* Opinions, says, [illegible]

The first of these Divine Properties or Attributes here mentioned is God's *Oneness*, or *Unity* This Attribute is a Corollary or Consequence of the Self-existence of God, or his being the first or Original Cause of all things, for as it is necessary that there must be something which was eternally Existent without having any Cause, so there is no necessity of there being more than the one Cause, which being the Fountain of all Causality does necessarily include Unity But the Antient Christians, who vindicated this Attribute of the Deity against the Heathen Idolaters, made use of more popular Arguments, that were better accommodated to the Capacities of ordinary People, and were for the most part as strong and conclusive

Unity of the Deity proved from the Testimony of the wisest Heathens

The first was drawn from the Opinion of the wisest and most learned of the Heathens themselves As that of *Orpheus*,

> Εἷς ἔστ' αὐτογενης, ἑνὸς ἔκγονα πάντα τέτυκται
> [illegible] αὐτοῖς αὐτὸς περιγίγνεται ὀδέ τις αὐτὸν
> Εἰσοράᾳ ψυχῶν θνητῶν, αὐτὸς δὲ γε πάντας ὁρᾶται
>
> *There is one Self-existent God, who made*
> *All things that are, his own great Self being [illegible] them*
> *Invisible to all, yet seeing all Things*

Those noted Verses of *Sophocles* are quoted by most of the Apologists upon this Head

> Εἷς ταῖς ἀληθέιαισιν εἷς ἐστιν Θεὸς
> Ος ὀυρανον τ' ἔτευξε ϗ γαῖαν μακρὰν
> Πόντου τε χαροπὸν οἶδμα κἀνέμων βίας,
> Θνητοὶ δὲ πολλοὶ καρδίᾳ πλανώμενοι
> Ἱδρυσάμεσθα πημάτων παραψυχὰς
> Θεῶν ἀγάλματα ἐκ λίθων τε ϗ ξύλων
> Ἢ χρυσοτεύκτων, ἢ ἐλεφαντίνων τύπους,
> Θυσίας τε τούτοις, ϗ κακὰς πανηγύρεις
> Τεύχοντες, οὕτως ευσεβεῖν νομίζομεν
>
> *There is but One in Truth, One only God*
> *Who did create the Heav'n and the wide Earth,*
> *The boistrous Waves of Sea, and force of Winds.*
> *But foolish Mortals have, instead of these,*
> *Made to themselves, for solace of their guilt,*
> *The Images of Gods, of Stone and Wood,*
> *Or Statues made of Gold, or Ivories white*
> *To these they Sacrifice, to these they Festial Days*
> *Do dedicate And this they call Devotion*

To the same purpose *Hesiod*

> Αὐτὸς γὰρ πάντων βασιλεὺς, ϗ κοίραν☉ ἐστι
> Ἀθανάτων οὐδ' ἄτ' ἐρισεται Θεὸς ἄλλ☉
>
> *He is the King of all, the Sovereign of th' Immortals,*
> *Nor can there any other God be found than He*

The

The same was the Doctrine of the great Father of the Ethnick Philosophy, *Socrates*, who died a Martyr for this Truth, as *Cicero* says, *ab Anyto quodam Divite & Melito Poeta & Lycone Oratore accusatus quasi Deos communes non coleret being accused by a certain strict Man called* Anytus, *by* Melitus *a Poet, and* Lyco *an Orator, because he did not worship the ordinary Gods* Cic de Or Lib 3 His Opinion of the Deity, and that of his Scholar *Plato*, is thus related by *Plutarch* Σωκράτης κὴ Πλάτων τὸ ἓν τὸ μονοφυὲς κὴ αὐτοφυὲς, τὸ μοναδικὸν τὸ ὄντως ἀγαθὸν Socrates *and* Plato *taught, that the Deity was a single Self-existent Being, of one simple Nature, truly Good* Plut de Plac Phil But not to enter into a long detail of Citations out of the ancient Philosophers and Poets, any one may observe in reading the Books of not only *Plato*, but *Aristotle*, *Tully*, *Seneca*, &c that when they speak strictly and philosophically of the Deity, they use the word *God*, as we Christians do, in the singular Number, and, when they mention the word *Gods* in the plural, they only accommodate themselves to the Language and Capacity of the Vulgar whom they conversed with So that unless we will Balance the Opinion of the Rabble against the Doctrine of the most wise and learned Men of the several respective Ages, we have the Testimony even of Heathen Antiquity on our side, for the Unity of the Divine Nature

From the Incongruity of the Divine Nature being communicated to more than one

Another Argument for the Unity of the Deity is drawn, from the Incongruity of the Divine Power being communicated to more than one God, because this would infer several infinite Powers, and infinite Goodness's For if one of them had all Power and all Goodness, the other would have no Power and no Goodness at all For thus *Athenagoras* Εἰ ἦσαν ἐξ ἀρχῆς δύο ἢ πλείους θεοί, ἤτοι ἐν ἑνὶ κὴ ταυτῷ ἦσαν, ἢ ἰδίᾳ ἕκαστος αὐτῶν ... [illegible] *If from the beginning there were two or more Gods, they were either conjoined in one and the same Nature, or they were singly separate. They cannot have one and the same Nature For the Gods are not alike For some of them are unborn, and some of them born, and therefore not alike Those that are unborn are unlike, as neither produced by any one, nor according to any exemplar* Athen Seq pro Christ In the like manner *Lactantius* argues, *Si plures partiantur orbem, minus & virium singuli habebunt, cum intra præscriptam portionem se quisque contineat Eodem etiam modo Dii, si plures sunt minus valebunt, aliis tantundem in se habentibus, If more Governours should divide the World between them, each of them would have less Power, because they would have a limited Power In the same manner the Gods, if there be a Plurality of them, will not have an omnipotent Power, each of them having but a share of it* Lactan Inst Lib 1 And again. *Si autem* [Dii] *sunt multi, dum habent singuli potestatis aliquid, ac numinis, summa ipsa decrescit nec poterunt singuli habere totum, quod est commune cum pluribus, unicuique tantum deerit, quantum cæteri possidebunt If there are many* [Gods] *whilst each of them have some Power or Portion of the Deity, the Total of the divine Power will be lessened for each of them cannot have the whole which is common to more for so much will be wanting to every one which the rest possess* Lact de Ira Dei, cap 2

Unity of the Godhead, proved from the Contrariety of the Wills of different Gods

Another Argument for the Unity of God, is taken from the Contrariety of Judgment and Will, which must necessarily be, in a supposed Plurality of Gods, and the hurry and tumult which would from thence arise in the Government of the World For thus *Athanasius* argues. Καὶ ἡ τάξις δὲ αὕτη τῆς διακοσμήσεως, κὴ ἡ τῶν πάντων μετ' ὁμονοίας ἁρμονία ... [illegible] *For from the Order of Administration, and the Harmony of Consent, the Scripture shews, that there are not many Gods, but one Ruler and Governour of the World For if there were more Governours of the World, the Order of all things could not be preserved But all things would be out of Order by reason of those many Governours, one drawing all things to his Will, and opposing the other* Athan contr Gent Both this and the former Argument are joyned together in these Verses of *Prudentius*

Aut unus Deus est, rerum cui summa potestas,
Aut quia jam duo sunt, minuuntur dispare summo,
Porro nihil summum, nisi plenis viribus unum
Distantes quoniam, proprium dum quisq, revulso
Vindicat imperio, nec summa nec omnia possunt

The Chief God must be One for were there two
Chief Deities, Omnipotence it self would lessen,
God therefore must be One, with plenitude of Power
For different Gods would always be a scrambling
For Rule, and none of them possess Omnipotence
Prud. in Hamartig

b *Living*] This Title of *Living* is added here, in the Enumeration of the Divine Attributes, because in the holy Scriptures it is so frequently ascribed to God in Opposition to the Heathens, who gave this Title to their Idols, who were inanimate and senseless Gods without Life For nothing was more common, not only among the vulgar Heathen, but among their Writers, to call an Image a God For so *Horace*

Olim truncus eram ficulnus, inutile lignum
Cum faber incertus, scamnum facerene Priapum
Maluit esse Deum

I was a Fig-tree's Stump, that sorry Wood
The Carpenter uncertain what to make me,
Whether a Bench, or Image of Priapus,
At last he'd have me be a God —— Hor Lib I Ser 8

To the like propose *Martial*

Qui fingit sacros auro vel marmore vultus,
Non facit ille Deos qui rogat ille facit

He that of Gold or Marble makes an Image
Don't make them Deities, but their Votaries Prayers.
Mar Lib VIII. Ep 44

Upon this account *Moses* distinguishes the true God from the fictitious Deities and dumb Idols of the Heathens, by the Name of the *living God. Ye have heard the Voice of the living God*, Deut v 26 So *Joshuah*, *Hereby ye shall know that the living God is among us*, Jos iii 10 And *David*, *Who is this uncircumcised Philistine, that he should defy the Armies of the living God*? 1 Sam xiv 26 It was also a Custom among the *Jews* to Swear by *the living God*. *As the Lord liveth*, &c 1 Sam xiv 39 1 Sam xix. 6. xx 21 xxvi 10 1 *Kings* ii 24 2 *Kings* v 20 The same form is used by the *Jews*, when they put any to their Oath by way of Adjuration, as appears clearly by the Oath put to our Saviour at his Trial *I adjure thee by the living God* Mat xxvi 23 And as the *Jews* thought this the most sacred and binding of all Oaths, so they did not think the swearing by any other Oath, or at least by any of the Heathen Deities, binding As appears by that of *Martial* concerning a *Jew*

Ecce negas jurasq, mihi per templa Tonantis
Non credo jura, verpe, per Anchialum.

Tho' you deny and swear by th' Thunderer's Temple,
I don't believe you, Jew, *swear by* Anchialus
Mart Lib xi. Ep xcv.

Which is a plain Allusion to the Jewish form of Swearing, *Chaieloh im*, or *Chaieloha, as the Lord liveth*, or as they then pronounced it *Chiala*, from which the Poet formed the word *Anchialus*

What is meant by the LIFE of God

But when Life is ascribed to God, it must not be understood any new Vigor added to the Deity, or ascititious Act joined to his Essence, as when one is added to one it makes two or any Effect resulting from a Soul added to his Being, as the Life of Man is, the Separation of which occasions Dissolution or Death or any thing which depends upon a prior Cause for its Original or Conservation, as the Life of Angels does but the Divine Nature it self considered as eternally perceiving and enjoying its own Excellence and Good, independent of any other Cause, but continuing by its own Power, without any decay or diminution Upon which account God is said in a peculiar manner, beyond any of his Creatures, to live in Scripture, *I live for ever*, Deut. xxxii 40 *Who liveth for ever and ever*, Rev iv 9 *Who only hath Immortality*, 1 Tim vi 16. *Who giveth to all things Life, Breath, and all Things*, Acts xvii. 25 Hence some

lasting, without Body, Parts, or Passions, of | lasting *e* without Body, | *incorporeus, impartibilis, immensæ potentiæ,*

some of the Fathers call him αὐτοζωὴ who has Life in himself, and communicates it to all others *Dion Areop de Div Nom* cap ii Sect 8 And in this Sense Life is an incommunicable Attribute of God, which none of his Creatures do partake of.

c *True*] God is said to be True in several Respects 1 With relation to the Reality of his Deity, in opposition to the feigned Gods of the Heathens And in this respect he is mostly called in Scripture by the Title of the *true God* *The Lord is the true God*, Jer x 10 *This is eternal Life to know thee the only true God*, John xvii 3 *Ye turned to God from Idols, to serve the living and true God*, 1 Thess i 9 2*dly*, In Respect of his Intellectual Truth, or the exact Conformity of his Understanding to the true nature of Things, by which he is uncapable of all Error or Mistake or change of his Judgment 3*dly*, In respect of his Moral Truth or Faithfulness Hence he is called *the God of Truth*, Psal xxxi 5 *the Lord holy and true*, Rev vi 10 *Abundant in Goodness and Truth*, Exod xxxiv 6 *God is not a Man, that he should lie, neither the Son of Man that he should repent, hath he said and shall not he do it?* &c Which is agreeable to what *Plato* says concerning both the Intellectual and Moral Truth of the Divine Nature Οὐ γὰρ οὐδὲν ἕνεκα θεὸς ψεύδοιτο, &c Κομιδῇ ἄρα ὁ θεὸς ἁπλοῦν καὶ ἀληθὲς ἔν τε ἔργῳ καὶ λόγῳ καὶ οὔτε αὐτὸς μεθίσταται (forte μεθοδεύεται) οὔτε ἄλλους ἐξαπατᾷ οὔτε κατὰ φαντασίας οὔτε κατὰ λόγους οὔτε κατὰ σημείων πομπάς, οὐδ' ὕπαρ, οὐδ' ὄναρ *For, what reason is there that God should lie? [he having shewn before that he has no one to fear, no one who can oppose or contradict him] God is simple and true, both in Word and Deed, he is neither himself changed [or deceived] nor does he deceive others, neither by false Appearances, or Revelations, or by Signs, or Visions, or Dreams* Plat de rep Lib ii

What is meant by the TRUTH *of God*

d *Everlasting*] Our *English* word *Everlasting* here used does answer to the *Greek* αἰώνιος, and the *Latin æternus*, and does denote something that has lasted or continued before the present time, and will last or continue to all Eternity after it, for this is the true Notion of Everlastingness or Eternity So *Origen* defines Eternity, *Æternum propriè dicitur quod neq, initium ut esset habuit, neq, cessare unquam potest esse* *That is properly said to be Eternal, which never had a beginning to be, and can never cease to be* Or Periarch cap 3 The Reasoning of *Gregory Nazianzen*, as well as his Eloquence, upon this Head is very just Διχῆ δὲ τῷ ἀπείρῳ ἐπινοουμένῳ κατὰ τε ἀρχὴν, καὶ τέλος, &c *Infinite time is considered in a twofold respect, namely with relation both to beginning and end*, &c ὅταν μὲν εἰς τὸν ἄνω βυθὸν, &c *For when the Mind looks back into the profound Abyss of time past, and cannot tell where to set her Foot, relying upon its imaginations which it has of the Deity, at length it gives a name to this interminable tract of time which it cannot go over, and calls it without beginning, and when it descends to the lower or future times, she calls it immortal, and which never hath an end, and when she has joined both together, she calls it Eternal*, Naz Orat xxxviii The like Description the Apostle gives of Eternity, having *neither beginning of Days, nor end of Life*, Heb vii 3 So that when we speak of God's being Everlasting or Eternal, we mean he had eternal Existence without any Beginning, and shall continue in the Possession of it without end

Now that God was eternally Existent without Beginning, may be proved, Because he is the first Cause of Things For if he never was caused or produced, he must always be Upon this reason is grounded that Answer of *Thales* in *Plutarch* Τί πρεσβύτατον, θεὸς, ἔφη Θάλης, ἀγέννητον γάρ ἐστι *What is the oldest of all Beings? God, says Thales, because he never was produced* Plut in Convivio So likewise *Philo* argues from the necessary Connexion between Uncreatedness and Eternity Γενητὸς, οὐδεὶς ἀληθείᾳ Θεὸς, ἀλλὰ, δόξῃ μόνον, τὸ ἀναγκαιότατον ἀφῃρημένος ἀΐδιότητα *No one that was ever created can in truth be a God, but only a Titular one wanting that which is necessary to the Godhead, Eternity.* Philo de Philaut.

God's ETERNITY, *ex parte ante*

God's future Eternity is demonstrated, Because there is no Power Superior to him to destroy his Being, Therefore, as the Divine Nature now is, and always was, so it must always be Upon which account *Plato* says, τοῦ μὲν [illegible] ἀεὶ κατὰ ταὐτὰ ὂν *That which was always and never had a beginning, must always continue in the same manner*, Plat in Tim And so S. *Austin* Reasons *Summum bonum quo superius non est, Deus est & per hoc immutabile bonum est & ideo vere æternum & immortale* *The chief Good which has no Superior is God, who for this reason does admit of no Alteration, and consequently is Eternal and Immortal* Aug de Nat boni contr Manich 'Tis upon Account of this Attribute, which is so essential to the Divine Nature, that the Holy Scripture does so frequently join this Compellation to the Name of God, *The Eternal God*, Deut xxxiii 27 *The King Eternal*, 1 Tim i 17 *The everlasting God*, Gen xxi 33 *The everlasting Father*, Isa ix 6 *Everlasting King*, Jer x 10.

God's ETERNITY, *ex parte post*

e *Without Body Parts*] There was a stupid sort of Hereticks which started up in *Egypt* about the latter end of the fourth Century, who contended that God was of Human Shape, grounding their ridiculous Opinion upon that Passage of *Genesis*, *Let us make Man after our Image*, and upon the *Eye*, *Hand*, &c of God being frequently mentioned in Scripture, *Socr* Lib vi c 7 *Soz* Lib viii c 11 But these Passages of Holy Writ may easily be accounted for, by saying that by the first is understood the rational Soul of Man, which bears a nearer Similitude to the Deity, than any other Parts of the Creation And that by the *Eye of God* is meant his Providence, by the *Hand* of God is meant his Power, &c which was occasioned by the narrowness of the *Hebrew* Tongue, which wanted words to express abstracted Notions, and which were afterwards coined in those Nations where the *Pagan* Philosophy was cultivated And the *Hebrew* Criticks lay down several very excellent Rules for the understanding any of these Metaphorical Expressions in Scripture, and for reducing them to a strict and proper Sense *Vid Maimon More Nevoc* Lib i *Buxt Lex in voc.* [illegible] The belief of God's Incorporeity is so fundamental a Part of Religion, that God in his Revelation to the *Jews* made it one of the first Precepts of the Jewish Religion not to make any Image of him, lest it should lead them into the gross Error of the Idolatrous Heathen Nations, of God's being of an Human Shape or any other Bodily Figure, *Exod* xx *Deut* iv 12 And our Saviour informed us, whilst he was teaching us the Doctrines of Christianity, *That God is a Spirit*, John iv 24 We likewise are instructed by Reason, that God is an Incorporeal Being, which the Ancients draw from several very Excellent Topicks. (1) From the Superior Excellency of a Mind beyond that of Body, now since these are the two great Classes to which all Beings are reduced, it is necessary, that God who is the most perfect of all Beings should be a Mind rather than a Body For thus *Maximus Tyrius* argues, Ποῖ τοίνυν τοῦτον τὸν θεὸν τάττωμεν, πότερα ἐν τῷ ἀνθρωπίνῳ, ἀλλὰ εὐφημεῖν ἄξιον. λείπεται δὴ ὥσπερ εἰς ἀκρόπολιν ἀναβιβάσαντας τῷ λόγῳ τὸν θεὸν ἱδρῦσαι κατὰ τὸν νοῦν αὐτὸν τὸν ἀρχηγικώτατον *Under which rank of these shall we place God? Among the crowd of Bodies? God forbid It remains therefore, that our Dissertation place him, as in the highest Tower of Beings, a Mind the chief Governing Principle of all*, Max Tyr Diss. 1 (2) Because Corporeity would be inconsistent with the Simplicity of the Divine Nature For thus a learned Platonick argues upon this Head Εἰ γὰρ σῶμα ὁ Θεὸς, ἐξ ὕλης ἂν εἴη καὶ εἴδους διὰ τὸ πᾶν σῶμα συνδυασμά τι εἶναι ἐκ τῆς ὕλης, καὶ τοῦ σὺν αὐτῇ εἴδους, &c ἄτοπον δὲ τὸν Θεὸν ἐξ ὕλης εἶναι καὶ εἴδους, οὐ γὰρ ἔσται ἁπλοῦς, οὐδὲ ἀρχικός *If God were a Body, he would be compounded of Matter and Form, because every Body is a Composition of these Two*, &c *But it is absurd*

No Countenance from the Scripture Phraseology, for God having a Body

The INCORPOREITY *of the Deity proved, from the Excellency of Mind beyond Body*

Because inconsistent with the Simplicity of the Deity.

to

infinite Power, Wis- Parts, or[f] Passions, of[g] infi- *sapientiæ & bonitatis,*

to say God is compounded of Matter and Form, for then he would neither be a Simple, nor yet the primary Being, &c Alc c 10 (3) Because Corporeity does infer a Capability of Dissolution, which is repugnant to the first Notion of a God For thus *Alcinous* reasons [Greek] *If God were a Body, he would be subject to Corruption, and Generation, and to Change But 'tis the greatest Absurdity to attribute any of these to him,* Alc ibid The same Argument is prosecuted with greater force by *Gregory Nazianzen* [Greek] *How is God worthy of Adoration if he be a circumscrib'd Body? And then how shall we avoid saying that he is compounded of the Elements, and is resolved into them again, and consequently wholly dissolvable? For Composition is the Cause of Strife, Strife of Division, and that of Dissolution But Dissolution is incompatible with the Nature of God, and the first Cause Therefore there is no Division in the Divine Nature, because there can be no Dissolution, nor Strife, because there is no Division, nor Composition, because there is no Strife and therefore God has no Body because he has no Composition* Greg. Naz Orat xxxiv

Because it would infer a Possibility of Dissolution.

f *Passions.*] Altho' the Holy Scriptures do frequently represent God as being subject to such Emotions of Mind as we commonly call Affections or Passions, as when he is said to Love, to Fear, to Hate, to be Angry, yet we must understand these Expressions as being Condescensions made to our Capacities, and are only Representations of the Tendencies of the Divine Will, by the Idea we have of our own Inclinations But when it is requisite to speak more strictly concerning the Divine Nature, the Holy Scripture perfectly excludes from it, all the Perturbation and Commotion of Human Affection, making God devoid of all Affection or Passion properly so called. For thus *Samuel* speaks of God *The strength of Israel will not lie nor repent for he is not a Man that he should repent,* 1 Sam. xv 29 So God himself in the Prophet *Hosea* declares against his having any vindictive Temper in him, like that of Man, *I will not return to destroy Ephraim for I am God and not Man,* Hos xi 9 The same is deducible from the Dictates of human Reason, which cannot possibly conceive a God, but it must at the same time conclude that he is not subject to the Uncertainties and Fluctuations of Passion This the Ancients argue from several very proper Topicks

God's IMPASSIBILITY proved from Scripture

1 From the Perfection and Dignity of the Divine Nature, which is too great and excellent to submit to the Weaknesses and Wants and Changeableness which Passion does imply. The very *Epicureans,* who had the grossest Thoughts of any of the Philosophers concerning the Deity, could nevertheless acknowledge that the Divine Nature could not be subject to Passion

Proved from the Dignity of the Divine Nature

Quicquid enim Divum natura necesse est, &c
Nam privata Dolore omni, privata periclis
Ipsa suis pollens opibus, nihil indiga nostri
Haud bene promeritis capitur, nec tangitur ira.

For what so e'er's Divine———
———*Must be from* Fears *and* Dangers *free,*
Sufficient to its own Felicity
Must nothing want, *nor* joyously *be glad*
For well-done Acts, nor storm *against the bad*

Lucret Lib 1

Plato, who always speaks very justly concerning the Deity, says [Greek] *God, who is endowed with the Divine Nature, must necessarily be without either Grief or Joy exercising a most perfect Wisdom and Understanding* Plat, Epin *Athenagoras* does with great Strength of Reason expose the Heathen Theology. [Greek] *But if they shall say they are of a fleshly Nature, and that they have Blood and Seed, and are subject to the Passions of Anger and Desire, this is Trifling and Ridiculous, for in God there is neither Anger, nor Lust, nor Desire, nor Child-begetting Seed* Athan Leg pro Christ

2 They argue the same from the Immutability of the Divine Nature, and the most absurd Consequence which would ensue thereupon, a tendency to Dissolution and Destruction *Sallust* reckons it as a [Greek], a common Maxim that which all Mankind agree in, [Greek] &c *That God is without Passions, and unchangeable,* &c. Sallust de Mund The Absurdity of attributing Passion to the Deity, is thus urged by *Arnobius* *Ubi est ullus affectus ibi necesse est esse Passionem Ubi passio sita est, perturbationem consentaneum est consequi Ubi perturbatio ibi dolor & ægritudo est, imminuitioni & corruptionijam locus est Quæ duo si vexant, adest vicinus interitus, mors omnia finiens, & cunctis adimens sentientibus vitam Where there is Affection there must needs be Passion Where Passion is settled there must of course be Perturbation Where there is Perturbation there must be Grief and Pain Under the vexation of which, Dissolution must be nigh, and Death which makes an end of all, and puts a period to Life* Arnob contr. Gent. Lib 1 To the same purpose *Lactantius* *Pertinaciter mentes convertit nos, semper universos animorum affectus ignotos Diis esse, consentaneum est credere nunquam Deos irasci ——quicquid enim vexatur rei alicujus, e motu passibile esse constat, & fragile, quod Passioni fragilitatique subjectum est, id necesse esse mortale Ira autem vexat, & patientes se solvit Ergo esse mortale dicendum est, quod passionibus Subjectum est We ought constantly to remember, that all Affections are for ever unknown to the Gods, and that 'tis agreeable to believe that the Gods are never angry ——For whatsoever is disturb'd by any thing, it is plain from the Perturbation that it is passible and fragil, because it is subject to Passion and Fragility, and must therefore be mortal But Anger disturbs, and tends to the Dissolution of those who suffer by it Therefore that must needs be Mortal which is subject to Passions.*

Because Immutable and Incorruptible

g *Of infinite Power*] The Holy Scripture is very express in setting forth this great Attribute of God He is called *God Almighty,* Gen xxxv 2 it is there said that he *can do every thing,* Job xlii. 2 that *with God nothing shall be impossible,* Luke i 37 *with God all things are possible,* Mat xix. 26 that *he is mighty in Strength, who hath hardned himself against him?* Job ix 4 *Thine, O Lord, is the Greatness, and the Power, and the Glory, and the Victory, and the Majesty,* &c Chron xxix. 2 *O house of Israel, cannot I do with you as this Potter? saith the Lord. Behold as the Clay is in the Potter's hand, so are ye in my hand, O house of Israel* Jer xviii 6 Besides this, there are several Arguments used by the Ancients, which do either prove or confirm this principal Attribute of God

God's OMNIPOTENCE proved from Scripture

1. The first is drawn from his being the great Creator and Governor of the World, to which such a plenitude of Power is necessary, both for the first producing it, and afterwards for the keeping it in good Order And this is that, which the Ancient Poets do so frequently insist upon, thus he is called in *Orpheus* his Hymns, [Greek] *The Mover of all things, or Director of them at his Pleasure* *Homer* calls him

Because the Governor of the World

——[Greek]

The Father (i e The Creator and Governor) *of Gods and Men*

And elsewhere speaking of God's Almighty Power, he says,

[Greek] Il π

That his determination can over-rule Mens Actions

Pῖα

dom and Goodness, nite Power h Wisdom, and creator & conservator

Ῥεῖα Θεὸς γ' ἐθέλων ᾗ τῆλ θεν ἄνδρα σαώσαι

That when he is pleased he can at a distance succour any one. Odyss. 2

——Θεοὶ δέ τε πάντα δύνανται

——*That the Gods can do all things* Odyss. 2

For the same Reason *Virgil* calls him

Pater Omnipotens, rerum cui summa potestas

The Almighty Father, who has the chief Power over all things. Virg Æn 10

And *Horace*

Reges in ipsos imperium est Jovis,
Cuncta supercilio moventis

The Empire of God is over Kings, he disposing of all things at his Pleasure Hor Lib III Od 1

Because the Origin of all Power 2 Another Argument for God's Omnipotence is drawn from his being the first Cause or Origin of all Power, so that nothing can be Powerful enough to resist him from whom that and all other Power came And this is the meaning of that Sentence of *Callimachus* quoted by *Plutarch* Εἰ θεὸν οἶσθα, ἴσθι ὅτι ᾗ ῥέξαι θεῷ δυνατόν *If you know what God is, you must know, that he can do all things* Plut Lib I. de plac Phil. On this Head *Cicero* argues thus *Materiam enim rerum, ex qua, & in qua, omnia sint, totam esse flexibilem & commutabilem, ut nihil sit, quod non ex ea quamvis subito fingi convertique possit, ejus autem universæ fictricem & moderatricem divinam esse providentiam Hanc igitur quocunque se moveat, efficere posse quicquid velit For Matter, out of which, and in which, all things do consist, must be flexible and changeable, so that there can be nothing, which may not out of that be suddenly changed and turned the Framer and Governour of which is the divine Providence And this, whithersoever it turns it self, it can do whatsoever it pleases* Cic de Nat.Deor Lib III The like is urged by several of the Christian Writers, from the same Power remaining in God still, which he was vested with, when he made the World out of Nothing, the most stupendous Instance of an Almighty Power, For thus *Theophilus Antiochenus* [illegible] *We have a Demonstration of God's Almighty Power in this, that he made all things which he pleased out of Nothing,* Theoph ad Autol Lib. II. To the same purpose *Eusebius Emissenus, Cuncta, quæ non erant, tanquam subito aliunde producta, ante nutum ejus, velociter adstiterunt, nulla apparente materia Origo fuit rerum, efficax Creatoris imperium All which things were not, being produced of a sudden stood before him at his Pleasure, tho' there was no matter to make them of The efficacious Power of the Creator was the Original of things* Euseb Emiss Hom I de Symb

God does not do all that he Can But then there are some Rules to be observed, in stating the Doctrine of God's Omnipotence 1 The *first* is, That Men should not conclude, that God has actually done, or will do, all that he can Which is of good use to confute the Errors of those, who oftentimes under the Shelter of God's Almighty Power, would give Countenance to their own groundless Fancies, *Tertullian* speaks very well in this Case *Plane nihil Deo difficile Sed si tam abrupte in præsumptionibus nostris hac sententia utamur, quidvis de Deo confingere poterimus quasi fecerit, quia facere potuerit. Non autem, quia omnia potest facere, ideoq; credendus est, illum fecisse etiam quod non fecerit, sed an fecerit requirendum There is nothing difficult with God, but, if without Consideration we shall apply this Maxim to all our Fancies, we may feign any thing of God, as if he had done, what he could have done For, because he can do all things, it must not therefore be believed, that he has done what he has not, but we ought to look out whether he has done it or no* Tertull. adv. Prax.

Cap 8 To the same purpose speaks *Athanasius* [illegible] &c *It was possible that Christ might not have come, and that God might have dissolved the Curse, only by a word But we ought to consider what was most expedient for Men, and not in all things to judge what God is able to do,* &c

God cannot do Contradictions 2. The *Second* Rule is, not to ascribe to God the Power of doing any thing which implies a Contradiction This was a Truth so obvious, that the Heathens could not but take Notice of it

Μόνου γὰρ αὐτοῦ καὶ Θεὸς στερίσκεται
Ἀγένητα ποιεῖν ἅσσ' ἂν ᾖ πεπραγμένα

God's Power is bounded by one thing alone,
To make things undone, which have once been done
Agathon the Poet in *Aristotle*'s Ethicks, Lib VI cap 2.

And *Plotinus* gives the Reason of this, because it would be [illegible], to do that work, which he had with the greatest Wisdom done before, which is contrary to the Perfection of the Divine Nature for, says he, [illegible] *to be able to do Contradictions, is an Inability to continue in what is best* Plot Ennead 6 Lib VIII c 21 The like is to be said concerning God's making Matter not to be extended, that two and two should not be four, that Ten should be Twenty, &c which does not proceed from any defect of Power in the Deity but that he has already willed what the respective Natures must be Or as St *Cyril* in a like Case says, [illegible] *This is no sign of Imperfection in God, but it shews only a sort of a steadiness and unshakeable Consistency in the Nature of things, which is in each of these Particulars, and which he knows does naturally and unchangeably operate in them* Cyril Comment in Joh vi

God cannot do any thing contrary to his Holiness. 3 The *Third* Rule is not to ascribe to God the doing of any thing, which implies Moral Obliquity, or which is contrary to his Holiness and Purity Thus in the holy Scriptures, it is declared of God, that he *cannot lye* Tit 1 2 Heb. vi 18 The Reason of which is thus given by *Origen* [illegible] *God cannot do any vicious things, because then it could be in the Power of God not to be God For if he could do any thing vitious, he would not be God* Orig Lib iv. contr Cels The same Argument is used by S *Ambrose* *Quid ergo Deo impossibile? Illud utique quod naturæ ejus contrarium est, non quod virtuti arduum Impossibile est (inquit) ei mentiri, & impossibile istud non infirmitatis est, sed virtutis & majestatis, quia veritas non recipit mendacium, nec Dei virtus levitatis errorem. What therefore is impossible to God? that which is contrary to his Nature, not that which is too hard for his Power It is impossible* (he says) *for him to lye, but that Impossibility does not argue his Infirmity, but his Power and Majesty, because he who is Truth does not admit of a Lye, nor the Power of God the error of Levity* And so St *Chrysostom* Ὥσπερ γὰρ ὅταν λέγωμεν ἀδύνατον εἶναι τὸν Θεὸν ἁμαρτεῖν, [illegible] *When we say, that it is impossible for God to Sin, we do not bespeak any Weakness in him, but only declare an unspeakable Power which belongs to him* Chrys Hom. xxviii in Joh

h *Wisdom*] To make up the Character of perfect Wisdom two things are Necessary, First a perfect Understanding of the Nature and Circumstances of things, and Secondly a Wise Ordering of them Both of which Qualifications are in the Deity, in an Infinite degree of Perfection

Of

Of God's Intellectual Wisdom, or his Knowledge

In speaking of which it will be requisite to Observe,

God's KNOWLEDGE different from ours

I That the Understanding of God is a thing vastly different from our Understanding both in Nature and Manner as well as in Degree For in us Understanding is a Quality, which Improves and Exerts it self gradually, and in short is something new superinfused upon the Mind, but God who is one pure simple Act cannot admit of any such Habit, and therefore the Knowledge of God is only the very Essence of God considered as Knowing or Understanding So that on this Account, *Aristotle* argues very justly, that if God's Understanding were a Habit, εὔλογον ἐπίπονον εἶναι τὸ συνεχὲς αὐτῷ τῆς νοήσεως, *his perpetual Cogitation* (or thinking of such a number of things together) *would be laborious to him.* Arist Met 12 Cap 9 And thus *Plotinus* Δεῖ δὲ νοῦν λαμβάνειν, εἴπερ ἐπαληθεύσομεν τῷ ὀνόματι, μὴ τὸν δυνάμει, μηδὲ τὸν ἐξ ἀφροσύνης εἰς νοῦν ἐλθόντα Εἰ δὲ μή, ἄλλον πάλιν πρὸ αὐτοῦ ζητήσομεν ἀλλὰ τὸν ἐνεργείᾳ καὶ ἀεὶ νοῦν ὄντα ... μὴ ἐπακτὸν τὸ φρονεῖν ἔχει *If we would speak properly, we ought not to consider the Divine Mind as a Habit, or as making a Progress from Ignorance to Knowledge For then we must seek out further for some other Mind But we ought to consider it as a Mind which is in Act, and always in being For otherwise it would have an Adscititious Understanding, i e it would be beholding to something without to perfect it* Plot Enn v Lib 9 c 5

Understands all things that are

II That God has a perfect Knowledge of all things that have a Being, and 1st, of the most transcendent of all Beings, Himself For, as *Alcinous* says, ἐπεὶ δὴ ὁ πρῶτος νοῦς κάλλιστος, δεῖ καὶ κάλλιστον αὐτῷ νοητὸν ὑποκεῖσθαι, οὐδὲν δὲ αὐτοῦ κάλλιον· ἑαυτὸν ἂν οὖν καὶ τὰ ἑαυτοῦ νοήματα ἀεὶ νοοίη *Forasmuch as the first Mind is the most excellent, it is necessary that that, which is the most excellent, should be the Object of its Understanding But nothing is more excellent than its self, therefore it must understand it self and its own thoughts* Alcin c 10 And to the like purpose *Plotinus* ὅταν αὐτὸ τι αὐτὸ νοῇ, ὁ δὴ κυρίως ἔστι νοεῖν *when God contemplates himself, then he is most properly said to understand*, Plot. Lib V c 13 2dly, Of all other things (1) Because of the admirable Penetration of the Divine Nature, and the inherent Light and Clearness of its Understanding From this Topick *Philo* reasons thus Ἰδοὺ γὰρ Θεῷ ὡς ἐν αὐγῇ καθαρᾷ πάντα ἀεὶ δῆλα· ὅς γε ἄχρι τῶν τῆς ψυχῆς μυχῶν φθάσας, ἃ τοῖς ἄλλοις ἐστὶν ἀθέατα, τηλαυγῶς ὡς ἐν φωτὶ καθορᾷν, καὶ προμηθείᾳ καὶ προνοίᾳ χρώμενος, οἰκείαις ἀρεταῖς, οὐδὲν ἀπελευθεριάζειν, καὶ ἔξω τῆς ἑαυτοῦ κατάληψεως βαίνειν ἐᾷ ... ἐπεὶ οὐδὲ ἐν τοῖς μέλλουσιν ἀδηλότης αὐτῷ συμβαίνει· οὐδὲ γὰρ ἄδηλον, οὔτε μέλλον ἐστὶ Θεῷ οὐδέν *All things are manifest to God as in a pure Light For penetrating to the inward parts of the Soul, he by his own Nature clearly sees things which are unobservable by others and making use of his Wisdom and Providence, and proper Excellencies, suffers nothing to pass by and to escape his Understanding Forasmuch as the Obscurity of future things is obvious to him For nothing is uncertain or future to God* Phil Lib de Immutab Dei

Because all things are present to him

(2) Because all things are present to him And to this Head relate those *Orphick* Verses.

> Ὄμμα μέγα τρομέουσιν ὃ καὶ γαίην ὑπένερθεν
> Αἰθέρα καὶ πόντοιο μεγάλου βένθος, ὅ τε τε κεύθει
> Νῦν, ἐφορῶντα· τὸν οὐ τι κέκευθεν χρόνος, ἀλλὰ πάρεστι
> Πάντα Θεῷ ——

> *Let's tremble at that mighty Eye, which looks*
> *Into the Ground, and over all the Ocean,*
> *Which sees what Men desire to conceal,*
> *Whose Sight no time impairs for every thing*
> *Is present unto God*——

Upon which Consideration the *Ægyptians* framed their Hieroglyphical Representation of the Deity, hanging up in their Temples Eyes and Ears of Gold, to denote that God sees and hears all things *Clem Alex* Lib V *Strom*

Because all things are made and preserved by him

(3) Because all things are made and preserved by God, who upon that account must most intimately know them For thus *Ammonius* in his Commentary upon *Aristotle*'s Book of Interpretation writes, Ἀλλ' ἀγνοῶν μὲν οὐδὲν ... αὐτοὺς ἐνδέχεται τὰ πάντα παραγόντας τε, καὶ διακοσμοῦντας *The Gods cannot be ignorant of any things that are, since they produced them and put them in order* And thus St *Clement* of *Alexandria* excellently speaks Κινδυνεύουσι τοίνυν οἱ φάσκοντες, &c *They that say that Philosophy did not come hither from God, seem to say that 'tis impossible that God should see all things and that he is not the cause of all good things, if they be particulars For 'tis plain that nothing can be without the Will of God But if all things are by his Will, then Philosophy is from God, who would have it be as it is for their sakes, who would upon no other account abstain from evil For God knows all things, not only those things which are, but those which are to come, and how every one of these is. foreseeing all their particular Motions, provides for all things and hears all things, seeing the naked Mind of every one, has an eternal Understanding of all particulars And, as it is in a Theatre, where People see distinctly all that is before them and about them, so it is in God, ἀθρόως τε γὰρ πάντα καὶ ἕκαστον ἐν μέρει μιᾷ προσβολῇ προσβλέπει, He sees all things at one view, and every particular thing with the same glance of his Eye* Clem Al Lib VI Protr Therefore it is greatly to be wondered at, how it should enter into the Thoughts of so learned, and in some things so acute a Man, as St *Jerom*, to deny the Knowledge of God as to all the particulars of Nature *Absurdum est* (says he) *ad hoc Dei deducere majestatem, ut sciat per momenta singula quot nascantur culices, quotve moriantur, quæ cimicum & pulicum & muscarum sit in terra multitudo, quanti pisces in aqua natent, & qui de minoribus majorum prædæ cedere debeant It is absurd to bring down the Majesty of God to take notice, how many Gnats are every moment born, or die, what number of Gnats or Flies there is in the World; how many Fishes swim in the Sea, and what little Fishes are to be a prey to the greater* Hier in 1 Cap Habac. Now take this, either to relate to God's Knowledge, or Providence, it is certainly a very irreligious Thought: and 'tis much the Atheists do not defend this Paradox of his, after the Example of some others who have vindicated his Fancy of the Identity of the Orders of Bishops and Presbyters. But it is no wonder, that this Father should depreciate the Dignity of Bishops, when he has made so bold with the Omniscience of Almighty God

Knows all future Contingents

III God has a perfect Knowledge of all future Contingents This some of the Heathen Philosophers denied, but others with greater force of Reason maintain'd *Cicero*, or at least his Interlocutor, in his Book of Divination, was of the negative side *Nihil enim est tam contrarium rationi & constantiæ, quam fortuna ut mihi ne in Deum quidem cadere videatur, ut sciat quid casu & fortuito futurum sit Si enim scit, certe illud eveniet. Sin certe eveniet, nulla fortuna est Est autem fortuna. rerum igitur fortuitarum nulla est præsensio There is nothing so contrary to Reason and Constancy, as Fortune So that I do not think it is in the Power of God, to know what casual things shall come to pass For if he does know them they will certainly come to pass If they certainly will come to pass, then there is no Fortune But there is Fortune, therefore there is no knowing fortuitous things* Cic de Div. Lib II The force of this Objection will be hereafter answered in a more proper Place. In the mean time let us see what Arguments there are to evince the Truth of God's knowing future Contingents

This proved from the Predictions in Scripture

1. This a Truth confirmed both by the Doctrine and by the Predictions of Holy Scripture. From the Prophet *Isaiah* we learn, that this Knowledge is one of the Characteristicks of the true Deity For thus, insulting the Heathen Deities, God speaks *Shew the things that are to come hereafter, that we may know that ye are Gods*, Isa. xli 23. And again, *I am the first and I am the last, and besides me there is no God And who, as I, shall call and shall declare it*, &c *and the things that are coming, and shall come?* Is xliv 6, 7 The Sins of the Jews are foretold, *Is* lii 1 Our Saviour foretels his Passion, *Mat.* xx 17, 18 and that he should be betrayed by *Judas*, *Mat.* xxvi 21 That *Peter* should deny him thrice, *Mat* xxvi 34 The coming of false Prophets is foretold, *Mat* xxiv. 5 1 *Tim* iv 1. and of Anti Christ, 2 *Thess* ii. 3, &c. The same Truth is evinced by Reason.

The want of which would argue Imperfection of the Deity

(1) Drawn from the Excellence of the Divine Mind, the want of which Qualification would argue great Imperfection, which in all Thoughts and Words relating to the Deity ought to be avoid-

ed

the Maker and Pre- | [l] Goodness, the [k] Maker | *omnium, tum visibili-*

ed For thus *Origen*, Τὸ προκαταγγέλλειν τὰ μέλλοντα ... θεότητος ἐπαγγελία. *The foretelling of future things is the Character stick of the Deity* Orig cont. Cels Lib vi And in another Passage of his, cited by *Eusebius*, ὅτι μὲν ... ὁ Θεὸς ... δυνάμεως τοῦ Θεοῦ *That God does foreknow every thing which is to come, altho' the Scripture said nothing of it, yet this would be manifest from the Nat. of God, which every one must acknowledge, who Understands the Dignity of the Divine Power*, Euseb de Prep Lib vi (2) Because God makes and orders all things, and therefore cannot but know their future Conditions For thus *Ammonius* the Philosopher reasons ... *It must be said that the Gods do know all things, that have been, and are, and shall be, in that manner which is agreeable to the Gods that is, by one defined and immutable Knowledge And therefore they must be endowed with the Knowledge of Contingents, as those who produce all things that are in the World* Ammon in Com de Lib Arist de Interp To the same purpose St *Ambrose* *Ideo non potuit Creator omnium ignorare quod fecit, nescire quod donavit Novit ergo diem qui fecit, &c Ergo qui fecit quæ futura sunt, eo genere quo futura cognovit The Creator of all things cannot be ignorant of what he has made, and not know what he has given Therefore he knows the day which he made, &c Upon the whole, he who made those things which are to come, knows them, in that manner that futures are known*, Lib v de fide, c 7 (3) He knows these by an infallible Knowledge, not from conjecture For thus *Ammonius* argues ... *The Gods know Contingents in a more excellent manner, than according to their Nature For since they have an undefined Nature, and may happen or not happen, they (the Gods) in a more excellent manner than this, have an anticipated Knowledge of them, and know them definitely* Ammon ibid. And so likewise *Plotinus* ... *The knowledge of future Events, if they* [the Gods] *have it, is not such as that of Conjecturers, but like that of those who have a firm persuasion that a thing shall be For this is of those who have all things in their Power, to whom nothing is uncertain or doubtful For with them there is a steady Knowledge of Futures, as well as Presents, as to their Stability* (4) That this Knowledge is not inconsistent with the freedom of human Will And this, 1 because God does not so much determinably will things to be future, as he looks upon them in their future state as present which Intuition does not lay any force upon Man's Will For thus *Boetius* argues upon this Point *Atque Deus ea futura, quæ ex arbitrii libertate proveniunt, præsentia contuetur, Hæc igitur ad intuitum relata divinum necessaria fiunt per conditionem divinæ notionis per se vero considerata, ab absoluta naturæ suæ libertate non desinunt God looks upon those futures which depend upon the Liberty of the Will, as things present Therefore these things as they relate to the Divine Knowledge are necessary, but considered by themselves, they do not vary from the absolute Liberty of their Nature* Boet de Cons. Lib v 2 Because to foresee is not to determine, as *Origen* excellently well Reasons ... &c "To whom we answer, That, "when God designed to make the World out of No-"thing, he took a view of all things, and saw this was to "be, and this was to be consequent upon it But if this "come to pass, then that will follow But if this be so, "something else will happen And so going on to the end, "he knows whatever things shall come to pass but yet "not so, as to cause those things which he knows to come "to pass As he that sees that one who walks carelesly "will slip, his looking on and foretelling his fall is not "the cause of his slipping So it must be understood, that "God does foresee whatever each Person will do, but "his looking on is not the Cause of this Man's doing ill, "or that Man's doing well

Because he makes and orders all things

God does not know Contingents only by Conjecture

God's Knowledge of future Contingents not inconsistent with human Will

Of God's Wisdom in the Disposal and Ordering of things

I need not here speak much concerning this Branch of the Divine Wisdom, because I shall have occasion to insist more fully of it in treating of Providence in the Note *l* I shall only observe, (1) That this Attribute is frequently ascribed to God in holy Scripture *He is mighty in Strength and Wisdom* Job xxxvi 5 *Blessed be the name of the Lord for ever and ever, for Wisdom and Might are his* Dan ii 20 Particularly with relation to the Creation of the World *O Lord how manifold are thy works, in Wisdom hast thou made them all*, Psal civ 24 *He hath established the world by his Wisdom, and stretched out the Heavens by his discretion*, Jer x 12 And so with relation to the Redemption of the World Upon this account Christ is called the *Wisdom of God* 1 Cor i 24 And the Gospel is called the *Hidden Wisdom of God, and the manifold Wisdom of God*, Eph iii. 10 Nay, Wisdom in Scripture is in a peculiar manner ascribed unto God, as in a true and proper manner belonging to no one else The Consideration of this made St *Paul* to cry out, *O the depth of the riches, both of the Wisdom and Knowledge of God* Rom xi 33 and to say, that *the Lord knoweth the Thoughts of the wise that they are but vain*, in comparison of the Divine Wisdom, 1 Cor iii 20 (2) The same is deducible from human Reason Because the want of Wisdom would argue a great Imperfection, and it would be the highest degree of Arrogance for Creatures to claim Wisdom to themselves, and to deny it to their Creator Besides, if this Perfection were wanting in God, the rest of his Perfections would be to little purpose For what would signify infinite Power, to be able to do all things, and to want Wisdom to Conduct those mighty Actions? This would only serve, to fill the whole Creation with Irregularities and Blunders, and set all things jarring and fighting with one another What would it signify, to know the respective Natures and Tendencies of all things, and not to be able to dispose them to wise and good purposes? This would occasion such untoward Combinations of Causes and Effects, as would put the whole World into disorder But when infinite Wisdom is joyned with the like Knowledge and Power, it cannot but produce that Harmony and Regularity, which are observable in every part of Nature, and in every Branch of the Divine Providence

WISDOM of God proved from Scripture

Want of this would imply the greatest Imperfection in the Deity

l Goodness] The Goodness of God does denote all that is Excellent Holy, and Bountiful in the Divine Nature Therefore his Goodness is branched into these three Parts, 1 His Metaphysical Goodness, *i e* his Excellency, or Perfection 2 His Moral Goodness, *i e* his Purity or Holiness 3 His beneficial Goodness, *i e* his Bounty or Favour to his Creatures, particularly to Mankind

Of God's Metaphysical Goodness, or his Excellency

The Name of Good in Scripture is generally applied to God's Moral or Beneficial Goodness, but his Metaphysical Goodness or Essential Perfection is usually expressed by *Excellent*, *Gen* xv 7 *Psal* cxxxviii 13 *Psal* cl 2 *Is* xxviii 29 or Great, *Deut* x 17 *Chron* xvi 25 *Psal* xlviii 1 *Job* xxxvi 26 *Jer* xxxii 18 tho' perhaps that Passage of our Saviour may be interpreted in this Sense, *None is good save one*, *Luke* xviii 19 none has an original, inherent and perfective Goodness, or an Accumulation of all Excellencies, but God Now this Branch of the Divine Good-

God's Essential GOODNESS proved from his Perfection

Goodness may be proved (1) From the Essential Perfection of the Divine Nature, which contains in it all that is Good and Excellent Hence the Platonists call God the τἀγαθὸν, *The Good*, by way of Eminence And Proclus makes a Distinction, between *good* and *The good* [illegible] *The good it self, and be that is good, are very different* Procl Lib in Timaeum And [illegible] *The good it self is not any good thing, but that which is simply good*, ibid And, he says, that every created Being is only [illegible] *only something like to good, and such by Participation, but the* Good it *self is primarily good*, ibid In like manner, Origen speaks [illegible] *The Good which is so substantially, is not like that which is Good-ness by accident, and by the by* Orig contr Cels Lib vi (2) Because he is the Fountain from which all Excellency is derived For, thus Alcinous reasons [illegible] *nothing* [illegible] *it self sufficient, that is, wanting nothing* [illegible] *but perfect in every respect, being the Goodness, the Substance* [illegible] THE GOOD Alcin de doct Plat Cap x And thus Dionysius [illegible] *The just Person is so called Perfect, because* [illegible] *but is always Perfect and never Diminished,* [illegible] *containing all things in its self, according to one superabundant* [illegible] *Bounty, by which he perfects all things, and fills them up with his own Perfection* Dionys Cap iii de Div Nom (3) Because he Possesses, in the most Eminent manner, every thing, that is good and perfect And thus an acute Philosopher writes, upon this Argument [illegible] *The Original Good, or the Good it self,* [illegible] *to be above all things, and only good, having nothing in its self but good,* [illegible] *else, above all, and the Cause of all* Plot Enn v Lib v

Of God's Moral Goodness

God's Moral GOODNESS proved from Scripture

This is in Scripture called by the general Name of Holiness He is said to be *Holiness* it self, *Psal* xxx the *holy one*, Hab. i. 12 *holy in all his ways and works*, Psal cxlv 17 And all moral Obliquity is denied of him, in Holy Scripture *A God of Truth and without iniquity*, Deut xxxii 4 [illegible] 1 Sam xv 29 *Far be it from God that he should do wickedness*, Job xxxiv 10 And Reason dictates the same thing I That God is endowed with such an Essential Rectitude of Nature, that he cannot do any thing contrary to the Rules of Moral [illegible] And for this the ancient

From Reason [illegible]

Divines assign several Reasons (1) God cannot Sin, Because he is eternal and uncreated, &c, since all Sin does proceed from some Weakness or other, viz. want of Power, [illegible] of Shame, or Punishment, &c the great Creator of all things, being free from these Imperfections, is not liable to Sin This Argument is prosecuted by S Austin with great strength against the *Manichees* Aug contr *Ful* Lib i (2) Because his Nature is unchangeable S *Austin* says, *Malorum nonnulla* [illegible] *bonum, & à summo Deo,* [illegible] *qui bona omnia condidit, institutu* [illegible] *There would be no Evil,* [illegible] *changeable Nature which being* [illegible] *God who is an unchangeable Good,* [illegible] Aug de Civ Dei Lib [illegible] The same Reason is assigned by *Philo* There is [illegible] λῆς, [illegible] *Something unmoveable and unchangeable, and is not like Man who never stands at the same stay, but is subject to continual Changes, whose* [illegible] *unhappy Creature! being tripped up (for his whole Life is a slip) suffers a grievous fall* Philo de nom comm (3) Because of the innate Goodness of his Nature For thus Gregory Nyssen reasons on this Argument, tho' with particular Relation to the second Person of the Trinity [illegible] *Whereas the Divine Will is able to do all things, it has no manner of Propension to evil* [illegible] *a Propension to Evil is perfectly foreign to the Divine Nature But all that is good it does necessarily Will and being* [illegible] *able to do it and being thus able does not fail* [illegible] *every good, which it has made its choice of* Greg Nyss Catech c i

Because of his innate Goodness

II That he cannot be the Author of Sin This is proved (1) from the Essential Goodness of God For thus Plato reasons [illegible] *Since God does not hurt, does he do any evil?* [illegible] *that which does no evil, is the cause of no evil* Plat de rep Lib II And again blaming Homer for imputing this to the Gods, [illegible] &c. *That breaking of Oaths and Leagues, which was occasioned by Pandarus, tho' any one impute it to Pallas or Jupiter, we will not ascribe it to him, neither will we suffer our young Men to hear* [illegible] *Aeschylus says*,

God cannot be the Author of Sin, Because of his Essential Goodness

— [illegible]
[illegible]

— Jove makes a Family be wicked,
When e'er he pleases to destroy it Ib

And to the like purpose *Philo*, [illegible] &c *Nor does Moses as some wicked Persons do, make God the Cause of Sin* &c Phil Quod det pot And elsewhere, [illegible] *In our selves are the Treasures of all evil things, but in God of good things* Phil de Prof (2) Because otherwise the guilt of Sin could not be chargeable upon Men Which Argument is thus excellently urged by Origen [illegible] *to us (i e the Heathens Objection, of the Christians making God the Author of Sin) that Evils* [illegible] *Actions which flow from them, are not caused by God* [illegible] *could they teach the Doctrine of a future judgment, that wicked Men shall be punished for their evil deeds according to the nature of their Crimes, and that they shall be rewarded by God, who live according to the Rules of Virtue, and do virtuous actions, if God be the cause of those Sins?* Orig contr Cels Lib VI (3) Because this is a blasphemous Opinion, and very injurious to the Honour of Almighty God For *Methodius* very justly says, [illegible] *From whence it appears, that God the Creator of all things is not the cause of Evil, which is an impious Opinion* Method apud Photium To the same purpose St *Basil* writes more expressly [illegible]

Because, otherwise, Men could not be charged with Sin

Because, this is a blasphemous Opinion

[illegible] *He is a Fool and void of Mind* [illegible] *Sense, who says there is no God. And like to him, and little different from him in Folly, is he that says God is the* [illegible] *And I think the Crime of both of these is* [illegible] *because both of these do deny the good God; he* [illegible] *his Being, the other* [illegible] *him to be Good* [illegible] *if he be the Author of Sin he is not good. Wherefore* [illegible] *of these Opinions is a denying of God.* Basil Hom. Quod [illegible]

JUSTICE of God in not letting Sin go unpunished.

III. That he will not suffer Sin, or the Violation of his Laws, to go unpunished, nor Virtue, or the diligent Observance of them, to be unrewarded. This branch of the Divine Goodness is generally called God's JUSTICE. And this is evidently proved out of Holy Scripture. As for God's vindicative Justice we learn it from Rom. i. 18. *The Wrath of God is revealed from Heaven against all Ungodliness and Unrighteousness of Men, who hold the Truth in Unrighteousness.* And 1o Eph. v. 6. *This ye know that no* [illegible] *Man who is* [illegible] *hath any Inheritance in the Kingdom of Christ* [illegible] *of God.* We [illegible] therein [illegible] [illegible] *righteous thing with God to recompense* [illegible] *to them* [illegible] [illegible] 2 Tim. iv. 6, 7. [illegible] *for me a Crown of Righteousness, which the Lord the Righteous Judge shall give me at that Day.* 2 Tim. iv. 8. *God is not Unrighteous to forget your work and labour of love.* Heb. vi. 10. This, indeed, is not strictly due to our Merits, nor does it flow as an Original Debt from the Divine Justice, but so flows only from God's gracious Promise, which he has engaged himself, that he will bestow upon us, and therefore only consequentially, by virtue of that and our performing the Conditions of the Covenant on our side, he finds obliged to confer it upon us. This is shortly summed up by St. Basil [illegible] *There is Justice sent down from Heaven by the righteous Judge, the one* [illegible] *the other* [illegible] Basil in [illegible] To the same effect Clemens of Alexandria [illegible]

[illegible] *which is the only* [illegible] Clem. Alex. in Protrept.

MERCY of God in not inflicting Punishment till Men are Incorrigible.

IV. That God is not disposed to inflict that extremity of Punishment, which his Justice might exact and demand of Men, for their Sins, whilst they are capable of growing better. This branch of the Divine Goodness is called his MERCY. Now because, in this State of Imperfection, it is impossible for us to perform an unsinning Obedience, and our manifold Violations of God's most Holy Laws do expose the best of Men to his Justice, therefore it has pleased God, for our Comfort, to reveal to us this gracious Disposition, to rescue us from this Misery which our Sins make us liable to, upon our complying with those Conditions which he has made known to us in the Gospel. This gracious Disposition of the Divine Nature, which is an admirable temperament of God's Justice, is stiled in the Scripture Language his *Mercy*, [illegible] Metaphor drawn from that Tenderness, which we find in our human Nature, when we have a miserable or distressed Object before our Eyes. And we learn (1) That there is such an Affection in the Divine Nature, whereby he is inclined to rescue us from the Misery and Punishment entailed upon Sin. *God who is rich in Mercy, for his great Love wherewith he loved us, even when we were dead in Sins, hath quickened us together with Christ.* Eph. ii. 4, 5. *Who hath called you out of darkness into his marvellous Light; which in time past were not a People, but are now the People of God, which had not obtained Mercy, but now have obtained Mercy.* 1 Pet. ii. 9, 10. *Be ye merciful as your Father in Heaven is merciful.* —— *Who according to his abundant Mercy hath begotten us again unto a lively hope.* 1 Pet. i. 3. (2.) That this Life is the only proper time for exerting God's Mercy, his Justice being to be display'd most in the other. This is evident from the whole Tenor of the Gospel, and the Apostolical Writings, which are designed to exhort Men to make their Peace with God, and to make the best Preparation for another World, during their stay in this; but more especially the Parable of D[illegible] and L[illegible], and that of the wise and foolish Virgins, with our Saviour's most terrible Discourse thereupon, of Men's final Doom to be awarded at the Resurrection, And [illegible] to Christians, that this Life only is the Time [illegible] Mercy, at least, as far as Revelation has [illegible] of. Upon which St. Cyprian well enlarges [illegible]

[illegible] Cyp. contr. Demetr. [illegible] to the same Sense St. Athan. [illegible] *that shall* [illegible] *Day* [illegible] Hesych.

Of God's Perfect Goodness

This is the most delightful and amiable to us of all God's Attributes, because it comes to us fraught with such innumerable Blessings and Favours, which our natural Selfishness [illegible] upon us to think upon. [illegible] is the Beauty of the Deity. [illegible] Zech. ix. 17. Now that this [illegible] does belong to Almighty God, we shall prove it from these following Topicks, from Scripture, from Reason, from Experience.

GOD'S BOUNTY from Scripture.

I. In the most early Revelation made by God to [illegible] he manifests his [illegible] this Character [illegible] [illegible] The Hebrew [illegible] [illegible] God [illegible] [illegible]

II. [illegible] teaches us, That [illegible] most [illegible] to Men, that God [illegible] God, that the Heathens could not help the [illegible] to the Persons whom they Worshipped for the Supreme God. Wherefore [illegible] Jupiter [illegible] the Title given by the Greeks to [illegible], and among the Latins, Jupiter Optimus Maximus. [illegible] (2.) Because this is the chiefest of God's Excellencies, which [illegible] others, that viewed by themselves, look of a rougher and harsher Nature. For what would be Almighty Power without Almighty Goodness, but only an infinite Tyranny, which all must Obey, but no one could love? Infinite Wisdom would only be an all-over-reaching Craft, unless Goodness inclined to punish the Wicked, and reward good ones, to [illegible] by [illegible] On [illegible] Reason [illegible] *Greatness*, Sen. de Ben. (3.) Because there is [illegible] this Perfection observable in God's Creatures, which does very much indear them to him, and render them beloved.

Reason from the Goodness of God.

Because God's [illegible] *Excellencies.*

Because [illegible] *Creature.*

[illegible] and therefore it must certainly be a most Eminent Divine, in the Creator [illegible] This Reason is the Author of the Book of the Trinity, [illegible] the Goodness of the whole [illegible] [illegible] *The whole World is the* [illegible] *of the Goodness of God, which he had not made, had he not been good. For if all things are to* [illegible] *good by consequence, and with very good Reason,* they prove the *Maker of them to be good.* De Trin Cap 4 But 'tis [illegible] by the Expressions of the Heathen, that they [illegible] had the greatest Thoughts of God's Beneficent Goodness, by their stiling those extraordinary Persons, who were benefactors to them by the Name of *Divi*, [illegible], &c because they thought, that by reason of their Goodness and Beneficence, they resembled God, and were a sort of lesser Deities which they would not have [illegible] had they not thought that the Deity was [illegible] Good and Beneficent

From Experience III Our Experience informs us, how highly we [illegible] indebted to the Divine Beneficence This the Ancient Divines and Philosophers have reduced to several Heads, according to the several Ways and Methods, by which we are befriended by the Divine Goodness I)

Because he confers [illegible] without Compulsion. I his beneficent Goodness is remarkably display'd, by the free Communication of it, whereas he might if he had pleased, being all-sufficient, have enjoyed his Happiness to himself alone On this Account thus *Hierocles* expresses himself [illegible Greek] *By God's Goodness all things were brought to be good For no other [illegible] of the making of all things can be assigned, but [illegible] Goodness For he was good by his Nature [illegible] at any time, upon this account, [illegible] are assigned for God's [illegible] the World, [illegible]* Hier in Aur Carm Pyth But this was no more than what he learned from *Plato*, who on the same account speaks almost in the same words [illegible Greek] *Let us enquire what was the cause which moved God to the making of the World He was good Now no Envy comes near Goodness Being without this, he made all things like himself This is the [illegible] reason of God's making the World, which I have learned from wise Men, and which ought as a true [illegible] to be received* Plat in Tim

Without prospect of Advantage (2) God Almighty bestows his Benefits upon us, without any prospect of Advantage to himself For thus *Plato* remarks [illegible Greek] *We receive all good things from the Gods, and they nothing from us* Plat in Eutyphron And so St *Chrysostom.* [illegible Greek] *God has made us without expecting any Advantage by us For he has demonstrated that he did not want us by making us so late For if he had wanted [illegible], he had made us long before* Chrys Hom in Ep ad Phil And to the like purport St *Austin* speaks *Non [illegible] Deum [illegible] [illegible] nemo [illegible] dixerit God does not enjoy [illegible], but makes use of us for if he did enjoy [illegible] as a good to himself, he would stand [illegible] need of us, which no Man in his Senses will assert* Aug de Christ Doctr

With the greatest readiness (3) God confers his Benefits upon us with the greatest readiness, without our making us wait for them (like other Benefactors) and tiring us out with Expectations This Observation is admirably well pursued by *Seneca* Of Human Benefits he remarks this *Plerique hoc [illegible] est, &c Most Men are [illegible] out of an evil Ambition [illegible] their Promises, least the crowd of their Adherents should be less —They do nothing quickly, they do [illegible] Their Injuries are very quick, but their Benefits are slow* Sen de Ben Lib ii cap 5 But of God's conferring his Favours, he speaks thus *Quocunque te flexeris, [illegible] ipse implet Wheresoever you turn you, [illegible] there is nothing void of him he fills his whole work.* id Lib iv cap 8 See the whole Vth and VIth Chapter of this Book.

Because he is good to all (4) Others are bountiful only to some few, but God is good to all Who, as our Saviour remarks, *maketh his Sun to shine upon the evil and the good*, Mat. v 45 *Seneca* speaks to the same purpose, and almost in the same words *Si deos imitaris, da & ingratis beneficia Nam & sceleratis Sol oritur, & Piratis patent maria If you would imitate the Gods, do good turns even to ungrateful Persons For the Sun arises upon the wicked, and the Seas are open to the very Pirates*, Sen de Benef Lib iv cap 26

Because he is good at all times (5) Mens Benefits are conferred oftentimes by fits, as their Humour leads, or Opportunity serves them, but God at all times disperses his Favours This is excellently well expressed by *Gregory Nyssen* [illegible Greek] *Is there any mark of true Goodness? This is, not to be profitable only to some particular thing, not to be sometimes profitable and other times unprofitable, not to be good to one and to another not so, but to be [illegible] good, to every one, and at all times*

Because he is particularly bountiful to Mankind (6) God's benefits are in a peculiar manner extended to Mankind And this with Relation both to his Body and Soul The Books of the Ancient Poets, and Philosophers, do abound with Observations on this Head For thus *Ovid*

Pronaque cum spectent animalia cætera terram,
Os homini sublime dedit cælumque tueri
Jussit, & erectos, ad sidera tollere vultus

Whilst other Animals look to the Ground,
He gave to Man a Face which upwards looks,
And bad him raise his Countenance to Heaven
Ovid Met Lib i

And thus *Manilius*

Quis dubitet posthæc hominem conjungere cælo?
[illegible] dedit lingamque capaxque
Ingenium [illegible] quem denique in unum
Descendit Deus, atque habitat, ipsumque requirit

Who then can doubt to join Man unto Heaven?
To whom a nimble Tongue Nature has giv'n,
A Wit capacious, and a sprightly Soul,
Into whose Breast alone God does descend,
And dwell therein, and does with Care look after.
Manil Lib ii

Juvenal makes the same Observation.

Sortiti ingenium, divinorumque capaces,
Atque exercendis capiendisque artibus apti,
Sensum a cælesti demissum traximus arce

We have a Wit capable of things Divine,
For Learning, and for exercising Arts
Dispos'd having a Soul from Heav'n descended.
Juvenal Sat xv.

Cicero, in many places, employs his Eloquence upon the same Subject, in his Offices, Lib i de Finibus Lib v. but particularly in this Passage of his Book of Laws "*Ipsum hominem eadem natura, non solum celeritate mentis ornavit, sed & sensus quasi satellites attribuit ac nuncios, & rerum plurimarum obscuras & necessarias intelligentias enudavit, quasi fundamenta quædam scientiæ figuramque Corporis habilem & aptam ingenio humano dedit Nam cum cæteras animantes abjecisset ad pastum, solum hominem erexit, & ad cæli, quasi cognationis domiciliique pristini, conspectum excitavit Tum speciem ita formavit oris, [illegible] Et oculi, quam [illegible] loquuntur & is, qui appellatur vultus, qui nullo in animante esse præter hominem potest, indicat mores*" *Nature has adorned Man not only with a ready Mind, but has likewise given him Senses to be as it were Centinels and Messengers for his use has cleared up for him many obscure but necessary Problems as the Foundation of his Knowledge, has made the figure of his Body fitable* *suitable to his Wit* For when he had made other Animals look downward, to their Food, he raised up Man alone and made him look upwards, as it were to take a view of his heavenly Kindred, and his antient Habitation* Cic de Leg. Lib 1 St *Chrysostom* makes the same Observation, but draws a further Use from the erect Shape of Man's Body [Greek illegible] *Man is made looking upwards to Heaven, that he may look about the things there, and Philosophize upon them, that he may make Observations upon them, and have the Eye of his Soul sharp-sighted* Chrys in Psal cxxi And elsewhere he draws a like Consequence, *viz* that Man should for this Reason, [Greek illegible] *That he should have nothing common with the Earth, that he should not be dragged or creep downward, but constantly fly upwards, and look up to the Sun of Righteousness*, Id. Hom xxiv in 1 Cor The same Father argues the Bounty of God, to Man, because all things are made for his Use [Greek illegible] *Man is a great and an admirable Animal, more dear to God than all other Creatures, for whom the Heaven and the Earth and the Sea, and all the rest of the Creatures were made* Hom ii Tom v But the greatest Benefits of all, which God has bestowed upon Mankind, are those which he confers upon us, with relation to our Souls, the State of future Glory, which he has prepared for us, and the Methods of Grace in order to it To omit the many Passages of Scripture, wherein this Truth is illustrated, and innumerable others in the Writings of the Fathers, let this Passage of *Basil* of *Seleucia* suffice [Greek illegible] *For thee, O Man, God appeared among Men for thy sake was the distribution of the Holy Spirit, the destruction of Death, and the hope of the Resurrection the divine Commandments which perfect thy Life the way to God by the Precepts of Religion the Kingdom of Heaven was made ready, and the Crowns of Righteousness, prepared, for those who do not decline to suffer for Virtue's sake* Bas Orat in *Verba Mosis* Attende tibi ipsi

k *Maker*] The words *Maker of all things visible and invisible* are taken out of the *Nicene* Creed as it now stands, or out of the Confession of Faith delivered by *Eusebius* to that Council [Greek illegible] *We believe on God the Maker of all things visible and invisible* Socr Hist Eccl Lib 1 cap 7 ed Steph Bishop *Pearson* has remarked that this Expression is not found in many of the antient Creeds, but the Substance of it seems to be contained in the word [Greek illegible] But however *Irenæus* makes it to be of Apostolical Tradition, *Quia sit unus Deus omnipotens, qui omnia condidit per verbum suum—sive visibilia sive invisibilia, sive sensibilia, sive intelligibilia, sive temporalia, sive æterna* *That there is one Almighty God, who has made all things by his word—whether Visibles or Invisibles, whether Temporal or Eternal* Iræn Lib 1 cap 19 And again, *Unum Deum fabricatorem cœli & terræ—Ecclesia omnis per universum orbem hanc accepit ab Apostolis traditionem.* *That there is one God, the Creator of Heaven and Earth—the whole Church throughout the universal World has received it as a Tradition from the Apostles* Iræn. Lib iii cap 9 And the Profession of it seems to be grounded upon an Opposition,

God declared to be the Maker of the World, in opposition to those who held the Eternity of it

1. To those Philosophers, who maintained the Eternity of the World, principally from the necessary Emanation of God's Goodness, who being essentially Good, could not but necessarily from all Eternity communicate his Goodness but this was a mistaken Notion of God's communicative, or beneficial Goodness, or an undue Confusion of it with his Moral Goodness For God is of necessity morally Good, because no time can be assigned in which he could have done Evil But it cannot be said of his Beneficent Goodness, that he must always communicate it, for this would restrain his Liberty, when it does not imply Imperfection, which does as essentially agree to him as any other of his Attributes. Upon which consideration, *Clemens* of *Alexandria* thus argues, concerning the Deity [Greek illegible] *God creates by his mere Will, and Production follows his willing it* Clem. Alex in Protrep Besides, the Absurdity of this Opinion is urged even by Philosophers of other Sects, as particularly, because no Action of considerable Antiquity is remembred,

Præterea, si nulla fuit genitalis origo
Terrarum & cœli, semperque æterna fuere,
Cur supra Bellum Thebanum & funera Trojæ
Non alias alii quoque res cecinere Poetæ?

But grant the World Eternal, grant it knew
No Infancy, and grant it never new
Why then no Wars our Poets Songs employ
Beyond the Siege of Thebes, or that of Troy?
Why former Heroes fall without a Name,
Why not their Battles told by lasting Fame?
Lucr Lib v cx vers Creech

And so again he argues from the late Invention of Arts

Quare etiam quædam nunc artes expoliuntur,
Nunc etiam augescunt, nunc addita navigiis sunt
Multa, &c

And therefore Arts that lay but rude before
Are polish'd now, we own new Ars the Store
We perfect all the old, and first find more
*Shipping's improv'd——*Ibid

In opposition to those Hereticks who would have it made by Angels

2 In opposition to those Hereticks who pretended that the World was made either by Angels, or, as others of them more wickedly, by an evil Principle, or the Devil *Simon Magus*, the Founder of this abominable Spawn of Hereticks, asserted [Greek illegible] *That the World was made by Angels* Theod Ep Hær Lib So did *Menander*, Iræn Lib 1 cap 21 *Saturninus*, id Lib 1 cap 21 as likewise the *Basilidians*, Theodor de Hær Lib and *Carpocrates* Epiph contr Hær. *Marcion* taught, [Greek illegible] *That there was a God greater than he that was Maker of the world*, Just Apol ii And *Cerdon* taught that there were *duos deos, unum bonum & alterum sævum, bonum superiorem, sævum hunc mundi Creatorem* *Two Gods, one good, and the other cruel the good the superior God, the other the Creator of the World* Tert de Præscr contr Hær But this was (as *Irenæus* observes) not only a wicked but a foolish Reflection of theirs upon God's Omnipotence *Qui non credunt quidem, quod ex ipsam materiam, cum sit potens, & dives in omnibus Deus, creavit, nescientes quantum potest Spiritualis & Divina Substantia* *Who do not believe that God could make Matter, when as he is mighty and rich in all things, being ignorant of the Power of a spiritual and divine Substance*, Iræn ad Hær Lib ii cap 10.

In opposition to those who asserted the Pre-existence of Matter.

3 In opposition to those Philosophers and Hereticks who asserted the eternal Pre-existence of Matter. For that many of them did so, St *Chrysostom* does in very few words inform us [Greek illegible] *Altho' the Manichee come and say, That Matter does Pre-exist, tho' Marcion and Valentinus, and the Greek Philosophers, tell them that in the beginning God created the Heaven and the Earth* Chrys Hom ii in Gen But the Orthodox Christians always maintained, that the World was created by God out of Nothing, and not out of any Matter Pre-existing And this Doctrine they grounded chiefly upon the word of God For, tho' the word *barach* in the first of *Genesis*, God *created the Heaven and the Earth*, does not in the strict Sense of the word denote a Creation out of nothing, it being used promiscuously with the word *gnasa* and *gnatzar*, which signify to make or to form any thing, tho' out of preceding Matter, yet that God did Create the World out of nothing, is more manifestly evident

 dent

dent from other places of Scripture, which do denote that this firft Production was out of nothing For that Expreffion of St *Paul* is a plain Allufion to this Senfe *Which calleth thofe things which be not as though they were* And more plainly in the Epiftle to the Hebrews *Through Faith we underftand that the Worlds were framed by the Word of God fo that things which are feen, were not made of things which do appear*, Heb xi 3 This feemed fo evident a Truth, that St *Chryfoftom* expreffes himfelf thus [Greek illegible] *To fay that things which are were made out of Pre exiftent Matter, and not to confefs that they were made out of nothing, is a fign of the laft degree of Frenzy*. Chryf Hom ii in Gen

Providence of God every where afferted in Scripture

[l] *Preferver*] I The Holy Scripture is full of Inftances, wherein the Providence of God in Preferving and Governing all things is declared, and Examples thereof recorded As *O Lord thou preferveft Men and Beafts*, Pfal xxxvi 6 *God giveth to the Beaft his Food, and to the young Ravens which cry*, Pfal cxlvii 9 *He giveth to all Life, Breath, and all things*, Acts xvii 25 And our Saviour teaches us, that God preferves the Fowls of the Air and the Lilies of the Field, *Mat* vi 26 And that a Sparrow does not fall to the Ground without his Permiffion, *Mat* x 29 And not only in Preferving them but in Governing them *Who maketh his Sun to rife upon the evil and upon the good*, Mat.v 45 *Who covereth the Heaven with Clouds and prepareth Rain for the Earth*, Pf cxlvii 8 *who gives us Rain from Heaven and fruitful Seafons, filling our Hearts with Food and Gladnefs*, Acts xiv 17 *The Lord from the place of his Habitation looketh upon all the Inhabitants of the earth He fafhioneth their Hearts alike he confidereth all their works*, Pfal xxxiii 14, 15 *The ways of Man are before the Eyes of the Lord, and he pondereth all his goings*, Prov v 21

Proved from Reafon

Becaufe Preferv ation requires the fame Omnipotent Power as Creation.

II Reafon affures us, that God does preferve and take care of all things, Becaufe it equally requires the fame Omnipotent Power to preferve things, as it did at firft to create them For thus St *Chryfoftom* argues [Greek illegible] *To preferve the World is not a lefs thing than to make it Nay, to fay fomething which may feem extraordinary, it is a greater thing For to create is only to produce a thing out of nothing, but to preferve is to keep from falling into nothing, and alfo to keep jarring Principles in order* Chryf Hom ii in Ep ad Heb

A Confequent of God's Goodnefs

III Becaufe, fince it has pleafed God to make all things, his Goodnefs will incline him to take care of them Which Argument is thus purfued by *Philo*. [Greek illegible] *Reafon dictates, that a Father, or a Maker, muft take care of what is produced by them For a Father takes care of his Children, and an Artificer of his Work driving away from them all things that may hurt them, and providing them with all Neceffaries* Phil de Op Mund And the like is faid by St *Ambrofe* *Quis operator negligat opera [illegible] Quis [illegible] & defti[illegible], quod ipfe condendum [illegible] [illegible] eft regere, nonne eft major injuria fec iffe? Cum el [illegible] non feciffe nulla injuftit a fit non curare quod feceris, fumma inclementia What Workman will neglect the care of his work? Who will defert and leave expofed that which he has thought fit to make? If* (as the Atheifts pretend) *it be an Injury to govern things, is it not a greater Injury to make things, and to take no care of them? For 'tis no Injuftice not to have made them, but tis the greateft Act of Inclemency, not to take care of them after they are made* Ambr Off Lib [illegible] c 13 This is no more than what was obferved by *Plato* [Greek illegible] *The Gods being moft perfect in all Virtue, take all convenient care of [illegible]* Plat Tim

Providence proved from the Regularity of every part of Nature

IV Becaufe of the great Regularity and Conftancy which is obfervable in every part of Nature As (1) In the Heavenly Bodies, all whofe Motions and Viciffitudes are performed in the exacteft Order, without the leaft Variation or Change For thus *Cicero* urges this Argument *Quis hunc hominem dixerit, qui cum tam certos cæli motus, tam ratos aftrorum ordines, tamque omnia inter fe connexa, & apta viderit, neget in his ullam ineffe rationem [illegible] [illegible] dicat, qua quanto confilio gerantur nullo confilio affequi poffumus? Who can call him a Man who when he fees the Motions of the Heavens fo conftant, and the Orders of the Stars fo fixed, and all things among themfelves fo connected and fitted, fhall deny that there is a Reafon which governs them, [illegible] that all this is done by Chance which [illegible] greateft Wifdom cannot comprehend the Wifdom by which they are guided?* Cic de Nat Deor Lib ii (2) In the Order which is obferved in the production of the Species, and the Prefervation of the Individuals, among irrational Creatures For thus *Nemefius* reafons upon this Topick [Greek illegible] *How fhould a Man be begotten of a Man, a Bull of a Bull, and all other Creatures after their own kind, if there were no Providence?* Nemef de Nat Hom cap 42 St *Ambrofe* urges the fame from the natural tendency they have to things which contribute to their Health. *Cui [illegible] animantiis cognitum eft, quemadmodum fuam [illegible] [illegible] Si viribus fuppetit, refiftendo fi velocitas, fugiendo fi aftutia prævalendo Quis eas ufum medendi, [illegible] [illegible] [illegible] notitiam? Homines fumus, & fæpe fpecie herbarum fallimur, & plerumque quas falebras pi[illegible] [illegible] Quoties inter dulces epulas [illegible] [illegible] [illegible] pfit, & inter ipfas Aulicorum excubias [illegible] vitalia Regum fecalis efca penetravit? Fera folo [illegible] odore [illegible] & profutura difcernere nullo prævio, nullo prægufta tore, [illegible] herba nec lædit Melior enim magiftra [illegible] [illegible] natura eft*, &c *Every living Creature knows how to preferve its own Safety If it has ftrength, by refifting if it has fwiftnefs, by flying if it has cunning, by caution [illegible] [illegible] them the ufe of Medicine, and the knowledge of Herbs? We are Men, and yet we oftentimes miftake one Herb for another and what we think to be Medicinal we find to be Deadly How frequently are Princes poifoned in their Food, tho' they have all their Courtiers about them attending? But Animals by their fmell know what is deadly to them, they bite upon an Herb without a Tafter, and yet it never hurts them Therefore Nature is the beft Miftrefs of Truth*, &c Ambr 6 Hexaem cap 4

From God's Prefervation and Government of Mankind.

V But particularly God's Providence is demonftrable, from his Prefervation and Government of Mankind The care which God takes of the irrational part of the Creation relates only to their Bodies, but the Prefervation and Providence which he extends to Men, relates to their Souls as well as Bodies Which Acts of God's gracious Providence are manifeft,(1) In defending them from Dangers, and fupplying them with all bodily Comforts Some of which are common to all Men, others but to the generality of Men, but fome are of fo particular and concerning a Nature, that they do demonftrably infer the Interpofition of an immediate Providence Of which Perfons may fay, as *Homer* faid of *Ulyffes*,

[Greek illegible]
[Greek illegible]

I never faw the Gods fo plainly love
A Man, as *Pallas* him, whom She always fuccour'd
Odyff iii

[illegible] (2) By

good, by consequence, and with very good Reason, they prove the *Maker of them to be good* De Trin. Cap 4 But 'tis plain, even by the Expressions of the Heathen, that they naturally had the greatest Thoughts of God's Beneficent Goodness, by their stiling those extraordinary Persons, who were Benefactors to them, by the Name of *Divi*, Ἡμίθεοι, Σωτῆρες, Θεοὶ &c because they thought, that by reason of their Goodness and Beneficence, they resembled God, and were a sort of lesser Deities which they would not have done, had they not thought that the Deity was in the highest degree Good and Beneficent

From Experience

III Our Experience informs us, how highly we stand indebted to the Divine Beneficence This the Ancient Divines and Philosophers have reduced to several Heads, according to the several Ways and Methods, by which we are befriended by the Divine Goodness (1)

Because he confers it without Compulsion

This beneficent Goodness is remarkably display'd, by the free Communication of it, whereas he might if he had pleased, being All-sufficient, have enjoyed his Happiness to himself alone On this Account thus *Hierocles* expresses himself [illegible] ἀγαθότης, ἀγαθὸς ... *By God's Goodness all things were brought to be good For no other reasonable cause of the making of all things can be assigned, but his own Goodness For he was good by his Nature But no Envy could at any time, upon any account, ... And whatsoever other causes are assigned, for God's making the World, they savour more of human Affections, than of God* ... Hier in Aur Carm Pyth but this was no more than what he learned from *Plato*, who on the same account speaks almost in the same words Λέγωμεν δὴ δι' ἥν τινα αἰτίαν γένεσιν καὶ τὸ πᾶν τόδε ὁ ξυνιστὰς ξυνέστησεν. ἀγαθὸς ἦν, ἀγαθῷ δὲ οὐδεὶς περὶ οὐδενὸς οὐδέποτε ἐγγίγνεται φθόνος· τούτου δ' ἐκτὸς ὢν πάντα ὅτι μάλιστα ἐβουλήθη γενέσθαι παραπλήσια αὐτῷ. Ταύτην δὲ γενέσεως ... ἀρχὴν ... παρ' ἀνδρῶν φρονίμων ἀποδεχόμενος, ὀρθότατα ἀποδέχοιτ' ἄν. *Let us enquire what was the cause which moved God to the making of the World He was good Now no Envy comes near Goodness Being without this, he made all things like himself This is the justest reason of God's making the World, which I have learned from wise Men, and which ought as a true one to be received* Plat in Tim

Without prospect of Advantage.

(2) God Almighty bestows his Benefits upon us, without any prospect of Advantage to himself. For thus *Plato* remarks Πάντα τὰ ἀγαθὰ παρ' αὐτῶν λαμβάνομεν, ... δὲ παρ' ἡμῶν οὐδέν *We receive all good things from the Gods, and they nothing from us* Plat in Euthyphron And so St *Chrysostom* Οὐδὲ ... ὁ Θεὸς τῶν παρ' ἡμῶν ... ἐπεδείξατο, ... *God has made us without expecting any Advantage by us For he has demonstrated that he did not want us by making us so late For if he had wanted us he had made us long before* Chrys Hom iii in Ep ad Phil And to the like purport St *Austin* speaks *Non fruitur nobis Deum sed utitur nam si frueretur egeret bono nostro, quod nemo sanus dixerit God does not enjoy us, but makes use of us for if he did enjoy us as a good to himself, he would stand in need of us, which no Man in his Senses will assert* Aug de Christ Doctr

With the greatest readiness

(3) God confers his Benefits upon us with the greatest readiness, without making us wait for them (like other Benefactors) and tiring us out with Expectations This Observation is admirably well pursued by *Seneca* Of Human Benefits he remarks this *Plerisque hoc vitium est*, &c *Most Men are faulty out of an evil Ambition in deferring their Promises, least the crowd of their Addresses should be less.* ——*They do nothing quickly, they do nothing at once Their Injuries are very quick, but their Benefits are slow* Sen de Ben Lib ii cap 5 But of God's conferring his Favours, he speaks thus *Quocunque te flexeris, ibi illum videbis occurrentem tibi nihil ab illo vacat opus suum ipse implet Whersoever you turn you, you shall find him meeting you there is nothing void of him he fills his whole work.* Id. Lib iv cap 8 See the whole Vth and VIth Chapter of this Book

Because he is good to all

(4) Others are bountiful only to some few, but God is good to all. Who, as our Saviour remarks, *maketh his Sun to shine upon the evil and the good*, Mat v 25 *Seneca* speaks to the same purpose, and almost in the same words *Si deos imitaris, da & ingratis beneficia Nam & sceleratis Sol oritur, & Piratis patent maria If you would imitate the Gods, do good turns even to ungrateful Persons For the Sun arises upon the wicked, and the Seas are open to the very Pirates*, Sen de Benef Lib iv cap 26

Because he is good at all times

(5) Mens Benefits are conferred oftentimes by fits, as their Humour leads, or Opportunity serves them, but God at all times disperses his Favours. This is excellently well expressed by *Gregory Nyssen* Τίς γὰρ χαρακτὴρ ... ἀγαθότητος, τὸ μὴ μόνοις τοῖς ... ἔχειν, ... *Is there any mark of true Goodness? This is, not to be profitable only to some particular thing, nor to be sometimes profitable and other times unprofitable, not to be good to one, and to another not so, but to be it its self and its own Nature good, to every one, and at all times*

Because he is particularly bountiful to Mankind

(6) God's Benefits are in a peculiar manner extended to Mankind And this with Relation both to his Body and Soul The Books of the Ancient Poets, and Philosophers, do abound with Observations on this Head For thus *Ovid*

Pronaque cum spectent animalia cætera terram,
Os homini sublime dedit cælumque tueri
Jussit, & erectos, ad sidera tollere vultus

Whilst other Animals look to the Ground,
He gave to Man a Face which upwards looks,
And bad him raise his Countenance to Heaven

Ovid. Met Lib I

And thus *Manilius*

Quis dubitet posthæc hominem conjungere cælo?
Eximium naturæ dedit linguamque capaxque
Ingenium volucremque animum quem denique in unum
Descendit Deus, atque habitat, ipsumque requirit

Who then can doubt to join Man unto Heaven?
To whom a nimble Tongue Nature has giv'n,
A Wit capacious, and a sprightly Soul,
Into whose Breast alone God does descend,
And dwell therein, and does with Care look after

Manil Lib ii

Juvenal makes the same Observation

Sortiti ingenium, divinorumque capaces,
Atque exercendis capiendisque artibus apti,
Sensum a cælesti demissum traximus arce

We have a Wit capable of things Divine,
For Learning, and for exercising Arts
Dispos'd having a Soul from Heav'n descended

Juvenal Sat xv

Cicero, in many places, employs his Eloquence upon the same Subject, in his Offices, Lib i de Finibus Lib v but particularly in this Passage of his Book of Laws "*Ipsum hominem eadem natura, non solum celeritate mentis ornavit, sed & sensus tanquam satellites attribuit ac nuncios, & rerum plurimum obscuras & necessarias intelligentias enudavit, quasi fundamenta quædam scientiæ figuramque Corporis habilem & aptam ingenio humano dedit Nam cum cæteras animantes abjecisset ad pastum, solum hominem erexit, & ad cæli, quasi cognationis domiciliique pristini, conspectum excitavit Tum speciem ita formavit oris, ut in ea penitus reconditos mores effingeret Et oculis, quum admodum ... affectus ... loquuntur & is, qui appellatur vultus, qui nullo in animante esse præter hominem potest, indicat mores*" *Nature has adorned Man not only with a ready Mind, but has likewise given him Senses to be as it were Centinels and Messengers for his use has cleared up for him many obscure but necessary Problems as the Foundation of his Knowledge, has made the figure of his Body suitable*

suitable to his Wit For when he had made other Animals look downward, to their Food, he raised up Man alone and made him look upwards, as it were to take a view of his heavenly Kindred, and his antient Habitation Cic de Leg Lib 1. St *Chrysostom* makes the same Observation, but draws a further Use from the erect Shape of Man's Body Οὗτος ὀρθὸς πρὸς τὸν οὐρανὸν τέταται, ἵνα τὰ ἐκεῖ περισκοπῇ καὶ ἐν ἐκείνοις φιλοσοφῇ, καὶ ἐκεῖνα φαντάζηται, καὶ ὀξυδερκὲς ἔχῃ τὸ ὄμμα τῆς ψυχῆς *Man is made looking upwards to Heaven, that he may look about the things there, and Philosophize upon them, that he may make Observations upon them, and have the Eye of his Soul sharp-sighted* Chryf in Psal cxvi And elsewhere he draws a like Consequence, *viz* that Man should for this Reason, μηδὲν πρὸς τὴν γῆν κοινὸν ἔχειν μηδὲ κάτω σύρεσθαι καὶ ἕρπειν, ἀλλ᾽ ἄνω πέτεσθαι διηνεκῶς, καὶ πρὸς τὸν ἥλιον τῆς δικαιοσύνης ὁρᾷν *That he should have nothing common with the Earth, that he should not be dragged or creep downward, but constantly fly upwards, and look up to the Sun of Righteousness,* Id Hom xxiv in 1 Cor The same Father argues the Bounty of God, to Man, because all things are made for his Use Ἄνθρωπός ἐστι τὸ μέγα ζῶον καὶ θαυμαστὸν καὶ τῆς κτίσεως ἁπάσης τῷ Θεῷ τιμιώτερον, δι᾽ ὃν οὐρανὸς καὶ γῆ καὶ θάλαττα, καὶ τὸ λοιπὸν ἅπαν τῆς κτίσεως σῶμα *Man is a great and an admirable Animal, more dear to God than all other Creatures, for whom the Heaven and the Earth and the Sea, and all the rest of the Creatures were made* Hom ii Tom v. But the greatest Benefits of all, which God has bestowed upon Mankind, are those which he confers upon us, with relation to our Souls, the State of future Glory, which he has prepared for us, and the Methods of Grace in order to it To omit the many Passages of Scripture, wherein this Truth is illustrated, and innumerable others in the Writings of the Fathers, let this Passage of *Basil* of *Seleucia* suffice Διὰ σὲ Θεὸς ἐν ἀνθρώποις, πνεύματος ἁγίου διανομή, θανάτου κατάλυσις, ἀναστάσεως ἐλπὶς ... θεῖα παραγγέλματα, τελειοῦντά σου τὴν ζωὴν, ὁδὸς ἡ πρὸς τὸν Θεὸν διὰ τῶν ἐντολῶν, βασιλεία οὐρανῶν ἕτοιμος ... *For thee, O Man, God appeared among Men for thy sake was the distribution of the Holy Spirit, the destruction of Death, and the hope of the Resurrection the divine Commandments which perfect thy Life the way to God by the Precepts of Religion the Kingdom of Heaven was made ready, and the Crowns of Righteousness prepared, for those who do not decline to suffer for Virtue's sake* Bas Orat in *Verba Mosis* Attende tibi ipsi

k *Maker*] The words *Maker of all things visible and invisible* are taken out of the *Nicene* Creed as it now stands, or out of the Confession of Faith delivered by *Eusebius* to that Council Πιστεύομεν εἰς ἕνα Θεὸν τὸν ... ἁπάντων ὁρατῶν τε καὶ ἀοράτων ποιητήν *We believe on God the Maker of all things visible and invisible.* Socr Hist Eccl Lib 1. cap 7 ed Steph Bishop *Pearson* has remarked that this Expression is not found in many of the antient Creeds, but the Substance of it seems to be contained in the word παντοκράτορα But however *Irenæus* makes it to be of Apostolical Tradition, *Quia sit unus Deus omnipotens, qui omnia condidit per verbum suum—sive visibilia sive invisibilia, sive sensibilia, sive intelligibilia, sive temporalia, sive æterna That there is one Almighty God, who has made all things by his word—whether Visibles or Invisibles, whether Temporal or Eternal* Iræn Lib 1 cap 19 And again, *Unum Deum fabricatorem cœli & terræ—Ecclesia omnis per universum orbem hanc accepit ab Apostolis traditionem That there is one God, the Creator of Heaven and Earth—the whole Church throughout the universal World has received it as a Tradition from the Apostles* Iræn Lib ii cap 9 And the Profession of it seems to be grounded upon an Opposition,

God declared to be the Maker of the World, in opposition to those who held the Eternity of it

1 To those Philosophers, who maintained the Eternity of the World, principally from the necessary Emanation of God's Goodness, who being essentially Good, could not but necessarily from all Eternity communicate his Goodness but this was a mistaken Notion of God's communicative, or beneficial Goodness, or an undue Confusion of it with his Moral Goodness For God is of necessity morally Good, because no time can be assigned in which he could have done Evil But it cannot be said of his Beneficent Goodness, that he must always communicate it, for this would restrain his Liberty, when it does not imply Imperfection, which does as essentially agree to him as any other of his Attributes. Upon which consideration, *Clemens* of *Alexandria* thus argues, concerning the Deity Ψιλῷ τῷ βούλεσθαι δημιουργεῖ, καὶ τῷ μόνον ἐθελῆσαι αὐτὸν ἕπεται τὸ γεγενῆσθαι *God creates by his mere Will, and Production follows his willing it* Clem Alex in Protrep Besides, the Absurdity of this Opinion is urged even by Philosophers of other Sects, as particularly, because no Action of considerable Antiquity is remembred,

Præterea, si nulla fuit genitalis origo
Terrarum & cœli, semperque æterna fuere,
Cur supra Bellum Thebanum & funera Trojæ
Non alias alii quoque res cecinere Poetæ?

But grant the World Eternal, grant it knew
No Infancy, and grant it never new
Why then no Wars our Poets Songs employ
Beyond the Siege of Thebes, or that of Troy?
Why former Heroes fell without a Name,
Why not their Battles told by lasting Fame?
Lucr Lib v ex vers Creech.

And so again he argues from the late Invention of Arts

Quare etiam quædam nunc artes expoliuntur,
Nunc etiam augescunt, nunc addita navigiis sunt
Multa, &c.

And therefore Arts that lay but rude before
Are polish'd now, we now increase the Store.
We perfect all the old, and first invent more
*Shipping's improv'd——*Ibid

In opposition to those Hereticks who would have it made by Angels

2 In opposition to those Hereticks who pretended that the World was made either by Angels, or, as others of them more wickedly, by an evil Principle, or the Devil *Simon Magus*, the Founder of this abominable Spawn of Hereticks, asserted ὑπὸ τῶν ἀγγέλων δημιουργηθῆναι τὸν κόσμον *That the World was made by Angels* Theod. Ep Hær Fab So did *Menander*, Iræn Lib 1 cap 21 *Saturninus*, id Lib 1 cap 21 as likewise the *Basilidians*, Theodor de Hær Fab and *Carpocratians* Epiph contr Hær. *Marcion* taught, ἄλλον τινὰ νομίζειν μείζονα τοῦ δημιουργοῦ θεὸν *That there was a God greater than he that was Maker of the world,* Just Apol ii. And *Cerdon* taught that there were *duos deos, unum bonum & alterum sævum, bonum superiorem, sævum hunc mundi Creatorem Two Gods, one good, and the other cruel the good the superior God, the other the Creator of the World* Tert de Præscr contr Hær But this was (as *Irenæus* observes) not only a wicked but a foolish Reflection of theirs upon God's Omnipotence *Qui non credunt quidem, quoniam ipsam materiam, cum sit potens, & dives in omnibus Deus, creavit, nescientes quantum potest Spiritualis & Divina Substantia Who do not believe that God could make Matter, when as he is mighty and rich in all things, being ignorant of the Power of a spiritual and divine Substance,* Iræn ed Hær. Lib ii cap 10.

In opposition to those who asserted the Pre-existence of Matter.

3 In opposition to those Philosophers and Hereticks who asserted the eternal Pre-existence of Matter For that many of them did so, St *Chrysostom* does in a very few words inform us Κἂν Μανιχαῖος προσελθὼν λέγῃ ... προϋπάρχειν, κἂν Μαρκίων, κἂν Οὐαλεντῖνος, κἂν Ἑλλήνων παῖδες, λέγε πρὸς αὐτοὺς, ἐν ἀρχῇ ἐποίησεν ὁ Θεὸς τὸν οὐρανὸν καὶ τὴν γῆν *Altho' the Manichee come and say, That Matter does Pre-exist, tho' Marcion and Valentinus, and the Greek Philosophers, tell them that in the beginning God created the Heaven and the Earth* Chryf Hom ii in Gen But the Orthodox Christians always maintained, that the World was created by God out of Nothing, and not out of any Matter Pre-existing And this Doctrine they grounded chiefly upon the word of God For, tho' the word *Barach* in the first of *Genesis*, God *created the Heaven and the Earth*, does not in the strict Sense of the word denote a Creation out of nothing, it being used promiscuously with the word *gnasa* and *gnatza*, which signify to make or to form any thing, tho' out of preceding Matter, yet that God did Create the World out of nothing, is more manifestly evident

server of all things, and [1] Preserver of all things, *tum tum invisibilium,*

dent from other places of Scripture, which do denote that this first Production was out of nothing For that Expression of St *Paul* is a plain Allusion to this Sense. *Which calleth those things which be not as though they were* And more plainly in the Epistle to the Hebrews *Through Faith we understand that the Worlds were framed by the word of God, so that things which are seen, were not made of things which do appear,* Heb xi 3 This seemed so evident a Truth, that St *Chrysostom* expresses himself thus Τὸ δὲ λέγειν, ἐξ ὑποκειμένης ὕλης τὰ ὄντα γεγενῆσθαι, καὶ μὴ ὁμολογεῖν, ὅτι ἐξ οὐκ ὄντων αὐτὰ παρήγαγε ὁ τῶν ἁπάντων δημιουργὸς, τῆς ἐσχάτης παραφροσύνης ἂν εἴη σημεῖον *To say that things which are were made out of Pre-existent Matter, and not to confess that they were made out of nothing, is a sign of the last degree of Frenzy* Chryf. Hom ii in Gen

Providence of God every where asserted in Scripture

1 *Preserver*] I The Holy Scripture is full of Instances, wherein the Providence of God in Preserving and Governing all things is declared, and Examples thereof recorded As, *O Lord thou preservest Men and Beasts,* Psal xxxvi 6 *God giveth to the Beast his Food, and to the young Ravens which cry,* Psal cxlvii 9 *He giveth to all Life, Breath, and all things,* Acts xvii 25. And our Saviour teaches us, that God preserves the Fowls of the Air and the Lilies of the Field, *Mat* vi 26 And that a Sparrow does not fall to the Ground without his Permission, *Mat* x 29 And not only in Preserving them but in Governing them *Who maketh his Sun to rise upon the evil and upon the good,* Mat v 45 *Who covereth the Heaven with Clouds, and prepareth Rain for the Earth,* Pf cxlvii 8 who *gives us Rain from Heaven and fruitful Seasons, filling our Hearts with Food and Gladness,* Acts xiv. 17. *The Lord from the place of his Habitation looketh upon all the Inhabitants of the earth He fashioneth their Hearts alike he considereth all their works,* Psal xxxiii 14, 15 *The ways of Men are before the Eyes of the Lord, and he pondereth all his goings,* Prov v 21

Proved from Reason
Because Preservation requires the same Omnipotent Power as Creation.

II. Reason assures us, that God does preserve and take care of all things, Because it equally requires the same Omnipotent Power to preserve things, as it did at first to create them For thus St *Chrysostom* argues Τὸ γὰρ συνέχειν τὸν κόσμον οὐχ ἧττόν ἐστι τὸ ποιῆσαι ἀλλ' εἰ δεῖ καί τι θαυμαστὸν εἰπεῖν, καὶ μεῖζον τὸ μὲν γὰρ, ἐξ οὐκ ὄντων ἐστὶ τὶ παράγειν τὸ δὲ γενόμενα εἰς τὸ μὴ εἶναι μέλλοντα ἀπαχθῆναι, συνέχειν τε καὶ συγκρατεῖν πρὸς ἄλληλα διαστασιάζοντα *To preserve the World is not a less thing than to make it. Nay, to say something which may seem extraordinary, it is a greater thing For to create is only to produce a thing out of nothing, but to preserve is to keep from falling into nothing, and also to keep jarring Principles in order* Chryf Hom ii in Ep ad. Heb

A Consequent of God's Goodness

III Because, since it has pleased God to make all things, his Goodness will incline him to take care of them Which Argument is thus pursued by *Philo.* Τὸ μὲν γὰρ γεγονότος ἐπιμελεῖσθαι τὸν πατέρα καὶ ποιητὴν αἱρεῖ λόγος· καὶ γὰρ πατὴρ ἐγγόνων, καὶ δημιουργὸς τῶν δημιουργηθέντων στοχάζεται τῆς διαμονῆς· καὶ ὅσα μὲν ἐπιζήμια καὶ βλαβερὰ μηχανῇ πάσῃ διωθεῖται, ὅσα δὲ ὠφέλιμα καὶ λυσιτελῆ, κατὰ πάντα τρόπον ἐκπορίζειν ἐπιποθεῖ *Reason dictates, that a Father, or a Maker, must take care of what is produced by them For a Father takes care of his Children, and an Artificer of his Work driving away from them all things that may hurt them, and providing them with all Necessaries* Phil de Op Mund And the like is said by St *Ambrose* *Quis operator negligit operis sui curam? Quis deserat & destituat, quod ipse condendum putavit? si injuria est regere, nonne est major injuria fecisse? Cum aliquid non fecisse nulla injustitia sit, non curare quod feceris, summa inclementia. What Workman will neglect the care of his work? Who will desert and leave exposed that which he has thought fit to make? If* (as the Atheists pretend) *it be an Injury to govern things, is it not a greater Injury to make things, and to take no care of them? For 'tis no Injustice not to have made them, but tis the greatest Act of Inclemency, not to take care of them after they are made* Ambr Off. Lib i c 13 But this is no more than what was observed by *Plato* Οὐδὲ ὡς ἀγαθοί γε ὄντες πᾶσαν ἀρετὴν, τῶν ἑαυτῶν ἐπιμελεῖσθαι οἰκειότατα αὐτοῖς ὄντα γεγόνασι *The Gods being most perfect in all Virtue, take all convenient care of their Creatures* Plat Tim

Providence proved from the Regularity of every part of Nature

IV. Because of the great Regularity and Constancy which is observable in every part of Nature As (1.) In the Heavenly Bodies, all whose Motions and Vicissitudes are performed in the exactest Order, without the least Variation or Change For thus *Cicero* urges this Argument. *Quis hunc hominem dixerit, qui cum tam certos cæli motus, tam ratos astrorum ordines, tamque omnia inter se connexa, & apta viderit, neget in his ullam inesse rationem, eaque casu fieri dicat, quæ quanto consilio gerantur nullo consilio assequi possumus? Who can call him a Man who when he sees the Motions of the Heavens so constant, and the Orders of the Stars so fixed, and all things among themselves so connected and fitted, shall deny that there is a Reason which governs them, and say all this is done by Chance, which the greatest Wisdom can't comprehend the Wisdom by which they are guided?* Cic de Nat Deor Lib ii (2.) In the Order which is observed in the production of the Species, and the Preservation of the Individuals, among irrational Creatures For thus *Nemesius* reasons upon this Topick Πῶς γὰρ ἂν ἐξ ἀνθρώπου ἄνθρωπος, καὶ ἐκ βοὸς βοῦς ἐγεννᾶτο, καὶ ἐπὶ τῶν ἄλλων ὁμοίως, μὴ προνοίας οὔσης; *How should a Man be begotten of a Man, a Bull of a Bull, and all other Creatures after their own kind, if there were no Providence?* Nemef de Nat Hom cap 42 St *Ambrose* urges the same from the natural tendency they have to things which contribute to their Health. *Cuique animanti cognitum est, quemadmodum sibi suam tueatur salutem. Si vires suppetant, resistendo; si velocitas, fugiendo; si astutia procavendo. Quis eas tam remedii sui, herbarumque docet habere notitiam? Homines sumus, & sæpe species herbarum fallimur, & plerumque quas salubres putamus, noxias reperimus. Quoties inter dulces epulas cibus lethalis irrepsit, & inter ipsas Aulicorum excubias non strontinum vitalia Regum feralis esca penetravit? Feræ solo norunt odore noxia, & projiciunt discernere nullo prævio, nullo prægustatore, corripit herbam nec lædit. Melior enim magistra veritatis natura est, &c Every living Creature knows how to preserve its own Safety. If it has strength, by resisting If it has swiftness, by flying if it has cunning, by caution Who taught them the use of Medicine, and the knowledge of Herbs? We are Men, and yet we oftentimes mistake one Herb for another and what we think to be Medicinal we find to be Deadly How frequently are Princes poisoned in their Food, tho' they have all their Courtiers about them attending? But Animals by their smell know what is deadly to them, they bite upon an Herb without a Taster, and yet it never hurts them Therefore Nature is the best Mistress of Truth,* &c Ambr 6 Hexaem cap 4

From God's Preservation and Government of Mankind

V But particularly God's Providence is demonstrable, from his Preservation and Government of Mankind The care which God takes of the irrational part of the Creation relates only to their Bodies, but the Preservation and Providence which he extends to Men, relates to their Souls as well as Bodies Which Acts of God's gracious Providence are manifest, (1.) In defending them from Dangers, and supplying them with all bodily Comforts Some of which are common to all Men, others but to the generality of Men, but some are of so particular and concerning a Nature, that they do demonstrably infer the Interposition of an immediate Providence Of which Persons may be said, as *Homer* said of *Ulysses,*

Οὐ γάρ πω ἴδον ὧδε θεοὺς ἀναφανδὰ φιλεῦντας,
Ὡς κείνῳ ἀναφανδὰ παρίστατο Παλλὰς Ἀθήνη

I never saw the Gods so plainly love
A Man, as *Pallas* him, whom She always succours.
Odyss iii

(2) By

both Visible and Invisible. And in Unity of

both [m] Visible and [n] Invisible; and in the Unity of this

& in unitate ejus divinæ naturæ, tres sunt

(2) By supports of his Grace in Temptations and Sufferings This is admirably set forth by St *Chrysostom* Τίς γὰρ οὐκ ἐκπλαγήσεται, &c *Who does not wonder, when he sees a Man of the same make with himself, who has conversed among Men, letting, as if he were an Adamant, his sufferings make no Impression upon him? Nay being stronger than an Adamant, when in the midst of Fire, and Swords and Beasts, he conquers all these for righteousness sake? who blesses when he is reviled, who praises them who speak ill of him, who when he is injured prays for those who do him harm, and does Courtesies to those that are designing and plotting against him* Ταῦτα γὰρ καὶ τὰ τοιαῦτα, τῶν οὐρανῶν πολλῷ μᾶλλον δοξάσει τὸν θεόν *This and such a like Temper of Mind, do more than the Heavens declare the Glory of God* Chryf Hom xviii in 1 Cor (3) By making them to account for their Actions, they being endowed with a freedom of acting, which renders them accountable upon their Transgression of the Laws of their Creator From this Head *Basil* of *Seleucia* proves the Punishment due to Sin, as deservedly incurred, because Men are to give an Account of their Actions, which their Reason and Freedom makes them liable to, which irrational Creatures are not Τὰ μὲν γὰρ ἄλλα τῶν ζώων ... &c *The Creator, making other kind of Animals, has bound them to the Laws of Nature, neither is there a free Will in them occasioning an exercising of their Faculties indifferently on either side, neither a Judgment of Reason weighing the choice of what they are to do But Nature at the same time commands and forces them to do, not troubling it self about giving out a Precept But Man being endowed with Reason, is adorned with an Elective Faculty*, &c Bas Sel Or de Adam.

VI That this Providential Care of God does not imply any Operosiness, or Anxiety, in the Deity This is only a foolish Notion of the Epicureans, as *Velleius* speaks in *Tully* *Nisi quid clam, nihil beatum est Deum hominum commoda vitasque tueatur, is ille est implicatus molestis negotiis & operosis There is nothing happy but what is quiet Whilst God looks after the Concerns and the Lives of Men he must needs be distracted with a very busy and troublesome Employ* Cic de Nat Deor Lib 1 But this is, as one very well observes, ... *The reasoning of Men who measure God's Understanding by their own, and charge their own weakness upon him* Ammon in Ar de Interp *Plotinus* exposes this Objection, because it makes God to have need of the adscititious helps of Memory and Computation ... Plot. En 4 Lib. 4

God's Providence creates no Anxiety

VII That it is no Objection against God's providential Care, That bad Men sometimes have a greater share of the good things of this World than good Men have (1) Because if good Men were always to be happy in this World, and bad Men the contrary, there would be no variety in the Dispensations of Providence, and the Designs of an all-wise God would be subject to every common Understanding And therefore *Plotinus* blames those who accuse Providence, for these seeming unequal Dispensations, thus Ἡμεῖς δὲ ὡς ἄπειροι γραφικῆς, ... *Whilst we accuse Providence we are like them who not understanding the Art of Painting, blame the Painter for not putting the finest Colours in every place, whilst he chose to set them in the most convenient places Or if any one should find fault with a Play because all are not Heroes in it, or because a Slave or a Country Man, or any Person of mean Condition, speaks in it For the Beauty would be lost, if you take away any of these meaner Parts, which complete the whole* Plot Enn 3 Lib. 3 (2) Because God turns the Evils which befal Good Men in this World into good, and pursues thereby the wise and righteous Designs of his Providence. Wherefore St *Austin* says very well *Maleficæ virtutes in mundo Divinæ providentiæ est ... The Power which is permitted to wicked Men is the ... of the Divine Providence* Lib xvi cont Faust And to *Synesius* ... *The Evils which are excogitated by some are made by God to tend to a good and profitable end, and tho' they seem evil they carry good with them* Synes Ep 57 St *Basil* the great speaks more expresly in explaining those words of the Prophet *I the Lord create Evil*, Is xlv. 7 Κτίζει ... *Create Evil that is, reforms it and makes it good, so that they lay aside their evil Nature and take the Nature of good upon them* Bas. Mag Or ... and then he very accurately distinguishes, between the several kinds of Evil ... *One thing is evil, respect of our Senses another is evil in its own Nature This which is by Nature evil, is in our Power to avoid, but the accidental and the painful Evil, is sent to us by a wise and good Master, and tends to our Advantage* And so again ... *Sin which is only properly an Evil, and truly deserves the name of Evil, depends upon our Will But for other Evils, some of them are only afforded to us as Combats, or Exercises for the Proof of our Manhood, others as Examples to make those who are liable to fall into Sin to act more warily* Ibid. (3) Because, if any Obliquities happen in the administration of the Divine Providence in this World, they will abundantly be made up in the distribution of Rewards and Punishments in the next For thus *Just*in *Martyr* argues for the certainty of a future State ... *If there be no Resurrection of the Dead, why shall not the reasons be the same, who cause the Martyrs agonies, as theirs who suffer them? If this be unjust, why then is it not unjust that there should be no Resurrection of the Dead, in which alone a difference is made in Judgment, by the Punishment of evil Deeds, and the Reward of good ones?* Just Mart Quest & Resp ad Gr And in like manner St *Chrysostom* ... *In this world many who have been great Sinners have died unpunished many who have lived a Life of Virtue, have died suffering grievous Calamities Therefore, since God is just, how will he reward these Mens goodness, or punish the others wickedness, if there be no Hell, if there be no Resurrection?* Chryf Hom vi in Ep ad Phil

Objections against Providence answered

m *Visible*] This Expression of *Visible and Invisible* is used here in Imitation of the antient Creeds, which join to the Πατέρα the words ... *The maker of all things Visible and Invisible* But the Expression was originally taken out of Scripture, and refers to that Passage of the Apostle Ὅτι ἐν αὐτῷ ἐκτίσθη τὰ πάντα τὰ ἐν τοῖς οὐρανοῖς καὶ τὰ ἐπὶ τῆς γῆς, τὰ ὁρατὰ καὶ τὰ ἀόρατα *For by him were all things created that are in Heaven, and that are in Earth, Visible and Invisible*, Col i 16 Which Language of the Apostle seems to be purely Philosophical, and does exactly agree with the Language of *Plato*, who frequently uses the word ὁρατὸν for a sensible or visible Being, and ἀόρατον or νοητὸν for an Invisible or Spiritual one *Plat. in Tim. Pol Lib vii. Phæd & alibi passim*

By the word Visible the material World understood

By

By the word *Visible* here is understood the Frame of the whole material World, consisting of all the numerous Bodies both Cœlestial and Terrestial, which are compendiously related by *Moses* in the first Chapter of *Genesis*, in such an extraordinary Strain of Majestick Eloquence, that it very much affected one of the greatest Masters of it, *Longinus*, who for that Reason calls him [illegible] *no mean Person* Long. [illegible]. And *Theophilus Antiochus*, in a Strain of Admiration, at the matters related there in, speaks thus [illegible] *No one can explain as he ought the History of the Creation, and the Order and Disposition of things there related, if he had a thousand Mouths and a thousand Tongues; or if he should live innumerable Ages in this Life could he speak as much of it as it deserves, by reason of the excessive greatness and riches of the Divine Wisdom discovered in this History of the Six Days work.* Theoph. Ant. ad Autol. Lib. ii.

By Invisible is understood Angels.

How called in Scripture.

[And] *Invisible*.] The Articles having declared God to be the Maker of the Visible or the Material World, proceed to declare him to be the Maker of the Immaterial or Invisible, which does consist of Angels and Spirits. That there are such Beings that are invisible to our Eyes, is frequently notified unto us in Scripture under several Appellations. The most common Name which is given to them, is that of *Malachim*, Angels or Messengers, *Gen.* xvi. 7. ix. 10, 11. xix. 1, &c. They are sometimes called *Abarim*, The strong, or mighty, *Psal.* lxxviii. 29. *Elim*, the powerful, *Job* xx. [illegible], the Lords, *Gen.* xxxi. 24. *Job* xxxviii. 7. *Psal.* viii. 6. xcvii. 8. *Ben elohim*, the Sons of God, *Deut.* xxxii. 8. *Job* i. 6. xxxviii. 7. And in one place *Eshdath*, the fiery Order, *Deut.* xxxiii. 2. Our Translation and most others render it a *fiery Law*, or *Law of Fire*, but the Septuagint Translate it [illegible], Angels, probably taking it to allude to the igneous Nature which Angels were supposed to consist of, or which they used to make their Appearance in. Now since there is so frequent mention made of Angels, not only in the Hagiographers and the Prophets, but also in the Mosaical Writings, which every Sect among the Jews did acknowledge to be Divinely inspir'd, it seems matter of no little wonder, how the Saducees, who professed themselves Jews, and pretended to acknowledge the Authority of the Mosaical Writings, should deny the Existence of Angels and Spirits, *Mat.* xxii. 27. as they seem to have done. *Grotius* has not unhappily conjectured, that they did not universally deny the Existence of Angels, but were only of the Opinion of those Jews, mentioned by *Justin Martyr*, who said that the Angels were [illegible] *That these were certain indivisible and inseparable Powers of God, which he made upon occasion to go out from himself, and then made them return into himself again.* In opposition to which Opinion that Father maintains, [illegible] *That the Angels were permanent Beings, and not after this manner dissolvible.* Just. Coll. cum. Tryph. But whether this were their Opinion or no, it is certain, that they must maintain some Opinions, contrary to the current Doctrine of the Jewish Church, with relation to Angels. Now it was usual among the Jews, to go upon Pneumatick or Spiritual Principles, in explaining the ordinary *Phænomena* of Nature. They did not explain the Nature of Winds, by the Exhalation of Vapors, but by Angels moving the Air at the Divine Command, *who maketh his Angels Spirits* or Winds; nor did they explain the Production of Lightening by the Explosion of a sulphureous Substance in the Air, but by the energetical Power of Angels who presided in those Regions, *his Ministers a flaming Fire*, Psal. civ. 4. Which words plainly relate to the Meteors in the Air, which the Psalmist is in that place speaking of, from the words that immediately precede it, *Who layeth the Beams of his Chambers in the Waters, who maketh the Clouds his Chariot, who walketh upon the Wings of the Wind.* So they explained Plagues, not by the arising of Pestilential Vapors from the

The Jews Opinion of Angels.

Earth, but by the destroying of an Angel, 1 *Chr.* xxi. [illegible] In Allusion to which the Psalmist attributes a personal Action to the Plague, *The Pestilence which walketh in Darkness*, &c. *Ps.* xci. [illegible] the Angel who causes the Plague. Therefore 'tis but natural to imagine, that the Saducees who had learned some Maxims of the Heathen Philosophy, and thereupon explained these Occurrences by material Principles, very much displeased their Adversaries the Pharisees, by this Ethnick way of Philosophizing, who thereupon to be sure would not fail to load them with the remotest and most invidious Consequences of their Opinion, so that they were in the Opinion of the Vulgar looked upon to deny the very Being of Angels, which in reality they could not do, unless they had renounced the Books of *Moses*, that so frequently make mention of Angels, which it does not appear that they ever did.

The Opinion of the Heathens concerning Angels.

The Doctrine of Angels and Spirits, being universally received in the Jewish Church and Nation, was in all Probability derived from them to the *Ægyptians*, and by their means, to the *Greeks*. Or perhaps *Pythagoras*, who was the first who taught the Doctrine of Angels or Spirits, among the *Greeks*, might have it immediately from the Jews. For he is Recorded to have been initiated into [illegible] *the Rites of the* Barbarians, [illegible] *that he was conversant among the* Chaldæans, *and the* Magi. Diog. Laert. in vita Pythag. His Doctrine concerning Spirits or Angels was [illegible] *That the Air was full of Spirits, which were called Demons or Heroes, and from these Dreams were sent to Men, and Signs of Diseases, and of Health, and not only to Men, but to all other Beasts*, [illegible] From his Principles his Followers learnt their Doctrine of Demons, Angels, Archangels, which their Books were so full of [illegible]. It is not improbable that *Plato* derived his Doctrine of Dæmons or Angels, from the same Fountain, his Writings being full of it. He says they are called Dæmons from their Knowledge, and for that Reason *Hesiod*, who first used the word *Dæmon*, called the Heroes of the Golden Age by that Name, and [illegible] *he called them Demons, because they were wise and knowing.* Plat. in Cratyl. He says an Angel or Dæmon is a *Spirit*, [illegible] *a middle Being between God and Man*, Plat. Symp. That these are [illegible] *Co-adjutors to God* in Polit. and more particularly that [illegible] *That they are Interpreters and Embassadors of the Gods to Men, and from Men to the Gods. That they present the Prayers and Sacrifices of the One, and that they carry the Commands and Answers upon Sacrifices to the Others.* Plat. in Sympos.

Whether Angels have Bodies.

II. There is no constant, whether these Superior Beings have Bodies, or whether they are pure Spirits. The Scripture is altogether silent therein, and tho' it speaks of *Angel's Food*, and the *Tongue of Angels*, yet these and the like are supposed to be only figurative Expressions, to denote an excellent Food, such as Angels, if they did eat, might be supposed to feed on, and an eloquent Tongue, such as Angels, if they did speak, might be supposed to speak with. Therefore the Ancient Divines of the Church have taken their Liberty to decline severally their Opinions, on each side of this Question. The more ancient Fathers were for their having Bodies, of a yielding Aereal Nature, like the [illegible] or Vehicles of the Platonists. *Justin Martyr* seems to have too gross Conceptions, when he argues their Corporiety from the Angels Eating when they were entertained by *Abraham*, Gen. xviii. and from Manna being called the Food of Angels [illegible] *'Tis plain that they are nourished, tho' they do not feed on the same food as* [illegible]. Just. Martyr. Dial. cum Tryph. *Origen* in his *Meudo* [illegible] will allow it only to be the Property of God, *esse sine materiali substantia* [illegible]. St. *Basil* says, that their Substance [illegible] *an Aerial Spirit, or a Fire without gross Matter.* De Spir. Sanct. cap. 16.

St. Cyril

S Cyril of *Alexandria* following *Origen*, will allow God Almighty only to be ἀσώματον, but that the Angels πνεύματα are circumscribed, or inclosed with Bodies σωματα γὰρ εἰ καὶ μὴ παντα τυχον, οποῖα τὰ ἡμέτερα, *though, perhaps their Bodies are not such as ours are*, Cyr in Joh *Tertullian* asserts, that the Angels, *Corporis alicujus, sui tamen generis, incarnem autem hi manam transfigurabiles, ad tempus enclosed with a certain Body, of their own sort, so that for a time they can put on our Flesh* Tert de car Christ S *Hilary* says, that they do *corpoream naturæ sua substantiam sortiri, partake of a corporeal Substance, peculiar to them* Hil in Mat cap v And S *Ambrose* will allow Immateriality only to agree, but to the Blessed Trinity *Nos autem nihil materialis compositionis immune, atque alienum putamus, præter illam solam venerandæ Trinitatis substantiam* Lib II de Abrahamo S *Austin* says, that they do *Corpus sumere, cui non subduntur, sed subditum regunt, in species, quas volunt, accommodatas, atque aptas actionibus suis mutare change their Bodies, to which they are not subject, but entirely govern, and adapt to their actions*, Aug de Trin Lib II

Several of the other Fathers take the opposite side of the Question and maintain that Angels are pure Spirits, devoid of all manner of Body *Eusebius* calls them, ἀσωματους τινὰς, νοερὰς, ... δυνάμεις ἀγγέλους τε καὶ ἀρχαγγέλους, αὐλα τε, καὶ τὰ ... πνεύματα *unbodied Intelligences, ... Powers, the Angels and Archangels, devoid of all Body, and pure Spirits*, Euseb de Dem Lib iv cap ... St *Chrysostom* speaking of them says, God made ... ἀσωμάτους οὐσίας *Angels, archangels, and other immaterial Substances*, Hom ... in Mat ... calls them ... *Intellectual Spirits*, Orat ... *Simple, Intelligent, and Pellucid*, Carm ... de Vire *Gregory Nyssen* says, that the Angelick Nature is ... *a simple and ... immaterial Nature, free from all Bodily Circumscription, and at large*, Cat c 6 The Latin Fathers, about the 6th and 7th Century, held the same Opinion *Isid de diff* c 12. *Greg. Mag* iv *Dial* c 29 But this latter Opinion was so far from being an established Doctrine of the Church, that *John* Bishop of *Thessalonica* disputes strenuously against it, in the 2d Council of *Nice*, A 787, saying, περὶ τῶν ἀγγέλων καὶ ἀρχαγγέλων καὶ τῶν ὑπὲρ αὐτοὺς ἁγίων δυνάμεων, προστίθημι δὲ καὶ τὰς ἡμετέρας ψυχὰς ἡ καθολικὴ ἐκκλησία ... νοερὰς μὲν αὐτοὺς ... ἀσωμάτους ... *Concerning Angels and Archangels, and the Powers above them, nay, I will farther add the Souls of us Men, the holy Church acknowledges them to be intelligible, but not altogether without any Body*, or *Insensible* For which Opinion he vouches the Authority of *Basil* the Great, *Athanasius* and *Methodius* Conc Nic ii Act 5 And, what is remarkable, the Council does not contradict this Doctrine Some Ages after, the School Divines, striking in with the latter Doctrine, made it more current, and then it was confirmed as the true Orthodox Opinion by the *Lateran* Council, under *Innocent* the Third, A D 1215 in these words *Deus utramque de nihilo condidit creaturam, Spiritualem, & Corporalem, Angelicam videlicet & Mundanam God created both sorts of Creatures, the Spiritual and the Corporeal, namely the Angelick and the Worldly* Conc Lat. sub. In iii cap 1 After this the current Doctrine of Divines was, for the pure Spirituality of Angels.

Beings of great Understanding

III They are endowed with a very great degree of Knowledge and Understanding (1) For this the Holy Scripture informs us of, when it declares, that the Revelations which God Almighty was pleased to make to Mankind, were handed to them by the Ministry of Angels, *Act* vii 53 *Gal* iii 19 A wise Prince is said to be as the *Angel of God to discern good and bad*, Act xiv 17 which words shew the common Notion of those times, concerning the Superior Knowledge of Angels. (2) But however their Knowledge is limited For it is recorded in Scripture, that they are ignorant of *the Day of Judgment*, Mar xiii 32 And the antient Writers of the Church teach us the same. Αἱ ἀόρατοι δυνάμεις οὔτε προΐσασιν, οὔτε ἴσασιν ἅπαντα, μόνη γὰρ ἡ θεία φύσις ταύτην ἔχει τὴν γνῶσιν ἄγγελοι δὲ καὶ ἀρχάγγελοι, καὶ αἱ ἄλλαι τῶν ἀοράτων δυνάμεων συμμορίαι, τοσαῦτα ἴσασιν, ὅσα διδάσκονται *The Invisible Powers neither foreknow nor know all things. for the divine Nature only has this Knowledge But Angels and Archangels, and the other Companies of Invisible Powers, know so much as they are taught* Theod. in *Psal* xviii So *Isidore Pelusiot*. Αἱ τάξεις ἀγγέλων, οἷα τῷ ὄντως ... τὰ μέλλοντα ... ἀγνοοῦσι *The Orders of Angels, as being our fellow Creatures, are ignorant of things not yet Present*, Isid Pel Lib 1 Ep 195. (3) Their Knowledge is very different from ours This seems to be grounded upon what we find in Scripture revealed concerning a future State, and the Superior degree of Knowledge which the Soul shall be possessed of there. *Now we see through a glass darkly, but then face to face now I know in part, but then I shall know even as I am known*, 1 Cor xiii 12 And whereas it is likewise told us by our Saviour, that we shall be *as the Angels of God*, Mat. xxii 30 it follows, that the Angels of God, at present, do enjoy that eminent share of Knowledge, that so extraordinarily clear and distinct view of things, which we shall partake of hereafter Divines, both Antient and Modern, have, perhaps, explained this Angelical Knowledge with more licences and particularity, than they have ground for. One of them calls it an Ἐνοειματική αἴσθησις, καθ' ἣν ὁρῶσιν αἱ ψυχαὶ ἑαυτάς τε, καὶ τὰ ὑπ' αὐτάς. ἔτι δὲ καὶ τοὺς ἀγγέλους τε, καὶ τοὺς δαίμονας ... ψυχὴ ψυχὴν, οὔτε ἄγγελος ἄγγελον, οὔτε δαίμων δαίμονα, ἀλλὰ κατὰ τὴν ... ἐννοηματικὴν αἴσθησιν ὁρῶσιν ἑαυτούς τε καὶ ἀλλήλους ἔτι δὲ καὶ τὰ σωματικὰ πάντα *A Cogitative Perception by which Souls see themselves, and things under them as also Angels and Dæmons For a Soul does not perceive or see a Soul, nor an Angel an Angel, nor a Dæmon a Dæmon, but according to the forsaid Cogitative Perception, they see themselves and one another, and also all bodily things* Auth. Qu ad Orthod apud Just Mart Q 76 *Dionysius* explains the Knowledge of Angels after a like manner, who says, τὰς ἀπλᾶς καὶ μακαρίας ἔχουσι νοήσεις ... οὐκ ἀπὸ μεριστῶν, ἢ αἰσθητῶν, ἢ λόγων διεξοδικῶν συναγουσαι τὴν θείαν γνῶσιν, οὐδὲ ὑπό τινος κοινῶ πρὸς ταῦτα συμπεριαγόμεναι, παντὸς δὲ ὑλικοῦ, καὶ πλήθους, ἀθαρεῖσαι, νοερῶς, ἀΰλως, ἑνοειδῶς τὰ νοητὰ τῶν θείων νοοῦσι *They have simple and blessed Understandings, not as Divisibles nor from Divisibles, or the Senses, collecting the divine Knowledge from tedious Discourse, but being purged from every thing that is material, and from multiplicity, they understand intelligibly, immaterially and singly* Dionys de Div nom c 7 This was the Foundation of the Intuitive Knowledge of Angels, and a great many other fanciful Opinions, which are taken up at a venture without Countenance from Scripture, in the Divinity of the Schools

Not in their own Nature Mortal

IV These excellent Beings are Immortal, and not subject to the Laws of Death and Dissolution, as we Men are (1) Of this our Blessed Saviour has particularly informed us, when he declared the Nature of our Bodies, after the Resurrection *Neither*, says he, *can they die any more, for they are equal to the Angels*, Luke xx 36 Which clearly denote, that the Angels are not subject to the Laws of Mortality (2) But then it must be observed, that they are not endowed with such an Essential Immortality, as that of Almighty God, who may if he pleases at any time by his Omnipotent Authority put a Period to their Being, this being only owing to that firmitude of their Nature, whatever it be, which God was pleased to bestow on them, which renders them uncapable of Dissolution, by the Power of any created Being Upon which Consideration St *Athanasius* makes this Observation Μόνος ὁ Θεὸς ἔχει ἀθανασίαν, ὅτι ὁ Θεὸς αὐτὸς ἐστὶν ἀθανασία ... ἄγγελοι ... ἀθανασίας ... *God only has Immortality, because he is Immortality it self but Angels are Immortal by the Participation of his Immortality* And *Theophylact* says, that God only κυρίως καὶ οὐσιωδῶς ἔχει τὸ ἀθάνατον ἄγγελοι γὰρ, εἰ καὶ ἀθάνατοι ἀλλ' οὐ φύσει, ... ὡς τι ... ἔχουσιν, ἀλλὰ μετέχουσι. *God only properly and essentially has Immortality but Angels, though they are Immortal, are not so by Nature but by Grace so that they cannot be so properly said to have Immortality as to partake of it* Theoph on 1 Tim vi 16. *Who only hath Immortality*, &c.

Angels Beings of vast Power

V They are endowed with a very large share of Power, which is evident from their being employ'd as God's Agents, in executing his great Designs As the Angels that were sent to destroy *Sodom* and *Gomorrah*, *Gen* xix and as that single Angel who could in one Night destroy all the first born in *Ægypt*, *Exod.* xii. 29 and another who killed 185000 of the Army of *Senacherib* 2 *King*. xix. 25 Wherefore *Nazianzen* says, δύο ταῦτα ... ἄγγελος *There are two things, which are not to be resisted, God and an Angel.* Greg Naz.

Naz Orat xxviii And again in his Poems he thus speaks of the Angels, executing the Divine Commands

——νόες εἰσὶν ἐλαφροὶ,
Πῦρ, καὶ πνεύματα θεῖα, δι' ἀέρος ὠκα θέοντες,
Ἐσσυμένως μεγάλοισιν ὑποδρήσσουσιν ἐφετμαῖς.

——*Nimble Minds,*
All Flame and Spirit Divine, that through the Air
The swiftly, to discharge their King's Commands
Greg Naz Car II

Created by God

VI They were created by God, and were not Eternal Beings. (1) This is manifest from Holy Scripture. For the Psalmist, when he calls upon all the Parts of the Creation to praise God, excites the Angels to do the same, *Praise him all ye Angels*, Psal cxlviii 2 Adding this reason, *Let them praise the Name of the Lord, for he commanded and they were created*, v 5 And for this Reason the Title of the *Sons of God* is given to Angels, *Job* i 6, 7. *Job* xxxviii 7 Whereupon *Theodoret* thus expresses himself Ὅτι κτιστὴν ἔχουσι φύσιν καὶ Ἄγγελοι καὶ Ἀρχάγγελοι, καὶ ἔτι ἕτερον ὅτιν ἀσώματον, πλὴν τῆς ἁγίας Τριάδος, ἡ θεία σαφῶς ἡμᾶς διδάσκει γραφή. *That Angels and Archangels, and whatsoever else is incorporeal, except the Divine Trinity, have a created Nature, the Scripture does expresly teach* Theod Qu. ii in Gen. And for holding the contrary Opinion, by the Imperial Edict, they are to be Excommunicated τὰς μὴ ὁμολογοῦντας κτίσμα εἶναι θεοῦ τὰς Ἀγγέλους, *who do not confess that Angels are created by God*, Nov cxxxii (2) But, as to the time of their Creation, that is not so exactly agreed upon by Divines, the Scripture being silent therein, and they having nothing left them to steer by, but their own Ratiocinations and Conjectures. There are two considerable Reasons offered by the Antients for this Silence of the Scripture therein One is given by St *Athanasius* Γινώσκων ὁ Θεὸς τὸ φιλειδωλον καὶ πολύθεον τῶν ἀνθρώπων, καὶ μάλιστα τῶν Ἰουδαίων, τούτου χάριν ἀπέκρυψεν ἐν τῇ γενέσει τὸ περὶ τῶν Ἀγγέλων λόγον, ἵνα μὴ καὶ αὐτοὺς θεοποιήσωσιν ὡς Θεοὺς *Because God knew that Men, especially the Jews, were inclined to Idolatry, and to believe a multitude of Gods, therefore he omitted to speak any thing of the Generation of Angels, least they should worship them as Gods* Athan Qu iv ad Antioch The other is given by St *Chrysostom* Ἐπειδὴ Ἰουδαίοις, &c *Forasmuch as* Moses *spake to the Jews, who were detained only by the love of things present, and could conceive nothing but that which fell under their Senses, he represents God to them as the Creator of the material Universe, that learning from the Creation of things the Creator of them, they may adore him who made them, and not cleave to the Creature* Chrys. Hom i in Gen. And again, Οὐδὲν περὶ τῶν ἀοράτων, &c. *He speaks nothing of the Invisible Powers, neither does he say God created Angels or Archangels, which he did not without good design omit For speaking to the Jews, who look'd only after present things, and could not frame their Minds to conceive Intelligibles, he raises them by Sensibles to the Creator* Hom. ii in Gen The greater number of the Antients would have them, to be created a considerable time before the Creation of the Material World This was *Origen*'s Opinion, who in his first Homily upon *Genesis* speaks thus *In Principio & ante omnia dicitur factum, omnem spiritualem substantiam intelligit, super quam, velut in throno quodam, & sede Deus requiescit* In the beginning, &c *he understands every spiritual Substance, after the making of which God for some time rested as it were in a Throne or a Seat* And S *Basil*'s, who says, Ἦν τις πρεσβυτέρα τῆς τοῦ κόσμου γενέσεως, &c *There was an ancienter State than that of the Creation of the World, agreeable to the* Supra Mundan *Powers, before time and sempiternal For the Creator, and Worker* (δημιουργὸς) *of all things, then produced his Creatures the Intelligible Light of them, who, agreeably to their Happiness, love God, the purely reasonable and invisible Natures, and all the Orders of Intelligibles, and whatsoever excels our Nature, whose Names we cannot discover They fill up the Substance of the Invisible World, as St* Paul *teaches us, when he says,* For in him all things were created, whether Visibles, &c. Of the same Opinion is St *Chrysostom* Ἐποίησεν ἀγγέλους, ἀρχαγγέλους καὶ τὰς ἄλλας τῶν ἀσωμάτων οὐσίας, &c μετὰ δὲ τούτων δημιουργίαν ποιεῖ καὶ τὸν ἄνθρωπον *God made Angels and Archangels, and the rest of the Incorporeal Substances, &c After the Creation of these he created Man.* Chrys in i. Lib, ad Stag. And so *Nazianzen* Ἐπεὶ δὲ τὰ πρῶτα καλῶς εἶχεν αὐτῷ, δεύτερον ἐννοεῖ κόσμον ὑλικὸν καὶ ὁρώμενον *After he had first well established his first Creation (viz of Spirits) he then thought of making the Material and Visible World* Naz Or xxxviii St *Ambrose*, in maintenance of the same Opinion, says *Angeli, Dominationes & Potestates, etsi aliquando ceperunt, erant tamen jam, quando hic mundus est factus. The Angels, Dominions and Powers, tho' they once had a beginning, yet they were in being at that time when the World was made*, Ambr i in Hexaem c 5 So St *Hierom* *Sex millia necdum nostri orbis implentur anni, & quantas prius æternitates, quanta tempora, quantas sæculorum origines fuisse arbitrandum est, in quibus Angeli, Throni, Dominationes cæteræque virtutes servierint Deo, & absque temporum vicibus atque mensuris, Deo jubente, substiterint? Six thousand Years of our World are not yet compleated, but how many Eternities before that, what vast times, what Series of Ages, must we think to have passed, wherein the Angels, Thrones, Dominions, and other Powers serv'd God in, and had a Being, according to the Divine Will, before the Vicissitudes and Measures of Time?* Hier. in Cap i Epist ad Tit

But *Epiphanius, Theodoret*, and some others, will have the Angels created at the same time with the Material World Στερεώματος γῆς καὶ οὐρανοῦ καὶ ἀρχαγγέλοι ἅμα σὺν τούτοις γεγόνασιν *The Firmament, the Heaven and Earth, and the Angels were made together* Epiph Hær lxv And *Theodoret* Εἰκὸς τὰς ἀγγέλους σὺν οὐρανῷ ἐκτίσθαι καὶ γῇ *It is probable that the Angels were made with the Heaven and the Earth* Theod Qu iv in Gen Therefore upon the whole, the Scripture being silent in this matter, and the greatest Divines being divided in their Opinions upon it, we are at liberty to hold which side of the Question seems most probable to us

Several Ranks of these Beings

VII There is great Reason to think, that there are several distinct Orders and Ranks of these Angelical Natures (1.) Because several places of Scripture seem to intimate so much As when the Apostle says, that Christ is set *far above all Principality and Power, Might and Dominion*, Eph i 21 And when he declares, that *by him were all things created that are in Heaven and that are in Earth, Visible and Invisible, whether they be Thrones or Dominions, Principalities or Powers*, Col i 16 So, *nor Angels, nor Principalities, nor Powers*, &c. Rom viii 38 These Passages seem plainly to refer to several sorts of Invisible Beings, which the Jews of that time thought the Angels were ranked into. *Grotius* thinks, that this ranging of the Spiritual Beings into these distinct Orders, took its rise from the Form of the *Persian* Government, which the Jews for some time lived under That the *Principalities* allude to the *Rabrebani*, the *Princes*, mentioned *Dan* v 2 that the *Powers*, the *Powers*, relate to the *Sharim*, the great Men or *Princes* invited to the Feast by *Hester*, Est ii. 18 that the κυριότητες, or *Dominions* refer to the *Hashaloth*, the *Dominions*, spoken of *Dan* xi 4, 5 vid Grot in *Rom* viii Which Conjecture does not appear to be improbable, since the modern Jews have divided the Angels into Ranks, according to the Scriptural Names Thus *Maimonides* calls one Order of them *Haioth Hakadhosh*, the Sacred *Living Creatures*, Ez i 14 Another the *Ophanim*, or the Wheels, Ez i 16 x 10 A third the *Oralim* or the Powerful, *Is* xxxiii 7 So the *Chasmalim*, or the Order of the *Amber*, Ez i 4 The *Seraphim* or the *Burners* The *Malachim* or the *Messengers* The *Elohim* or the Gods The *Cherubim* or the *Oxen-heads* The *Beni elohim*, or the *Godsons* The *Ishim* or the *Men* Maimonides de fund. Leg Cap ii (2) Because the most considerable of the Ancient Christian Writers do maintain this Doctrine One of the most early Writers of them all, *Ignatius*, plainly declares in favour of this Opinion For he says that he was, δυνάμενος τὰ ἐπουράνια καὶ τὰς τοποθεσίας τὰς ἀγγελικὰς, καὶ τὰς συστάσεις τὰς ἀρχοντικὰς ὁρατά τε καὶ ἀόρατα. *able to speak of heavenly things, the site of Angels, the Constitutions of* Archons *or Principalities, things Visible and Invisible* Ign ad Trall. Which words, as they do clearly refer to some of the forementioned Words of St *Paul*, so they do plainly acknowledge them to be meant of Angelical Orders. Besides it is evident, that the most principal of the other Fathers do explain St *Paul*'s words in the like Sense Thus do *Epiphanius*, Hær lxiv Sect 33 *Greg Naz.* Orat xxxiv *Cyr Hier* Cat 7 *Athan* Ep ad Serap. Hier in i. Eph The Counterfeit *Dionysius* has made many fanciful Observations about these Orders, their Laws and Oeconomy, without Ground from Scripture, which being taken into the

the School Divinity has begotten a world of curious Questions among those Writers, which tend little to Edification or Improvement

God's Ministers for Mens good. VIII They are employ'd as God's Ministers for the Benefit of good Men for their Preservation from Danger *For he shall give his Angels charge over thee, to keep thee in all thy ways*, Psal xci 2 and delivering them from it *The Angel of the Lord encampeth round about them that fear him, and delivereth them*, Psal xxxiv 7 Examples of which we have in *Lot*, Gen xix *Jacob*, Gen xxxii 1 *Elias*, 2 King vi *Peter*, Act xii in conducting their Souls to a State of Happiness, *Luke* xvi 22 Upon which Account *Nazianzen* says, that all the Host of Heaven have their several Posts assigned them, for this purpose, Λειτουργὸς θεία θελήματ⊕, δυνατὰς ἰσχύι συστῶτε ᾗ ἐπίκτητο παντα ἐπιτορευομένα, πάσι παντα χῦ παρέσας ἑτοίμας, προθυμία τε λειτουργίας ᾗ κουφότητι φύσεως, ἄλλας ἄλλό τι ἐγκεχειρισμένας, ⊕ διειληφότας, ἢ ἄλλω τινι τῦ παντὸς ἐπιτεταγμένας, *They being Ministers of the Divine Pleasure, traverse all places, being prepared to be present at any Place, by the promptness of their Administration and the swiftness of their Nature, some being dispatched to one part of the World, and some to another*, Greg Naz Or xxxiv And *Gregory Nyssen* says, that the λειτουργία τῶν πνευμάτων τούτων ἐστιν ἐπὶ ὠφέλεια τῶν σωζομένων ἐκπέμπεσθαι *The Ministry of these Spirits is to be sent out for working the means of Mens Salvation* Greg Nyss Lib i contr Eunom

Whether Guardian Angels? IX But whether every Person has a Guardian Angel assigned him, is a matter not so certain (1) There is one Passage of Scripture, which seems to offer something in Favour of this Opinion, which is this *Take heed that ye despise not one of these little ones, for I say unto you, that in Heaven their Angels do always behold the Face of my Father which is in Heaven*, Mat xviii 10 (2) This seems to be countenanced by the general Opinion of the Wise, who were enlightened by no Revelation *Menander* says,

"Απαντι δαίμων ἀνδρὶ συμπαρίσταται
Εὐθὺς γενομένῳ, μυσταγωγὸς τῦ βίε
'Αγαθὸς——

As soon as every Man is born,
A gentle Dæmon is set o'er him,
A Guardian for his Life ——
Menand apud Euseb de Præp Lib xiii

Horace speaks of the same in that Verse

Scit Genius, natale comes, qui temperat astrum,
Naturæ Deus humanæ ——

My friendly Genius knows, who rules my Fate,
The God of human Nature ——
Hor Ep Lib ii Ep 2

So *Seneca*, *Unicuique nostrum Pædagogum dari Deum, non quidem ordinarium, sed hunc inferioris notæ ex eorum numero quos Ovidius dicit* de plebe Deos *Every one of us has a Tutor God afforded him, not any one of the commonly known Gods, but one of inferior Rank, but such an one of those whom* Ovid *calls* Heavens Commonalty Sen Ep cx Which was the general Opinion of the Stoicks, as appears by that of *Arrian* 'Επίτροπον ἑκάστῳ παρέςησε, τὸν ἑκάστου δαίμονα, ᾗ παρέδωκε φυλάσσειν αὐτὸν αὐτῷ, ᾗ τοῦτον ἀκοίμητον ᾗ ἀπαραλόγιστον *God has set over every one of us a Tutor, and delivered us into his Hands to preserve us, one that does not sleep and cannot be imposed upon* Arr in Epict. Lib i c. 14 (3) Besides, the most eminent Writers of the antient Church have espoused this Opinion, and grounded it upon the forementioned words of our Saviour. This Passage of St *Chrysostom* concerning this matter is remarkable. Τὸ πρῶτον κατ' ἀριθμὸν ἐθνῶν ἦσαν οἱ ἄγγελοι νῦν δὲ ἐ κατ' ἀριθμὸν ἐθνῶν, ἀλλὰ κατ' ἀριθμὸν τῶν πιστῶν. πόθεν δῆλον, 'Ακϛε τῦ Χριςῦ λέγοντ⊕ ὁρᾶτε, μὴ καταφρονήσατε, &c 'Εκαςος γὰρ πιςὸς ἄγγελον ἔχει *At first, there were Angels according to the number of the Nations, but now not according to the number of the Nations, but according to the number of the Faithful How does this appear? Why, hear Christ himself speaking*, Take heed that ye despise not, &c *Every faithful Person has an Angel*, &c Chrys. Hom. iii in Ep ad Col S *Basil* speaks with more assurance Συνεῖναι ἑκάςῳ τῶν πιςῶν ἄγγελον, οἷον παιδαγωγόν τινα ᾗ νομέα τὴν ζωὴν διευθύνοντα, ὐδεὶς ἀντερεῖ, μεμνημέν⊕ τῶν τῦ κυρίυ λόγων, εἰπόντ⊕, Μὴ καταφρονήσατε, &c. *That every one of the faithful has an Assistant Angel, as a certain Tutor or Pastor for the Government of his Life, is a Truth which no one will contradict, who remembers what our Lord has said*, Take heed that ye despise not, &c Bas Lib iii contr Eunom *vid Auth. Q & R ad Orthod Q* xxx *Theod Ep divin Decr cap* 7 *Orig Hom* xxxv *in Luc* But *Clement* of *Alexandria* is something particular in his Opinion, when he says, that a Christian may arrive to such a Degree of Perfection, as to live without the conduct of his Angel Οὐ γὰρ δεῖ ἀεὶ ἀγγέλω. Coπθεῖ. ἐπειδὴ ἔτι ἀξιω βέλτιον τῦτον παρ' ἑαυτῦ ὁ ἄξιον γενόμενος λαμβάνει, ᾗ τὴν φρουρὰν ἔχειν παρ' ἑαυτῦ, δι' ἣν ἔπιμελ. ας *He will not always have him wanting the Assistance of Angels, but, when he is grown worthy, to take his own Government upon himself, and look after himself, by reason of his tractableness* Clem Alex Strom vii Therefore those Persons talk too roughly, who call this a Popish Doctrine, which so many great and Orthodox Divines have maintained It is only a Theological Opinion, which all Persons are at liberty, either to embrace or refuse

Not to be worshipped. X These blessed Spirits are not to be worshipped (1) This is evident from Scripture, where we are forbid *to be beguiled with the worshipping of Angels*, Col ii 18 and we read, that the Angels refused any worship offered them *And I fell at his Feet to worship him, and he said unto me, See thou do it not, I am thy fellow-Servant*, Rev xix 10 Which words, upon the like occasion, are again repeated, Cap xxii 9 (2) The Primitive Christians tenaciously adhered to this Doctrine *Origen says, That tho' they are called Gods in Scripture*, ἀλλ' ὐχ ὥςε προσκυνεῖσθαι ἡμῖν, &c *Yet we are not commanded to worship and adore them as God, for all our Prayers and Intercessions and giving of thanks must be sent up to God who is over all, by our High-Priest who is the* Logos *and God, and above all Angels*, Orig cont Cels Lib i *Theodoret* speaks thus, Ἐγὼ ὁμολογῶ μὲν, &c *I confess, the Holy Scripture has taught us, that there are certain invisible Powers, who praise their Creator, and minister unto his Will But these we do not esteem them as Gods, neither do we pay divine Worship unto them, neither do we parcel out our Adoration between him and them. We think them greater than Men, but yet we look on them to be our Fellow-Servants* Theod. Serm iii Tom iv

Of Evil Angels

That there are Evil Angels. I Under Invisible Beings are contained Evil Angels likewise, the Prince or Chief of which is termed in Scripture Satan, or the Devil Frequent mention is made of these in Holy Scripture, as having Idolatrous Worship paid to them, and that in the most barbarous manner, as when the Idolatrous Nations, and sometimes the Jews in compliance with them, offered their *Sons and Daughters unto Devils*, Psal cvi 37 as tormenting the Bodies of Men who were *possessed with Devils*, Mat iv 24. viii 16 Mar i 22 Luke viii 36 Luke iv 41 as disseminating false Doctrines, which are therefore called the *Doctrines of Devils*, 1 Tim iv 1 Frequent mention is likewise made of Satan, the Chief of these accursed Spirits As *Job*, cap i and ii who is called the *Accuser of the Brethren*, Rev xii 8 And *our Adversary the Devil*, 1 Pet v. 8 who is called the *Father* of wicked Men, *John* viii 44 whose *works Christ came to destroy*, 1 John iii 8 whose *wiles* we are commanded to *stand against*, Eph vi 2 and to take care that we *fall not into their Snares*, 2 Tim ii. 26 Wherefore the Antients call him ὁ ἀνθρωποκτόν⊕ θήρ, *a Wild Beast that destroys the Souls of Men*, Ign ad Philad and the inferior Devils πονηρὰ πνεύματα *wicked Spirits*, Ep ad Philip St *Chrysostom* calls him κοινὸν τῆς οἰκουμένης ἐχθρὸς *the common Enemy of the World*, Chrys in Psal ii. *Gregory Nyssen* calls him, βασιλέα τῆς κακίας, *the King of Mischief*, Tract ii. in Psalm. And θανάτε δημιεργὸ, *the Creator of Death*, Orat iv contr Eunom *Nazianzen* styles him ψυχῶν λῃςὴν ᾗ τύραννον *The Robber and the Tyrant of Souls*, Orat xvi

Fell through Pride and Disobedience II They were created good and happy, but fell into this wicked and wretched Estate, by their Pride and Disobedience to their Creator This is plainly revealed to us in Scripture *God spared not the Angels that sinned, but cast them down to Hell, and delivered them into Chains of Darkness, to be reserved unto Judgment*, 2 Pet ii 4 *The Angels which kept not their first estate, but left their own Habitation, he hath reserved in everlasting Chains under Darkness, unto the Judgment of the great Day*, Jude 6. Some of the Antients have entertained very fanciful Opinions concerning the fall of these mighty Spirits,

this Godhead are three God-head there be ° three *Personæ ejusdem essen-*

Spirits, as that they had indulged themselves in sensual Lusts, Fornication, &c. *Athanag de Leg Just Mart. Apol* 1. *Clem Alex Pædag & Strom. Lib* m *Tertul. de Idol* ix *Lanctant Lib* ii *cap* 15 But, the more general Opinion of the Antients was, that the Sin which occasioned the Fall of the Evil Angels, was Pride, which incited them to refuse the payment of their Worship and Subordination to their Creator, and to transfer it to the Chief of their Order, who headed their Rebellion For this Opinion the Writer of the Treatise under the Name of *Athanasius* prefers to the fanciful Opinion which some had conceived concerning the Lust of Angels Ο γὰρ Σαλανᾶς οὐχ᾽ ἕνεκεν πορνείας, ἢ μοιχείας, ἢ κλοπῆς κατενέχθη ἐκ τῶν οὐρανῶν ἀλλ᾽ ἡ ὑπερηφανία αὐτὸν κατέβαλεν εἰς τὰ κατώτερα μέρη τῆς ἀβύσσου *Satan was driven out of Heaven, not upon account of Fornication, or Adultery, or Theft: but Pride threw him down headlong into the lowest Abyss* Athan in Orat de Virg St. *Chrysostom* says that the reason of their being thrown out of Heaven was, μεῖζον τῆς ἀξίας φρονήσαντες because they *arrogated more to themselves than was their due* Chrys Hom xxii in *Gen S. Cyril* of *Alexandria* says, that Satan being ἐπίσημος ἐν ἀγγέλοις, ἔπεσε καὶ συνετρίβη περιφανῶς ὑπέρογκα καὶ τῇ μόνῃ πρέπουσαν τῇ ὑπεράτῃ φύσει τιμὴν τε καὶ δόξαν ἁρπάσαι τολμήσας *An Angel of high dignity, fell and was crushed by God, for his insolent attempts, and for his endeavouring to ravish away the honour and glory, which was due alone to the divine Nature* Cyr Comm ii in Is The same is expressed by *Gregory Nazianzen* in the Verses

Λάμψας ὁ πρώτιστος ἑωσφόρος ὕψος ἀερθεὶς
("Η γὰρ δὴ μεγάλοιο θεοῦ βασιληΐδα τιμὴν
Ἤλπετο κῦδος ἔχων πρέσβυς οἱ) ἄλεσεν ἀγλαΐην
Καὶ πέσεν ἐνθάδ᾽ ἄτιμος——

For high-rais'd Lucifer, *of Angels Chief,*
Hoping to share the Great God's Regal Honour,
His Splendor lost, in which he did excell,
And fell from Heaven inglorious——
Greg Naz. Car vi Arcan.

And so another Christian Poet

——*Tanquam conditor esset*
Ipse sui, rabido concepit corde furorem
Auctoremque negans, Divinum consequar (inquit)
Nomen, & æternam ponam super æthera sedem
Excelso similis, summo nec viribus impar

——*As if he were*
The Maker of himself, conceiv'd mad Rage
Within his Breast, denying his Creator.
I'll have the Honours of Divinity
(Said he) paid me I'll have a Throne erected
Like the Eternals, in Power not inferior
Alc Avitus Lib. ii

III That since their Fall, they retain an inveterate Malice against God and his Workmanship, particularly Mankind, whom, upon all Occasions, they endeavour to seduce to a like Wickedness with their own, and to involve them in their Punishment This the Holy Scriptures do expresly inform us of They began the exercise of this malicious purpose, soon after the Creation, by deceiving our first Parents. Upon which account, that crafty Spirit, who was the Occasion of this Miscarriage, is called in Scripture *the old Serpent, called the Devil and Satan which deceiveth the whole World,* Rev xii 9. and the *Serpent which beguiled Eve, through his subtilty,* 2 Cor xi 3 He is said *to go about as a roaring Lion, seeking whom he may devour,* 1 Pet v. 8 That we have a continual Combat with him, and all his wicked Associates *For we wrestle, not against Flesh and Blood, but against Principalities and Powers, against the Rulers of the darkness of this world,* Eph vi 12 Whereupon *Macarius,* in one of his Homilies, well says, Ὁ πολέμιος καὶ ἐχθρὸς παύσεως πολεμῶν ὁ Σαλανᾶς ἐστιν ἀσπλαγχνὸς ὢν καὶ μισάνθρωπος διὸ καὶ παντὶ ἀνθρώπῳ πολεμῶν ἐστι *He is an Enemy which wages a continual War with all Men for Satan is void of all Bowels of Compassion, and a Hater of Mankind, therefore he never ceases to wage War with Man* Mac Hom xv These Wiles of the Devil are pushed on, with more Vehemence and Application, against those that are eminent for Piety Which S *Chrysostom* very finely remarks Ὥσπερ γὰρ οἱ λῃσταί, οὐκ ἔνθα χόρτος ἢ ἄχυρον ἢ καλάμη, ἀλλ᾽ ἔνθα χρυσίον καὶ ἀργύριον, ἐκεῖ διορύττουσι, καὶ συνεχῶς ἀγρυπνοῦσιν οὕτω καὶ ὁ διάβολος τούτοις μάλιστα ἐπιτίθεται τοῖς πνευματικῶν ἀπολαύουσι πραγμάτων *As Thieves, who, not where there is Hay, or Chaff or Reeds, but where there is Gold and Silver, there break through, there they watch so the Devil there makes his Attacks, where he finds Men eminent for Spiritual Virtues,* Chrys Orat Stat i

° *Three*] Hitherto the Articles have been declaring those Affections of the Divine Nature, which are demonstrable from the Dictates of human Reason, as well as from the Attestation of God's Word They now proceed to declare some other Affections, which we are entirely beholding for to Revelation, That we have any Notice thereof And the first is the Doctrine of the ever blessed Trinity, which informs us, That God is not so altogether one, but that his Unity does admit of a Trinity of Persons, which are, in an ineffable and incomprehensible manner, One This great Article of our Faith is chiefly grounded upon Scripture, and the uninterrupted Tradition of the Catholick Church in all Countries and Ages, but it has likewise some Foundation in the Doctrine, both of the Jewish and Heathen Writers, who may not be without good Reason supposed to have some Traces thereof left among them, from some antient Revelation made in some very early Ages of the World, to the Progenitors both of the Jews and the Heathens, or else the latter copied it from the former For

Trinity of the Jews

The Doctrine of a Trinity in the Divine Nature was received among the Jews For this some of their celebrated Rabbies, as well as the Christian Doctors, do infer from the first Verse of *Genesis Barosh elohim,* &c *The Gods created the Heaven and the Earth* no, it is not written so, *but he the* Gods *created,* &c Bereshith Rabba *Amar Rabb. Eliezer* &c Rabbi Eliezer said, The *World was not created but by the* WORD *of the* Lord *and Rabbi Simeon said, God breathed from the* SPIRIT *of his Mouth, and the World was created,* ibid So in the *Midrash Tehillim,* or antient Commentary upon the *Psalms,* Psal l i *Elohim Jehova dabar,* &c The *Gods the Lord hath spoken,* &c *Lamma hazakir,* &c *Why did Asaph remember the name of the holy and blessed God three times? To teach you, that with these three names God created his Ages or his Universe, his three Proprieties in which the World was created, and these are his Wisdom, his Knowledge and his Understanding* Some of the Rabbins will have the *Jod, He* and *Vau* in the name of *Jehova* to denote God's three essential Proprieties *R Abrah in Lib Jetzira* And that Passage of *Maimonides* in his Book of the Foundations of the Law is very remarkable. *Hou hodhiang,* &c *God is the Knower, the Thing known, and Knowledge, So that these three, or* (hacol achadh) *all these are one* Vid Raimund Martin Pugion Fid p 396 Galatin Lib ii c 4 *Philo* the Jew speaks yet more expresly of the Trinity Δορυφορούμενος ὢν ὁ μέσος, &c *God being on each side guarded by his Powers, affords to a perceiving Understanding, sometimes the Idea of* ONE *and sometimes of* THREE *Of* ONE *when the Mind is throughly purged, and has not only gotten over the multitude of number, but even the Dyas (or number of two) next to the Monad (or Unit) and centers in the unmixed Incomposit, and Self-existent Of* THREE, *when not yet initiated into great Mysteries it is conversant in lower matters, and cannot conceive a Being from its self, but considers it either as creating, or governing* Phil Lib de Abrahamo. Their Cabbalistical Doctrine of the *Kepher* the Crown, *Bina* Prudence, *Cochmah* Wisdom, the Principal or Original Sephiroths, may not improbably be thought to be a part of antient Tradition among them, vid Dr *More's* Works, *Lat p* 431 *Vol* II

Heathen Trinity.

II The Heathens likewise had a Notion of the Trinity, and that so clearly, that the Heretical Opposers of this Doctrine do accuse it (though very falsely) for being derived from their Philosophy *Plato,* who learned his Theology from the Eastern Nations, speaks of this

this great Mystery in the Divine Nature, thus. Φραστέον δ' αὐτῷ δι' αἰνιγμῶν ἵν' ἄν τι ἡ δέλτος ἢ πόντου ἢ γῆς ἐν πτυχαῖς πάθῃ, ὁ ἀναγνοὺς μὴ γνῷ ὧδε γὰρ ἔχει περὶ τὸν πάντων βασιλέα πάντ' ἐστί, κἀκείνου ἕνεκα πάντα, κἀκεῖνο αἴτιον ἁπάντων τῶν καλῶν δεύτερον δὲ περὶ τὰ δεύτερα, καὶ τρίτον περὶ τὰ τρίτα *I must now express my self to you some things, by Mysteries or Riddles, which if the Letter miscarries either by Land or by Sea, he that reads it will not Understand it. It is this All things are about the King of all things for his sake all things were, he is the Cause of all that is excellent second things are about the second and third things about the Third* Plat Epist Dionys cited by *Eusebius*, Præp Ev Lib ii He elsewhere makes mention of a πρῶτος Θεὸς the first or Original Deity, the δημιουργός, or the Creator, and the κόσμου ψυχή *the Soul of the Universe*, which *Eusebius* says he makes his Θεὸν τρίτον, the third Person of his Trinity The later Platonists followed their Master in this Doctrine For thus *Proclus* speaks Ἀπὸ τῶν πληθῶν ἐπὶ τὰς ἑνάδας ἀνατρέχειν εἰώθ. ἡ πᾶσα δὲ τάξις ἀπὸ μονάδος ἄρχεται δι. μὲν γὰρ τέλειος θεῖος ἀριθμὸς τριάς ἀλλὰ πρὸ τῆς τριάδος ἡ μονάς *Plato says, we are wont to run up from a multitude to Unity But all the divine Order begins from One For tho' the divine number must be a Trinity, yet before that Trinity there was an Unity* Procl in Tim Where likewise he cites *Numenius* for delivering a like Doctrine. Νουμήνιος μὲν γὰρ τρεῖς ἀνυμνήσας θεοὺς, πατέρα μὲν καλεῖ τὸν πρῶτον, ποιητὴν δὲ τὸν δεύτερον, ποίημα δὲ τὸν τρίτον ὁ γὰρ κόσμος κατ' αὐτὸν ὁ τρίτος ἐστὶ θεός ὥστε ὁ κατ' αὐτὸν δημιουργὸς διττός, ὅ τε πρῶτος καὶ ὁ δεύτερος θεός τὸ δὲ δημιουργούμενον ὁ τρίτος *Numenius preaching up three Gods, he calls the first the Father, the second the* Worker, *and the third the Work For the World according to his Opinion is the third God Therefore according to his Opinion, there is a twofold Worker, the first and the second God and that which is made is the Third* Procl ib It may be objected indeed, that these Trinities of the Jews, and Platonists, do not exactly agree with the Christian Trinity. And the like may be said of their way of treating of Moral Virtues for we Christians explain Justice, Mercy, Charity, Humility, &c in a different manner from both Jews and Heathens, but no reasonable Person will for this reason conclude, that the Jews and Heathens acknowledged no Natural Religion, or Moral Virtue. And tho' it should be granted that those, who have prosecuted at large the Arguments, for the establishing this Christian Doctrine, drawn from the Jewish and Heathen Trinities, have mixed sometimes too much Fancy in their Writings, their Opposers in their turns have discovered too much unreasonable Prejudice, and what is worse, not a little Confidence and Buffoonery

Trinity revealed in Scripture.

III This Doctrine is revealed in Scripture. The word *Trinity* indeed is not to be found in Scripture But there are several Places which afford unexceptionable Ground for the use of this word, for there are three distinct Divine Persons mentioned there, these may with the exactest Propriety of Expression be called the Trinity, and if there be other Places, which do assert there is but one God, it must necessarily be concluded, that these Persons are a *Trinity* in *Unity*, which makes up the whole Idea of the Christian Trinity The Passages for the Unity of God have been mentioned before, in the Note concerning the Unity of God And other Places, which evince, the Son and the Holy Ghost to be God, shall be taken notice of hereafter. I shall at present only set down some Texts, which prove these Three to be One *When the Comforter is come, whom I will send unto you from the Father, even the Spirit of Truth, which proceedeth from the Father, he shall testify of me*, John xv 26 *When he the Spirit of Truth is come, he will guide you into all Truth for he shall not speak of himself, but whatsoever he shall hear, that shall he speak and he will shew you things to come He shall glorify me for he shall receive of mine, and shall shew it unto you*, John xvi 13, 14 In which Places, not only the Three distinct Divine Persons are mentioned, but the particular Derivation of their Essence is illustrated The Form of Baptism is a further Proof of this great Truth *Go ye therefore and teach all Nations, baptizing them in the Name of the Father and of the Son and of the Holy Ghost*, Mat xxviii 19 There are those Hereticks, who would have the Son to be a Creature, and the Holy Ghost a Quality, do fasten very great Inconsistencies upon this Form of Baptism, in setting a Creature upon the Level with its Creator, and ascribing a personal relation to a mere Accident, which, with no Propriety of Speech, can be said to have a Name, which Proselites should be baptized in The same may be proved from the Apostles Form of Blessing *The Grace of our Lord Jesus Christ, the Love of God, and the Fellowship of the Holy Ghost be with you all* Amen 2 Cor xiii 13 And so likewise from that remarkable Text of S *John* *There are three that bear record in Heaven, the Father, the Word and the Holy Ghost, and these three are one* 1 Joh v 7. But because this last Text of Scripture is excepted against, as being wanting in some Manuscripts, and not being cited by several of the Antient Fathers in their Disputes with the *Arians* and *Macedonians*, something ought to be said in the Defence thereof

Vindication of 1 Joh v 7

IV It must be granted that there are many both Greek and Latin Manuscripts, where this controverted Clause is omitted as in the *Alexandrian* MSS in the Queen's Library, and in several others of the *French* King's, cited by Father *Simon* in his Critical History of the New Testament, &c But then on the other side there are many others, of as good Authority, which have it The Divines of *Louvain* took great Pains in their Edition of the New Testament, comparing it with all the MSS which they could procure, and yet they testify that it was wanting only in five *Robert Stephens* made use of sixteen MSS Copies, the greater part whereof had it *Lucas Brugensis* made use of many MSS of which he confesses that five Latin ones wanted it But says, that all the Greek ones had it, *taceo omnes Græcos Par fieri, ... Codices ... est qui diffideat* *Erasmus* indeed was so wrought upon by the Antiquity of some of these MSS which wanted it, as to publish an Edition of the Greek Testament without the Verse in Controversy, *A D* 1516 but, afterwards, in his maturer Years, and upon better Conviction, he publisht his later Editions with it If the Antiquity of the MSS where the Verse is wanting be pretended, as Father *Simon* and others set much upon this Head, it may be answered very justly, that the antienter they are the higher they come to those Times, when the *Arians* and other Antitrinitarian Hereticks prevailed, to whose charge the expunging the clause is laid The Truth is, almost all MSS of 6 or 700 Years standing have the Clause, of those of 1000 or 1200 Years some retain it, others omit it But then these carry us upon or near the time of Arianism, and higher than that there are no MSS at all But that there were Copies of the new Testament, which had the Clause, before the time of Arianism, is plain from S *Cyprian*, who in his book of the Unity of the Church says, *Dicit Dominus Ego & Pater unum sumus & iterum de Patre & Filio & Spiritu Sancto ... scriptum est Et tres unum sunt* *The Lord saith, I and my Father are One and again, of the Father, the Son and the holy Ghost, and these Three are One* Sandius says this Passage is an Interpolation but offers nothing in Proof of it Father *Simon* says he meant it only of the *Spirit*, *the Water and Blood*, but S *Cyprian*'s plain Words better explain his Meaning than the Father's Comment on them But however *Fulgentius* was as capable of understanding them as this *French* Critick *Beatissimus Martyr Cyprianus in Epistola de Unitate Ecclesiæ confitetur, ... qui ... Christi ... Ecclesiam ... colligit, Christi Ecclesiam spargit ... de Scripturis ... Dominus, ego & Pater unum sumus, & iterum de Patre & Filio & Spiritu Sancto scriptum est, & hi tres unum sunt* *The blessed Martyr S Cyprian in his Epistle concerning the Unity of the Church confesses, saying, he that breaks the Peace ... of Christ acts against Christ ... that Gathers ... elsewhere than in the Church scatters abroad And to prove that there can be but one Church of one God, he brings Testimonies from Scriptures, as that of our Lord, I and my Father are One and again, of the Father, the Son and the holy Ghost, and these Three are One* Fulgent Contr Object Ar

Quoted by S Cyprian

By S Jerom

St *Jerom* lived when the *Arian* Controversy flamed, who setting forth a New Translation of the Bible, put Prologues or Prefaces before the particular Books, and one before the Catholick Epistles which has these words *In qua (1 Ep Joh) ab infidelibus Translatoribus multum erratum fuisse a fidei veritate comperimus, trium tantummodo vocabula, hoc est, aquæ, sanguinis & spiritus in ipsa sua editione ponentibus, & Patris Verbique ac Spiritus Testimonium omittentibus, in quo maxime & fides Catholica roboratur & Patris ac Filii ac Spiritus sancti una divinitatis substantia comprobatur* *We find that great Faults have been committed by by the Heretical Translators, putting only the three Words, i. e. the Water, the Blood and the Spirit, in their Edition, and leaving out the Testimony of the Father, the Word and the Spirit, by which the Catholick Faith is very much strengthened, and the one Substance of the Father, the Son and the holy Spirit is proved.* When *Erasmus* was pressed with this Passage by his Adversary *Stunica*, he falls foul upon S. *Jerom*, and says, *violentus est, parumque pudens, sæpe varius parumque sibi constans. That he was a violent and confident Man, and often times inconsistent with himself,* adding that he suspected he had not acted a fair part in putting in this Verse, the Copies of his Time not warranting to do it. *Erasm. An. in 1 Joh. v.* But by the way, this is as Confident and as Angry, and gives as much Suspicion of Unfairness, as any thing to be met with in S. *Jerom.* Thus he thinks to elude the force of St *Jerom*'s Authority. But Father *Simon* taking another Course, without Sense or Wit, denies S. *Jerom* to be the Author of the Epistle, as if he had Understood S. *Jerom*'s Style better than *Erasmus*, who had dealt so much in his Works, and would have taken this Method of getting rid of S. *Jerom*'s Authority which pressed him so hard, if he had found any Pretence for it. Father *Simon* will have the Epistle to be written by some one who collected together all the Books of S. *Jerom*'s Version, in S. *Jerom*'s Name. Alledging no Proof for this Assertion but only, that the Epistle is in one or two MSS. of the New Testament without a Name, and in some few others there is the Preface though the Verse be wanting. But after this way of reasoning it may be concluded that *Virgil* never wrote his *Æneids*, nor *Ovid* his *Fasti*, so much we he must be laid upon the Blunders of Transcribers. And considering what ignorant People they were, we may very well think that they were like enough to put S. *Jerom*'s Prefaces to an Arian Bible which they had copied. Not long after S. *Jerom* lived *Victor Uticensis*, who in the Confession of Faith delivered to King *Hunrick* quotes the Verse thus, *Et ut adhuc luce clarius unius divinitatis esse cum Patre & Filio Spiritum sanctum doceamus, Johannis Evangelistæ testimonio comprobatur: ait namque tres sunt qui testimonium perhibent in cælo Pater Verbum & Spiritus sanctus & hi tres unum sunt.* And to make the Unity of the Divine Persons as clear as Light, it is proved by the Authority of S. *John*, who says, *There are Three*, &c. *Bibl. Patr. Mag. Vol.* iv. p. 707. These words are cited likewise by *Vigilius Tapsensis. Audisti superius Evangelistam Johannem in Epistola sua tam absolute testantem, tres sunt qui testimonium dicunt in cælo Pater,* &c. *You have heard before* John *the Evangelist so absolutely witnessing in his Epistle, There are Three which bear witness in Heaven, the Father,* &c. de Trin. Lib. c. 5.

By Victor Uticensis

By Vigilius Tapsensis

And to this, that the Greek Church have the Verse, in their Ἀπόστολος or Book of Epistles, which are read in their Church.

This is sufficient to prove, that there were Copies, in these several Ages, wherein this Verse was read. But what must be said, to account for the Omission of it by *Oecumenius* among the Greeks, and *Bede* among the Latins, who have written Notes upon this Epistle. That it should not be mentioned, either by *Gregory Nazianzen*, *Gregory Nyssen*, nor even by *Athanasius* nor St *Austin*, whose Controversies with the Arians, or other Oppofers of the Trinity, seem'd to invite them to the Citation of this Text, had it then been in their Bibles? This must be allowed to be a considerable Objection, but which may be accounted for, from the very great Corruption of Copies occasion'd, as S. *Jerom* intimates, by the Antitrinitarian Hereticks. And a fair Opportunity was given for this, by the mighty prevalency of the Arian Bishops in the East, towards the rise of that Heresie, and afterwards in the West by the Power of the Gothick Kings, who were Favourers of that Opinion. Besides, as all Books of the Holy Scripture were scarce, and to be perused mostly in Libraries, so the Catholick Epistles were less read, as appears by so few of the Fathers writing Commentaries upon them, and because that when they were defending Articles of Faith, they chose to make use of Proofs chiefly drawn from the Gospel, which being generally the words of our Saviour himself, were thought to carry the greatest Authority with them: which may be the reason why they cited more frequently, *I and my Father are one,* for the Proof of the Unity in the Godhead, than the Text before mentioned.

V. The Doctrine of the Trinity was the received Doctrine of the Church, before it was established by the Council of *Nice*. The Antitrinitarians indeed pretend, That it was the Invention of that Age, and That that Council innovated in the Christian Faith, by establishing this Doctrine. But it is certain, that the Christian Writers, who lived long before this Council, did maintain this Doctrine, though some of them do express themselves in somewhat a different manner, from the Divines who lived after it. For the frequent Debates which happened at and after that Council, concerning the particular controverted Points in this Doctrine, occasioned a new sort of Language among Divines, which was unknown to their Predecessors. So that it is no wonder if those antient Writers expressed themselves differently from the latter, and did not make use of a set of Words and Expressions, which were coined after their time. But however, they had for the most part the same Meaning concerning the Trinity which the others had, tho' their way of expressing it was not altogether the same. It shall content me to mention a few, of a great many which may be alledged, referring the Reader to those who have written at full upon this Argument. To begin with *Ignatius*. One can hardly think, that this Father would have expressed himself as he does, if the Doctrine of the Trinity had not been the received Doctrine of his time. Πάντες οὖν ὡς εἰς ἕνα ναὸν συντρέχετε Θεοῦ, ὡς ἐπὶ ἓν θυσιαστήριον, ὡς ἐπὶ ἕνα Ἰησοῦν Χριστὸν, τὸν ἀφ' ἑνὸς πατρὸς προελθόντα, καὶ εἰς ἕνα ὄντα καὶ χωρήσαντα. *Do you all run as to one Temple of God, as to one Altar, as to one Jesus Christ, who goeth out from the one Father, and returneth again to him being One.* Ign. Ep. ad Mag. Εἷς Θεός ἐστιν ὁ φανερώσας ἑαυτὸν διὰ Ἰησοῦ Χριστοῦ τοῦ υἱοῦ αὐτοῦ, ὅς ἐστιν αὐτοῦ λόγος ἀΐδιος. *There is one God who has manifested himself by his Son Jesus Christ, who is his Eternal Word.* Ib. *Just. Martyr* speaks of the Trinity in these express words. Ὁμολογοῦμεν τῶν τοιούτων νομιζομένων θεῶν ἄθεοι εἶναι, ἀλλ' οὐχὶ τοῦ ἀληθεστάτου καὶ πατρὸς δικαιοσύνης καὶ σωφροσύνης, καὶ τῶν ἄλλων ἀρετῶν, ἀνεπιμίκτου τε κακίας Θεοῦ· ἀλλ' ἐκεῖνόν τε, καὶ τὸν παρ' αὐτοῦ υἱὸν ἐλθόντα καὶ διδάξαντα ἡμᾶς ταῦτα, &c. πνεῦμά τε τὸ προφητικὸν σεβόμεθα καὶ προσκυνοῦμεν, λόγῳ καὶ ἀληθείᾳ τιμῶντες. *We confess we are Atheists in denying the Being of your supposed Gods, but not with relation to the true God, the Father of Righteousness and Temperance and of other Virtues, and who is a God unmixed with Evil: Him, together with his SON who came from him, and taught us these things,* &c. *as also the Prophetick SPIRIT, we adore and pay honour to, both in word and truth.* Just. Martyr Apol. ii. And thus *Athenagoras*, Καὶ μή μοι γελοῖόν τις νομίσῃ τὸ υἱὸν εἶναι τῷ Θεῷ. Οὐ γὰρ ὡς ποιηταὶ μυθοποιοῦσιν, οὐδὲν βελτίους τῶν ἀνθρώπων δεικνύντες τοὺς θεούς, ἢ περὶ τοῦ Θεοῦ καὶ πατρὸς ἢ περὶ τοῦ υἱοῦ πεφρονήκαμεν. Ἀλλ' ἐστὶν ὁ υἱὸς τοῦ Θεοῦ λόγος τοῦ πατρὸς ἐν ἰδέᾳ καὶ ἐνεργείᾳ· πρὸς αὐτοῦ γὰρ καὶ δι' αὐτοῦ πάντα ἐγένετο, ἑνὸς ὄντος τοῦ πατρὸς καὶ τοῦ υἱοῦ· ὄντος δὲ τοῦ υἱοῦ ἐν πατρὶ καὶ πατρὸς ἐν υἱῷ ἑνότητι καὶ δυνάμει πνεύματος, νοῦς καὶ λόγος τοῦ πατρὸς ὁ υἱὸς τοῦ Θεοῦ. *There is no reason that any one should think it ridiculous, that God should have a Son. For we have not the same thoughts of God the Father and the Son, as the Poets, who make their Gods not better than Men. For the SON is the word of God the FATHER in Idea and Energy. For by him were all things made, God the Father and God the Son being One: the Son being in the Father and the Father in the Son, by the unity and power of the HOLY GHOST.* Athenag. Leg. pro Chr. The Doxology used by *Clement* of *Alexandria* is an express Declaration of the Doctrine of the holy Trinity. Τῷ μόνῳ πατρὶ καὶ υἱῷ καὶ τῷ ἁγίῳ πνεύματι, πάντα τῷ ἑνί, ἐν ᾧ τὰ πάντα, δι' ὃν τὰ πάντα ἕν, δι' ὃν τὸ ἀεί, οὗ μέλη πάντες, οὗ δόξα, αἰῶνες, τῷ πάντα ἀγαθῷ, τῷ πάντα καλῷ, τῷ πάντα σοφῷ, τῷ δικαίῳ τὰ πάντα, ᾧ ἡ δόξα καὶ νῦν καὶ εἰς τοὺς αἰῶνας, ἀμήν. *To the one FATHER, SON and holy SPIRIT, who are all things ONE: in whom are all things, and by whom is Eternity: whose Members all Men are: from whom proceed the glory and the Ages: who is altogether wise, and altogether righteous: to whom be glory both now and for ever. Amen.* Clem. Pæd. Lib. iii. in the Conclusion of the Book. *Irenæus* has proved this Doctrine from the tenor of the Creed which is professed all over the World, to believe in Father, Son and Holy Ghost. *Iren. adv. Hær. Lib.* i. c. 2. *Tertullian* has several Passages in his Works, for the Support of it. Particularly this. *Protulit Deus sermonem,*&c. "God has produced his WORD "as a Root its Branch, as a Fountain its River, as the Sun "its Ray. Because every Original is a Parent, and every "thing

Trinity a Doctrine of the Church before the Council of Nice

Persons, one Substance, Power, and Eternity; the Father, Son and Holy Ghost.	p Persons of one Substance Power and Eternity; the Father, Son and Holy Ghost.	tiæ, potentiæ & æternitatis, Pater, Filius & Spiritus sanctus

And he is Everlasting, MSS C C 1571

" thing which is produced by the Original is an Offspring Much more the word of God has obtained the " Name of a Son. Neither is the Branch divided from " the Root, neither the River from the Fountain neither " the Ray from the Sun · so neither is the Word divided " from God Therefore according to the form of these " Examples, I profess my self to call God and his Word, " the Father and the Son, two For the Root and the " Branch are two, but United and the Fountain and the " River are two, but yet undivided and the Sun and the Ray " two, but yet are coherent Every thing that is generated of " any thing, must be of the Nature of that by which it is " generated, but yet not so as to be separate from it " There is a second where there are two, and a third " where there are three But the Spirit is a third proceeding from God and the Son as the Fruit is a third issuing from the Root and the Branch, as a Rivulet is a " third from the Stream And the Point of the Ray is a " third from the Sun Neither is there any Separation " made from the Original Deity, from whence they receive their Properties So that the Trinity by these continued and connected Degrees taking its source from " the Father, is not capable of any jarring in the Divine " Government and Dispensation *Tert adv Prax* cap viii After him S *Cyprian* declares in favour of this Doctrine, grounding it upon the Baptismal Form, and using the word Trinity it self *Dominus post resurrectionem suam Discipulos suos mittens, quemadmodum baptizare deberent, instituit & docuit dicens, data est mihi omnis potestas in cœlo & terra ite ergo & docete gentes omnes baptizantes eos in nomine Patris & Filii & Spiritus sancti. Insinuat Trinitatem cujus Sacramento Gentes baptizarentur Our Lord after his Resurrection, being about to send his Disciples, instructed and taught them how they should baptize, saying, to me is given all power in Earth, go therefore and teach all Nations, baptizing them in the name of the Father, Son and holy Ghost. He intimates a Trinity, by whose Sacrament the Nations should be baptized* Cypr ad Jub This is sufficient to shew, that the Doctrine of the Trinity was the current Perswasion of the Church, before the starting of the Arian Heresie

p *Persons*] The word *Person*, as it denotes one of the Subsistencies of the Divine Nature, which are in Holy Scripture called by the Name of Father, Son and Holy Ghost, is not indeed to be found in the inspired Writings, but it owes its rise to Ecclesiastical Usage, being a Term which is very properly accommodated to denote that Distinction in the Deity

The Original use of the word Person

I The word *Persona* which we translate Person does primarily signify a Visor or Mask, which was anciently, for the most part, worn in the acting of Plays From whence by an easy Metaphor, it came to signify the part which any one acted, or the Character which he sustained Hence that of *Cicero* *Tres personas unus sustineo, meam, adversarii, judicis* I sustain three Persons, my own, that of an Adversary, and that of a Judge Sometimes it was used to signifie those remarkable Qualities which distinguished one Man from another, and fixed the Notices of difference and Individuation The former was the civil Law Sense of the word, and the latter the Grammatical, but it was upon this account, that the first, second and third Person had their Names given to them in Grammar

Tertullian the earliest Church Writer, who uses it

II. The earliest Writer that we have, who has applied this word to the Trinity is *Tertullian* As particularly in this Passage in his Book against *Praxeas*, *Hic erit Deus, & sermo Dei Filius Videmus duplicem statum, non confusum sed conjunctum in una* PERSONA, *Deum & Hominem Jesum Here will be God, and the word the Son of God We see a twofold State, not confounded but conjoyned in one* PERSON, *God and the Man Jesus*. Tert adv. Prax Cap xxvii He is followed by the Author of the Book *de Trinitate*, supposed to be *Novatian*, who calls Christ *secundam personam post Patrem* the second Person next to the Father Cap xxi The same word is used by S *Hilary* *Una substantia, si non personarum subsistentiam per unitatem nec tantam substantium partitam in duos dividat, religiose prædicatur The Trinity may be religiously said to be one Substance, if thereby we do not destroy personal Subsistence, or divide one Substance into two* Hil Lib de Synod And by S *Ambrose* *Sicut Deus Pater, Deus Filius, Deus Spiritus sanctus est, non tamen tres Dii sunt, sed unus Deus tres habens Personas ita & anima intellectus, anima voluntas, anima memoria non tamen tres animæ in uno Corpore, sed una anima tres habens dignitates As the Father is God, the Son is God, and the Holy Ghost is God, and yet there are not three Gods but one God, but one God having three* PERSONS *so the Understanding is the Soul, the Will is the Soul, and the Memory is the Soul, and yet there are not three Souls in one Body, but one Soul having three Powers.* Ambr de dign cond hom By S *Jerom*, *Sed quæ illa sola natura est perfecta, & in tribus personis Deitas una consistit, quæ est vera & una natura est*, &c. *But the one Nature only is perfect, and the one Deity which is one Nature consists of three* PERSONS, &c Hier. Ep [illegible] Dam And S *Austin*, *Itaque loquendi causa de ineffabilibus, ut fari aliquo modo possemus, quod effari nullo modo possumus, dictum est a nostris Græcis, una essentia, tres Personæ quia, sicut jam diximus, non aliter in sermone nostro, i e. Latino, essentia quam substantia solet intelligi Now to speak of ineffable things, the Greeks say there is one Essence and three Persons because as we observed before, in our Latin Tongue, Essence signifies the same with Substance.* Aug. vii Trin c 4 This Doctrine of the Latin Fathers concerning the Personal Subsistence in the Deity being taken into *Peter Lombard*'s Sentences, was delivered down to the Schools, who branched it out into many Niceties, *vid Thom Sum Par i Bann in i Thom.* Q 29 &c

The Greeks expressed the same by Hypostasis

III But it must be noted that, as the Latins used the word Person to denote the particular Subsistences in the Divine Nature, so the Greeks used the word [illegible], to signify the same, and sometimes the word [illegible] For thus *Gregory Nazianzen* [Greek illegible] *We acknowledge one, indeed as to Essence, indivisible, or Adorations, but three, as to Hypostases, or Persons*, Greg. Naz O xxxii And so *Theodoret* [Greek illegible] *As Man is the common Name of his Nature, so have we learned to denote the Trinity but the word Hypostasis does denote one of the Persons, either Father, Son or Holy Ghost. For following the Determinations of the holy Fathers, we take Hypostasis, Person and Propriety to signify the same thing* Theod Dial 3 Tom iv But then it must be considered, that it was some time before the whole Greek Church could be brought to an universal Use of this word to signify *Person* For some of the Orthodox used the word [illegible] to signify the Essence of the Deity, which Differences were endeavoured to be settled by the Council of *Alexandria*, A D 362 soon after which the Greeks constantly Understood the same by [illegible] that the Latins did by *Persona*

And by [Greek illegible]

The word [illegible], as it was not subject to the like Ambiguity in the Greek Language with [illegible], so it was not liable to the same Exceptions This is frequently used by S. *Basil* [Greek illegible], &c *If there be any among you, who say Father, Son and Holy Ghost, are in one Subject, confessing three perfect Persons*, &c Bas Ep 349 So likewise by *Epipha-*

nius

ARTICLE II.

II *Of the Word of God made very Man*

Of the Word or Son of God, who was made very Man.

II * De Verbo five Filio Dei, qui verus Homo factus est

The Son which is the

The [a] Son which is [b] the Word

Filius, qui est verbum

* Verbum dei verum hominem esse factum. Art Ed VI

mus [Greek] *The Proprieties of the subsistent Persons of Father, Son and Holy Ghost, the Orientals call Hypostases* Eph Hær lxxiii n 17 But then to these Personalities they allowed but one Sameness of Essence. Indeed the Similitudes which are used by the Antients, as for Instance, of three Individual Men being one in their common Specifick of Nature of Humanity, have given an handle for some to fancy, that some of the Fathers have taught that Father, Son and Holy Ghost, were as distinct Persons from each other as *Peter*, *James* and *John*, but as those Similitudes are not to be carried further, than they are designed to illustrate what they are brought for, so the same Fathers sometimes speak with more Caution and Exactness S. *Athanasius* writes [Greek] *The Divinity of the Son is the Divinity of the Father And so the Father in the Son takes care in the Providence of all things* Ath Orat. iv. Again [Greek] *The Unity of the Deity is inseparable and indivisible* id Or v *Gregory Nazianzen* speaking of the three Persons of the Deity says [Greek] *Every Person has not only Unity with that with which it is joyned, but also with it self, by reason of the sameness of Essence and Power*. Greg Naz Orat xxxvi So S *Basil* [Greek] *Although they be two in number by Nature they are not divided neither he that asserts two Persons, does infer two different Beings There is one God and Father, and one God and Son and yet there are not two Gods For the Son has the same Essence with the Father* Bas contr Sabell S *Cyril* speaking of the Son thus expresses himself [Greek] *He is one with his Father according to his natural Sameness yet he exists and understands according to his proper Hypostasis*. Cyr Lib x cont Jul And again [Greek] *The Father is Father, the Son Son, and the Holy Ghost the Holy Ghost, but yet the Sameness of their Essence collects them into an Unity* id Lib iv contr Jul.

---

a *Son*] The Places of Scripture are innumerable in which our blessed Lord is called the *Son of God*, and emphatically *the Son* It is foretold to the blessed Virgin before his Nativity, *that the holy thing which shall be born of her shall be called the Son of God*, Luke i 35 S *Mark* entitles his History *The Gospel of Christ the Son of God*, Mark i. 1 God the Father declares by a Voice from Heaven, *This is my beloved Son*, Mat iii 17 The very Devils own the same, *What have we to do with thee Jesus thou Son of God*, Mat. viii 29 S *John* bears record that he is the *Son of God*, John i 34 St *Paul* says, that he *lived by the Faith of the Son of God*, Gal ii 20 and that the Jews *crucified the Son of God* Nay 'tis particularly remarkable that about our Saviour's Time the Title of the *Son of God* was a synonymous Name with that of the Messias For *Nathaniel* owns our Saviour to be the Messias in these words, *Rabbi, thou art the Son of God, thou art the King of Israel*, John i 49 The Devils use the same Expression, which the Text explains to be meant of the Messias *The Devils also came out of many, crying out and saying, Thou art Christ the Son of God And he rebuking them suffered them not to speak, for they knew that he was Christ*, Luke iv 41 *Martha* declares her Faith in confessing, *I believe that thou art the Christ the Son of God, which should come into the World*, John xi. 27 St *Peter*'s remarkable Confession denotes the same, *We believe and are sure, that thou art that Christ the Son of the living God*, John vi 69

He is in other Places called emphatically *the Son*, and the *only begotten Son of God* *No Man knoweth the Son, but the Father*, Mat xi. 27 *He that believeth on the Son hath everlasting Life*, John iii 36. *The Father loveth the Son*, John iii 35 *The Father hath sent the Son*, 1 John iv 14 *He that hath not the Father hath not the Son*, 1 John v 12 He is elsewhere called the *only begotten of the Father*, Joh i 14 And God in sending Christ is said to *give his only begotten Son*, John iii 16 The Author to the *Hebrews*, says, that God *offered up his only begotten Son*, Heb xi 17 And S *John* that *he sent his only begotten Son that we might live*, 1 John iv 9 Now there are two Reasons principally assignable, why Christ should be called the Son of God The first is, that he was born by the miraculous Power of God, and not after the ordinary way of human Generation And this Reason the holy Scripture gives for this Appellation, when it relates the Address of the Angels to the blessed Virgin *The holy Ghost shall come upon thee, and the power of the highest shall overshadow thee. Therefore also that holy thing which shall be born of thee, shall be called the Son of God*, Luke i 35 The second Reason is, because God the Father communicated the Divine Essence to him, after the same Nature and Similitude of his own infinite Existence. Upon which account the Apostle calls him, *the Image of God, the brightness of his Glory, and the express Image of his Person*, 2 Cor iv 4 Heb i 3 Which ineffable Generation the Apostle does infinitely prefer to that of Angels *For unto which of the Angels said he at any time, thou art my Son, this day have I begotten thee?* Heb i. 5

b *The Word*] This Expression of *the Word* to denote the Son of God or the second Person of the Trinity, seems to have taken its rise originally from the Jews For the Jewish Paraphrasts, some of which are older than Christianity, do frequently make use of it For so *Gen* xxviii 20 *If the Lord shall be with me*, Onkelos paraphrases *im jehi meimrah dayah besangedhi*, *If the* WORD *of the Lord shall be to my Assistance* So Deut xiv 20 *Whosoever will not hearken unto my words which he shall speak in my name, I will require it of him* Onkelos paraphrases *If any man shall not obey my words which he shall speak in my name, my* WORD *shall require it of him* So Isa xlviii 5 *I made the earth, and men and beasts on the face of the earth* The Paraphrase explains it *I bemeiri by my* WORD *made the earth*, &c Nor is this peculiar only to *Onkelos*, but the other Targums do the same For on Gen iii 22. *The Lord God said, behold man is become as one of us*, &c. The Targum of *Jerusalem* comments thus The WORD *of the Lord God said* &c And so on Gen xix 24 *The Lord rained upon Sodom and Gomorrah brimstone and fire* The Targum of *Jerusalem* Paraphrases, *The* WORD *of the Lord made to descend the rain*, &c And the Targum of *Jonathan*, *The* WORD *of the Lord sent down rain*, &c So on Exod xx 1 *God spake all these words saying*, The

The WORD to denote the Son of God first used among the Jews

Word of the Father, took Man's Na- | of the [c] Father, [d] begotten from Everlasting of the Father; | Patris, ab æterno a patre genitus, verus

The Targum of *Jerusalem* paraphrases, *Umalhl meira*, &c. *The WORD of the Lord spake all the praise of these Words.* It would be tedious to cite more of the like Passages, whereof these Paraphrases are full, from whence may be learned that the Doctrine of the *Word*, as being a Person of the Divine Essence, or at least an energetical or demiurgical Power by which God acted, was commonly received among the Jews, when these Commentaries were written. And it must be further observed, that *Philo*, agreeable to his Country-men the Targumists, attributes the Divine Actions, in making and governing the World, to the λόγ⊕ or Word. This he calls δεύτερον θεὸν *a second God*, Phil. Quæst & Sol and sivs, ὁ λόγ⊕ τοῦ θεοῦ ὑπεράνω παντός ἐστι τοῦ κόσμου καὶ πρεσβύτατ⊕ καὶ γενικώτατ⊕ τῶν ὅσα γέγονε. *The Word of God does excel the whole World, and is more antient and more noble than any thing that is made*, Leg. Alleg. Lib. ii. He elsewhere calls the Word ὄργανον θεοῦ δι' οὗ ὁ κόσμ⊕ κατεσκευάσθη. *The Agent of God by whom he made the World*. Lib. de Caino. And in another Place he thus describes the λόγ⊕ or Word, ὁ δὲ ὑπεράνω τούτων λόγ⊕ θεῖ⊕, εἰς ὁρατὴν οὐκ ἦλθεν ἰδέαν ... αὐτὸς εἰκὼν ὑπάρχων θεοῦ, τῶν νοητῶν ἁπάντων ὁ πρεσβύτατ⊕, ὁ ἐγγυτάτω, μηδενὸς ὄντ⊕ μεθορίου διαστήματ⊕, τοῦ μόνου ὃ ἔστιν ἀψευδῶς ἀφιδρυμέν⊕. *The divine Word is more excellent than all things, there is no Idea of it, nor can it come under Perception, it self being the Image of God, the most antient of all the Intelligibles, between whom and the most high there is no intermediate Being, being most truly like unto him.* Phil. de Profug. Besides, that the Jews generally received the Doctrine of the *Logos*, we have the Testimony of *Celsus* in *Origen*, who personated a Jew. Εἰ δὲ ὁ λόγ⊕ ἐστὶν ὑμῖν υἱὸς τοῦ θεοῦ, καὶ ἡμεῖς ἐπαινοῦμεν. *If among you the* Logos *be esteemed the Son of God, we agree with you in this.* Or. adv. Cels. Lib. ii. Indeed *Origen* denies this to be the Doctrine of the Jews, and the learned Bishop *Pearson* thinks, that the Jews had changed their Opinion, between the time of *Celsus* his Writing his Book, and *Origen*'s Answer, which was about 60 Years. But that does not appear. It is more probable, that the Jews whom *Origen* had conversed with, did dissemble the received Opinion of the Jews, than that they had laid that Doctrine aside. The *Jerusalem*-Targum was in all probability written after *Origen*'s time, for some where or other it mentions the Kingdom of *Lombardy*, which was not erected in *Italy* till 500 Years after Christ, and yet we find frequent mention of the *Meimrah* or *Logos* in that Paraphrase. The Cabbalistical Jews lived after the compiling of this Paraphrase, and yet we find that they are not only very express as to the *Logos* or second Person of the Trinity, but also to all the three Persons. Witness that remarkable Passage of an antient Cabbalist cited by *Grotius* in his Annotations upon the first of S. *John*. *Abh elohim eloseim*, &c. *The Father is God, the Son is God, the Holy Ghost is God, three in one, and one in three.* Now it being the received Doctrine of the Jewish Church, that the Messias was to be the Son of God, and also that the Son of God was what they called the *Meimrah* or *Logos*, S. *John* applied this Appellation to our blessed Saviour, who being the true Messias had a right to that Title.

c *Father.*] I. The first Person of the blessed Trinity is, in holy Scripture, most usually stiled by the Name of the Father, as Mat. xi. 27. *All things are delivered unto me of my Father, and no Man knoweth the Son but the Father, neither knoweth any Man the Father save the Son.* So Mat. xxviii. 19. *Go therefore and teach all Nations, baptizing them in the Name of the Father*, &c. John i. 14. *We beheld his Glory, as of the only begotten of the Father.* John iii. 35. *The Father loveth the Son*, &c. John v. 22. *The Father judgeth no Man, but hath committed all Judgment unto the Son.* and verse 23. *That all Men should honour the Son as they honour the Father.* John viii. 19. *Ye neither know me nor my Father.*

First Person of the Trinity called Father in Scripture.

II. But besides the alledging these and other Passages of Scripture, the antient Fathers do deduce the Paternity or Fatherhood of the Divine Nature, from the natural Fecundity of it, and the Absurdity of admitting a Sterility in the Godhead. For thus S. *Cyril* argues. Τέλει⊕ ὁ θεὸς, οὐχ ὅτι μόνον ἐστὶ θεὸς, ἀλλ' ὅτι πατήρ ἐστι ... εἰ τὸ πατέρα ... ἀναιρήσεις τῆς θείας φύσεως ... μηκέτι τὸ τέλειον ἔχοι, λείποντ⊕ αὐτῇ τοῦ γεννᾶν ... τοῦ εἶναι τελειότητ⊕ ἡ καρπογονία, καὶ σφραγὶς τοῦ ... εἶναι τέλειον, ὁ ἐξ αὐτοῦ προελθὼν ἀχρόνως υἱός. *God is perfect, not only because he is God, but because he is a Father. For if you take the Fatherhood from God, you will take away the Fecundity of the Divine Nature, which will take off from his Perfection, since he will then want the Power of generating, for Fecundity is a mark of Perfection, and the Son's eternally going out from the Father is a Seal or sure Mark that God is perfect.* Cyr. Thes. v. With a like Argument *Athanasius* exposes the Absurdity of the Arian Doctrine. Εἰ δὲ μὴ καρπογόν⊕ ἐστιν αὐτὴ ἡ θεία οὐσία, ἀλλ' ἔρημ⊕ κατ' αὐτοὺς, ὡς φῶς μὴ φωτίζον, καὶ πηγὴ ξηρά, πῶς δημιουργικὴν ἐνέργειαν αὐτὸν ἔχειν λέγοντες, οὐκ αἰσχύνονται, ... τὸ κατὰ φύσιν ... ἀρνούμενοι. *But if the Divine Nature be not fruitful, but barren, as the Arians pretend, like a Light which does not enlighten, or a Fountain which is dry, how are they not ashamed to allow him a creative Energy? for when they have taken away from him that which is according to Nature, they may be ashamed to allow him that which he has according to his Will.* Athan. Orat. ii.

Paternity of God proved from the Fecundity of the Deity.

III. It is observed, that Fatherhood is more properly attributed to God the Father, than it is to any Creature. This Observation is very much insisted on by several of the Antients. St. *Athanasius* expresses himself upon this Head thus. ... τοῦ θεοῦ ... μόνος ὁ Πατὴρ κυρίως Πατήρ ἐστι, καὶ ὁ υἱὸς κυρίως υἱός ἐστι ... καὶ μόνων ... ἀεὶ ... ὁ υἱὸς ἀεὶ υἱός ἐστι. *The Father only in the Divine Nature is properly a Father, and the Son properly a Son, and in these only it comes to pass, that the Father is always a Father, and the Son is always a Son.* Athan. Orat. ii. So *Faustinus* in his Treatise against the Arians. *Deus solus proprie verus est Pater, qui sine initio & fine Pater est. Non enim aliquando cœpit esse quod Pater est, sed semper Pater est, semper habens filium ex se genitum. Only God is properly a true Father, because he always was a Father, and always will be. For he never began to be a Father, but is always a Father, having always a Son begotten of himself.* Gregory *Nazianzen* argues the same Propriety of Fatherhood, from the Father's not being a Son, nor the Son a Father. Πατὴρ κυρίως, ὅτι μὴ καὶ υἱὸς ... υἱὸς κυρίως, ὅτι μὴ καὶ πατήρ ... ἡμῖν ... ἀμφω ... ἡμεῖς, &c. *He is with exact Propriety a Father, because he is no Son, and again, the Son is most properly a Son, because he is no Father. But as for us, we can properly be called by neither Name, because we are both Fathers and Sons, not one more than the other, and being born not of one, but two Parents, we are divisible*, &c. Greg. Naz. Orat. xxxv.

God more properly a Father than any Creature.

IV. God the Father by this Communication of his Essence is the Fountain of the Deity, from which the two other Persons derive their Natures, by an eternal flux of the Godhead. And therefore the antient Divines, for this reason, call him emphatically the *Principle*, the *Cause*, the *Unbegotten*, the *first Light*, &c. *Nazianzen* calls him ἀρχὴ, ... αἴτιον, ... πηγήν: *The Principle, the Cause, the Fountain*, Or. xxxv. S. *Chrysostom* says, Πατὴρ αἴτι⊕ τοῦ υἱοῦ κατὰ τὸ πατὴρ εἶναι. *The Father is the Cause of Christ as he is the Father.* Chrys. Hom. in 1 ad Cor. *Alexander*, Bishop of *Alexandria*, calls him, in his Letter, ἀγέννητον πατέρα, οὐδένα τοῦ εἶναι αὐτῷ τὸν αἴτιον ἔχοντα. *The unbegotten Father, who has no cause of his Essence.* Theod. Hist. Eccl. Lib. i. cap. 3. He is stiled by *Athanasius*, ἀγέννητος καὶ ἀναίτι⊕ καὶ ἀπάτωρ. *Unbegotten, without Cause, without Father.* Athan. Dial. i. contr. Maced. *Dionysius* speaking of Christ says, δι' οὗ τὴν πρὸς τὸ ἀρχίφωτον πατέρα προσαγωγὴν ἐσχήκαμεν. *By whom we have access to the Original Light the Father.* Dionys. Hier. Cap. i. num. 2.

God the Father the Fountain of the Deity.

d *Begotten from Everlasting.*] I. This may be concluded from the holy Scripture, which does in several Places point out to us this eternal Generation. This may be proved from

Eternal Generation of the Son proved from Scripture.

ture in the Womb of the [e] very and [f] eternal God, *& æternus Deus ac Pa-*

those Places of Scripture, which do assert our Saviour's Pre-existence before the World was made As that of our Saviour, *O Father glorify thou me with thine own self, with the glory which I had with thee before the World was,* John xvii. 5 *By him all things were created,* Col i 16 *By whom he made the Worlds,* Heb i 2 *All things were made by him,* John i 3 And particularly from the first Verse of that Chapter, *In the beginning was the Word, and the Word was God* Where the Antients understood the Words *in the beginning* of Eternity For thus *Theophylact,* Ἐν ἀρχῇ ἦν τὸ ἦν ἀεὶ, ἢ ἀπείρως, δηλωτικὸν δὲ *The words* in the beginning *do denote an Infinite and Eternal Existence* And before him S *Chrysostom* Ἐν ἀρχῇ ἦν, οὐδὲν ἕτερόν ἐστιν, ἀλλ' ἢ τὸ εἶναι ἀιδιότητα δηλωτικὸν ἢ ἀπείρως εἶναι *In the beginning is nothing else but a Demonstration that the Word had a Being from eternity and infinitely* Chrys Hom ii in *John* But when the Apostle sets the Generation of the Son far above that of Angels, Heb i 5 *Unto which of the Angels said he at any time, Thou art my Son,* &c it follows that the Generation of the Son must be Eternal

Universal Doctrine of the Church, till opposed by Arius

II This was the Universal Doctrine of the Church, till it was contradicted by *Arius* For this eternal Generation of the Son was a thing which he could not brook, and therefore bent all his Thoughts to oppose it And therefore in his Letter heavily complains, that he was deposed by *Alexander* his Bishop, for not espousing the Doctrine of the eternal Generation Ἐπειδὴ οὐ συνφωνοῦμεν αὐτῷ δημοσίᾳ λέγοντι, ἀεὶ θεὸς, ἀεὶ υἱὸς, ἅμα πατὴρ, ἅμα υἱὸς, συνυπάρχει ὁ υἱὸς ἀγεννήτως τῷ θεῷ ἀειγενής, ἀγεννητογενής οὔτε ἐπινοίᾳ, οὔτε ἀτόμῳ τινὶ προάγει ὁ θεὸς τοῦ υἱοῦ, ἀεὶ θεὸς, ἐξ αὐτοῦ τοῦ θεοῦ ὁ υἱός. *Because we will not agree with him when he publickly teaches, that the Son was always God, was always a Son, that there was always a Father, and always a Son, that the Son did co exist* (ἀγεννήτως as the Arians would make the Orthodox speak, but as they expressed themselves ἀγεννήτως) unmade *with God eternally begotten, begotten of the unbegotten, that God was not in thought or so much as a moment of time before the Son that the Son was always God, and Son of God himself* Epiph Hær lxix Sect 6 In which words whilst he endeavours to expose the Orthodox Faith, he shews the very Spirit and Soul of his Heresie.

In Opposition to this Heresie, and others that were derived from it, the Antients have advanced several Arguments, (besides the several Texts of Scripture, and the necessity of a Person which does partake of the Divine Nature having an eternal Existence) for the support of the Doctrine of Christ's eternal Generation

Eternity of the Son necessary from the Eternity of the Father

III Because he derives his Being from an eternal Father, and therefore he must be an eternal Son For thus S *Cyril* of *Alexandria* argues Τὸ ἐξ ἀϊδίου γεννηθὲν πατρὸς, ἀΐδιος τε διὰ τοῦτο ὑπάρχων, καὶ αὐτὸς ἐπάγεται γὰρ ἀναγκαίως τὸ τοῦ τεκόντος ἀξίωμα *The Son because he is born of an eternal Father did eternally Exist for his Father's Dignity was communicated to him Substantially* Cyr Lib. vi. in *John* S *Hilary, Quod ab æterno nascitur, habet æternum esse quod natum est That which is born of an Eternal, must have Eternity likewise by virtue of its Birth* Hilar cont. Ar Lib xii

Because of the Perfection of the Divine Being

IV Because God is a perfect Being S *Cyril* having shewn that even the Creatures of God, when they come to Maturity and Perfection, do produce their Species, concludes, Τί ἂν ἐκώλυε τελείαν οὖσαν τὴν οὐσίαν τοῦ πατρὸς, τίκτειν τὸ ἐξ αὐτῆς ἀχρόνως εἰς συναΐδιον αὐτῇ, οὐ γὰρ δήπου φαίησεν ἄν τις ὡς ἐν χρόνῳ τὸ τέλειον ἔσχεν ἡ τοῦ πατρὸς οὐσία, ἀεὶ ὡσαύτως ἔχουσα καὶ οὔτε προσθήκης τινὸς δεομένη, οὔτε μείωσιν ἀποσῆναι δυναμένη *What should hinder why the Substance of the Father, when it was perfect, should beget that which is born of it, before all time and Co-eternal to it self? For it cannot be said, that the Substance of the Father gained Perfection in time, which always was the same, nor was capable of Increase or Diminution,* Cyr Thes v The same Argument is thus urged by *Plotinus* Καὶ πάντα δὲ ὅσα ἤδη τέλεια, γεννᾷ τὸ δὲ ἀεὶ τέλειον, ἀεὶ, καὶ ἀΐδιον γεννᾷ *Those things that are perfect generate something, therefore that which was always perfect, did eternally Generate, and that an eternal Being* Plotin Enn v Lib i Cap 6 *Athanasius* urges the same with something more force Ἀνθρώπων μὲν γὰρ ἴδιον τὸ ἐν χρόνῳ γεννᾷν διὰ τὸ ἀτελὲς τῆς φύσεως θεοῦ δὲ ἀΐδιον τὸ γέννημα διὰ τὸ ἀεὶ τέλειον τῆς φύσεως *It is the property of Men to generate in time, by reason of the Imperfection of their Nature but the Generation of God is Eternal, because of the eternal Perfection of his Nature* Athan Or ii

Because the Wisdom of God

V Because the Son is the Wisdom of God Therefore since God did from all Eternity Understand, his Son which is his Divine Λόγος or his Wisdom or Understanding, must likewise eternally Exist For thus S *Austin. Quænam est illa generatio, quæ in Principio erat Verbum,* &c *vel quod est hoc verbum, quod dictum us antea non silebat quo dicto non siluit qui dicebat quod est verbum sine tempore, per quod facta sunt tempora? Verbum quod laxa nullius aperuit captum, clausitve finitum? What is that Generation, by which in the beginning was the Word,* &c *Or what is that Word, which when he was about to speak he was not silent before and being spoken, he that did speak was not silent? What is that Word without time, by which the times were made? A Word which never began to be spoken, and never will cease?* Aug Ser i de Div Nat All which is an Allusion to the Platonick Notion of the *Logos,* and the Eternity of the Divine Ideas εἰ γὰρ αἱ ἰδέαι νοήσεις θεοῦ αἰώνιοί τε καὶ αὐτοτελεῖς *The Ideas and Understandings of God are Eternal and Self-perfecient* Alcin C 9

Because of God's Immutability

VI Because God is immutable, and therefore could never come to be a Father, having not been Eternally so For thus S *Ambrose Si Pater esse cæpit, Deus ergo primo erat, postea Pater factus est Quomodo ergo immutabilis Deus? si enim antea Deus postea Pater, utique generationis accessione mutatus est? If he began to be a Father, he was first God and afterwards a Father How then is God immutable? But if he be first God and afterwards a Father, he is then changed by the Accession of Generation.* Ambr Lib i de fid

[e] *Very and eternal God*] I Our Saviours being the true and eternal God, as it is an essential Article of our Faith, grounded upon the clear Doctrine of the holy Scriptures, and the uninterrupted Tradition of the Catholick Church, so there have not been wanting some Hereticks, who in several Ages of the World have opposed this fundamental Truth, though the main Body of Christians have in the several Ages maintained it

Hereticks who opposed our Saviour's Divinity

The first Person who opposed this Truth was *Cerinthus,* who lived very early in the Church, and poisoned several with his Heresie before the Apostle St *John* wrote his Gospel, which occasioned that Apostle to be more express in his Writings concerning the Divinity of our blessed Lord, than the rest of the Evangelists *Epiph. Her.* lix In the second Century the same Heresie was revived by *Theodotus,* who upon that account was excommunicated by *Victor* I Bishop of *Rome Euseb Hist. Eccl Lib* v. *Theod Hær Fab Lib* ii *cap* v After these followed, in the same pestilent Doctrines, *Sabellius, Samosatenus* and *Plotinus,* who (as *Theodoret* speaks *Dial.* ii) ἄνθρωπον μόνον ψιλὸν εἶναι τὸν Χριστὸν *Taught that Christ was only Man* In the beginning of the fourth Century, this Truth, though in a different manner, was opposed by *Arius* who allowing his Pre-existence denied him to be true God, and eternally Co-existent with the Father, and asserted him only God by a temporary Participation of the Divine Essence, that he was only a κτίσμα, a ποίημα a *Creature or a Workmanship* Athan Or i. Ep Hær lxix. All which was, as *Sozomen* well remarks, at that time very novel Doctrine among Christians Ὡς τοῦτο πρῶτον παρ' ἑτέρου οὐ εἰρημένον τολμῆσαι ἐν τῇ ἐκκλησίᾳ ἀποφῆναι, τὸν υἱὸν τοῦ θεοῦ ἐξ οὐκ ὄντων γεγενῆσθαι, καὶ εἶναί ποτε ὅτε οὐκ ἦν, καὶ αὐτεξουσιότητι κακίας, καὶ ἀρετῆς δεκτικὸν ὑπάρχειν καὶ κτίσμα καὶ ποίημα *That he was the first that dared to vent in the Church, That the Son of God was of things that are not, and That there was a time when he was not, That he was endowed with a freedom of Will to do evil as well as good, that he was a Creature and God's Workmanship* Soz Lib i. c. 15

II But notwithstanding these Oppositions, the Orthodox Truth made its way, by the force of the Arguments, in behalf of our Saviour's Divinity, drawn from Scripture, as also by the Declaration and Judgment of several General Councils, which attested the Doctrine of the respective Churches in the several Parts of the World, and condemned the Opposers thereof for Innovators.

Now

Scriptural Passages which prove our Saviour's Pre-existence.

Now the Scriptural Authority does establish this Doctrine 1 By such Passages which positively assert, or necessarily infer, our Saviour's Pre-existence, whereby the Errors of the *Photinians*, *Samosatenians*, *Sabellians*, &c and such like Hereticks, who would not allow our Saviour to have had in Existence before his Incarnation, are confuted 'Tis plain by the Evangelical History, that *John* the Baptist was some Months older than our Saviour, and yet the same Baptist himself positively declares, our Saviour's having a Being before him *This is he of whom I spake, He that cometh after me is preferred before me, for he was before me*, John i 15. Our Saviour himself frequently mentions his coming down from Heaven He said, he was the *living Bread which came down from Heaven*, John vi 51 *I came down from Heaven not to do my own Will, but the Will of him that sent me*, John vi 38 *He that cometh from Heaven is above all*, John iii 31 *I came forth from the Father and came into the World again, I leave the World and go to the Father*, John xvi 27, 28 These were such strong and evident Proofs of our Saviour's Pre-existence, that they perfectly silenced the old *Photinians* and *Samosatenians*, so that their Heresies soon dwindled away The Socinians who have revived those Heresies, have employed all their Subtilty to evade the force of them, but in vain and have at last been forced to take up with a ridiculous Fable of their Invention, that Christ during the time of his Retirement into the Wilderness, ascended up into Heaven, to be more perfectly instructed in the Will of his Father, and that to this imaginary Ascent and Descent these Texts refer *Socin Christ Rel Inst ejus Resp ad Aad Vola*, C ell de Uno Deo Patre *Volkelius* Lib 3 De Rel c 5 *Smalc* Hom in cap *John* But this is an impudent Subterfuge of these Hereticks, to feign such an important Part of the Gospel History, which the sacred Writers mention not one word of, nay which they expresly contradict For S *Luke* says expresly, that he was *forty Days tempted of the Devil*, Luke iv 2 And S *Mark* as expresly says, That *he was in the Wilderness forty Days tempted of Satan*, Mark i. 13 Now to be in *Heaven*, according to the Socinian Supposition, and to be in the *Wilderness*, are two very different things, and to be *tempted of the Devil*, and to be *instructed by God*, have not a much nigher Relation But granting this idle Fancy had some weight in it, yet it would serve only to evade the force of some of the Texts before mentioned, but it would avail nothing against other most express Passages of our Saviour's Pre-existence As that of S. *Paul*, *When the fulness of time was come, God sent forth his Son made of a Woman made under the Law*, Gal iv Which words do suppose, that the Son who was sent forth was with the Father, before his Mission And that of S *John*, *The Word was made Flesh and dwelt among us*, John i 14 Which words imply that the Word had a Being, before it was *made Flesh*, and before it came to *dwell among us* This plainly proves our Saviour's Pre-existence some time before his Nativity There are other Passages which prove his Existence, during the most Antient times of the History of the Old Testament That he had an Existence in the time of *David*, does appear from *Psalm* cx *The Lord said unto my Lord*, &c which our Saviour himself says, is to be understood of the Messias, *Mat* xxii 44 *Mark* xii 36 *Luke* xx 44 For if he was *David's Lord*, he must necessarily have a Being in *David's* time Nay, before that he had a Being, *viz* in *Moses* his time, when the *Israelites* were in the Wilderness For this the Apostle S *Paul* does witness, when he says, *Neither let us tempt Christ as some of them also tempted*, 1 Cor x 9 Now if Christ was tempted by the *Israelites*, he must have a Being at the same time when he was tempted To go yet farther backwards, he had a Being in the time of *Abraham*, as appears by the express Attestation of our Saviour himself, who said *Before* Abraham *was I am*, John viii. 58 S *Paul* dates his Being to have existed *before all things*, Col i 17 And our Saviour himself speaks of his Existence in Glory before the Creation of the World *And now O Father glorifie thou me with thine own self, with the glory which I had with thee, before the World was*, John xvii 5 These Texts which have been alledged do carry our Saviour's Existence to an indeterminable Time, before the Creation of the World, and do perfectly overturn the *Photinian* and Socinian Heresies, for notwithstanding the Espousers of them have essayed to give other Interpretations of these Passages, they are generally so forced and strained, that by the same Liberty of expounding, one may make any the plainest words to speak a quite different Sense So that, though these Passages do not prove our Saviour to be God, they evince him to have had a Being long before the Creation of the World, and consequently that he is more than Man

Passages of Scripture which prove our Saviour to be very God particularly his creating the World

2 But *secondly*, There are other Passages of Holy Scripture, which do clearly prove him to be God There can not be a more certain Characteristick of Divinity than the Creative Power For since Nothing is infinitely distant from Something, to produce Something out of Nothing does betoken an infinite Power which none has but God Now since the Creation of the World is ascribed to our Saviour in Scripture, it necessarily follows, that he is God And that the Creation of the World is ascribed to him, is evident to any one who reads the Books of the New Testament S *John* in the beginning of his Gospel, in inculcating this important Truth, because no one should mistake his Meaning, redoubles his Expression *All things were made by him, and without him was not any thing made that was made*, John i 3 The same Truth is delivered by the Author to the *Hebrews* *By whom also he made the Worlds*, Heb i 2 And probably the same Author means the same thing when he says, *Through faith we understand that the Worlds were framed by the Word of God*, Heb xi 3 And by S *Paul* in his Epistle to the *Colossians*, who speaking of our Saviour says, *Who is the Image of the invisible God, the first-born of every Creature For by him were created all things that are in Heaven and that are in Earth, Visible and Invisible, whether they be Thrones or Dominions, or Principalities or Powers all things were created by him and for him And he is before all things, and by him all things consist*, Col i 15, 16 17 The Socinians, to maintain their Errors, would strain all these Passages to a Metaphorical Sense, as if they meant only a Spiritual Creation, or Regeneration But as they rack and tenter the Texts contrary to all the Rules of Criticism and Interpretation, so they have the whole bent of Antiquity against them, even of the *Antenicene* Fathers, who took those Texts as we do, to be understood of the material Creation *Justin Martyr* concludes from the Supposition of the undoubted Truth of Christ creating this World, that he shall likewise create the New Heaven and the New Earth, *Dial cum Tryph* And in his Exhortation he speaks thus of the *Logos*, δι' ὧ ὁ οὐρανὸς καὶ ἡ γῆ καὶ πᾶσα κτίσις γέγονε, ὡς ἐδίδαξαν ἡμᾶς αἱ θεῖαι τῶν ἁγίων γραφαί *By whom the Heaven and the Earth and every Creature was made, as the holy Scriptures teach us* Just. Cohort ad Gr *Irenæus* says, *Quemadmodum* & *Johannes Domini Discipulus ait de eo, Omnia per ipsum facta sunt, & sine ipso factum est nihil In omnibus autem est & hic qui est secundum nos mundus. As S* John *says of him*, All things were made by him and without him there was not any thing made that was made *he means by all things what we commonly call the World*, Iren adv Hær Lib ii *Clemens Alexandrinus* asserts the same, Ὁ δὲ ἀγαθὸς παιδαγωγὸς ἡ σοφία, ὁ λόγος τῦ Πατρὸς, ὁ δημιουργήσας τὸν ἄνθρωπον, ὅλυ κήδεται τῦ πλάσματος. *But the good Instructer, the Wisdom, the Word of the Father, who made Man, takes care of his whole Creation* Clem Alex Lib i Pædag So *Tertullian In principio erat sermo In quo principio Deus fecit cœlum & terram Et sermo erat apud Deum, & Deus erat sermo Omnia per ipsum facta sunt In the beginning was the Word In which beginning God made the Heaven and the Earth, and the word was with God*, &c Tert. adv. Hermog cap xx And S *Cyprian*, who says, *Christum Primogenitum esse, & ipsum esse Sapientiam Dei per quam omnia facta sunt Christ is the first Born, and the Wisdom of God, by which all things were made*

The Divine Attributes ascribed to our Saviour in Scripture

3 Our Saviour's being very God may be proved, from the incommunicable Attributes of the Deity being attributed to him in Scripture (1) As Immensity or Omnipresence. For our Saviour declares, *Where two or three are gathered together in his Name there he is in the midst of them*, Mat. xviii. 20 *Lo I am with you always unto the end of the World*, Mat. xxviii 20 *No Man hath ascended up into Heaven, but he that came down from Heaven, even the Son of Man which is in Heaven*, John iii 13 (2) Omnipotence *I am Alpha and Omega, the beginning and the*

the ending saith the Lord, which is and which was and which is to come, the Almighty, Rev i 8 *upholding all things by the word of his Power*, Heb i 3 *All Power is given unto me in Heaven and in Earth*, Mat xxvii 18. (3) Omniscience, or the Knowledge of all things *Lord, thou knowest all things*, John xxi 17 *Now we are sure that thou knowest all things*, John xvi 30 *All the Churches shall know that I am he which searcheth the Reins and the Hearts*, Rev ii 23 *He knew their Thoughts, and said unto the Man with the withered Hand*, &c Luke vi 8 *Jesus did not commit himself unto them, because he knew all Men*, John ii. 24 (4) Immutability or Unchangeableness. *They shall perish but thou remainest*, &c *and as a vesture shalt thou fold them up, and they shall be changed, but thou art the same and thy years shall not fail*, Heb i 11, 12 *Jesus Christ, the same yesterday, to day and for ever*, Heb xiii 8

Our Saviour called frequently GOD in Scripture.

4 Another Proof of our Saviour's being the true God, is his being so frequently called God in Scripture It cannot be supposed that the Holy Scriptures which were written to inform Christians and to guide them into the Truth, should be so penned as necessarily to mislead them in so important a Point as that of our Saviour's Divinity and that they should so frequently call our Saviour God, when in reality he is not so S *Paul* speaks thus to the Elders of the Church of *Ephesus* *Take heed unto your selves, and to all the Flock, over which the Holy Ghost hath made you Overseers to feed the Church of God, which he hath purchased with his own Blood*, Acts xx 28 Now since 'tis here plainly asserted that the Church (or all faithful Christians) is purchased by the *Blood of God*, Christ who made this purchase, 1 *Pet*. i 18 is God S *Thomas* addressed himself to our Saviour, in these words, *My Lord and my God*, John xx 28 He is several times called so in the Epistles of S *Paul* *Without controversy great is the mystery of Godliness, God was manifested in the Flesh, justified in the Spirit, seen of Angels, preached unto the Gentiles, believed on in the World, received up into Glory*, 1 Tim iii 16 And in the Epistle to the *Romans*, St *Paul* speaking of the Jews, says, *out of whom, as concerning the flesh Christ came, who is over all God blessed for ever*, Rom. ix 5 If these Passages had been so penned, that they might lead Christians into a mistake, in thinking Christ to be God when really he was but Man, or some other Superior created Being, S *John* who wrote his Gospel after all the rest, would have set Matters right, and told the World that our Saviour was only a Creature, and that those Expressions which seemed to bespeak him God were only some high Metaphors, which must have a much lower Meaning put upon them But instead of this, S *John* is more express in this matter than any of the Apostles, who had written before him In the very Entrance into his Gospel he tells his Reader, who the Person is that he is to write the History of, That he was the *Logos* or Word, who from all Eternity was with God, and that this *Word was God* Words so express, that the Apostle must needs think they would necessarily misguide his Reader, if they had any other Meaning than what they naturally import

The Deity of our Saviour acknowledged by the Antient Fathers

III The Deity of our Saviour was owned by the antient Fathers of the Church, who lived before the *Nicene* Council, wherein this Doctrine was fully established. One of the most antient of the Ecclesiastical Writers, and who lived in or very near the Apostolical times, is *Hermas*, who in his Book entituled, *The Pastor*, has many Expressions relating to our Saviour which do either assert or imply his Divinity

Godhead of the Son acknowledged by HERMAS

At Nomen Filii Dei magnum est & immensum, & totus ab eo sustentatur orbis *The Name of the Son of God is great and immense, and the whole World is sustained by him*, and again, *Omnis Dei Creatura per Filium ejus sustentatur* *Every Creature of God is sustained by his Son* *Ignatius*, who lived not long after him, does in several Places of his Epistles stile him God

IGNATIUS.

Δοξάζω Ἰησοῦν Χριστὸν τὸν Θεὸν τὸν οὕτως ὑμᾶς σοφίσαντα *I glorify Jesus Christ, God, who has made you thus wise*, Ign Ep ad Smyrn And again in another Epistle, ἵνα ὦμεν αὐτοῦ ναοί, καὶ αὐτὸς ᾖ ἐν ἡμῖν Θεὸς ἡμῶν *That we may be his Temple and he God in us* Ign Ep ad Eph. So in another Epistle, ἐπιτρέψατέ μοι μιμητὴν εἶναι τοῦ πάθους τοῦ Θεοῦ μου *Suffer me to be an Imitator of the Passion of Christ my God*, Ign Ep ad Rom

CLEMENS

Clemens Romanus in his Epistles does not indeed directly assert our Saviour's Godhead, but he uses Expressions which are Tantamount thereunto He calls him the ἀπαύγασμα τῆς μεγαλωσύνης τοῦ Θεοῦ, *The Splendor of the magnificence of God*, Clem Ep i ad Cor And σκῆπτρον τῆς μεγαλωσύνης τοῦ Θεοῦ *The Scepter of God's magnificence*, ibid *Justin Martyr* blames them that deny, ὅτι ὁ υἱὸς τοῦ Πατρὸς τῶν ὅλων ὢν καὶ λόγος πρωτότοκος τοῦ Θεοῦ καὶ Θεὸς ὑπάρχει *That there is a Son to the Father of all things, which being the first-born Word of God is himself God* Just. Mart Apol ii In his Conference with *Trypho* the Jew, he asserts, τὸν Θεόν, τὸ μόνου καὶ ἀγεννήτου Θεοῦ υἱόν *That he is God because he is the Son of the only begotten God*, Dial cum Tryph

JUSTIN MAR

Athenagoras does assert not only the Godhead of the Son, but likewise of the Holy Ghost, together with the whole Order of the Blessed Trinity Τίς οὖν οὐκ ἂν ἀπορήσαι λέγοντας Θεὸν Πατέρα καὶ υἱὸν Θεὸν καὶ πνεῦμα ἅγιον, δεικνύντας αὐτῶν καὶ τὴν ἐν τῇ ἑνώσει δύναμιν, καὶ τὴν ἐν τῇ τάξει διαίρεσιν, ἀκούσας ἀθέους καλουμένους. *Who does not wonder, when he hears, that we who preach up God the Father, and God the Son and the Holy Spirit, setting forth the Power of them in Unity, and the distinction in Order, are called Atheists* Athen Legat pro Chr

ATHENAGOR

Theophilus Antiochenus says, that he is, Θεὸς ὢν ὁ λόγος καὶ ἐκ Θεοῦ πεφυκώς *That the Word is God, because he is born of God* Lib ii ad Autol

THEOPH ANTIOCH

Irenæus speaking of our Saviour, says, *Neque Dominum neque Spiritum S neque Apostolus, eum qui non esset Deus, definitive & absolute Deum nominasse aliquando, nisi esset verus Deus* *Neither our Saviour, nor the Holy Ghost nor the Apostles would have positively and absolutely have called any one God, unless he had been true God*. Iren. Lib iii c. 6 *Ipse igitur Christus cum Patre vivorum est Deus qui & locutus est Moisi, qui & Patribus manifestatus est* *Christ with the Father is the God of the Living, who also spake to Moses and was manifested to the Fathers* Iren Lib iv. cap 11 And again *Non enim infectus es, O homo, neque semper coexistebas Deo, sicut proprium ejus Verbum* *For, O Man, were not unmade, nor did you Eternally exist with God, as his Word did* Iren Lib. ii cap 43

IRENÆUS

The Godhead of our Saviour is owned by S *Clement* of *Alexandria*, who writes thus

CLEM ALEX

Λόγος οὗτος καὶ τὸ ζῆν ἐν ἀρχῇ μετὰ τοῦ πλάσαι παρασχὼν ὡς δημιουργός, τὸ εὖ ζῆν ἐδίδαξεν ἐπιφανεὶς ὡς διδάσκαλος, ἵνα τὸ ἀεὶ ζῆν ὕστερον ὡς Θεὸς χορηγήσῃ *The Word which heretofore, as a Creator, gave Life in the Creation, afterwards as a Teacher manifested himself, that afterwards he might give Eternal Life as a God.* Clem Alex Protrept And again, Ὁ θεῖος λόγος ὁ φανερώτατος ὄντως Θεός, ὁ τῷ δεσπότῃ τῶν ὅλων ἐξισωθείς ὅτι ἦν υἱὸς αὐτοῦ, καὶ ὁ λόγος ἦν ἐν τῷ Θεῷ *The Divine Word who is most manifestly the true God, being equalled to the Lord of the Universe, because he was his Son, and the Word was in God*, ibid

Tertullian says, *Quod de deo profectum est, Deus est & Dei filius, & unus ambo* *That which is born of God is God, and the Son of God, and both one*, Tert Apol He elsewhere says that Christ is, *Sermo Dei omnipotens, qui sermo Dei omnipotentis* *he is the Almighty God, as he is the Word of the Almighty God*, Tert cont Mar Lib iv cap 25.

TERTUL

Though *Origen*, in some Parts of his Works, makes use of some very improper and absurd Expressions, concerning the Generation of the Son, yet in his Books against *Celsus* which were written in his old Age, when his Thoughts grew Cooler, he very strenuously asserts our Saviour's Divinity, speaking of the Wise Men of the East bringing their Gifts to our Saviour, he says, φέροντα δῶρα ... σύμβολα ὡς βασιλεῖ τὸν χρυσόν, ὡς δὲ τεθνηξομένῳ τὴν σμύρναν, ὡς δὲ Θεῷ τὸν λίβανον *They offered these Symbols or Gifts, Gold as to the King, Myrrh as to one who was to die, and Frankincense as to a God*, Orig cont Cels. Lib i He says Christ had in him, θειότερόν τι ἢ τὸ βλεπόμενον ἀνθρώπινον, *something more Divine than what appeared in his human Shape* ib and afterwards calls him, Θεὸν ἐν ἀνθρωπίνῳ φανέντα σώματι ἐπ' εὐεργεσίᾳ τοῦ γένους ἡμῶν *God appearing in human Shape, for the Benefit of us Men*, ib He says, that the Body of Christ was, τὸν ἀληθῶς ναὸν Θεοῦ λόγου καὶ σοφίας καὶ ἀληθείας *The true Temple of God the Word, and of his Wisdom and Truth*, Orig cont Cels Lib ii He elsewhere gives him the Titles which the Platonists give to the Supreme God, αὐτοσοφία and αὐτοαλήθεια, and says, that τὸ μέγιστα περιφέρειν, καὶ τῆς ἐκείνου θειότητος κεκοινωνηκότα εἰς Θεὸν μεταβεβηκέναι

ORIGEN.

βιώσεως That he was endowed with the greatest Qualifications, enjoying with God a participation of the Godhead, id Lib iii S Cyprian
S CYPRIAN asserts Quod Homo & Deus Christus ex utroque genere concretus, ut Mediator esse inter Nos & Patrem possit That Christ is both God and Man, partaking of two Natures, that he might be a Mediator between Us and the Father, Cypr Test adv Jud Lib ii cap 9 In his Epistle to Cæcilius, he calls our Saviour, Dominum & Deum nostrum Our Lord and our God He elsewhere says, Deus cum homine miscetur, hic Deus noster, hic Christus est God is joyned with Man This is our God, our Christ Cypr. de Idol Van Arnobius and Lactantius were not very well versed in the Doctrines of Christianity, when they wrote their Books, which upon that account abound with several Errors, especially with relation to the more mysterious Points, but however they both of them do assert in general the Godhead of the Son, though they run into some mistakes in the Explication of

ARNOBIUS. it Arnobius, in answer to an Objection of the Heathen against Christ's Divinity. Sed est more hominis interemptus He was killed, as any ordinary Man. He answers, Non ipse neque enim cadere divinas in res potest mortis occasus Not the Christ or Word it self, for Death does not befal divine things, &c Arnob adv. Gent Lib i And elsewhere speaking of our Saviour he says, Cum vero Deus sit re certa, & sine ullius rei dubitationis ambiguo, inficiaturos arbitramini nos esse, quum maxime illum a nobis coli, & præsidem nostri Corporis nuncupari? Now since Christ is really God, and without all doubt, do you think that we should deny that we worship him, and that we own him to be

LACTANT the Head of our Body? ibid Lactantius in answer to an Objection made against the Christians for worshipping two Gods, Father and Son, he answers, Cum dicimus Deum Patrem & Deum Filium, non diversum dicimus nec utrumque secernimus. quia nec Pater sine Filio esse potest, nec Filius a Patre secerni. When we say God the Father, and God the Son, we do not assert two Gods, nor divide them both For the Father cannot be without the Son, neither can the Son be divided from the Father, Lact Lib iv. c 29

The Primitive Christians blamed by the Heathens, for esteeming Christ to be God

This is sufficient to shew, that the Council of Nice which established the Doctrine of Christ's Divinity by the highest Ecclesiastical Authority, did not make a new Faith as the Unitarians falsely pretend, but only declared the antient one which was generally received in the Church, throughout the several Ages which preceded that Council, and that when they declared in their Creed, that Christ was θεὸν ἀληθινὸν ἐκ θεοῦ ἀληθινοῦ, and γεννηθέντα καὶ οὐ ποιηθέντα Very God of very God, and begotten not made, said but the same thing which the Writers before cited, who all lived before this Council, had done

To these Testimonies of the Antenicene Fathers, we may add the further Testimony of the Heathens themselves, who, all along the first Ages of Christianity, upbraided the Christians for their esteeming Christ as their God Pliny tells the Emperor Titus, that the Christians of those times did Christo quasi Deo carmen dicere, sing Psalms to Christ as to a God All the foolish Calumnies of the Heathens concerning the Christians worshipping an Ass, and Onychites, &c were founded upon the Christians worshipping of Christ as a Person of the Godhead We meet with this Objection answered in all the Apologists who wrote for Christianity, and urged by all the Adversaries who wrote against it This is Trypho's Objection in Justin Martyr Τὸ δὲ λέγειν σε προϋπάρχειν θεὸν ὄντα πρὸ αἰώνων τοῦτον, εἶτα καὶ γεννηθῆναι ἄνθρωπον γενόμενον ὑπομεῖναι, καὶ ὅτι οὐκ ἄνθρωπος ἐξ ἀνθρώπων, οὐ μόνον παράδοξον δοκεῖ μοι εἶναι, ἀλλὰ καὶ μωρόν It looks to me not only as a Paradoxical but as a foolish Notion, to think that this Christ should be from all Eternity and yet be born a Man and being made Man to continue as Man, not coming of a Man Celsus objected the same thing in his Book written against the Christians, which Origen answered He ridicules the Wisemen, προσκυνοῦντας κατὰ τὸ νήπιον ὡς θεόν For worshipping Christ in his Infancy as a God Or. cont Cels Lib i And so he does the History of Christ's flight into Ægypt, θεὸν οὐκ εἰκὸς ἦν περὶ θανάτου δεδοικέναι 'Tis undecent that a God should be afraid of Death id Lib ii. c 29 And likewise the History of his Passion, καὶ τὸν θεὸν ὄντα οὔτε φεύγειν ἔδει, οὔτε δεθέντα ἀπάγεσθαι, It was no ways agreeable that a God should fly, or be lead away Prisoner, ibid. So the Heathens in Arnobius argue against the Christians Non ideirco Dii vobis infesti sunt, quod omnipotentem colatis Deum, sed quod Hominem natum, & quod personis infame est vilibus, crucis supplicio interremptum, & Deum fuisse contenditis, & superesse adhuc creditis, & quotidianis Supplicationibus adoratis The Gods are not angry with you, because you worship the Almighty God, but because you worship a Man that was born, and (what is a scandal to the vilest Person) one crucified, whom you would have to be a God and to be still in being, and whom you worship with your daily Supplications Now can we think, that the Heathens would have so constantly objected this, and the Apologists have no where denied the Imputation, if the first Christians had not looked upon Christ as God?

f Eternal God] Some of the antient Hereticks who really denied the Godhead of Christ, would allow him to be stiled God in a large Sense, but when they explained themselves, they asserted οὐκ ἀεὶ ἦν ὁ λόγος, ἀλλ' ἐξ οὐκ ὄντων γέγονεν He was not always the Word but was made out of nothing vid Alex Epist apud Socr Hist Eccl Lib i. Upon this account the Nicene Fathers do Anathematize, τοὺς λέγοντας, ἦν ποτε ὅτε οὐκ ἦν, Those that say there was a time when the Son was not, Socr ibid. Athan Ep ad Jovin The modern Unitarians have covered themselves under the same Ambiguity Socinus says, Falsissimum est nos palam affirmare, Christum non esse verum Deum Soc Resp ad 4 Priora cap Wick And so Schlichting u, Christus est verus Deus, sed quatenus verus opponitur falso, non quatenus opponitur non summo, in John iv 23 And Crell, Benedicendus in secula, ostendit quantus Deus [illegible] Christus, Crell in John x 33 To avoid therefore [illegible] Ambiguity, and all Subterfuge of Heretical Pravity, the [illegible] is here added Which is no more than what the Holy Scriptures do warrant, which ascribe Eternity to the second Person of the Trinity For that was [illegible] probably S John's Meaning, when he said, In the beginning was the Word, i e from all Eternity, John i especially since he begins his Epistles with the like Expression, That which was from the beginning, 1 John i 1 The same is signified by S Paul, who says, that Christ was before all things Col i 17 But this is a Truth, which the Arians of old, as well as the Socinians of late have denied, but on the other side all the Orthodox Antiquity, not only the Fathers of the middle Ages, but those who lived before the Council of Nice, do affirm

IGNATIUS asserts, ὅτι εἷς θεός ἐστιν ὁ φανερώσας ἑαυτὸν διὰ Ἰησοῦ Χριστοῦ τοῦ υἱοῦ αὐτοῦ, ὅς ἐστιν αὐτοῦ λόγος ἀΐδιος: There is one God who has manifested himself by his Son Jesus Christ, who is his Eternal Word, Ign Ep ad Mag.

JUSTIN Martyr speaking of God the Son says, Οὗτος ὁ ἀπ' ἀρχῆς, ὁ καινὸς φανεὶς καὶ παλαιὸς εὑρεθεὶς καὶ πάντοτε νέος ἐν ἁγίων καρδίαις γεννώμενος· οὗτος ὁ ἀεὶ, ὁ σήμερον υἱὸς λογισθείς. This is he who was from the beginning, who late appeared, and always born anew in the Hearts of the Saints Ist Ep ad Diogn Irenæus asserts the same in these words Exclusa est omnis contradictio dicentium, si ergo tunc natus est, non erat Christus Ostendimus enim, quia non tunc cœpit Filius Dei existens semper apud Patrem All Contradiction is excluded of them that say, if he was then born he was not Christ For we have shewn, that he did not then begin to be, but always was with the Father Iren Lib iii c 20 And elsewhere, semper autem coexistens Filius Patri, olim & ab initio semper revelat Patrem, id Lib ii cap 55.

CLEMENT of Alexandria speaks of him thus. Αἰδίου υἱὸς, ὅπως εἷς, ὁ μέγας ἀρχιερεὺς τοῦ ἑνὸς θεοῦ καὶ αὐτοῦ πατρὸς This is the one Eternal Jesus, the great High Priest of the one God, his Father, Clem Protrept The same Father in his Hymn calls him,

Λόγος ἀέναος. Word Everlasting,
Αἰὼν ἄπειρος, Infinite Æon,
Φῶς ἀΐδιον Light Eternal
Clem Alex Pædag in fine

ORIGEN calls him ἀπαύγασμα φωτὸς ἀϊδίου The Splendor of the Eternal Light, Lib v cont Cels Athanasius quotes from him this remarkable Sentence Τολμήσας τις ἀρχὴν εἶναι υἱοῦ πρότερον οὐκ ὄντος; πότε γὰρ ἡ ἄρρητος καὶ ἀκατονόμαστος καὶ ἄφθεγκτος ὑποστάσεως τοῦ πατρὸς εἰκὼν ὁ χαρακτὴρ ὁ λόγος, ὁ γινώσκων τὸν πατέρα οὐκ ἦν, κατανοείτω γὰρ ὁ τολμῶν καὶ λέγων ἦν ποτε ὅτε οὐκ ἦν ὁ υἱὸς ὅτι ἐρεῖ καὶ σοφία ποτε οὐκ ἦν, Who dares to ascribe a beginning to the Son, as if there were a time in which he yet was not? For when was not that ineffable, unnameable and undeclarable Hypostasis,

the Blessed Virgin, of one [g] Substance with the Fa- *tri consubstantialis, in*

Hypostasis, the Image, the Character, the Reason which knows the Father? Let him think with himself who dares say, that there was a time when the Son was not that he says, that there was a time when Wisdom was not, when Reason was not, when Life was not Athan in Lib de decret Syn Nic *Athenagoras, Tatian, Theophilus Antiochenus, Tertullian* and *Lactantius*, have several Expressions to the like purpose, though it must be owned there be some Passages which occur in them that seem to make against the Eternity of the *Word*, whom they declare to have been begotten by the Father some time before the Creation of the World, God making use of him as his Agent or Instrument in the creating all things But it must be considered, that most of the Antients had a Notion, That the Son lay from all Eternity quiescent in the Bosom of the Father, That in time he made his [Greek] or *going forth*, as *Athenagoras* speaks, That then by the Divine Eructation [Greek] the *internal Word*, he became the [Greek] the *spoken Word*, which was looked upon as another begetting or Production of the second Person of the Trinity, and to this refer those Passages in the forementioned Writers, which seem to make against the Eternal Generation of the Word This is, with great force of Reason and Learning, unexceptionably made out by the late excellent Bishop *Bull*, in his *Defensio fide Nicena* Sect iii Cap 5, 6, 7, 8, 9, 10

Consubstantiality of the Son proved from Scripture

g *Of one Substance*] This Expression answers to the Greek [Greek], which was used by the Antients, to denote the Unity of Essence which was between the Father and the Son The Foundation of this Expression was grounded upon these Texts of Scripture. *There are three that bear Witness, &c and these three are One*, 1 John v 7 And that of the Evangelist, *I and my Father are One*, John x 30 which does import a Unity of Essence and not of Consent, as may be proved by our Saviour's own Explication of his Meaning in other Words, *The Father is in me and I in him*, v 38 and by the Sense the Jews understood him in, as being a Pretention to the Divine Nature *For a good Work we stone thee not, but for blasphemy, and because that thou being a Man makest thy self God*, v 33

The Homoousion used before the Council of Nice, or Controversy with Arius

After the Divinity of our Saviour came to be denied by some of the Hereticks which had crept into the Primitive Church, the Orthodox made use of the Word [Greek] to be a Test upon them, making them declare that our Saviour was not a Creature, or a Titular God only, but God of the same Nature and Essence with the Father This *Athanasius* says was [Greek] *A Bulwark against the impious Opinions of the Arians* Athan de Syn Arim and Seleuc *That it was the Hypocrisy of the Eusebians that made the Orthodox*, [Greek], *express them more clearly, and say that the Son was of the same Substance with the Father*, Athan de Conc Nic Decret The Hereticks on the other side clamoured against this Expression, [Greek] *being unscriptural*, Epiph Hær lxix to which the Orthodox replied, [Greek] *Though this and such like Expressions are not in Scripture, yet the purport of them is found there*, Athan de Decret Syn Nicen Besides, not only the Unitarians of late, but the *Arians* of old, did object against the Orthodox the Novelty of this Expression, saying that it was not more antient than the Controversy between *Alexander* Bishop of *Alexandria* and *Arius*, and was soon after followed by the *Nicene* Council, who did [Greek] *By their Synodical Voices meet together, to declare the* [Greek] *or Sameness of the Son with the Father, and to condemn* Arius Philost Hist Eccl Lib i Sect vii But this was a false Suggestion For the very Word was used by several Divines much more antient *Eusebius*, who is not generally thought to be a partial Witness in this Case, owns, [Greek] *We have known some of the Antients, both famous Bishops and Writers, who disputing concerning the Divinity of Christ, have used the Word* [Greek] Euseb Ep ad Cæsarienf apud Soc Hist. Eccl Lib i cap 8 *Origen*, who lived cxxx Years before the *Nicene* Council, in his Dialogue against the *Marcionites* says, That [Greek] *God the Son, or the Word is of the same Substance with the Father* And *Dionysius* Bishop of *Alexandria*, who lived near 100 Years before this Council writes, as *Athanasius* quotes him, [Greek] *That Christ is of the same Substance with God* Ath de Decr. Conc Nicen. And in his Epistle to *Paulus Samosetanus* which is still extant, he says it was a common Expression used by the Divines long before his time [Greek] *He that is by Nature the Lord and the Word of the Father, and whom the Holy Fathers call* [Greek], *of the same Substance with the Father* Dion Ep in bib Patr magn Tom xi

Consubstantiality of the Son, owned by the Antenicene Fathers

But if we have regard to the Purport and Sense of the Word, almost all the Ecclesiastical Writers of the Church from the beginning of Christianity, have declared in favour of this Doctrine We have before given several Instances out of *Hermas, Clement, Ignatius*, &c of Christ's being the true God, which does virtually infer the Sameness of Essence For as *Athanasius* very well observes, [Greek] *The purport of the Word* [Greek] *is known by this, that the Son is not a Creature or any thing made*, Athan Epist ad Afr Ep Op Tom i

JUSTIN Martyr insists the same, when he says of Christ he is [Greek] *He alone is truly God's Son*, alluding to the Sameness of kind, which a Son has with his Father *Just Apol* i and presently after [Greek] *He is only in a proper Sense the Son of God* ibid. In his Dialogue with the Jew, he expresses his Consubstantial Generation, in the same manner with the *Nicene* Council, *Light of Light* [Greek] *As we see one Fire kindled by another without Diminution, the first remaining the same, though more Fires are kindled by it* Just Dial cum Tryph

ATHENAGORAS speaks of him thus [Greek] *The Son and the Father are one, the Son being in the Father, and the Father in the Son by Unity and Power of the Spirit* Athan Leg pro Christ And elsewhere in the same Treatise he expresses himself thus. [Greek] *We confess God and his Son, the Word and the Holy Ghost, United in Power. For the Son is the Mind, Word and Wisdom of the Father, and the Holy Ghost is an Effluence as Light from the Fire*, ibid Which is a clear Profession of a Consubstantial Trinity

IRENÆUS professes the same when he says, *Ipse igitur Christus, cum Patre, vivorum est Deus, qui & locutus est Mosi, qui & Patribus manifestatus est Christ*, together with the Father, *is the God of the living, who spake to Moses, and revealed himself to the Fathers*, Iren Lib iv cap 11 So again, *Et bene qui dixit ipsum immensum Patrem, in Filio mensuratum Mensura enim Patris Filius, quoniam & capit eum He speaks well, who says the Infinite Father is measured by the Son For the Son is the Measure of the Father because he contains him*, Iren Lib iv cap 8.

CLEMENS ALEXANDRINUS asserts the same [Greek] *God hates nothing, neither his Word, for they are both one, namely God*, Pædag. Lib i cap 8 So in another Place [Greek] *O thou Governor, Father, and Charioteer of Israel, be Propitious to thy Children, O Son and Father both one, O Lord* ibid in fine Pædag

TERTULLIAN abounds with Instances, which assert the Son to be of the same Substance with the Father. *Nam etsi soles duos faciam, tamen & solem & radium ejus tam duas res & duas species unius indivisæ substantiæ numerabo*

of her Substance So ther, h took Man's Substance *utero beatæ Virginis,*

...abo quam Deum & sermonem ejus, quam Patrem & Filium For though I should say there are two Suns, meaning the Sun and his Rays, I might reckon these to be two Species of the same undivided Substance, as well as God and the Word the Father and the Son Tert adv Prax cap. 13 And so in another Treatise, he says, *Christum & Spiritum substantiam esse Creatoris, & eos qui Patrem non agnoverint nec Filium cognoscere potuisse per ejusdem Substantiæ conditionem That Christ and the Spirit is the Substance of the Creator, and they who do not acknowledge the Father, cannot know the Father by the Condition of the same Substance* Lib iii contr Marc cap 6 And so again, *Filium non aliunde deduco, quam de substantia Patris. I do not derive the Son from any other cause, but from the Substance of the Father,* id adv Prax cap 4

St *CYPRIAN* asserts the same, when he says, *De Patre, Filio & Spiritu sancto scriptum est, Hi tres unum sunt,* de Un Eccl cap 4 And in his Epistle to *Jubeianus* he says, *ipse Christus gentes baptizari jubet in plena & adunata Trinitate*

LACTANTIUS, in some particulars, does not seem to have the justest Notions of the Holy Trinity, but yet concerning the Consubstantiality he thus expresses himself *Cum dicimus Deum Patrem & Deum Filium, non diversum dicimus, nec utrumque secernimus, quia nec Pater sine Filio esse potest, nec Filius a Patre secerni, siquidem nec Pater sine Filio nuncupari, nec Filius potest sine Patre generari Cum igitur & Pater Filium faciat & Filius Patrem, una utrique Mens, unus Spiritus, una Substantia est When we say God the Father, and God the Son, we do not say two, because the Father cannot be without the Son, nor can the Son be divided from the Father, because a Father cannot be denominated without a Son, nor a Son be generated without a Father Whereas therefore a Father makes a Son and a Son a Father, they must both have one Mind, one Spirit and one Substance* Lact Lib iv. cap 29

The Humanity of Christ proved from Scripture

h *Took Man's Substance*] I There cannot be clearer Proof of any matter of Fact, than that our Saviour took upon him human Nature, and was truly Man The Prophecies which foretel the Messias, do declare likewise that he was to be *Man*. It was predicted as early as the Fall of Mankind, *That the Seed of Woman shall break the Serpent's Head*, Gen iii 15 And in another Prediction of the Messias, it is foretold, that *a Virgin shall conceive and bear a Son*, Isa vii 14 The Angel who notified his Conception to the blessed Virgin said, *She shall conceive in her Womb, and bring forth a Son*, Luke i 31 He was subject to all the Properties and Accidents which human Nature is liable to He *grew*, Luke ii 40 and *increased in Stature*, Luke ii 52 was *hungry*, Mat iv 2 and *thirsty*, John xix 28 he *wept over Jerusalem*, Luke xix 41 he *slept*, Mark iv 38 and *died*, Mat xxvii 50 Mark xv 37 Luke xxiii 46 John xix 30

Opposed by various Hereticks

II But notwithstanding these so many and plain Assertions of the Holy Scripture, great numbers of Hereticks heretofore have denied Christ's Humanity, probably out of a foolish Conceit that it reflected a Dishonour on the Deity to be united with human Body and that the matter of the Redemption might be transacted, by a seeming shew of an human Body here upon Earth, without the reality of it Some maintained this odd Opinion as early as the Apostolical times viz the *Gnosticks*, who asserted [Greek illegible] *That Christ was not born of the Virgin Mary, but only shewn by her That he did not take upon him flesh, but only the Appearance thereof* Epiph Hær xli And 'tis probably these that *Ignatius* means, when he says, [Greek illegible] *There are some Atheistical Persons, that is Unbelievers, that say Christ was born Man only in Appearance, that he seemed only to die and to suffer, and not in Reality* Ign Ep ad Trall After them *Saturninus* (or as others call him) *Saturnilus*, maintained the same fantastick Opinion, declaring as *Tertullian* says, that Christ did in *phantasmate tantum venisse Come only by way of phantom*, Tert de præscr cap 46 or, as *Irenæus* relates, *putative tantum hominem, That he was only taken to be Man*, Iren Lib 1. c. 22. The same foolish Opinion was maintained by *Cerdo*, *Marcion* and *Manes*, who as *Theodoret* says, [Greek illegible] *said that Christ appeared as Man, having nothing of human Nature*, Hæret Fab Lib i cap 11 The same before their time was asserted by *Basilides*, who moreover taught, that Christ himself did not suffer, but *Simon* of *Cyrene* was crucified in his stead *Iren Lib i* ... *Alex Strom Lib xiv* The like was maintained by *Valentinus* and his Scholars, *Epiph Hær xxx* *Tert de Præscr* cap 49 There were an odd sort of Hereticks called *Ophites*, who worshipped the Serpent that deceived *Eve*, who like wise asserted as *Tertullian* speaks, *Christum non in substantia carnis fuisse, that Christ was not in the Substance of the Flesh*, Tert de Præscr cap 50 or as *Theodoret* relates their Opinion, [Greek illegible] *That Jesus is different from Christ, that Jesus was born of the Virgin, and Christ came from Heaven* Theod Lib i cont Hær. cap 14 *Origen*, in his Book against *Celsus*, relates of a certain Heretick, that when any were admitted into this Sect, they cursed ... as I understand it, renounced Christ's Humanity There was another spawn of Hereticks, who denied that Christ had a truly human Body, but I know not what Body made of the Substance of the Stars or Æther, they owe their rise to one *Appelles*, the Scholar of the Heretick *Marcion*, and were from him called *Appelitæ Theodoret* thus relates his Opinion [Greek illegible] *He declared Christ was not born of the Virgin, but made out of the Substance of the World* Theod Hær Fab Lib i cap 25

III But the Orthodox Christians constantly maintained the true human Nature of Christ For thus *Ignatius* [Greek illegible] *He was carried in the Womb, during certain Periods of time, as we are, he was truly born, as we were, he ... took of the same common meat and drink with us* Ign Ep ad Trall To the like purpose St *Chrysostom* speaks, when he says, that our Saviour did [Greek illegible] *came into the Virgin's Womb, was carried there nine Months, was suckled, and underwent all things agreeable to human Nature.* Chrys Hom ... Joan ... Lo Sit But not to trouble the Reader with more Passages out of the Antients upon this Head, which every where occur in their Books written against the Hereticks and in their other Writings, I shall only set down their Reasons which they give, why it was necessary, that Christ should take upon him an human Body

De ... ... Orthodox

Reasons why Christ took on him an human Body

IV And first it was requisite that Christ should take upon him an human Body, to be qualified thereby to suffer and die and to perform the other Parts of our Redemption, thereby to destroy the Empire of the Devil, and to work out our everlasting Salvation. This is declared by the great Council of *Nice* in their Creed [Greek illegible] *Who for us Men and for our Salvation, came down from Heaven, was incarnate and made Man*. And so *Athanasius*, [Greek illegible] *It was our cause that gave him the occasion of descending from Heaven, it was our Transgression that made the divine Word take upon him the humanity, that the Lord came to us and appeared among Men We were the cause of his Incarnation.* Athan de Incar And thus *Prudentius*

1 To transact our Redemption

Mortale corpus induit,
Ut concitato corpore,
Mortis catenam frangeret,
Hominemque portaret Patri.

A Mortal Body he put on,
That by the means of this he might
The chain of Death asunder snap,
And to his Father carry Man.

Prudent Cathem Hymn xi

2 *To make us the Sons of God, &c.*

2 He became Man to make us the Sons of God, to bring us again into his favour, and to make us Partakers of his Grace Which Reason is thus expressed by *Athanasius*, Υἱὸς ἀ. θε. τὸ γέγονεν ἵνα οἱ υἱοὶ τοῦ ἀνθρώπε, τυτέσι Ἀδὰμ, υἱοὶ τοῦ Θεοῦ γένωνται *Christ was made the Son of Man, that the Sons of Man, that is of* Adam, *might be made the Sons of God* Athan de Human Nat Suscept. And thus by S. *Chrysostom*. [illegible] *The true and genuine Son of the immortal God, vouchsafed to be called the Son of* David, *that he might make thee the Son of God* Chryf Hom 1 in Mat S *Basil* declares the like, with particular relation to the Grace obtained by Christians, through Christ's Incarnation [illegible] *For this reason God appeared in the Flesh, because it was necessary that this Flesh that was under the curse should be sanctified, that being infirm it might be strengthened, that being alienated from God it might be reconciled to him, that being thrown out of Paradise it might be received into Heaven.* Bas. Hom xxv de Natal This *Prudentius* expresses in the following Verses

Ergo animalis homo quondam nunc Spiritus illum
Transtulit ad superi naturam Seminis, ipse m
Infundendo Deum mortalia vivificantem
Nec nova materies, solidata intercute flatu ,
Materies, sed nostra tamen, de Virgine tracta,
Lanit ant quæ corrupta exordia Vitæ,
Immortale bonum proprio spiramine sumens.

Man once an Animal Nature had, but now
The Spirit has giv'n him, from a Heav'nly Seed,
A Nature all Divine, to him transfusing
A God that quickens his Mortality.
The Virgin birth has giv'n him a new Substance,
Has alter'd quite his former Composition,
And breath'd into him an immortal Life
Prud in Apotheosi

3 *To discharge the Mediatorship by partaking of both Natures*

3. He took our Nature upon him, that he might thereby be better qualified to be our Mediator with God, by partaking of the Natures of both Parties, which he was to reconcile This is most elegantly in short expressed by *Gregory Thaumaturgus* [illegible] *Thou, O Christ, by taking upon thee a human Body, hast joyned as it were by a Bridge Heaven and Earth together* Greg Thaum Orat in Epiph The same is thus illustrated by S Cyril of *Alexandria* [illegible] *Christ is properly said to be a Mediator for this Reason, because he joyns those things which were at the greatest distance, the Divinity and the Humanity, and as he has shewn these united in himself, so he has thereby united us to God* Cyr Dial 1 de Trin To the like purport *Novatianus* *Si ad hominem veniebat, ut mediator Dei & hominum esse deberet oportuit illum cum eo esse, & Verbum carnem fieri, ut in semetipso concordiam confibularet terrenorum pariter, atque cælestium, dum utriusque partis in se connectens pignora, & Deum homini, & hominem Deo copularet Since he came among Men, to be a Mediator between God and Man, he must be with God, and the Word likewise must be made Flesh, that he might establish an Agreement between Heavenly and Earthly things, and that taking as it were a Pledge of both Parties, he might joyn God to Man, and Man to God* Novat de Trin cap xiii

4. *To teach Men Religion.*

4 He took upon him human Nature, that thereby, conversing among Men, he might teach them the Doctrines and Precepts of the most excellent Religion Which is thus expressed by *Lactantius Illum Filium suum primogenitum, illum opificem rerum, & Consiliatorem suum delabi jussit e Cælo, ut religionem sanctam Dei transferret ad gentes*, i e *ad eos qui Deum ignorabant God sent his only begotten Son, the Creator of the World and his Counsellor from Heaven, to transfer his Holy Religion to the Gentiles who were ignorant of it* Lact Lib iv cap 11 The same end of Christ's Incarnation is mentioned by *Clement* of *Alexandria* Διό μοι δοκεῖ, ἐπεὶ αὐτὸς ἧκεν εἰς ἡμᾶς οὐρανόθεν ὁ λόγος, ἡμᾶς [illegible] ἐπ' ἀνθρωπίνην ἰέναι μὴ χρῆναι διδασκαλίαν ἔτι, Ἀθήνας καὶ τὴν ἄλλην Ἑλλάδα, πρὸς δὲ καὶ Ἰωνίαν πολυπραγμονοῦντας εἰ γὰρ ἡμῖν ὁ διδάσκαλος, ὁ πληρώσας τὰ πάντα δυνάμεσιν ἁγίαις, δημιουργία, σωτηρία, εὐεργεσία, νομοθεσία, προφητεία, διδασκαλία, πάντα νῦν ὁ διδάσκαλος κατηχεῖ καὶ τὸ πᾶν ἤδη Ἀθῆναι καὶ Ἑλλὰς γέγονεν τῷ λόγῳ *Forasmuch as the Word has descended to us from Heaven, in my Opinion, we have now no longer necessity of human Discipline, nor to trouble our selves to go to* Athens *or any other part of* Greece, *or* Ionia *For since he is our Master, he fulfilles all things with holy Virtues, working in us, with Salvation, Beneficence, Legislature, Prophesy, Discipline he being our Master instructs us in all things, by reason of the Word, the whole World is now become* Athens *and* Greece. Clem. Alex in Protrept

5 *To be an Example*

5 Another end of Christ's Incarnation was to be an Example to us of Virtue. Which is excellently illustrated by S. *Chrysostom* Παραγενόμενος, &c *Christ coming into the World was willing to teach Men all manner of Virtue Now he that instructeth, not only teaches by Word but also by Work And this is the best way of teaching any Master. For the Pilot of a Ship making his Scholar sit by him, shews him how to manage the Rudder, speaking to him and working with him, neither always talking nor always working So an Architect when he teaches one to build an House, he shews him how to do it, not only by speaking but by working before him So does the Weaver, the Goldsmith and the Brasier, and every other Artificer, teach by Work as well as Word Therefore whereas Christ came to teach us all Truth,* καὶ λέγει τὰ πρακτέα καὶ ποιεῖ, *both tells things that are to be done, and himself does them* But above all other Virtues he did by his Example recommend the Virtue of Humility He speaks to all his Disciples and Followers, when he says, *Learn of me for I am meek and lowly in Heart*, Mat xi 29

And indeed this Lesson was not to be learned of any one else, for the Philosophers who valued themselves greatly for teaching other moral Virtues, overlooked this, nay contemned it as a meanness and poorness of Spirit Wherefore S *Austin* says very well, *Omnibus defuit divinæ Humilitatis exemplum, quod opportunissimo tempore, per Dominum nostrum Jesum Christum illustratum est There was no where to be found an example of Humility, and therefore our Saviour Jesus very opportunely illustrated it by his Example*, Aug Ep lvi

6 *To put a stop to Idolatry*

6 Another Reason of our Saviour's taking upon him human Nature was, to put a stop to Idolatry to which the World was so much enclined Upon which Observation *Athanasius* makes this Reflexion Ἐπειδὴ γὰρ οἱ ἄνθρωποι, &c *Forasmuch as Men are averse from the Contemplation of God, and being as it were plunged in the deep, having their Eyes fixed upon the Earth, they looked for God only in Nature and sensible things, making to themselves Gods out of mortal Men and Dæmons. For this reason the loving and common Saviour of us all, took to himself a Body, and as Man conversed among Men, taking to himself all human Affections, that Men understanding there was a God embodied, by those corporeal Actions which they beheld our Saviour to do, they might thereby come to understand the Truth, and be raised to the Knowledge of the Father.* Ath de Incarn S *Austin* expresses himself in a like manner *Maxime vero sua Incarnatione*, &c *The Incarnation of our Lord had this salutary effect, that whereas the generality of Men are Ambitious of paying their worship to God some way or other, they worshiping more presumptuously than piously the heavenly Powers, by Idolatrous Rites, which were rather Sacrileges than Sacred Ceremonies, on which account not Angels but Dæmons were worshiped by them , now Men might know, that God is so near to the Piety of Men, that he has taken upon him the Nature of Man, so that they need not seek to him, as if he were afar of, by intermediate Powers*, &c Aug. Ep iii

7 *That Sin might be remedied the way it came*

7 Another end assigned of our Saviour's taking human Nature upon him is, That the Remedy of Sin might come the same way that the Malady of it came Therefore S *Austin* says, *Melius judicavit, ut de ipso quod victum fuerat, genere assumeret hominem Deus, per quem generis humani vinceret inimicum God judged it more proper to take upon him the Nature of Man who was conquered, to gain a Victory over that Enemy of human kind* Aug xiii Trin. cap 18 So *Tertullian*, *Neque ad propositum Christi facere t, evacuantis peccatum carnis, non in ea carne evacuare illud, in qua erat natura peccati It would not have been conducible*

that two whole and perfect Natures, that is to say the Godhead and Manhood were joyned together in one Person, never to be divided, whereis one Christ, very God and very Man,

in the [i] Womb of the Blessed Virgin of her Substance; so that [k] two whole and perfect Natures, that is the [l] Godhead and the Manhood were joyned together in one Person never to be divided: whereof is [m] one Christ, very God and very Man.

exillius Substantia naturam humanam assumpsit: ita ut duæ naturæ, divina & humana, integrè atque perfectè in unitate Personæ fuerint inseparabiliter conjunctæ, in quibus est unus Christus, verus

conducible to Christ's design of cancelling a Sin of the Flesh, not to have cancelled it in that Flesh by which the Sin was committed Tert de car Christ c 16 S *Austin* carries the Analogy between the Malady and Remedy further. *Quia per mulierem in hunc mundum mors intravit, salus per Virginem redderetur,* &c *Ut ne perpetu reatus apud Viros opprobrium sustineret quia quæ culpam nobis transfuderat, transfudit & gratiam Because by a Woman Sin entered into the World, therefore Salvation must be restored by a Virgin,* &c *Because the Woman should not bear the Reproach of an eternal Guilt among the Men, the Woman, who first brought Guilt upon us, conveyed Grace to us* Aug Ser xiii de Nat

i *In the Womb of the Blessed Virgin of her Substance*] This Truth was denied by *Valentinus,* and some other of the Hereticks of the first times, who taught, as *Epiphanius* relates, 'Ανωθεν κατενηνοχέναι τὸ σῶμα, καὶ ὡς διὰ σωλῆνος ὕδωρ, διὰ Μαρίας τῆς παρθένου διελθεῖν μηδὲν δὲ ἐκ τῆς παρθενικῆς μήτρας εἰληφέναι *That Christ brought a Body from Heaven, and as Water passes through a Pipe, so did that through the Virgin* Mary, *but received no Substance from the Virgin's Womb* Ep Hær xxxi. But this foolish Notion is excellently thus refuted by S *Chrysostom* Εἰ τοῦτο ἦν, τίς χρεία τῆς μήτρας, εἰ τοῦτο ἦν, οὐδὲν ἔχει κοινὸν πρὸς ἡμᾶς, ἀλλ' ἀλλή τις ἐστιν ἐκείνη ἡ σὰρξ οὐ τοῦ φυράματος τοῦ ἡμετέρου· πῶς οὖν ἐκ τῆς ῥίζης Ἰεσσαί, πῶς δὲ ῥάβδος, πῶς δὲ υἱὸς ἀνθρώπου; πῶς δὲ μήτηρ ἡ Μαριάμ, πῶς δὲ ἐκ σπέρματος Δαυίδ; πῶς δὲ μορφὴν δούλου ἔλαβε, πῶς δὲ ὁ λόγος σὰρξ ἐγένετο; πῶς δὲ Ῥωμαίοις φησὶν ὁ Παῦλος ἐξ ὧν ὁ Χριστὸς τὸ κατὰ σάρκα, ὁ ἐπὶ πάντων Θεός, *If this be so* (i.e if Christ passed through the Womb of the Virgin as a Channel) *what need was there of the Womb of the Virgin at all? If this be so, Christ has nothing in common with us, he is another Flesh and not of the Mass of our Nature How is he then of the Root of* Jesse? *How is he the Branch? How is he the Son of Man? How is he of the Seed of* David? *How did he take upon him the form of a Servant? How can the Apostle to the* Romans *say, of whom according to the* Flesh Christ came, who is God over all? *Chrys Hom* iv *in Mat.*

This Clause of the Article, most probably, was not here inserted with so much Particularity, in Opposition to the Hereticks of old, as to the Tenets of some of the Anabaptists and Enthusiasts, of the time when the Articles were drawn up Two Years before King *Edward's* Articles were published, there was an obstinate Heretick burnt here in *England,* for maintaining the old *Valentinian* Heresy of Christ's passing through the Virgin *Mary's* Womb as through a Conduit Which is particularly noted by King *Edward* VI in his Diary *May* 2 1550 Joan Bochei, *otherways called* Joan of Kent, *was burnt for holding,* that Christ was not incarnate of the Virgin *Mary, being condemned the Year before, but kept in hopes of Conversion* And about the same time that Q *Elizabeth's* Articles were published, one *Adrian Hemsted* came out of *Zealand* into *England,* but was afterwards forced to leave this Nation, who maintained a Doctrine of the same kind, and, among other Heterodoxies, laid down, That to believe *That Christ was born of the Seed of the Woman, and that he was partaker of human Flesh, was no Article of the Christian Faith* Spond Contin Bar Vol ii p 784 Now because the Reformation might receive no Prejudice from these monstrous Opinions, it was by the Compilers of the Articles thought advisable to make an express Profession of our holding the true Catholick Doctrine in this particular.

k *Two whole and perfect Natures,* &c] These Words are added, in Opposition to the Tenets of some of the antient Hereticks, who held the human Nature of Christ to be imperfect, as wanting an human Soul, which they said was supplied by the Presence of the *Word,* which did perform all the Operations of a Soul in Christ's Body The Arians indeed were of this Opinion, but their greater Heresie in denying our Saviour's Divinity, made this Opinion of theirs less taken notice of But the Apollinarians, who divided from the Orthodox in this Point, have made this Heterodoxy chiefly to be attributed to them, concerning whom I shall premise a few Words

Of the Apollinarian Heresie

Apollinaris, when he broached his Heresie, and what it was

I These Hereticks owed their rise to one *Apollinaris,* who was Bishop of *Laodicea,* in the troublesome times of Arianism, when there were one or two Bishops of the several Factions in that City besides He had formerly been under some disgrace, having with his Father lain under an Excommunication, for their Familiarity with *Epiphanius* a Heathen Sophist *Socr Lib* ii. *cap ult Soz Lib* v *cap* 25 But the Son afterwards recovered his Credit among the Orthodox, by siding with them and espousing the cause of *Athanasius,* with whom he cultivated for some time a Friendship. *Epiph Hær* lxxvii *Leont contr Nest Lib* iii He was undoubtedly a very excellent Scholar, this being confess'd by his Adversaries *Epiphanius* says, he was παιδείας οὐ τῆς τυχούσης ὁ ἀνήρ *A Man of no ordinary learning* Epiph ibid *Vincentius Lirinensis* says of him, *Quid illo præstantius, acumine, exercitatione, doctrina? quam multas ille Hereses multis voluminibus oppresserit, quot inimicos fide confutaverit errores, indicio est opus illud triginta non minus librorum nobilissimum, ac maximum, quo insanas Porphyrii calumnias, magna probationum mole confudit? What can be more excellent than* Apollinaris, *in Smartness, in Stile, in Learning? How many Heresies has he silenced by his indefatigable Writing, how many Heretical Errors has he confuted, witness that noble Book of his consisting of no less than thirty Volumnes, in which he has so copiously confuted the Calumnies of* Prophyry? There seem to have been two Editions as it were of his Heresy The first at least he broached in his Father's time, in conjunction with him For, as *Socrates* relates, πρότερον μὲν ἔλεγον, &c *They first gave out, that there was no Soul taken by God the Word, in the Dispensation of the Incarnation but afterwards, retracting this Opinion, they corrected themselves, and allowed that there was a Soul taken,* νοῦν δὲ οὐκ ἔχειν αὐτὴν, ἀλλ' εἶναι τὸν Θεὸν λόγον ἀντὶ νοῦ εἰς τὸν ἀναληφθέντα ἄνθρωπον, *but that there was no Mind, God the Word being taken into Man, instead of a Mind* Socr Lib ii cap ult *Epiphanius* thus declares what his Doctrine was, *viz* εἶναι τέλειον ἄνθρωπον, ἐκ σαρκὸς καὶ ψυχῆς, καὶ θεότητος ἀντὶ τοῦ νοῦ: *That Christ was perfect Man as consisting of Flesh and a sensitive Soul, and that his Godhead was in lieu of his Mind* Epiph Hær lxxvii His Followers improved this Doctrine of his into a more monstrous and pestilential Heresie, *viz* asserting, that Christ's Body, or Human Nature, was consubstantial with his Divinity The detestableness of this Doctrine raised *Athanasius* into a pious Fervor, occasioning him thereupon thus to express himself Ποῖος ᾅδης ἐξηρεύξατο, &c *What Hell has exhaled this Doctrine, that the Body which was born of* Mary *should be consubstantial to the Deity? that the Word should be turned into Flesh, Bones, and the other Parts of human Body, and be changed from its own Nature? Who ever heard this from Christians, that the Son of God only in shew and fiction had a Body, but no natural and true One? Can any one break out in such Impiety as to assert and imagine, That that Deity which is consubstantial with the Father should be circumscribed, and from perfect made imperfect? That that which was fastened to the Cross should not be a Body, but the very Essence or Substance* (ουσια) *of him that made the World?* Athan Ep ad Epict His Heresie was several times condemned, first in a Synod held at *Alexandria, A D* CCCLXIII in another at *Antioch* CCCLXXVIII and lastly by the second General Council which was held at *Constantinople* These Fathers in Opposition to this Heresie declare thus Τὸν τῆς ενανθρωπήσεως ... λόγον ἀδιάστροφον σώζομεν, οὔτε ἄψυχον, οὔτε ἄνουν ἢ ἀτελῆ τὴν τῆς σαρκὸς οἰκονομίαν παραδεχόμενοι ὅλον δὲ εἰδότες τέλειον μὲν ὄντα πρὸ αἰώνων Θεὸν λόγον, τέλειον δὲ ἄνθρωπον ἐπ᾽ ἐσχάτων τῶν ἡμερῶν, διὰ τὴν ἡμετέραν σωτηρίαν γενόμενον. *We keep the Doctrine of the Lord's Incarnation inviolable, not allowing that the Oeconomy of the Flesh* (i.e Christ's human Nature) *is without a Soul, or without a Mind knowing that the Word was perfect from all Eternity, and that in these later Days he became perfect Man for our Salvation.* Theod. Hist Eccl Lib v. cap 9 Ed Hen. Steph

That Christ had an human Soul proved from Scripture.

II But the Holy Scriptures are perfectly against this Doctrine of the Apollinarians, they particularly asserting that our Saviour had an Human Mind or Soul, as well as a Body This is implied in the Words of the Apostle, *the Word was made Flesh*, John i 13 i e Man that being the Meaning of *Flesh* in many Places of Scripture, *Gen* vi 12 *Psal* cxlv 21. *Isa* lxvi 16 *Jer.* xxv 31 *Joel* ii 28 *Luke* iii 6

But besides our Saviour himself several times speaks of his Soul The following Passages are rendred in our Translation *Life*, but they are ψυχή Soul in the Greek *I lay down my Soul for my Sheep*, John x 15 *I lay down my Soul that I may take it again*, ib v 17 But there are other Passages which cannot but be understood of Christ's Rational Soul *Thou shalt not leave my Soul in Hell*, which Passage of the Psalmist St *Peter* applies to our Saviour's Soul in the State of Separation. *Acts* ii. 27 When Christ says, *My Soul is exceeding sorrowful even unto Death*, it must be meant of his Rational Soul, or Mind

Arguments for the same drawn from Reason
1 Because, otherways Christ could not be Man.

III. Moreover there are several very excellent Arguments drawn from Reason, whereby the Orthodox Doctrine is confirmed, and the Apollinarian Heterodoxy is confuted (1.) Because Christ could not be truly said to be Man, unless he had an human Soul as well as a Body For thus *Tertullian* reasons *Porro nec anima per semet ipsam homo, quæ figmento jam hominis appellato, postea inserta est nec caro sine anima homo, quæ post exilium animæ cadaver inscribitur The Soul it self is not Man, this being infused into that outward Shape or organical Figure which we call Man neither is the Body without the Soul Man, for when the Soul is separated from this it is no longer a Man, but a Carkase* Tert de Res Car cap 40 In like manner *Athanasius*, εἰ δὲ διὰ τοῦτο δι᾽ ἡμᾶς ὁ Θεὸς ἄνθρωπος γέγονεν ... τὸ σῶμα. *Since our Saviour was made Man for us, he could not have a Body without a Soul* Ath in Epist. Synod ad Antioch (2.)

2 Because all that was impaired by Sin must be repaired

Because Christ came into the World to repair as much of human Nature as was impaired, now because the Soul by Sin suffered more than the Body, Christ who was to make Satisfaction for this, must partake of human Soul as well as Body This is well expressed by *Theodoret* Ἠθέλησεν αὐτὴν ... τὴν φύσιν καταγαγεῖν ... ἀντίπαλον, ... καὶ σῶμα καὶ ψυχὴν ἀνέβαλε ... *He was willing to fight against the Adversary, in that Nature which he had worsted, and to gain a Victory over him, for this Reason he took upon him both a Soul and a Body* Theod Lib v contr Hær cap 11. And for the same reason *Athanasius* says, ... σῶμα ... ψυχὴν ... πρῶτον ὁ δεύτερος Ἀδάμ. *The second Adam took on him Soul and Body, and the whole Nature of the first* Athan de Sal adv (3.) Christ

3 Because the Soul required a Redemption as well as the Body

must have a Soul as well as a Body, that the whole Man might partake of the Benefits of Redemption Wherefore thus *Theodoret* Ὅλον γὰρ ἀνέλαβε τὸν ἄνθρωπον, ἵνα ὅλῳ τῷ πάθει αὐτὸν καὶ σὺν αὐτῷ τοὺς ... ζωοποιήσῃ. *Christ took upon him whole Man, that he might make alive whole Man, and all those that are dead,* Theod Dial. iii. This *Prudentius* expresses in these Verses

Totum hominem Deus assumit, quia totus ab ipso est,
Et totum redimit, quem sumpserat, omne redemens
Quicquid homo est istud tumulis, et illud Abysso

God on him takes the whole of human Nature,
For Man was wholly the Almighty's Creature.
From Man's each part he danger does repell,
This part from Grave he saves, and that from Hell.
Prud in Apotheosi.

I Godhead and Manhood] Our Articles asserting here that *two Natures were joyned together in Christ*, do in effect declare against the Heresie of *Eutyches*, who would allow but one Nature in Christ.

Of the Eutychian Heresie

The Rise and Progress of the Eutychian Heresie.

I *Eutyches* was a Presbyter of *Constantinople*, and advanced to the Dignity of an Archimandrite or Abbot When he was a Deacon he was of some considerable Note, usually being made of him to carry a Letter written to the Emperor in the Name of the Council of *Ephesus*, which condemned *Nestorius*, Eph Conc Par ii Act 3 His zeal against Nestorianism occasioned him to run into a contrary Error, which is a fate common to those, who oppose any Opinion without Discretion Besides several Errors which were imputed to him, as his asserting that Christ had not a like Body with ours, and that he brought a Body with him from Heaven, the chief Heterodoxy which he was remarkably distinguished by, was his asserting, *ante adunationem duas in Christo fuisse naturas, post adunationem vero unam factam esse, before the Union there were two Natures in Christ, and after the Union they were made one* Liber Brev c 11 The same account is given in the Acts of the Council of *Chalcedon* Ὁμολογῶ ἐκ δύο φύσεων γεγενῆσθαι τὸν Κύριον ἡμῶν πρὸ τῆς ἑνώσεως, μετὰ δὲ τὴν ἕνωσιν μίαν φύσιν ὁμολογῶ Soon after the broaching of his Heresie, he was cited to appear before a Synod of Bishops which met at *Constantinople*, under *Flavianus* Patriarch of the Place, but *Eutyches* for some time trifled with the Synod, now pretending he could not go out of his Abby, and otherwhiles giving out he was sick, but at last, being buoy'd up by the Power of *Chrysaphius* the Eunuch, a great Favorite of the Emperor *Theodosius*, who sent a Guard with him to the Synod, at last he appears before them, and, instead of recanting, makes an open Profession of his Heresie For which he is condemned by the Synod, and deprived of his Abby and his Priesthood *Conc Chal P.* i. *Act* i But *Chrysaphius* representing his Deposition to the Emperor, as a factious Proceeding of a few Bishops, obtains his Order that a new Council might be held of other Bishops less prejudiced to *Eutyches* at *Ephesus*, under *Dioscorus* Bishop of *Alexandria*, an *Eutychian* This Council rescinds the Acts of the Council of *Constantinople*, restores *Eutyches*, and deposes *Flavianus* By this the Affairs of the Church were involved in great Confusion, which occasioned the convening of the General Council of *Chalcedon*, which was ordered to meet by the Emperor *Marcianus* This great Council met in *October*, A D CCCCLI. *Dioscorus*, who had been the President of the late Council of *Ephesus*, and the Manager for *Eutyches*, appeared here in his Place, but the Council would not let him sit there as a Judge, whom they designed to bring before them as a Criminal, and therefore he was soon ordered to withdraw. In this Council the Acts of the *Ephesian* Synod are rescinded, the Bishops by them deposed restored *Dioscorus* is deposed as an Heretick and a factious Bishop, the Decrees of the Council of *Constantinople* with relation to the Condemnation of *Eutyches* are affirmed, and the Orthodox Faith declared to be τὸν αὐτὸν Χριστὸν, υἱὸν, κύριον μονογενῆ, ἐκ δύο φύσεων ἀσυγχύτως, ἀτρέπτως, ἀδιαιρέτως, ἀχωρίστως γνωριζόμενον οὐδαμοῦ τῆς τῶν φύσεων διαφορᾶς ἀνῃρημένης διὰ τὴν ἕνωσιν, σωζομένης δὲ μᾶλλον τῆς ἰδιότητος ἑκατέρας φύσεως, καὶ εἰς ἓν πρόσωπον, καὶ μίαν ὑπόστασιν συντρεχούσης. *That Christ is the Son and the only begotten Lord, that he does consist of two Natures, unconfusedly, unvariably, undistinguishably, unseparably That the difference of the Natures are not destroyed by the Union, the Properties of each Nature being preserved, they both making up one Person, and one Hypostasis.* Con Chalced Act. v. But the Determinations of this great Council were so far from destroying this Heresie, that they tended only to make it it flame the more, and spread it self into several Branches, the Greeks call them ... Horns, under different Denominations, with new Heterodoxies added to the old by means of which the Church was miserably distracted for a Century or more. *Alexandria* was all in Tumults upon the Deposition of *Dioscorus*, and *Proterius* being put in his Place, which last was murdered in his Church, by the Rable at the Instigation of *Timotheus Ælurus* an Eutychian Presbyter. And matters in other Places being carried on in a like tumultuous Manner, the Emperor *Leo*, in order to quiet Affairs, sends his Circular Letters to the Bishops in the several Provinces of the Empire, to declare their Mind about the Council of *Chalcedon*, who almost unanimously declare, *That they would defend that Council with their Blood*, Evag Lib ii cap 9 Upon this *Timotheus*, who had invaded the See of *Alexandria*, is banished by the Decree of the Emperor. Afterwards when *Zeno* came to be Emperor, the Eutychian Controversies were still kept on foot, wherefore to quiet the Spirits of the contending Parties, he published his *Henoticon* or Project of Union, *A D* CCCCLXXXII wherein he trimmed Matters between the Orthodox and the Eutychians. No mention of the *two Natures* being made in this Form of the Emperor, the Eutychians generally acquiesced therein, and thereby were restored to their Preferments among these was *Acacius*, who declared an Anathema against the Council of *Chalcedon*, and impiously added the Words, *who suffered for us*, to the end of the *Trisagium*, declaring thereby that the whole Trinity suffered, and giving rise to the Heresie of the *Theopaschites*, Evag Lib iii cap 16 Niceph Lib. xviii cap 51 Afterwards the Eutychians were divided among themselves some of them refused (with *Mogges* Bishop of *Alexandria*) to anathematize the Council of *Chalcedon*, others divided from him therein, whereupon they gained the Name of the *Acephali* i e *Men without a Head*, which Name afterwards was given to all the rigid Eutychians every where. The more moderate of these Hereticks, gained the Name of ..., the *Hesitants* or *Doubters* Leont de Sect From these Eutychians spawned some other Sects, as the *Phthartolatræ* who would have Christ's Body to be corruptible, and the *Aphthartodocetæ* who would have it to be incorruptible From the same arose the Tritheites who owned Three Gods, *Niceph Lib* xviii. *cap* 45 These Quarrels continued on till the Reign of *Justinian*, who was persuaded to publish an Edict, to condemn *Origen*'s Opinions, whose Books were in esteem among several of the Clergy This nettled *Theodorus* Bishop of *Cæsarea*, a great Admirer of *Origen*, and Favourer of *Eutyches* his Doctrine, to persuade the Emperor to publish an Edict likewise to condemn three Particulars or Heads of the Council of *Chalcedon* 1 That which countenanced the Writings of *Theodorus Mopsuestenus*. 2 The Epistle of *Ibas* 3 *Theodoret*'s Book against *Cyril* All of them Authors who had written contrary to the Eutychian Doctrine These are the *tria capitula* the three Chapters as they are called, that have made such a Noise in the World *Justinian*, according as was desired of him, publishes his Edict against the three Chapters, *A D* DXLVI Which *Vigilius* Bishop of *Rome* and most of the Western Bishops refuse to receive at last he does it faintly, qualifying it with the Clause *salvâ Concilii Chalcedonensis reverentia*. But the Emperor insists to have him recognize it absolutely this *Vigilius* refusing to do, is insulted by the Emperor's Guards, and pulled from the Altar of the Church he fled to, in a most scandalous manner The Emperor by this fierceness having brought matters to a worse state than he found them, thought to piece up all by a Council held at *Constantinople*, *A D* DLIII about the matter of the three Chapters, they condemning 60 Particulars in the Books of *Mopsuestenus*, but letting *Ibas* and *Theodoret* alone. This quieted Matters pretty well for a time in the East, but the Bishops of *Italy*, *Africa*, &c refused to condemn any thing in those Chapters, and this Controversy was not composed in the West till the time of *Gregory* the Great, who wrote several Epistles to put an end to it And in the East the Eutychian Doctrines broke out again, when the Heresie of the Monothelites arose, which is but another Branch of Eutychianism

The two Natures of Christ proved from Scripture

II But it must be observed that these Eutychian Notions are contrary to the Doctrine of the Holy Scriptures, which do plainly assert *two Natures* in Christ For all those Places of Scripture are a Proof of this, where our Saviour is declared to be God, and those where he is declared to be Man But there are several Passages in which both Natures are mentioned together As in that of S. *Paul*, *Concerning his Son Jesus Christ our Lord, who was made of the Seed of David according to the Flesh*, Rom. i 3 Where one part of the Verse relates to Christ's Divine, and the other to his human Nature In the first Chapter of the *Hebrews*, in respect of his Divinity he is said to be the *brightness of the Father's Glory*, and the *express Image of his Person*, in the next Chapter, it is said, *we see Jesus, who was made a little lower than the Angels for the suffering of Death crowned with Glory and Honour, that he by the Grace of God should taste Death for every Man*, which is plainly spoken of his Humanity, So Col i 14 in respect of his Humanity it is said, *In whom we have Redemption through his Blood, even the Forgiveness of Sins*, but the next Verse relates to his Divinity *Who is the Image of the Invisible God, the first born of every Creature*, Col i. 15

Reasons for asserting two Natures in Christ

III The Arguments drawn from Reason for the Confutation of the Eutychian Heresie, and for asserting the Distinction of the two Natures in Christ are chiefly these (1) Because Union does suppose Distinction or Division

1 Union supposes Distinction

For thus *Theodoret* argues ... *Without Distinction or Division, it is not to be understood how any thing can be united For he that supposes Union supposes likewise Division* Theod in Conf Anath 3 Tom.

2 The like Distinction in other Unions

... (2) Because a Distinction remains in other Unions Thus *Vincentius* on this Head *Sicut in homine aliud Caro & aliud Anima sed ... sic ... que homo Anima & Caro ... que ... Christo ... Substantiæ ...* As in Man the Flesh is one thing the Soul another, and yet both Flesh and Soul is one Man, So ... the same Christ, there are two Substances, the one Divine, the other Human

3 Because the Idioms of one Nature are communicated to the other.

(3) Because the Properties or Idioms, both of Christ's Divinity and his Humanity, are reciprocally communicable to one another For thus *Vigilius* in his Book against *Eutyches* *Si ergo me interroges utrum Christus habeat initium an non habeat, respondebo tibi, & habet & non habet habet secundum humanam mentem sed non habet secundum divinitatem suam* If you ask me, whether Christ hath a beginning or no I will answer he has and he has not He has according to his Humanity, and he has not according to his Divinity And again *Quicquid est proprium verbi est commune cum carne, & quicquid est proprium carnis commune cum Verbo est quoniam Verbum & Caro unus est Christus & una Persona* Whatever is proper to the Word is common to the Human Nature, and whatever is proper to the Human Nature is common to the Word: Therefore the Word is one Christ and one Person

in One Christ] The Words *One Christ* are here set down, partly in Agreement with the Holy Scriptures which assert the same, and partly in Opposition to the Nestorian Heresie, which asserted such a Distinction in the Natures of Christ as made them to be two Persons, or in effect two Christs We shall give a short account of the Rise of this Heresie, as we have done of the others, though, if we had observed the Order of Time, and not the Words of the Articles, we should have related this, before the Heresie of *Eutyches*.

Of the Nestorian Heresie

This Heresie was broached by *Nestorius* Bishop of *Constantinople* about the Year of our Lord CCCCXXX *Nestorius* was born at *Germanicia*, a little Town in *Syria*, and having travelled into several Countries to improve his Studies, and to exercise his Talent of Eloquence, which he was remarkable for, particularly the sweetness of his Voice, he at last settled at *Antioch* Socr Lib vii cap 29 Theod. Lib iv de Hær cap 12. He is said some time to have lead a Monastick Life *Nic Lib* xiv *cap* 36 but afterward taking Orders he became a celebrated Preacher, and was the more admired for the Gravity of his Temper, and for his studious Retirement *Evag Lib.* i *cap* 7 In the Year CCCCXXVIII *Sisinius* Bishop of *Constantinople* dying, the Emperors were willing that a Foreigner should rather succeed in that See than a Native, and *Nestorius* being of the same City from whence the famous *John Chrysostom* came, they cast their Eyes upon him, and

that two whole and perfect Natures, that is to say the Godhead and Manhood were joyned together in one Person, never to be divided, whereof is one Christ, very God and very Man,

in the [i] Womb of the Blessed Virgin of her Substance; so that [k] two whole and perfect Natures, that is the [l] Godhead and the Manhood were joyned together in one Person never to be divided: whereof is [m] one Christ, very God and very Man.

ex illius Substantia naturam humanam assumpsit: ita ut duæ naturæ, divina & humana, integrè atque perfectè in unitate Personæ fuerint inseparabiliter conjunctæ, in quibus est unus Christus, verus

conducible to Christ's design of cancelling a Sin of the Flesh, not to have cancelled it in that Flesh by which the Sin was committed Tert de car Christ c 16 S *Austin* carries the Analogy between the Malady and Remedy further. *Quia per mulierem in hunc mundum mors introivit, salus per Virginem redderetur*, &c *Ut ne perpetui reatus apud Viros opprobrium sustineret quia quæ culpam nobis transfuderat, transfudit & gratiam* *Because by a Woman Sin entered into the World, therefore Salvation must be restored by a Virgin*, &c *Because the Woman should not bear the Reproach of an eternal Guilt among the Men, the Woman, who first brought Guilt upon us, conveyed Grace to us* Aug Ser xiii. de Nat

i *In the Womb of the Blessed Virgin of her Substance*] This Truth was denied by *Valentinus*, and some other of the Hereticks of the first times, who taught, as *Epiphanius* relates, Ἀπὸ δὲ ἄνωθεν κατενηνοχέναι τὸ σῶμα, καὶ ὡς διὰ σωλῆνος ὕδωρ, διὰ Μαρίας τῆς παρθένου διεληλυθέναι μηδὲν δὲ ἀπὸ τῆς παρθενικῆς μήτρας εἰληφέναι *That Christ brought a Body from Heaven, and as Water passes through a Pipe, so did that through the Virgin* Mary, *but received no Substance from the Virgin's Womb* Ep Hær xxxi. But this foolish Notion is excellently thus refuted by S *Chrysostom* Εἰ τοῦτο ἦν, τίς χρεία τῆς μήτρας, εἰ τοῦτο ἦν, οὐδὲν ἔχει κοινὸν πρὸς ἡμᾶς, ἀλλ' ἄλλη τις ἐστιν σὰρξ ἐκείνη ἢ σὰρξ οὐ τοῦ συγκράματος τοῦ ἡμετέρου πῶς οὖν ἐκ τῆς ῥίζης Ἰεσσαί, πῶς δὲ ῥάβδος, πῶς δὲ υἱὸς ἀνθρώπου, πῶς δὲ μήτηρ ἡ Μαρία; πῶς δὲ ἐκ σπέρματος Δαυίδ, πῶς δὲ μορφὴν δούλου ἔλαβε; πῶς δὲ ὁ λόγος σὰρξ ἐγένετο, πῶς δὲ Ῥωμαίοις φησὶν ὁ Παῦλος ἐξ ὧν ὁ Χριστὸς τὸ κατὰ σάρκα, ὁ ἐπὶ πάντων Θεός, *If this be so* (i e if Christ passed through the Womb of the Virgin as a Channel) *what need was there of the Womb of the Virgin at all? If this be so, Christ has nothing in common with us, he is another Flesh and not of the Mass of our Nature How is he then of the Root of* Jesse? *How is he the Branch? How is he the Son of Man? How is he of the Seed of* David? *How did he take upon him the form of a Servant? How can the Apostle to the* Romans *say*, of whom according to the Flesh Christ came, who is God over all? *Chrys Hom* iv *in Mat*

This Clause of the Article, most probably, was not here inserted with so much Particularity, in Opposition to the Hereticks of old, as to the Tenets of some of the Anabaptists and Enthusiasts, of the time when the Articles were drawn up Two Years before King *Edward*'s Articles were published, there was an obstinate Heretick burnt here in *England*, for maintaining the old *Valentinian* Heresy of Christ's passing through the Virgin *Mary*'s Womb as through a Conduit Which is particularly noted by King *Edward* VI in his Diary *May* 2 1550 Joan Bocher, *otherways called* Joan *of* Kent, *was burnt for holding*, that Christ was not incarnate of the Virgin *Mary*, *being condemned the Year before, but kept in hopes of Conversion* And about the same time that Q *Elizabeth*'s Articles were published, one *Adrian Hemsted* came out of *Zealand* into *England*, but was afterwards forced to leave this Nation, who maintained a Doctrine of the same kind, and, among other Heterodoxies, laid down, That to believe *That Christ was born of the Seed of the Woman, and that he was partaker of human Flesh, was no Article of the Christian Faith* Spond Contin Bar Vol ii p 784 Now because the Reformation might receive no Prejudice from these monstrous Opinions, it was by the Compilers of the Articles thought advisable to make an express Profession of our holding the true Catholick Doctrine in this particular

k *Two whole and perfect Natures*, &c] These Words are added, in Opposition to the Tenets of some of the antient Hereticks, who held the human Nature of Christ to be imperfect, as wanting an human Soul, which they said was supplied by the Presence of the *Word*, which did perform all the Operations of a Soul in Christ's Body The Arians indeed were of this Opinion, but their greater Heresie in denying our Saviour's Divinity, made this Opinion of theirs less taken notice of But the Apollinarians, who divided from the Orthodox in this Point, have made this Heterodoxy chiefly to be attributed to them, concerning whom I shall premise a few Words

Of the Apollinarian Heresie.

Apollinaris, when he broached his Heresie, and what it was

I. These Hereticks owed their rise to one *Apollinaris*, who was Bishop of *Laodicea*, in the troublesome times of Arianism, when there were one or two Bishops of the several Factions in that City besides He had formerly been under some disgrace, having with his Father lain under an Excommunication, for their Familiarity with *Epiphanius* a Heathen Sophist. *Socr Lib* ii *cap ult Soz Lib* v *cap* 25 But the Son afterwards recovered his Credit among the Orthodox, by siding with them and espousing the cause of *Athanasius*, with whom he cultivated for some time a Friendship *Epiph Hær* lxxvii *Leont contr Nest. Lib* iii He was undoubtedly a very excellent Scholar, this being confess'd by his Adversaries *Epiphanius* says, he was παιδεία οὐ τῇ τυχούσῃ ὁ ἀνήρ *A Man of no ordinary learning* Epiph ibid *Vincentius Lirinensis* says of him, *Quid illo præstantius, acumine, exercitatione, doctrina? quam multas ille Hereses multis voluminibus oppresserit, quot inimicos fidei confutaverit errores, indicio est opus illud triginta non minus librorum nobilissimum, ac maximum, quo insanas Porphyrii calumnias, magna probationum mole confudit? What can be more excellent than* Apollinaris, *in Smartness, in Stile, in Learning? How many Heresies has he silenced by his indefatigable Writing, how many Heretical Errors has he confuted, witness that noble Book of his consisting of no less than thirty Volumnes, in which he has so copiously confuted the Calumnies of* Prophyry? There seem to have been two Editions as it were of his Heresy. The first at least he broached in his Father's time, in conjunction with him For, as *Socrates* relates, πρότερον μὲν ἔλεγον, &c *They first gave out, that there was no Soul taken by God the Word, in the Dispensation of the Incarnation but afterwards, retracting this Opinion, they corrected themselves, and allowed that there was a Soul taken,* νοῦν δὲ οὐκ ἔχειν αὐτὴν, ἀλλ' εἶναι τὸν Θεὸν λόγον ἀντὶ νοῦ εἰς τὸ ἀναληφθὲν ἄνθρωπον, *but that there was no Mind, God the Word being taken into Man, instead of a Mind* Socr Lib ii cap ult *Epiphanius* thus declares what his Doctrine was, *viz* τὸν τέλειον ἄνθρωπον, ἐκ σαρκὸς καὶ ψυχῆς, ἡ θεότητος ἀντὶ τοῦ νοῦ· *That Christ was perfect Man as consisting of Flesh and a sensitive Soul, and that his Godhead was in lieu of his Mind* Epiph Hær lxxvii His Followers improved this Doctrine of his into a more monstrous and pestilential Heresie, *viz* asserting, that Christ's Body, or Human Nature, was consubstantial with his Divinity The detestableness of this Doctrine raised *Athanasius* into a pious Fervor, occasioning him thereupon thus to express himself Ποῖος ᾅδης ἠρεύξατο, &c *What Hell has exhaled this Doctrine, that the Body which was born of* Mary *should be consubstantial to the Deity? that the Word should be turned into Flesh, Bones, and the other Parts of human Body, and be changed from its own Nature? Who ever heard this from Christians, that the Son of God only in*

 shew

shew and fiction had a Body, but no natural and true One? Can any one break out in such Impiety as to assert and imagine, That that Deity which is consubstantial with the Father should be circumscribed, and from perfect made imperfect? That that which was fastened to the Cross should not be a Body, but the very Essence or Substance (οὐσία) of him that made the World? Athan Ep ad Epict. His Heresie was several times condemned, first in a Synod held at Alexandria, A D ccclxii. in another at Antioch ccclxxviii and lastly by the second General Council which was held at Constantinople These Fathers in Opposition to this Heresie declare thus, [illegible] We keep the Doctrine of the Lord's Incarnation inviolable, not allowing that the Oeconomy of the Flesh (i e Christ's human Nature) is without a Soul, or without a Mind knowing that the Word was perfect from all Eternity, and that in these later Days he became perfect Man for our Salvation Theod. Hist Eccl Lib v cap 9 Ed Hen. Steph

II But the Holy Scriptures are perfectly against this Doctrine of the Apollinarians, they particularly asserting that our Saviour had an Human Mind or Soul, as well as a Body This is implied in the Words of the Apostle, the Word was made Flesh, John i 13 i e Man that being the Meaning of Flesh in many Places of Scripture, Gen vi 12 Psal cxlv 21. Is lxvi 16 Jer xxv. 31 Joel ii 28 Luke iii 6

That Christ had an human Soul proved from Scripture.

But besides our Saviour himself several times speaks of his Soul The following Passages are rendered in our Translation Life, but they are ψυχὴ Soul in the Greek I lay down my Soul for my Sheep, John x 15 I lay down my Soul that I may take it again, ib v 17 But there are other Passages which cannot but be understood of Christ's Rational Soul Thou shalt not leave my Soul in Hell, which Passage of the Psalmist St Peter applies to our Saviour's Soul in the State of Separation, Acts ii 27 When Christ says, My Soul is exceeding sorrowful even unto Death, it must be meant of his Rational Soul, or Mind

III. Moreover there are several very excellent Arguments drawn from Reason, whereby the Orthodox Doctrine is confirmed, and the Apollinarian Heterodoxy is confuted (1) Because Christ could not be truly said to be Man, unless he had an human Soul as well as a Body For thus Tertullian reasons Porro nec anima per semetipsam homo, quae figmento jam hominis appellato, postea inserta est nec caro sine anima homo, quae post exilium animae, cadaver inscribitur The Soul it self is not Man, this being infused into that outward Shape or organical Figure which we call Man neither is the Body without the Soul Man, for when the Soul is separated from this, it is no longer a Man, but a Carkass Tert de Res Car cap 40 In like manner Athanasius, [Greek text illegible] Since our Saviour was made Man for us, he could not have a Body without a Soul Ath in Epist. Synod ad Antioch (2) Because Christ came into the World to repair as much of human Nature as was impaired, now because the Soul by Sin suffered more than the Body, Christ who was to make Satisfaction for this, must partake of human Soul as well as Body This is well expressed by Theodoret [Greek text illegible] He was willing to fight against the Adversary, in that Nature which he had worsted, and to gain a victory over him, for this Reason he took upon him both a Soul and a Body Theod Lib v contr Hær cap 11 And for the same reason Athanasius says, [Greek text illegible] The second Adam took on him Soul and Body, and the whole Nature of the first Adam de Sal adv (3) Christ must have a Soul as well as a Body, that the whole Man might partake of the Benefits of Redemption Wherefore thus Theodoret [Greek text illegible] Christ took upon him whole Man that he might make alive whole Man, and all those that are dead, Theod Dial. iii. This Prudentius expresses in these Verses

Arguments for the same drawn from Reason

1 Because, otherways Christ could not be Man

2. Because all that was impaired by Sin must be repaired

3 Because the Soul required a Redemption as well as the Body

> *Totum hominem Deus assumit, quia totus ab ipso est,*
> *Et totum redimit, quem sumpserat, omne reducens*
> *Quicquid homo est istud tumulis, at illud Abysso.*
>
> *God on him takes the whole of human Nature,*
> *For Man was wholly the Almighty's Creature*
> *From Man's each part he danger does repell,*
> *This part from Grave he saves, and that from Hell.*
> Prud in Apotheosi.

I Godhead and Manhood] Our Articles asserting here that two Natures were joyned together in Christ, do in effect declare against the Heresie of Eutyches, who would allow but one Nature in Christ.

Of the Eutychian Heresie.

I Eutyches was a Presbyter of Constantinople, and advanced to the Dignity of an Archimandrite or Abbot When he was a Deacon he was of some considerable Note, use being made of him to carry a Letter written to the Emperor in the Name of the Council of Ephesus, which condemned Nestorius, Eph Conc Par ii Act 3 His zeal against Nestorianism occasioned him to run into a contrary Error, which is a fate common to those, who oppose any Opinion without Discretion Besides several Errors which were imputed to him, as his asserting that Christ had not a like Body with ours, and that he brought a Body with him from Heaven, the chief Heterodoxy which he was remarkably distinguished by, was his asserting, ante adunationem duas in Christo fuisse naturas, post adunationem vero unam factam esse, before the Union there were two Natures in Christ, and after the Union they were made one Liber Brev c 11 The same account is given in the Acts of the Council of Chalcedon [Greek text illegible] Soon after the broaching of his Heresie, he was cited to appear before a Synod of Bishops which met at Constantinople, under Flavianus Patriarch of the Place, but Eutyches for some time trifled with the Synod, now pretending he could not go out of his Abby, and other time giving out he was sick, but at last, being buoy'd up by the Power of Chrysaphius the Eunuch, a great Favorite of the Emperor Theodosius, who sent a Guard with him to the Synod, at last he appears before them, and, instead of recanting, makes an open Profession of his Heresie For which he is condemned by the Synod, and deprived of his Abby and his Priesthood Conc Chal P i Act i But Chrysaphius representing his Deposition to the Emperor, as a factious Proceeding of a few Bishops, obtains his Order that a new Council might be held of other Bishops less prejudiced to Eutyches at Ephesus, under Dioscorus Bishop of Alexandria, an Eutychian This Council rescinds the Acts of the Council of Constantinople, restores Eutyches, and deposes Flavianus By this the Affairs of the Church were involved in great Confusion, which occasioned the convening of the General Council of Chalcedon, which was ordered to meet by the Emperor Marcianus This great Council met in October, A D CCCCLI. Dioscorus, who had been the President of the late Council of Ephesus, and the Manager for Eutyches, appeared here in his Place, but the Council would not let him sit there as a Judge, whom they designed to bring before them as a Criminal, and therefore he was soon ordered to withdraw. In this Council the Acts of the Ephesian Synod are rescinded, the Bishops by them deposed restored, Dioscorus is deposed as an Heretick and a factious Bishop, the Decrees of the Council of Constantinople with relation to the Condemnation of Eutyches are affirmed, and the Orthodox Faith declared to be [illegible] That Christ is the Son and the only begotten Lord, that he does consist of two Natures, unconfusedly, unvariably, undistinguishably, inseparably That the difference of the Natures are not destroyed by the Union, the Properties of each Nature being preserved, they both making up one Person, and one Hypostasis Con Chalced Act. v. But the Determinations of this great Council were so far from destroying this Heresie, that they tended only to make

The Rise and Progress of the Eutychian Heresie.

it

it flame the more, and spread it self into several Branches, the Greeks call them [illegible] Horns, under different Denominations, with new Heterodoxies added to the old by means of which the Church was miserably distracted for a Century or more *Alexandria* was all in Tumults upon the Deposition of *Dioscorus*, and *Proterius* being put in his Place, which last was murdered in his Church by the Rable at the Instigation of *Timotheus Ælurus* an Eutychian Presbyter And matters in other Places being carried on in a like tumultuous Manner, the Emperor *Leo*, in order to quiet Affairs, sends his Circular Letters to the Bishops in the several Provinces of the Empire, to declare their Mind about the Council of *Chalcedon*, who almost unanimously declare, *That they would defend that Council with their Blood*, Evag Lib ii cap 9. Upon this *Timotheus*, who had invaded the See of *Alexandria*, is banished by the Decree of the Emperor Afterwards when *Zeno* came to be Emperor, the Eutychian Controversies were still kept on foot, wherefore to quiet the Spirits of the contending Parties, he published his *Henoticon* or Project of Union, A D CCCCLXXXII wherein he trimmed Matters between the Orthodox and the Eutychians No mention of the *two Natures* being made in this Form of the Emperor, the Eutychians generally acquiesced therein, and thereby were restored to their Preferments among these was *Acacius*, who declared an Anathema against the Council of *Chalcedon*, and impiously added the Words, *who suffered for us*, to the end of the *Trisagium*, declaring thereby that the whole Trinity suffered, and giving rise to the Heresie of the *Theopaschites*, Evag Lib iii cap 16 Niceph Lib xviii cap 51 Afterwards the Eutychians were divided among themselves, some of them refused (with *Moggus* Bishop of *Alexandria*) to Anathematize the Council of *Chalcedon*, others divided from him therein, whereupon they gained the Name of the *Acephali* i e *Men without a Head*, which Name afterwards was given to all the rigid Eutychians every where The more moderate of these Hereticks, gained the Name of [illegible], *the Hesitants or Doubters* Leont de Sect From these Eutychians spawned some other Sects, as the *Phthartolatræ* who would have Christ's Body to be corruptible, and the *Aphthartodocetæ* who would have it to be incorruptible From the same arose the Tritheites who owned Three Gods, *Niceph. Lib* xviii. *cap* 45 These Quarrels continued on till the Reign of *Justinian*, who was persuaded to publish an Edict, to condemn *Origen*'s Opinions, whose Books were in esteem among several of the Clergy This netled *Theodorus* Bishop of *Cæsarea*, a great Admirer of *Origen*, and Favourer of *Eutyches* his Doctrine, to persuade the Emperor to publish an Edict likewise to condemn three Particulars or Heads of the Council of *Chalcedon* 1 That which countenanced the Writings of *Theodorus Mopsuestenus* 2 The Epistle of *Ibas* 3 *Theodoret*'s Book against *Cyril* All of them Authors who had written contrary to the Eutychian Doctrine These are the *tria capitula* the three Chapters as they are called, that have made such a Noise in the World *Justinian*, according as was desired of him, publishes his Edict against the three Chapters, *A D* DXLVI Which *Vigilius* Bishop of *Rome* and most of the Western Bishops refuse to receive at last he does it faintly, qualifying it with the Clause *salvâ Concilii Chalcedonensis reverentia* But the Emperor insists to have him recognize it absolutely this *Vigilius* refusing to do, is insulted by the Emperor's Guards, and pulled from the Altar of the Church he fled to, in a most scandalous manner The Emperor by this fierceness having brought matters to a worse Issue than he found them, thought to piece up all by a Council held at *Constantinople*, *A D* DLIII about the matter of the three Chapters, they condemning 60 Particulars in the Books of *Mopsuestenus*, but letting *Ibas* and *Theodoret* alone This quieted Matters pretty well for a time in the East, but the Bishops of *Italy*, *Africa*, &c refused to condemn any thing in those Chapters, and this Controversy was not composed in the West till the time of *Gregory* the Great, who wrote several Epistles to put an end to it And in the East the Eutychian Doctrines broke out again, when the Heresie of the Monothelites arose, which is but another Branch of Eutychianism

II But it must be observed that these Eutychian Notions are contrary to the Doctrine of the Holy Scriptures, which do plainly assert *two Natures* in Christ For all those Places of Scripture are a Proof of this, where our Saviour is declared to be God, and those where he is declared to be Man But there are several Passages in which both Natures are mentioned together As in that of S *Paul*, *Concerning his Son Jesus Christ our Lord, which was made of the Seed of David according to the Flesh*, Rom i 3 Where one part of the Verse relates to Christ's Divine, and the other to his human Nature In the first Chapter of the *Hebrews*, in respect of his Divinity he is said to be the *brightness of the Father's Glory*, and the *express Image of his Person*, in the next Chapter, it is said *we see Jesus, who was made a little lower than the Angels for the suffering of Death crowned with Glory and Honour, that he by the Grace of God should taste Death for every Man*, which is plainly spoken of his Humanity So *Col* i 14 in respect of his Humanity it is said, *In whom we have Redemption through his Blood, even the Forgiveness of Sins*, but the next Verse relates to his Divinity *Who is the Image of the Invisible God, the first born of every Creature*, Col i 15

The two Natures of Christ proved from Scripture

III The Arguments drawn from Reason for the Confutation of the Eutychian Heresie, and for asserting the Distinction of the two Natures in Christ are chiefly these (1) Because Union does suppose Distinction or Division For thus *Theodoret* argues [illegible] *Without Distinction or Division, it is not to be understood how any thing can be united For he that supposes Union supposes likewise Division* Theod in Conf Anath 3 Tom 6 Cyr Op (2) Because a Distinction remains in other Unions Thus *Vincentius* on this Head [illegible] homine [illegible] *Caro & aliud Anima* [illegible] *idemque homo Anima & Caro* [illegible] *idemque Christo, duæ Substantiæ* [illegible], *altera Divina* As *in Man the Flesh is one thing and the Soul another, and yet both Flesh and Soul is one Man So* [illegible] *Christ, there are two Substances, the one Divine, the other Human* (3) Because the Properties or Idioms, both of Christ's Divinity and his Humanity, are reciprocally communicable to one another For thus *Vigilius* in his Book against *Eutyches* *Si ergo* [illegible] *Christus habeat initium, an non habeat* [illegible], *& habet & non habet habet secundum* [illegible] *habet secundum divinitatem* [illegible] *If you ask me whether Christ hath a beginning or no, I will answer, he has and he has not He has according to his Humanity, and he has not according to his Divinity* And again *Quicquid est proprium verum est communicatum carnis* [illegible] *est quoniam Verbum & Caro unus est Christus & una Persona Whatever is proper to the Word is common to the Human Nature, and whatever is proper to the Human Nature is common to the Word. Therefore the Word is one Christ and one Person*

Reasons for asserting two Natures in Christ

1 Union supposes Distinction.

2 The like Distinction in other Unions.

3 Because the Idioms of one Nature are communicated to the other

in One Christ] The Words *One Christ* are here set down, partly in Agreement with the Holy Scriptures which assert the same, and partly in Opposition to the Nestorian Heresie, which asserted such a Distinction in the Natures of Christ as made them to be two Persons, or in effect two Christs We shall give a short account of the Rise of this Heresie, as we have done of the others, though, if we had observed the Order of Time, and not the Words of the Articles, we should have related this, before the Heresie of *Eutyches*

Of the Nestorian Heresie

This Heresie was broached by *Nestorius* Bishop of *Constantinople*, about the Year of our Lord CCCCXXX *Nestorius* was born at *Germanicia*, a little Town in *Syria*, and having travelled into several Countries to improve his Studies, and to exercise his Talent of Eloquence, which he was remarkable for, particularly the sweetness of his Voice, he at last settled at *Antioch* Socr Lib vi cap 29 Theod. Lib iv de Hær cap 12. He is said some time to have lead a Monastick Life *Nic Lib* xiv *cap*. 36 but afterward taking Orders he became a celebrated Preacher, and was the more admired for the Gravity of his Temper, and for his studious Retirement *Evagr Lib* i *cap* 7 In the Year CCCCXXVII *Sisinnius* Bishop of *Constantinople* dying, the Emperors were willing that a Foreigner should rather succeed in that See than a Native, and *Nestorius* being of the same City from whence the famous *John Chrysostom* came, they cast their Eyes upon him, and

in

them and fiction had a Body, but no natural and true One? Can any one break out in such Impiety as to assert and imagine, That that Deity which is consubstantial with the Father should be circumcised, and from perfect made imperfect? That that which was fastened to the Cross should not be a Body, but the very Essence or Substance (οὐσία) of him that made the World? Athan Ep ad Epict His Heresie was several times condemned, first in a Synod held at Alexandria, A D ccclxii in another at Antioch ccclxxiii and lastly by the second General Council which was held at Constantinople These Fathers in Opposition to this Heresie declare thus, Τον τ ενανθρωπήσεως ... λογον αδιαστροφον σώζομεν, ὔτε ἄψυχον, ὔτε ἄνουν ... σαρκὸς οἰκονομίαν παραδεχόμενοι ὅλον ... τέλειον ... ἀνθρωπον ... We keep the Doctrine of the Lord's Incarnation inviolable, not allowing that the Oeconomy of the Flesh (i. e Christ's human Nature) is without a Soul, or without a Mind knowing that the Word was perfect from all Eternity, and that in these later Days he became perfect Man for our Salvation Theod Hist Eccl Lib v cap 9 Ed Hen. Steph

II But the Holy Scriptures are perfectly against this Doctrine of the Apollinarians, they particularly asserting that our Saviour had an Human Mind or Soul, as well as a Body This is implied in the Words of the Apostle, *the Word was made Flesh*, John i 13 i e Man that being the Meaning of *Flesh* in many Places of Scripture, Gen vi 12 Psal cxlv 21 Is lxvi 16 Jer xxv. 31 Joel ii 28 Luke iii 6

That Christ had an human Soul proved from Scripture.

But besides our Saviour himself several times speaks of his Soul The following Passages are rendred in our Translation *Life*, but they are ψυχὴ Soul in the Greek *I lay down my Soul for my Sheep*, John x 15 *I lay down my Soul that I may take it again*, ib v 17 But there are other Passages which cannot but be understood of Christ s Rational Soul *Thou shalt not leave my Soul in Hell*, which Passage of the Psalmist St Peter applies to our Saviour's Soul in the State of Separation, Acts ii 27 When Christ says, *My Soul is exceeding sorrowful even unto Death*, it must be meant of his Rational Soul, or Mind

III. Moreover there are several very excellent Arguments drawn from Reason, whereby the Orthodox Doctrine is confirmed, and the Apollinarian Heterodoxy is confuted (1) Because Christ could not be truly said to be Man, unless he had an human Soul as well as a Body For thus Tertullian reasons *Porro nec anima per semetipsam homo, quæ figmento jam homini appellato, postea inserta est nec caro sine anima homo, quæ post exilium animæ, cadaver inscribitur The Soul it self is not Man, tho' being infused into that outward Shape or organical Figure which we call Man neither is the Body without the Soul Man, for when the Soul is separated from th s it is no longer a Man, but a Carkase* Tert de Res Car cap 40 In like manner Athanasius, ... *Since our Saviour was made Man for us, he could not have a Body without a Soul* Ath in Epist. Synod ad Antioch (2) Because Christ came into the World to repair as much of human Nature as was impaired, now because the Soul by Sin suffered more than the Body, Christ who was to make Satisfaction for this, must partake of human Soul as well as Body This is well expressed by Theodoret Ἐβουλήθη αὐτὸν ... ἀγωνίσασθαι ... ἀντιπάλοις, ... σῶμα καὶ ψυχὴν ἀνέλαβε ... *He was willing to fight against the Adversary, in that Nature which he had worsted, and to gain a victory over him, for this Reason he took upon him both a Soul and a Body* Theod Lib v contr Hær cap 11 And for the same reason Athanasius says ... *The second Adam took on him Soul and Body, and the whole Nature of the first* Athan de Sal adv. (3) Christ must have a Soul as well as a Body, that the whole Man might partake of the Benefits of Redemption Wherefore thus Theodoret ... *Christ took upon him whole Man, that he might make alive whole Man, and all those that are dead*, Theod Dial. iii. This Prudentius expresses in these Verses.

Arguments for the same drawn from Reason
1 Because, otherways Christ could not be Man

2 Because all that was impaired by Sin must be repaired

3 Because the Soul required a Redemption as well as the Body

Totum hominem Deus assumit, quia totus ab ipso est,
Et totum redimit, quem sumpserat, omne reducens
Quicquid homo est illud tumulis, at illud Abysso

God on him takes the whole of human Nature,
For Man was wholly the Almighty's Creature
From Man's each part he danger does repell,
This part from Grave he saves, and that from Hell.
Prud in Apotheosi.

1 Godhead and Manhood] Our Articles asserting here that *two Natures were joyned together in Christ*, do in effect declare against the Heresie of Eutyches, who would allow but one Nature in Christ.

Of the Eutychian Heresie

The Rise and Progress of the Eutychian Heresie.

I *Eutyches* was a Presbyter of *Constantinople*, and advanced to the Dignity of an Archimandrite or Abbot When he was a Deacon he was of some considerable Note, use being made of him to carry a Letter written to the Emperor in the Name of the Council of *Ephesus*, which condemned *Nestorius*, Ep Conc Par ii. Act 3 His zeal against Nestorianism occasioned him to run into a contrary Error, which is a fate common to those, who oppose any Opinion without Discretion Besides several Errors which were imputed to him, as his asserting that Christ had not a like Body with ours, and that he brought a Body with him from Heaven, the chief Heterodoxy which he was remarkably distinguished by, was his asserting, *ante adunationem duas in Christo fuisse naturas, post adunationem vero unam factum esse, before the Union there were two Natures in Christ, and after the Union they were made one* Liber Brev c 11 The same account is given in the Acts of the Council of *Chalcedon* Ὁμολογῶ ἐκ δύο φύσεων γεγενῆσθαι τὸν Κύριον ἡμῶν πρὸ τῆς ἑνώσεως· μετὰ δὲ τὴν ἕνωσιν μίαν φύσιν ὁμολογῶ. Soon after the broaching of his Heresie, he was cited to appear before a Synod of Bishops which met at *Constantinople*, under *Flavianus* Patriarch of the Place, but *Eutyches* for some time trifled with the Synod, now pretending he could not go out of his Abby, and otherwhile giving out he was sick, but at last, being boy'd up by the Power of *Chrysaphius* the Eunuch, a great Favorite of the Emperor *Theodosius*, who sent a Guard with him to the Synod, at last he appears before them, and, instead of recanting, makes an open Profession of his Heresie For which he is condemned by the Synod, and deprived of his Abby and his Priesthood *Conc Chal P. i Act i.* But *Chrysaphius* representing his Deposition to the Emperor, as a factious Proceeding of a few Bishops, obtains his Order that a new Council might be held of other Bishops less prejudiced to *Eutyches* at *Ephesus*, under *Dioscorus* Bishop of *Alexandria*, an *Eutychian* This Council rescinds the Acts of the Council of *Constantinople*, restores *Eutyches*, and deposes *Flavianus* By this the Affairs of the Church were involved in great Confusion, which occasioned the convening of the General Council of *Chalcedon*, which was ordered to meet by the Emperor *Marcianus* This great Council met in *October*, A D CCCCLI. *Dioscorus*, who had been the President of the late Council of *Ephesus* and the Manager for *Eutyches*, appeared here in his Place, but the Council would not let him sit there as a Judge, whom they designed to bring before them as a Criminal, and therefore he was soon ordered to withdraw. In this Council the Acts of the *Ephesian* Synod are rescinded, the Bishops by them deposed restored. *Dioscorus* is deposed as an Heretick and a factious Bishop, the Decrees of the Council of *Constantinople* with relation to the Condemnation of *Eutyches* are affirmed, and the Orthodox Faith declared to be τὸν αὐτὸν Χριστὸν, υἱὸν, κύριον μονογενῆ, ἐν δύο φύσεων ἀσυγχύτως, ἀτρέπτως, ἀδιαιρέτως, ἀχωρίστως γνωριζόμενον οὐδαμοῦ τῆς τῶν φύσεων διαφορᾶς ἀνῃρημένης διὰ τὴν ἕνωσιν, σωζομένης δὲ μᾶλλον τῆς ἰδιότητος ἑκατέρας φύσεως, καὶ εἰς ἓν πρόσωπον, καὶ μίαν ὑπόστασιν συντρεχούσης. *That Christ is the Son and the only begotten Lord, that he does consist of two Natures, unconfusedly, unvariably, undistinguishably, unseparably That the difference of the Natures are not destroyed by the Union, the Properties of each Nature being preserved, they both making up one Person, and one Hypostasis* Con Chalced Act. v. But the Determinations of this great Council were so far from destroying this Heresie, that they tended only to make it it flame the more, and spread it self into several Branches, the Greeks call them [illegible] Horns, under different Denominations, with new Heterodoxies added to the old by means of which the Church was miserably distracted for a Century or more *Alexandria* was all in Tumults upon the Deposition of *Dioscorus*, and *Proterius* being put in his Place, which last was murdered in his Church, by the Rable at the Instigation of *Timotheus Ælurus* an Eutychian Presbyter And matters in other Places being carried on in a like tumultuous Manner, the Emperor *Leo*, in order to quiet Affairs, sends his Circular Letters to the Bishops in the several Provinces of the Empire, to declare their Mind about the Council of *Chalcedon*, who almost unanimously declare, *That they would defend that Council with their Blood*, Evag Lib ii cap 9 Upon this *Timotheus*, who had invaded the See of *Alexandria*, is banished by the Decree of the Emperor Afterwards when *Zeno* came to be Emperor, the Eutychian Controversies were still kept on foot, wherefore to quiet the Spirits of the contending Parties, he published his *Henoticon* or Project of Union, *A D* CCCCLXXXII wherein he trimmed Matters between the Orthodox and the Eutychians No mention of the *two Natures* being made in this Form of the Emperor, the Eutychians generally acquiesced therein, and thereby were restored to their Preferments among these was *Acacius*, who declared an Anathema against the Council of *Chalcedon*, and impiously added the Words, *who suffered for us*, to the end of the *Trisagium*, declaring thereby that the whole Trinity suffered, and giving rise to the Heresie of the *Theopaschites*, Evag Lib. iii cap 16 Niceph Lib xviii cap. 51 Afterwards the Eutychians were divided among themselves some of them refused (with *Moggus* Bishop of *Alexandria*) to Anathematize the Council of *Chalcedon*, others divided from him therein, whereupon they gained the Name of the *Acephali* or *Men without a Head*, which Name afterwards was given to all the rigid Eutychians every where The more moderate of these Hereticks, gained the Name of [illegible], the *Hesitants* or *Doubters* Leont de Sect From these Eutychians spawned some other Sects, as the *Phthartitæ* who would have Christ's Body to be corruptible, and the *Aphthartitæ* who would have it to be incorruptible From the same arose the Tritheites who owned Three Gods, *Niceph Lib* xviii *cap* 45 These Quarrels continued on till the Reign of *Justinian*, who was persuaded to publish an Edict, to condemn *Origen*'s Opinions, whose Books were in esteem among several of the Clergy This netled *Theodorus* Bishop of *Cæsarea*, a great Admirer of *Origen*, and Favourer of *Eutyches* his Doctrine, to perswade the Emperor to publish an Edict likewise to condemn three Particulars or Heads of the Council of *Chalcedon* 1 That which countenanced the Writings of *Theodorus Mopsuestenus* 2 The Epistle of *Ibas* 3 *Theodoret*'s Book against *Cyril* All of them Authors who had written contrary to the Eutychian Doctrine These are the *tria capitula* the three Chapters as they are called, that have made such a Noise in the World *Justinian*, according as was desired of him, publishes his Edict against the three Chapters, *A D* DXLVI When *Vigilius* Bishop of *Rome* and most of the Western Bishops refuse to receive at last he does it faintly, qualifying it with the Clause *salvâ Concilii Chalcedonensis reverentia* But the Emperor insists to have him recognize it absolutely this *Vigilius* refusing to do, is insulted by the Emperor's Guards, and pulled from the Altar of the Church he fled to, in a most scandalous manner The Emperor by this fierceness having brought matters to a worse Issue than he found them, thought to piece up all by a Council held at *Constantinople*, *A D* DLIII about the matter of the three Chapters, they condemning 60 Particulars in the Books of *Mopsuestenus*, but letting *Ibas* and *Theodoret* alone This quieted Matters pretty well for a time in the East, but the Bishops of *Italy*, *Africa*, &c refused to condemn any thing in those Chapters, and this Controversy was not composed in the West till the time of *Gregory* the Great, who wrote several Epistles to put an end to it And in the East the Eutychian Doctrines broke out again, when the Heresie of the Monothelites arose, which is but another Branch of Eutychianism

II But it must be observed that these Eutychian Notions are contrary to the Doctrine of the Holy Scriptures, which so plainly assert *two Natures* in Christ For all those Places of Scripture are a Proof of this, where our Saviour is declared to be God, and those where he is declared to be Man But there are several Passages in which both Natures are mentioned together As in that of S. *Paul*, *Concerning his Son Jesus Christ our Lord, which was made of the Seed of David according to the Flesh*, Rom i 3 Where one part of the Verse relates to Christ's Divine, and the other to his human Nature In the first Chapter of the *Hebrews*, in respect of his Divinity he is said to be *the brightness of the Father's Glory*, and the *express Image of his Person*, in the next Chapter, it is said, *we see Jesus, who was made a little lower than the Angels for the suffering of Death crowned with Glory and Honour, that he by the Grace of God should taste Death for every Man*, which is plainly spoken of his Humanity So Col i 14 in respect of his Humanity it is said, *In whom we have Redemption through his Blood, even the Forgiveness of Sins*, but the next Verse relates to his Divinity *Who is the Image of the Invisible God, the first born of every Creature*, Col i 15

The two Natures of Christ proved from Scripture

III The Arguments drawn from Reason for the Confutation of the Eutychian Heresie, and for asserting the Distinction of the two Natures in Christ are chiefly these (1) Because Union does suppose Distinction or Division For thus *Theodoret* argues [illegible] *Without Distinction or Division, it is not to be understood how any thing can be united For he that supposes Union supposes likewise Division* Theod in Conf Anath 3 Tom 6 Cyr Op (2) Because a Distinction remains in other Unions Thus *Vigilius* comments on this Head *Sicut homo alia caro & alia Anima sed unus idemque homo Anima & Caro Ita et [illegible] Christus duæ Substantiæ [illegible] sed una divina, altera humana* As in Man the Flesh is one thing and the Soul another, and yet both Flesh and Soul is one Man So [illegible] the same Christ, there are two Substances, the one Divine, the other Human (3) Because the Properties or Idioms, both of Christ's Divinity and his Humanity, are reciprocally communicable to one another For thus *Vigilius* in his Book against *Eutyches* *Si ergo me interroges utrum Christus habeat [illegible] an non habeat, respondebo tibi, & habet & non habet. habet [illegible] non habet secundum [illegible]. If you ask me, whether Christ hath a beginning or no, I will answer, he has and he has not He has according to his Humanity, and he has not according to his Divinity* And again *Quicquid est proprium verbi est commune [illegible] carni, & quicquid est proprium carnis [illegible] Verbo [illegible] Verbum & Caro unus est Christus & una Persona Whatever is proper to the Word is common to the Human Nature, and whatever is proper to the Human Nature is common to the Word: Therefore the Word is one Christ and one Person.*

Reasons for asserting two Natures in Christ

1 Union supposes Distinction

2 The like Distinction in other Union

3 Because the Idioms of one Nature [illegible] communicated to the other

in One Christ] The Words *One Christ* are here set down, partly in Agreement with the Holy Scriptures which assert the same, and partly in Opposition to the Nestorian Heresie, which asserted such a Distinction in the Natures of Christ as made them to be two Persons, or in effect two Christs We shall give a short account of the Rise of this Heresie, as we have done of the others, though, if we had observed the Order of Time, and not the Words of the Articles, we should have related this, before the Heresie of *Eutyches*

Of the Nestorian Heresie

This Heresie was preached by *Nestorius* Bishop of *Constantinople*, about the Year of our Lord CCCCXXX *Nestorius* was born at *Germanicia*, a little Town in *Syria*, and having travelled into several Countries to improve his Studies, and to exercise his Talent of Eloquence, which he was remarkable for, particularly the sweetness of his Voice, he at last settled at *Antioch* Socr Lib vii cap 29 Theod Lib iv de Hær cap 12 He is said some time to have lead a Monastick Life *Nic Lib* xiv *cap* 36 but afterward taking Orders he became a celebrated Preacher, and was the more admired for the Gravity of his Temper, and for his studious Retirement *Evag Lib* i *cap* 7 In the Year CCCCXXVII *Sisinnius* Bishop of *Constantinople* dying, the Emperors were willing that a Foreigner should rather succeed in that See than a Native, and *Nestorius* being of the same City from whence the famous *John Chrysostom* came, they cast their Eyes upon him, and in the Year CCCCXXVIII he was ordained Bishop of *Constantinople* At his first Entrance upon his Bishoprick, he was a fierce Prosecutor of the Hereticks He used a strange sort of Expression in a Sermon before the Emperor *Theodosius* *Give me, O Emperor, the World free from Hereticks, and I in lieu of it will give you Heaven Joyn with me in destroying the Hereticks, and I will joyn with you to Conquer the Persians* These Expressions though they were pleasing to some of the Catholicks, yet it alienated the Affections of many from him *Act Conc Eph Par* iii He had been acquainted with *Theodorus* of *Mopsuestia*, a Man of Heterodox Principles, from whom 'tis thought he received some Prejudices against the Doctrine of the Trinity *Evag Lib* i *cap* 2 These Notions he privately communicated to *Anastasius* a Presbyter, who was a Creature of his, declaring to him chiefly his dislike the Word of θεοτόκος, *the Mother of God*, or *she that brought forth God* *Anastasius* preaching a publick Sermon, at which *Nestorius* was present, used this Expression *Let no one call* Mary *the Mother of God, for* Mary *was a Women but 'tis impossible for a Woman to bring forth a God* Socr Lib vii cap 32 *Cyril* writes, that he persuaded one *Dorotheus* a Bishop who had Dependence upon him, to declare an Anathema against all that should call the Blessed Virgin θεοτόκος, Cyr Ep 9 This having been long used as a pious Expression without Offence, the People were highly displeased to have it thus opposed by Persons in holy Orders, but were more enraged when *Dorotheus* and *Anastasius* were defended by the Patriarch *Nestorius* himself, who in several Homilies to the People maintain'd what the others had said, supporting his Opinion with Arguments which were thought contrary to the Catholick Faith This made the greatest part of the City refuse to joyn Communion with him *Soc Lib* vii *cap* 28 *Nestorius* having given out some Copies of his Homilies, a Transcript of them got into *Ægypt*, and occasioned Doubts in the Minds of some simple and honest Men there This occasioned *Cyril* Bishop of *Alexandria*, suppressing his Name, to write a Letter to the Ægyptian Monks, to guard them against the Heterodoxy contained in *Nestorius's* his Homilies A Copy of this Letter getting to *Constantinople*, was highly satisfactory there, and confirmed many Persons in the Catholick Faith, who had been wavering on account of *Nestorius* his Doctrine, and it coming to be known that it was written by *Cyril*, the Magistrates of *Constantinople* writ a Letter of Thanks to him for it *Cyr Ep* 9 This Letter of *Cyril* nettled *Nestorius*, which *Cyril* perceiving wrote to him very kind Letters, persuading him to retract those Heterodox Notions which he had vented in those Homilies But, instead of this, *Nestorius* defends his Opinion of the different Personalities of Christ And after much Paper combat, they proceed to Anathematize one another *Cyril* draws up 12 Articles of Heresie against *Nestorius*, and *Nestorius* in his turn draws up as many against *Cyril*, Act Eph Con Great Troubles arising from this Controversie, the Emperor thought it convenient that a General Council should be called, to meet at *Ephesus* on *Whitsunday*, *A D* CCCCXXX Most of the Bishops from the several Countries met at the time appointed, only *John* Bishop of *Antioch*, who was a Friend of *Nestorius*, with some other Bishops whom he could influence, staid away during the beginning of the Assembly But however the Fathers there present proceed without them And from the Evidence of his own Homilies and Letters, they condemn him for Heresie in holding two Persons in Christ *Conc Eph Par* 2 Some Days afterwards the Party of *John* of *Antioch* arrived at *Ephesus*, who hearing of the Condemnation of *Nestorius*, refused to joyn with the Council, but form an Anti-Synod of themselves, and Anathematize *Cyril*, as the Fathers of the Council had done to *Nestorius* This Anti-Synod having the favour of the Counts *Irenæus* and *Candidianus*, loaded the Council with many Calumnies, much prejudicing the Emperor against them, the same Persons hindring the Letters, written by the Council in their Vindication, from coming to the Emperor's Hands, *Con. Epl ib* After this seven Deputies, from each Synod, are appointed by the Emperor to bring Matters to Agreement, but nothing is done, for the Deputies of the Council will not agree to the acquitting of *Nestorius* At length the Emperor takes the Matter into his Hands, confirms the Condemnation of *Nestorius*, but acquits *Cyril* and all others whom the Anti Synod had accused The See of *Constantinople* being thus void *Maximinianus* is chosen into his Place *Socr Lib* vii *cap* 35 And the Church had quiet, till it was disturbed again by the Heresie of *Eutyches*, which has been before related Indeed *Nestorius* and his Followers pretended, that He had hard Usage afforded him by the Synod, he never having in Words asserted that there were two Christs, or that Christ had two Persons But this *Cyril* says was owing to Heretical Craft Ἀλλ ἐπειδὴ σκοπὸς ἐκείνοις δύο λέγειν χριστοὺς, ᾗ δύο υἱὲς, ᾗ τ [illegible] ἄνθρωπον ἰδικῶς, τ δ θεὸν ἰδικῶς εἶτα μόνων τῶν προσώπων ποιεῖν τ ἕνωσιν, διὰ τοῦτο ποικίλλονται, ᾗ πεφωρασμένως [illegible] ἐν ἁμαρτίαις *Whereas their design is to assert two Christs and two Sons, and to make Christ to be singly Man and singly God, but having gained their Point in this to declare for an Unity of the Persons but in this they only act a part, and procure a Pretext for their Impiety* Cyr Ep 8 ad Cler Const The same is imputed to him, by other Writers who give an account of his Heresie. For *Leontius* says, that δύο ὑποστάσεις ἔλεγε ᾗ διαιρέσιν *He asserted two Personalities in Christ, and a Division of his Divinity and Humanity* Leon de Sect And *Vincentius Lirinensis* testifies *Nestorius, contrario Apollinari morbo, dum se duas in Christo Substantias distinguere simulat, duas introducit repente Personas & inaudito scelere duos vult esse filios Dei, duos Christos unum Deum, alterum hominem unum qui ex Patre, alterum qui sit generatus ex Matre* Nestorius, *falling into a contrary Heresie to that of* Apollinaris, *whilst he pretends to distinguish the two Substances in Christ, in the mean time introduces two Persons and by an unheard of Impiety, will have that there are two Sons of God and two Christs one God, the other Man one born of his Father, the other generated of his Mother* Most certain it is he was a bold positive Man, and talked and wrote many things very unjustifiable. There was not so much harm in his first opposing the use of the Word θεοτόκος for indeed this was an odd Expression, and occasioned many unwarrantable Honours, which were afterwards paid to the Blessed Virgin But what he said afterwards, to defend this Opposition, was directly contrary to the received Catholick Faith, and to the Holy Scriptures. He probably might have waved his Condemnation, had he managed himself with tolerable Temper or Discretion What he said just before his Trial at the Council, and was witnessed there by two Bishops, *Theodotus* and *Acacius*, do sufficiently shew the Temper and Opinion of the Man διμηνιαῖον ἢ τριμηνιαῖον μὴ δεῖν λέγεσθαι θεὸν 'tis *a shame to reckon him a God, that was once two Months, or three Months old* Conc Eph Par. ii Act i. Which Expression was the more scandalous, because it was one of the common Scoffs of *Celsus* and *Porphyry*, and other Enemies of Christianity.

II That Christ is one Person, is the Doctrine of the holy Scriptures, *The Word was made Flesh and dwelt among us*, John i. 14 The same Christ *which descended* (*i e.* the unbodied *Logos*) *was the same that ascended* (*viz* with his Body) Eph iv 10. The same Christ *who was in the form of God and thought it no robbery to be equal with God, took upon him the form of a Servant*, Phil iv 6, 7 *There is one Mediator between God and Men, the Man Christ Jesus*, 1 Tim ii 5

One Person of Christ proved from Scripture.

III The Reasons which have been urged for our Saviour's being one Person, are chiefly these (1) If the Divinity and Humanity of Christ made two Personalities, they would not be so Physically and Substantially United, that the Properties of the one should be attributed to the other, as we find they are in Scripture Now this could not be according to *Nestorius's* Hypothesis, who made Christ θεὸν ἰδικῶς and ἄνθρωπον ἰδικῶς, *God singly and Man singly* Wherefore the Nestorians avoided all Expressions, which might denote a Physical Union They avoided the use of the Word ἕνωσις which signified the being *made one*, and on that account seemed to bear too hard upon their Notion of two Persons, chusing rather to express themselves by ἐνοίκησις *Inhabitation* or *Indwelling* by συνάφεια *Consecration* by σχέσις or ἕξις *Familiarity* or *Friendship* vid Cyr cont Nest (2) Because if the Conjunction of the two Natures of Christ were not Physical, or if there were two different Personalities, the Divinity would not be United to Christ, more than to any Prophet who was inspired by God, or any good Man to whom God is present by his Grace. For thus S *Cyril* Reasons with great strength Κακούργως ταῦτα [illegible] ἐν ᾗ φύσει ᾗ ἀληθῶς υἱὸν ἐνανθρωπήσαντα, [illegible] σεσαρκωμένον διελόντες εἰς δύο παραιτοῦνται [illegible] ἕνωσιν, συνάφειαν δὲ ὀνομάζουσιν, ἣν ἂν ἔχοι τυχὸν ᾗ ἕτερός τις πρὸς θεὸν, ὡς [illegible] ἀρετῆς ᾗ ἁγιασμοῦ [illegible] συνῆμμένος *They act very craftily, after they have divided into two the one Christ who was made the Son of Man and incarnate, refuse to use the Word* ἕνωσις [Union] *but chuse rather to use* συνάφεια

Reasons for the single Personality of Christ

who truly Suffered, was Crucified, Dead and Buried, to reconcile his Father to us, and to be a Sacrifice, not only for Original Guilt, but also for Actual Sins of Men

n who truly Suffered, was Dead and Buried, o to reconcile his Father to us, and to be a Sacrifice not only for Orginal Guilt, but also for * Actual Sins of Men.

Deus & verus Homo, qui vere passus est, crucifixus, mortuus & sepultus, ut patrem nobis reconciliaret, essetque hostia, non tantum pro culpa originis, verum etiam pro omnibus actualibus hominum peccatis

* *All Actual Sins*, MS CCC 1571

ωσια [Sociation] *which any one may have with God being united to him by Virtue or Sanctification*, Cyr Tom.v ed Par 733 The same Argument is urged in these Verses of *Gregory Nazianzen*

Θεῷ [illegible] μετέσχεν ἀνθρώπου φύσις
Οὐχ ὡς Προφήτης, ἤ τις ἄλλ[illegible] Θεῷ
[illegible]
[illegible]

When Christ did Man become, he did partake
Of God in full, not like to Prophet,
Or other Man inspired, who don't partake
So much of God as of the things of God
The Union was Substantial, as the Rays
Are with the Sun United
Greg Naz Carm de vita sua

3 Because the like is observed in the Unions of other Substances, as particularly that of the Soul of Man with the Body For thus an antient Writer in these Controversies *Anima rationalis & Corpus hominis identitatem naturæ circa unitionem suscipiunt The Rational Soul and the Body of Man undergo the same Identity, as to matter of Union*, Rust Diac Dial contr Aceph The same Argument is advanced in the Athanasian Creed *As the reasonable Soul and Flesh is one Man, so God and Man is one Christ*

Reality of Christ's Suffering

n *Who truly Suffered*, &c] The History of our Saviour's suffering Death, and Burial, is so fully related in the Gospels, and owned by the Heathens themselves, who frequently upbraided them for their believing and worshipping a crucified Saviour, that nothing but unaccountable humour or stupidity could make any doubt of it But some there formerly were, who would have all Christ's Passion to be but mere Shew and Appearance, from whence they got the Name of *Docetæ* and *Phantasiasts*. They were as early as *Ignatius* his Time, whose Opinions he opposes several times in his Epistles, particularly in this Passage Ἔφαγε καὶ ἔπιεν ἀληθῶς, ἐσταυρώθη καὶ ἀπέθανεν ἐπὶ Ποντίου Πιλάτου ἀληθῶς [illegible] ἐσταυρώθη καὶ ἀπέθανε, βλεπόντων ἐπουρανίων, καὶ ἐπιγείων καὶ καταχθονίων *He truly Eat and Drank, and was crucified and died under* Pontius Pilate *He was, I say, truly crucified and died, and not in Appearance Those that were in Heaven and Earth and Hell viewing him* Epist ad Trall The same Heresie was maintained by some in *Athanasius* his Time, as appears from that of him, wherein he thus opposes the Phantasiasts [illegible] πάντα ἀληθῆ πιστεύειν, &c *We must either believe that all things in his History are true, and then we must own the Truth of his Passion, or if we say that he suffered impassibly, then we must account all other Passages of his to be Figure and Fancy If he did not suffer truly, neither did he arise truly If he did not truly tast of Death, neither did he extinguish the sting of Death we are still in our Sins, Death still reigneth over all, and we are still Strangers to the Inheritance* Athan adv eos qui Verb impat

o *To reconcile his Father to us*] These Words of the Article do plainly set forth the most necessary Christian Doctrine of Christ's Satisfaction, whereby our blessed Lord, out of his great Love to Mankind, was willing to suffer Death for our Sins, that thereby the Authority of God's Laws might be kept up and his Justice vindicated, and we might be delivered from the Punishment of Eternal Death The Socinians indeed do with all their Might oppose this Doctrine, because it has so nigh a Relation to Christ's Divinity, which they deny, and therefore will not allow, that Christ died to make Satisfaction for our Sins, but only to confirm the Doctrine which he taught, and to afford us an eminent Example of Patience Now for the better understanding of this Doctrine, it will be requisite to remark the following Particulars

Of the Satisfaction of Christ.

Necessity of Christ's Satisfaction.

I That it is necessary, that such a Satisfaction should be made for our Sins The Socinians are so far from allowing any such Necessity, that they will not own that God had any just Reasons at all to require any Satisfaction to be made, for the saving Men's Souls Some others, on the other extreme, deny it to be at all in the Power of God to have pardoned Sin, without this Satisfaction of his Son But as the former Opinion is contrary to the whole tenor of Scripture, so the latter seems to be too bold an Assertion it not having sufficient warrant from Scripture, and seems to entrench upon the Liberty and Power of the Divine Nature, which has Infinite ways of working, which we are not able to comprehend That of the Apostle ought to be a Check to such bold Determinations *Who hath known the Mind of the Lord, and who hath been his Counsellor?* Rom xi 34 *How unsearchable are his Judgments, and his ways past finding out!* Rom xi 33 The Antients were more modest in this point For *Athanasius* says, Ἠδύνατο γὰρ [illegible] μὴ [illegible] εἰπεῖν ὁ Θεὸς καὶ λῦσαι τὴν κατάραν [illegible] ἀλλ' σκοπεῖν δεῖ τὸ τοῖς ἀνθρώποις λυσιτελοῦν, [illegible] *God might, if he had pleased, without coming into the World, have by speaking a Word dissolved the Curse But we ought to consider what Method was more profitable for Man, and not to think in all things what God might have done* So S *Austin* declares, *non [illegible] modum possibilem Deo liberandi [illegible] Dei [illegible] [illegible]* *That God was not at a loss for other possible Methods of freeing us, but this was the more convenient Method of rescuing us from Misery* Therefore avoiding both these Extremes, we have very good Ground from Scripture to assert, That God had very just and sufficient Reasons moving him, to pursue this Method which he took, for the Redemption of the World, by the Satisfaction of his Son

God's Goodness a Motive to accept of Christ's Satisfaction for the Pardon of Sin.

(1) For he could not but, in general, be inclined to find out a way to Pardon Man's Sins, by his Goodness, and Mercy For when he is described in Scripture to be the *Lord God merciful and gracious*, Exod xxxiv 6 *the Lord good and ready to forgive*, Psal lxxxvi 5 when, after his Example, we are commanded, to *be merciful as our Father in heaven is merciful*, Luke vi 36 when we are informed of *the riches of his goodness*, and that *the goodness of God leadeth to Repentance*, Rom ii 4 we cannot but think this glorious Attribute did incline him to rescue us from Eternal Misery

His hatred of Sin a Motive to pardon Sin [illegible]

(2) When God had positively declared his Aversion to Sin *that he hated all the workers of iniquity*, Psal v 5 that *they who are of a froward heart are an abomination to the Lord*, Prov xi 20. that he will *visit for such things*, and that his *Soul will be avenged*, Jer v 31. All these and innumerable other Expressions in Scripture do denote God's great Detestation of Sin And having forbidden Sin by so many plain and positive Laws, and repeated Commands, given out by the greatest Authority, that of an Almighty Creator and which notwithstanding Men did continually break, by reason of the Violence of their Lusts and Passions, he was willing to adjust such a temperature of his Goodness and Mercy, as should mani-

 fest

fest at the same time both his hatred to Sin, and withal a regard for the observance of his Laws, so that by a commutation of the Punishment, his Authority might be preserved, and Mankind be freed from the Miseries, which their Disobedience subjected them to.

Truth of Christ's Satisfaction proved from his Mediation

II. That Christ did make a true proper Satisfaction for us, in dying for our Sins (1) Because Christ is frequently in Scripture called our Mediator, which does denote, that he was to make up a Difference which was between God and Man, and to procure our Peace with God, whom we had offended by our Disobedience, this being a Metaphor drawn from the usual Carriage of an offended Person, who will not admit to his Presence one who has grievously injured him, and therefore the Reconciliation must be adjusted by a third Person. Thus Christ is said to be the *Mediator of the New Testament, that by means of Death, for the Redemption of the Transgressions that were under the first Testament, they which are called might receive the Promise of eternal Inheritance*, Heb ix. 15. Which Words do imply more than a bare Mediation, moreover denoting that that Mediation would not be accepted, but only by the vicarious Suffering of the Mediator himself. And that we may not be mistaken in the true Sense of the Word Mediator, the Scripture, when it is mentioned, joyns something of Sacrifice, Propitiation, or vicarious Suffering. As *Heb* xii 24 *to Jesus the Mediator of the new Covenant, and to the blood of sprinkling, which speaketh better things than that of Abel*. And so 1 *Tim* ii 6 *One Mediator between God and Men, the Man Christ Jesus, who gave himself a ransom for all*. To avoid the force of these express Texts of Scripture, the Socinians pretend, that in Scripture Language a Mediator signifies an Interpreter, or one who makes known the Mind of one Person to another, and in this Sense *Moses* is called a Mediator, *Gal* iii. 19. because he made known God's Will to the People of *Israel*, by his Mediation or Interposition. But this is a Modern Quirk invented by these Hereticks, which the Antients knew nothing of. For they understood the forementioned Passages of Scripture, to denote Reconciliation or Satisfaction. *Gregory Nyssen* explaining the Sense of that Passage, 1 *Tim* ii 6 *One Mediator between*, &c says ὅλον ἡμῖν ε... αὐδα τὸ στοιχ... τῆς μυστηρίου διὰ τῆς μεσίτου λέξεως διακα... ... *By the Word Mediator he understands the whole Series of the Mystery of our Redemption*. Greg Nyss cont Eunom Lib 1. But long before him *Irenæus* declares what was the Notion of a Mediator in his Time. Ἔδει γὰρ τὸν μεσίτην θεοῦ τε καὶ ἀνθρώπων διὰ τῆς ἰδίας πρὸς ἑκατέρους οἰκειότητος, εἰς φιλίαν καὶ ὁμόνοιαν τοὺς ἀμφοτέρους συναγαγεῖν. *It was expedient there should be a Mediator between God and Men, that by partaking of both their Natures, he might reduce them both into Friendship and Concord*. Iren Lib iii cap 10. To the same purport speaks S *Chrysostom* ... δύο ... &c *As when two Persons are a fighting, one comes between them, and puts an end to the strife and difference, so did Christ do. God was angry with us, but we did not regard his anger, and slighted our kind Master, Christ threw himself (...) as a Mediator brought us into Friendship with one another, and he himself bore the Punishment of the Father which was due to us*. Chrys Hom de Ascens.

Truth of Christ's Satisfaction proved from his Redemption

(2) Christ by his Death made a true and proper Satisfaction for our Sins, Because he is so frequently in Scripture said to have redeemed us. The Apostle says his *Death was for the Redemption of the Transgressions that were under the first Testament, that they which are called might receive the promise of eternal Inheritance*. Heb ix 15. So again, *For all have sinned, and come short of the Glory of God, being justified freely by his Grace through the Redemption that is in Jesus Christ, whom God hath set forth to be a Propitiation*, Rom iii 23, 24, 25. And elsewhere, *In whom we have Redemption through his Blood, the Forgiveness of Sins, according to the riches of his Grace*, Eph i. 7. So S *James*, *Forasmuch as ye know, that ye are not redeemed, with corruptible things as Silver and Gold —— but with the precious Blood of Christ, as of a Lamb without blemish and without spot*. 1 Pet i 18, 19. The Greek Word which we translate Redemption is ἀπολύτρωσις, which signifies a Deliverance from a very sad and deplorable Condition, such as that of a Captive was before his Ransom was paid. Which Expression so frequently used by the Apostles in their Writings, was originally grounded on our Saviour's own Words *The Son of Man came to give his Life* (λύτρον) *a Ransom for many*, Mat. xx 28. Mark x 45. Therefore upon the whole, what tolerable Sense can be put upon these Words, but that our Souls being in an evil and lost Condition, like that of a Prisoner in Chains and doomed to Death, our Saviour paid down his own Blood as a λύτρον or Price of Ransom, to free us from this Misery? This the Antients took to be the Sense of these Passages. St *Basil* has a noble Expression in treating upon that place of the Psalmist, *No Man may deliver his Brother, nor make an Agreement unto God for him*, he says, Οὐ γὰρ δύναται ἄνθρωπος εὑρεῖν τι... ...τον, ἵνα δῷ ὑπὲρ λυτρώσεως τῆς ψυχῆς αὐτοῦ; Ἀλλ' εὑρέθη ἓν ὁμοῦ πάντων ἀνθρώπων ἀντάξιον· ὃ ἐδόθη εἰς τιμὴν λυτρώσεως τῆς ψυχῆς ἡμῶν, τὸ ἅγιον, καὶ πολυτίμιον αἷμα τοῦ Κυρίου ἡμῶν Ἰησοῦ Χριστοῦ, ὃ ὑπὲρ ἡμῶν ἐξέχεε πάντων ... καὶ τιμῆς ἠγοράσθημεν. *What can a Man find any thing that is of sufficient value to pay down as a ransom for a Soul? Yes, there is found that which is of value enough to ransom all Mens Souls, that which was given as a price of our Redemption, the most precious Blood of our Lord Jesus Christ, which he shed for us all*. Bas Hom. in Psal xlviii. S *Austin* understands the Redemption so frequently mention'd in Scripture, in the same Sense. *Tenebantur homines capti sub Diabolo & Dæmonibus serviebant, sed redempti sunt a captivitate. Vendere enim se potuerunt, sed redimere non potuerunt. Venit Redemptor & dedit pretium, fudit Sanguinem suum, & emit orbem terrarum. Quæritis quid emerit? videte quid dederit, & invenite quid emerit. Sanguis Christi pretium est. Tanti quid valet? Quid nisi totus orbis? quid nisi omnes gentes? All Men once were held captive by the Devil, serving wicked Spirits, but now they are redeemed from their Captivity. They were able to sell themselves, but they were not able to redeem themselves. Then comes a Redeemer, he pays down the Price, he pours out his Blood, and with it buys the whole World. Do you ask what he bought? see what he gave, and that will tell you what he bought. The price was the Blood of Christ. And what could come up to the value of that? What but the whole World? What but all Nations?* Aug Enar in Psal xcv. *Prudentius* teaches the same Doctrine in Verse.

Jesus resulsit omnium
Pius Redemptor gentium, &c.
Felix Johannes mergere
Illum tremiscit flumine,
Potest suo qui sanguine
Peccata mundi tergere.

The conquering Jesus did appear
All Nations great Deliverer, &c
The happy John *all trembling stood*
To plunge him into Jordan*'s Flood,*
Who by his Blood a way would find
To cleanse the Sins of all Mankind
Hymn in Epiph

From his Reconciliation

(3) Christ by his Death truly satisfied for our Sins, because the Scripture does imply this by so frequently asserting Christ's reconciling us to God, which does manifestly denote that God was displeased and angry with us before. Thus S *Paul*. *For when we were enemies, we were reconciled to God by the Death of his Son*, Rom v 10. *All things are of God, who hath reconciled us to himself by Jesus Christ, and hath given unto us the mystery of reconciliation, to wit, that God was in Christ, reconciling the World unto himself, not imputing their trespasses unto them*, 2 Cor. v 18, 19. And *(having made Peace thro' the blood of his Cross) by him to reconcile all things to himself*, Col i 20. That *he might reconcile both unto God in one body by the cross*, Eph ii 16. And that it may appear plainer, that this Reconciliation did imply an Anger, we may observe that in several Places of Scripture Christ is called a *Propitiation*, Rom iii 25. 1 John ii. 2. the original Words are ἱλαστήριον ἱλασμός, which signifie an appeasing of the Deity. For so the most antient Greek Authors use it

Ἔνθα δέ μιν ταύροισι, καὶ ἀρνειοῖς ἱλάονται
Κοῦροι Ἀθηναίων

Th' Athenian Youth with Goats and Lambs appease
The Goddess —— Hom Il. ii

Therefore *Hesychius* explains ἱλάονται by ...... to be made kind or favourable. The Socinians being pressed with the force of these plain Texts say, that God is not said to be reconciled to us, but we to God. but that is said for

for want of observing the use of the Words καταλλάττεσθαι and διαλλάττεσθαι in the New Testament, *Mat* v 24 1 *Cor* vii. 11 For the Greeks not having any reciprocal Conjugation answering to the Hebrew *Hithpael*, are forced to use a passive Verb So that when we are said to be *reconciled to God*, the Meaning is we are made reconciled, i e put in such a Condition that he is no longer Angry with us For so the Word is used when the offending Person is bidden to be *reconciled to his Brother*, Mat v 24 and the Wife to be *reconciled to her Husband*, 1 Cor vii 11 whereas in our ordinary way of speaking, he that had born the Injury should be said to be reconciled to the other and the Husband to the Wife

From the Substitution of his Person in our stead. (4) Christ truly made Satisfaction by his Death, Because he is so frequently in Scripture said to die *for us*, (i e in our stead Our *English* Word *for* is expressed by two Prepositions in the Greek, sometimes by ὑπὲρ, sometimes by ἀντί *God spared not his own Son but delivered him up* (ὑπὲρ) for *us all*, Rom viii 32 *In due time Christ died* (ὑπὲρ) for *the ungodly*, Rom v 6 *Christ died once for Sins, the just* (ὑπὲρ *for the unjust*, 1 Pet. iii. 18 *That he by the grace of God should tast of Death*, (ὑπὲρ παντὸς) *for every Man*, Heb ii 9 From which Expression it is clear that Christ died in our stead, and suffered Punishment for us, that we might escape it. For though the Præposition ὑπὲρ sometimes has other Senses, yet when 'tis joyned with Verbs, which denote *dying*, *suffering*, &c it signifies *instead of* So θνήσκω ὑπὲρ σέθεν, *I die for you*, Eurip in Alcest ἐρώτησον τούτους, μᾶλλον δὲ ἐγὼ ὑπὲρ σοῦ τούτους. *Ask these Persons, or otherways I will ask them, for you* Demonst pro Corona Therefore the Socinians talk ridiculously, when they would have the Word *for* to signifie *by occasion of* But there are two Texts of Scripture denoting the same thing which are expressed by the Præposition ἀντί Christ came to lay down his Life a Ransom (λύτρον ἀντὶ πολλῶν) *for many* Mat xx 28 Mark x 45 But this Præposition, not only in profane Authors, but likewise in Scripture, always signifies *instead of*, 1 Pet iii 9. Rom xii 17. Mat v 38 Heb xii. 16 And in this Sense the Antients always understood these Passages Thus *Justin Martyr*, Εἰ δὲ καὶ τὸν ἑαυτοῦ Χριστὸν ὑπὲρ τῶν ἐκ παντὸς γένους ἀνθρώπων ὁ πατὴρ τῶν ὅλων τὰς πάντων κατάρας ἀναδέξασθαι ἐβουλήθη εἰδὼς ὅτι ἀναστήσει αὐτὸν σταυρωθέντα καὶ ἀποθανόντα, &c *If therefore God the Father of all things was willing that his Christ should take upon him the Curses upon all Human kind, knowing that he would raise him up after he was crucified and dead* Coll cum Tryph So *Tertullian*, *Christum oportebat pro omnibus gentibus Sacrificium, qui tanquam ovis ad victimam ductus est, & velut agnus coram tondente*, &c *It was requisite, that Christ should be a Sacrifice for all Nations, who went as a Sheep to the Slaughter*, &c Tert adv Jud cap 13

From the Prophesies concerning him. (5 Christ's Death was a Satisfaction for our Sins, Because the Prophesies of his Death, do plainly denote a true Satisfaction, Expiation and vicarious Suffering To mention only the famous Prophesie of the liii of *Isaiah* Though the modern Jews and the Socinians, do attribute this Prophesie to *Jeremiah*, contrary to the Tradition both of the Jewish and Christian Churches, yet the antienter Jews interpreted it of the Messias *Jonathan* in his Targum, explains the Words which begin the Prophesie, *Behold my Servant shall deal prudently*, Isa lii 13 Hou jatzliach Meshica *My Servant the Messias shall prosper*, &c referring all that is said to the liv Chapter, unto the Messias So do *Rabbi Solomon*, *Beresh th Rabba*, and the *Midrash* upon *Ruth*, as may be seen at large in *Raymundus Martinus* Pug Fid P iii Disp 3 cap 10 Now can any thing express a Satisfaction, or vicarious Punishment more fully than this Prophesie? Christ is there described, as one that has *born our Griefs and carried our Sorrows*, Isa liii 4 *as wounded for our Transgressions, bruised for our Iniquities the chastisement of our peace was upon him with his stripes we are healed*, v 5 It is there said that *the Lord laid on him the iniquity of us all*, v 6 that *for the transgression of my people was he stricken*, v 8 that *he should make his Soul an Offering for Sin*, v 10 that *he should justify many* and *bear their iniquities*, v 11 Now if this be a Prophesie of Christ, as no good Christian ever doubted of it, there is such undeniable Evidence of Christs Satisfaction, that a reasonable Man need not require more The force of this Prophesie, and the fulfilling thereof in Christ, is excellently well set out by *Eusebius* Καὶ καθ' ὃ τὸ γοῦν τὸ ἀρνός, &c.

" For as much as when one Member suffers all the Members suffer with it, so many Members suffering and sinning, Christ according to the Laws of Sympathy (because being the Word of God it pleased him to take upon him the form of a Servant and to dwell in one of our Tabernacles) took the Griefs of the suffering Members upon himself, made our Infirmities his own, for our sakes to endure Cold and Labour, according to the Conditions of Humanity Nor did this Lamb of God only do this, but he suffered and underwent Torment for our sakes, which he did not deserve, but was the occasion that our Sins, for the multitude of Offenders, were pardoned who underwent Death for our sakes, and Scourgings and Reproaches, taking to himself those Disgraces which we had merited, was made a Curse for us, and drew upon himself the Curse which was due to us For what was he else but our ἀντίψυχον, the price of our Lives? Therefore the Prophesie speaks this in our Names, *By his Stripes we are healed*, *The Lord hath laid upon the Iniquities of us all* Eusebi Demon Evan Lib x c 1

Because the Types which prefigured him were expiatory (6) Christ made a true Satisfaction for our Sins, Because the Sacrifices of the Old Testament which were truly expiatory were but Types which did prefigure his Passion, and received their force and efficacy from that There is no doubt to be made but, that the Sacrifices of the Old Law were to attone for the Sins of those who had trespassed or offended, *Lev Cap* v, and *Cap* v Because it is frequently said that *the Priest shall make an attonement for him before the Lord, and his Sin shall be forgiven him.* And it is as plain that the Scripture does as expresly declare, that the Death of Christ was prefigured by the Sacrifices of the Old Testament Almost the whole Epistle to the *Hebrews* is a Proof of this Assertion But particularly it is declared, that *the Law was but a shadow of good things, and not the very Image of things*, Heb x 1 They are said to be *Patterns of heavenly things, which are purified with better Sacrifices* (i e) *the Blood of Christ*, Heb ix 24 The old Law is said to be *a shadow of things to come whose Body is Christ*, Col. ii 17 And whereas the Sacrifices of the Old Testament are said to derive their force and efficacy from the great Sacrifice of Christ, *Dan* ix 27 *Heb* vii. 9, 10 undoubtedly the Sacrifice of Christ, which was not only prefigured and represented by these but gave them their Expiatory force, by the Relation they had to their Antitype, this I say must undoubtedly it self have the Nature of a true and proper Expiation or Satisfaction

The Satisfaction of Christ was most perfect. III The Satisfaction of Christ was not only true, but was likewise most perfect And this, (1) Because of the unspotted Holiness and the Infinite Dignity of the Person who suffered For both these are requisite for rendring a Mediator between God and Man compleat For it is not to be supposed that one Sinner should be a Redeemer to another, who stands in need of a Redeemer himself Which is the Reason several times assigned in Scripture *For he hath made him who knew no Sin to be Sin for us*, 2 Cor. v 21 So Heb vii 26. *For such an high Priest became us, who is holy, harmless, undefiled, separate from Sinners* But besides this Innocency, for the Perfection of a Mediator it is requisite, that he should be of an Infinite Dignity likewise, the Infinite Merits of whom should counterbalance the Infinite Demerits of Sin. Now our Saviour being God as well as Man is Infinite Dignity has made his Satisfaction in the highest Degree perfect Whereupon S *Basil* thus expresses himself. Εὑρέθη ἓν μόνον πάντων ἀντάξιον, ὃ ἐδόθη εἰς τιμὴν λυτρώσεως τῶν ψυχῶν ἡμῶν, τὸ ἅγιον καὶ πολύτιμον αἷμα τοῦ κυρίου ἡμῶν Ἰησοῦ Χριστοῦ *There was one Sacrifice found, which was beyond all others, that was given for the Redemption of our Souls, and that was the holy and precious blood of our Lord Jesus Christ* Hom in Psal xlviii (2.) The Satisfaction of Christ is most perfect, Because of the Unity of it. The Apostle lays great stress upon this to prove the Excellence and Perfection of the Sacrifice of Christ's Death For having shewn the Imperfection of the Jewish Sacrifices from the necessity of their being so frequently repeated, *Every Priest standeth daily ministring and offering oftentimes, the same Sacrifices which can never take away Sins But this Man after he had offered ONE Sacrifice for Sins, for ever sat down on the right hand of God For by ONE offering he hath perfected for ever them that are sanctified*, Heb. x 11, 12, 13

ARTICLE III.

III *Of the going down of Christ into Hell.*

As Christ died and was buried for us, so also it is to be believed, that he went down into Hell, for the Body lay in the Sepulchre until the Resurrection, but his Ghost departing from him, was with the Ghosts that were in Prison or in Hell, and did Preach to the same, as the Place of St *Peter* doth testifie

Of the going down of Christ into Hell

As Christ died for us and was buried, * so also [a] it is to be believed, that he [b] went down into Hell. †

* *So also is it to be believed* MSS. CCCC 1571
† *For his Body lay in the Grave till the Resurrection, but his Soul being separate from his Body remained with the Spirits which were detained in Prison that is to say in Hell, and there preached unto them* MSS CCC 1562 *scored with Minium, but numbred*

III De descensu Christi ad Inferos

Quemadmodum Christus pro nobis mortuus est, & sepultus, ita est etiam credendus ad Inferos descendisse

a *It is to be believed*] This Article is added, because it is a part of the Creed, though it must be owned it came but late into it For till near 400 Years after Christ it was not looked upon as an Article of Baptismal Faith, which every Catechumen was obliged to assent unto, before he was admitted to Baptism, but only as a Point of Orthodox Belief, which all good Christians believed as being grounded on Scripture and Catholick Tradition There is nothing of it to be found in the antient Rules of Faith mentioned by *Irenæus*, Lib 1 cap 2 or by *Tertullian*, adv Prax de Prescr cap 13 Nor in any of the Confessions of Faith set forth by the Four first general Councils, nor in S *Cyril*'s, or S *Austin*'s Expositions of the Creed The first time we meet with it is in the Creed of *Aquileia*, which *Ruffinus* commented upon who says, *nos illum ordinem sequimur, quam in Aquileiensi Ecclesia per Lavacri gratiam suscepimus We follow that Confession of Faith which we were baptized into, in the Church of* Aquileia Ruff Exp Symb But *Ruffinus* there owns, *quod in Ecclesiæ Romanæ Symbolo non habetur additum*, Descendit ad inferna, *sed neque in Orientis Ecclesiæ habetur hic sermo That this Clause*, He descended into Hell, *was not in the Creed of* Rome, *nor in the Churches of the East* ibid Whether it was in any other Creeds, and how long it had been used in the Church of *Aquileia*, is a matter uncertain. About the sixth Century it was taken into many Creeds, and established by the Fourth Council of *Toledo*, A. D 633

b *He went down into Hell*] For the better Understanding what we are obliged to profess by these Words, it will not be unnecessary to observe these following Particulars 1 That by the Word *Hell*, by which we render the Greek ᾅδης, is meant the place of Receptacle of Souls in the State of Separation This cannot be denied by any, who have but the least Tast of the Greek Tongue For there is no Sense to be made of this Word in most of the Antients, if it were restrained to signifie a Place of Torments, as in that of *Pindar*.

Τοιαισιν οργαῖς εὔχεται
Ἀ[illegible] αιδαι, γη-
ρ[illegible] δεξάμενος πολιον
ο Κλεονίκου παις——

In this Degree of Happiness
The Son of Cleonicus
Does wish to go to Hades,
Or in the same t'arrive to
A venerable old Age——
Pind Isl Od 8

Now we cannot suppose any one in his Senses to wish for Hell's Torments Or when the Poet declares his Opinion that that Person is Happy,

[illegible] πύλας αἴδαο περῆσαι
καὶ [illegible] γῆς [illegible]

Who soon as born into the World, arrives
At Hades *Gates, and under Ground does lie*
Deep in the Earth——

Theogn Eleg

But to be Happy in a State of Misery is wholly inconsistent This Consideration has led several into an Opinion, that the Word ᾅδης does always denote the general State of the Dead, whether they be in Misery or in Torment Though perhaps some Passages of the Antients may be brought to Countenance that Opinion, yet I think this Notion, however common, is not altogether so well grounded. For I take the exact Notion which the Antients had of *Hades* was, that it was a Place or Receptacle of the ordinary Souls of the departed, which were neither remarkably Ill, nor distinguishably Good Those who were very Pious and Good, were supposed to be instated in *Elysium*, according to the Notions of the Heathen Theology, upon which they formed their Speech, and those that were very Bad were supposed to be doomed to *Tartarus*, both which Places were distinguished from the *Hades*, or the ordinary Receptacle of Souls *Homer* is the most antient Author extant who mentions the *Hades*, but he makes *Tartarus*, or the Place where wicked Persons were Punished, to be widely different from *Hades*, as appears by these Verses.

Ἢ μιν ἑλὼν ῥίψω ἐς Τάρταρον ἠερόεντα
Τῆλε μάλ' ἧχι βάθιστον ὑπὸ χθονός ἐστι βέρεθρον
Ἔνθα σιδήρειαί τε πύλαι καὶ χάλκεος οὐδὸς
Τόσσον ἔνερθ' αἴδεω ὅσον οὐρανός ἐστ' ἀπὸ γαίης

I'll throw him down into dark Tartarus,
Which is a Pit far off and vastly deep,
The Gates whereof are Iron, the Pavement Brass,
Deep below HADES, *as Heav'n than Earth is higher*
Hom Iliad viii.

He may be thought in his *Odysses*, to have made *Tartarus* a Part of *HADES*, when he makes *Ulysses* going thither to have a view thereof but

——Ἰέναι
Εἰς Ἀΐδαο δόμους——

is not to go to *Hades*, but to the Regions of *Pluto*, under whose Dominions both *Elysium* and *Tartarus* were contained. *Hesiod* likewise sets *Tartarus* at a vast Distance from *Hades*

Τόσσον ἔνερθ' ὑπὸ γῆς ὅσον οὐρανός ἐστ' ἀπὸ γαίης
Ἶσον γὰρ τ' ἀπὸ γῆς ἐς Τάρταρον ἠερόεντα

As far as Earth from Heaven distant is,
So far from Earth is the Dark Tartarus

But to leave the Poets, we find that *Plato*, who had as just Notions as any one of the Heathen Theology, did not allow all the Places or States of the departed Souls to be contained under *Hades*, as appears by this remarkable Passage in his Tenth Book of Laws Μεταβάλλει μὲν τοίνυν πάνθ' ὅσα μέτοχά ἐστι ψυχῆς, &c *All things that have a Soul*

Soul are changeable, they having the cause of Change in themselves and being changeable are disposed of according to the Laws of Fate Those that have committed but small Offences, wander about in a Region near the superficies of of the Earth, others that have been greater Sinners sink in to a more inferior Region (οὓς ᾍΔΗΝ τε καὶ τὰ τούτων ἐχόμενα τῶν ὀνομάτων ἐπονομάζοντες) *which we call* HADES *or some such like Name, there they do, as they did when they were joyned with Bodies, dream and fear But when a Soul is arrived at a greater pitch of Virtue or Vice when by a settled habit it adheres to divine Virtue, and is framed according to that, then it is translated to a better Place but when it is contrarily affected it is carried to live in a contrary Place:* So that according to him, *HADES* belongs neither to the very Good nor to the very Bad Souls, but to those of a middle Nature. The Latins wanted a Word to express the Greek ᾍδης, therefore they called *Hades*, *Elysium*, *Tartarus*, and all by the Name of *Inferi*, (i.e. the *People below* But *Virgil* in describing the Place follows the Opinions of the Heathen Theology, which he had from the Greeks, and distinguishes the Place of Punishment from the common *Hades* That was the *Hades*, properly so called, in which he saw *Dido*, *Deiphobus*, &c but having carried his Hero over that, he next comes to describe the two other Places, one of Punishment, the other of Happiness, and then he thus expresses himself

Hic locus est, partes, ubi se via findit in ambas,
Dextera, quæ Ditis magni sub mœnia tendit,
Hac iter Elysium nobis at læva malorum
Exercet pœnas, & ad impia Tartara mittit

—— *Here is a Place where two ways meet,*
The right hand leads unto great Pluto's *Palace*
And to Elysium *on the left are Punish'd*
The Bad, and a Road leads to Tartarus.
Virg Æneid Lib vi

But it must be observed, that, tho' Persons in the ordinary *Hades*, or that Repository of common Souls, which were neither remarkably Good nor Bad, shared neither Reward nor Punishment, yet it was generally looked on but as a Place of uncomfortable Condition, and less desirable than this World On this account *Homer* makes the Ghost of *Tiresias* thus to bespeak *Ulysses*, when he saw him Voluntarily come into the infernal Regions

Τίπτ᾽ αὖτ᾽, ὦ δύστηνε, λιπὼν φάος ἠελίοιο
Ἤλυθες, ὄφρα ἴδῃς νέκυας καὶ ἀτερπέα χῶρον;

Unhappy Man! to leave the Sun's clear Light
To see us Ghosts, and th' undelightsom Regions
Hom Odyss. Lib xi

And by the Latin Poets this is frequently called *Ripæ horrendæ, the frightful Banks* and *Tristia Regna, the Melancholy Kingdoms.* Virg Æn Lib. vi

Jewish Notion of Sheol *or* Hades, *from about the time of the Captivity to Christ*

The Jews seem to have had a not very different Notion of the *Hades* from the Heathen The Word which they had to answer to *Hades* was *Sheol* This Word though it does in several Places signify the Grave, yet in many others it signifies either a state of the Dead, or a subterraneous Repository of separate Souls. The first time we meet with the Word, is in the xxxvii of *Genesis*, *I will go down into* Sheol (Gr Hades) *unto my Son, mourning* Indeed we translate it, *I will go down into the Grave unto my Son mourning*, Gen xxxvii 34 But *Jacob* could not resolve upon that, because he supposed his Son had no Grave, as thinking him torn in Pieces and on the other side he could not take *Sheol* for a Place of Torment, for that would deter any one from resolving to go thither. Therefore 'tis probable he used that Word to signify the Repository of ordinary Souls after Departure There are several other Places which do manifestly denote a Local *Hades*, under Ground As that of *Job High as Heaven what canst thou do? deeper than Hell* (*Heb* Sheol *Greek* Hades) *what canst thou know?* Job xi 8 So in that of the *Psalms*, *If I ascend up into Heaven thou art there if I make my bed in* (Sheol) *Hell thou art there*, Psal cxxxix 7 In both which Places, Hell, supposed to be the lowest part of the Earth, is opposed to Heaven above So *Amos* ix 2 *Though they dig into Hell thence shall my hand take them*, Am ix. 2 All which are Allusions to a Local Hell, supposed to be deep under Ground

Nay 'tis not improbable, that the antient Jews had a Notion of a twofold *Sheol* or *Hades*, as the Greeks had, of a *Hades*, and a *Tartarus* For that of the Psalmist, *Thou hast delivered my Soul* (Heb *mesheol tachetijah*) Gr ἐξ ᾅδου κατωτάτου) *from the lowest* Hell, does suppose a difference between an Upper and a Lower Hell This S *Austin* long ago remarked, *Dicit Scriptura cui contradici non potest*, Eruisti meam animam ex inferno inferiori, *intelligimus tanquam duo inferna esse, superius & inferius Etenim, Fratres, propter duo ista inferna, missus est Filius Dei undique liberans Ad hoc infernum missus est nascendo, illud moriendo, &c The Holy Scripture, which must not be contradicted, says*, Thou hast delivered my Soul from the lowest Hell, *we understand it as if there were two Hells, an Upper and a Lower, to both of which Christ was sent a Deliverer, to the one by being born, to the other by dying* Aug. in Psal lxxxv He by too fanciful a Gloss, here, makes the Earth to be the Upper Hell but 'tis most probable it is an Allusion to the Distinction of the subterraneous World into the common *Hades* the Repository of ordinary Souls, and the *Tartarus* or the Place of Punishment for wicked Spirits The Jews of the latter times, seem to have held two distinct Places of the infernal Regions, one ordinary and common *Hades*, the other subject to Torment and Misery For thus the Son of *Syrach* speaks of the ordinary *Hades*, with relation to the Person whom *Elijah* raised up from the dead *O Elias, &c, who didst raise up a dead Man from death, and his Soul from the place of the Dead* (ἐξ ᾅδου) *by the Word of the most high* Ecclus xlviii 5. But the Hell of Torment we find thus described, under the Character of a Sinner prick'd in Conscience, in Consideration of what he is to suffer hereafter *Sleep came upon them out of the bottoms of inevitable Hell* (Hades) Wisd. xvii 14 *Whosoever there fell down was straitly kept shut up in a prison without Iron Bars*, v 16 *were all bound with one chain of darkness* v 17 *Over them was spread an heavy night, an image of that darkness which should afterwards receive*, v 21 Contrary whereunto is the Condition of Good Men *But the Souls of the righteous are in the hand of God, and there shall no Torment touch them*, Wisd iii 1

How Hades *used by the Writers of the New Testament*

To come to the Writers of the New Testament, it must be confessed that the Word ᾍδης is hardly ever used but for the Hell of Torment It is used four times in the *Revelations*, Rev i 18 vi 8 xx 13 xx 14 in the three first of which is understood the Place or State of the damned, and possibly in the last likewise It is used but three times in the Gospels, and in all the Places the Hell of the damned is understood The first is *Mat.* xi 23 *And thou Capernaum, which art exalted unto Heaven, shalt be brought down to* (Hades) *Hell* Where the highest Heaven is opposed to the lowest Hell; the one the Seat of the Blessed, the other of the Damned. The next Place where this Word is found is *Mat* xvi 18 *Upon this rock I will build my Church, and the Gates of* (Hades) *Hell shall not prevail against it* That is the Power of the Devils who are doomed to Hell. The last Place is *Luke* xv 23 *The rich Man in* (Hades) *Hell lift up his Eyes being in Torments* which cannot be any other *Hades* than the Place of the damned All the Question is concerning the Meaning of that Text, on which this Article is chiefly grounded, *David seeing this before spake of the Resurrection of Christ that his Soul was not left* (εἰς ᾅδου) *in Hell*, Acts ii 31

The Sense of more modern Jews concerning Sheol.

That we may the better come at the Meaning of this Word, it will be requisite to know what Sense the modern Jews had of the Word *Sheol*, which is used in that Passage of the *Psalms*, which this Text alludes to It is plain that the Jewish Writers have generally understood by *Sheol* the Hell of Torment by their adapting the Names of the Gates of Hell from several Passages of Scripture, where *Sheol* is mentioned As the *Gate in the Desert*, where *Corah*, *Dathan* and *Abiram* descended, because they are said to have gone *down alive into* Sheol, *Num* xvi 33 The *Gate of the Sea*, through which *Jonah* was supposed to have passed, when he cried unto God *out of the Belly of* (Sheol) Hell, *Jon* ii 2 It is manifest likewise that the Jewish Rabbies do ascribe to their Hell positive Torments, though they do, in their way, mix much Fancy therein In their most antient Book *Zoar*, the Torments of Hell consist in a vicissitude of intollerable Heat and Cold, *Buxtorf Lex* in voce גהנם which Opinion seems to have obtained among them before S *Jerom*'s time for in his Comment on *Mat* x he says (most probably

bably from the Jewish Writers) *Duplicem esse Gehennam unam ignis & frigoris, in Job plenissime legimus* That there are two Hells, one of Heat the other of Cold, we fully read in Job The Comment upon *Job*, which goes under S. *Jerom's* Name, 'tis true is not entirely his, but is attributed by many to *Bede* But there are many Passages therein whose Latinity is too good for *Bede* It is probably a motly Piece made out of several of S *Jerom's* Observations, mixed with others of later date But be it as it will, there is in it this Passage which contains this Notion of the Jewish Theology *Forte in ipsa gehenna talis sensuum erit usus fut illis ... in ea torquebuntur, ut nunc quasi ignem ardentem sentiant, nunc nimium algoris incendium & pœnalis commutatio, nunc frigus scatentibus nunc calor sit, ut quasi de loco ad locum transitus est ment Et fortasse inde Dominus ait in Evangelio, Mittite eum in tenebras exteriores, ibi erit fletus & stridor dentium* Perhaps, in Hell there shall be such a Torment of the Senses of the damned, that sometimes they shall feel a burning Fire, and sometime a pinching Cold and this change of Punishment shall be as they run from one place to another And perhaps, this is the reason of that Expression of our Saviour in the Gospel, Cast him forth into utter darkness, where there shall be weeping and gnashing of Teeth, *Hier in Job cap* xxiv But the Judgment of the Jews in this matter will be yet clearer, if we observe what they have commented upon those Places of Scripture, where *Sheol* is mentioned As on that of *Psal* ix 18 *The wicked shall be turned into* (Sheol) Hell For thus *Rabbi Solomon* on the Place, *Amar Rabbi Auba*, &c *Rabbi Ava the Son of Zabdi said, to the lower degree of Hell And why is it written they shall be turned? Because when they shall come out of Hell and stand in Judgment, they shall be turned back into the lower degree of Hell*, R Selom ad Psal ix v 18 *Rabbi Kimchi* on the same *Psalm* cites an antient Allegorical Comment called *Darash*, which says, *Lama amar leshcolah*, &c *L not He, in the end of a Word, the same as Lamed in the beginning? This is as much as to say into the lowest part of Hell*

The common Opinion of the Fathers for the first 400 Years, That Christ went to Hades *to rescue from thence the Souls of the Patriarchs*, &c

But to set aside these Jewish Authors, let us see how the Christian Writers interpreted this Passage of Scripture from the beginning of Christianity, and what Sense they had of Christ descending into *Hades*, or Hell It must be owned that the most early of the Fathers interpreted this Place by 1 *Pet* iii 18 *Being put to death in the flesh but quickened by the Spirit, by which he also went and preached to the Spirits in prison* This occasioned the antient Writers of the Church, for 4 or 500 Years together, to assert that Christ descended into *Hades* or Hell, to Preach the Gospel to those Souls which had departed before his coming, and to advance to Happiness those pious and well disposed Spirits, who did believe on him Thus *Justin Martyr* blaming the Jews for expunging several Passages of Scripture, which made for the Christians, from their Copies, mentions this for one. Ἐμνήσθη δὲ Κύριος ὁ Θεὸς Ἰσραὴλ τῶν νεκρῶν αὐτοῦ τῶν κεκοιμημένων εἰς γῆν χώματος, καὶ κατέβη πρὸς αὐτοὺς εὐαγγελίσασθαι αὐτοῖς τὸ σωτήριον αὐτοῦ *The Lord God of Israel remembred his dead and those that slept under the heap of the Earth, and descended to them to preach Salvation to them* Just Mart Dial cum Tryph Which Accusation, whether true or false, shews what was the general Doctrine of Christians in his Time *Clement* of *Alexandria* writes, Ὁ Κύριος δι' οὐδὲν ἕτερον εἰς ᾅδου κατῆλθεν ἢ διὰ τὸ εὐαγγελίσασθαι *Christ descended into Hell for no other Reason, than to preach the Gospel* Clem Alex Strom Lib vi *Irenæus* writes, *Et propter Dominum in ea, quæ sunt sub terra descendisse, evangelizantem & illis adventum suum, remissam peccatorum existentem his, qui credunt in eum For this Reason our Lord descended into the parts under the Earth, to preach to them his coming, and remission of Sins to those that believe on him* Iren Lib iv cap 45. And elsewhere he teaches, *tribus diebus conversatum esse, ubi erant mortui, & descendisse ad eos, & salvare eos the three days he conversed where the dead were, and descended to them to save them* Lib v cap 35 *Tertullian* says, *Nec ante ascendit in sublimiora cœlorum, quam descendit in inferiora terrarum, ut illic Patriarchas, & Prophetas compotes sui faceret He did not ascend to the highest parts of the Heaven, before he descended into the lowest parts of the Earth, that he might make the Patriarchs and Prophets Partakers of his Benefits* Lib de Anima cap 4 *Eusebius* says, Μέχρι θανάτου καὶ αὐτῶν νεκρῶν φιλανθρωπίας αὐτὸν ἐκκαλουμένης, ὡς ἂν καὶ τὰς πάλαι τεθνηκότων τὰς ψυχὰς ἀνακαλέσαιτο *The Laws of Humanity called him to death, that he might call back the Souls of them that were dead* Euseb de Demonstr Lib iv *Athanasius*, in Opposition to the Apollinarian Heresie, assigns the Reason of his Descent to be, ἵνα ψυχαῖς ταῖς ἐν δεσμοῖς κατεχομέναις μορφὴν ἰδίας ψυχῆς ἀντιδείξας ... *That for the sake of the Souls, that were detained in bonds, exhibiting the form of his own Soul, being present with them, he might break asunder the bonds of those Souls which were detained in* Hades Athan Lib de Incarn Christ S *Cyril* of *Jerusalem* says, that κατῆλθεν εἰς τὰ καταχθόνια, ἵνα κακεῖθεν λυτρώσηται τοὺς δικαίους *That he descended into the subterraneous parts, that he might redeem from thence the just* Cyr Cat iv These Writers, by *Hades* and the subterraneous Parts, seem to understand the common and ordinary *Hades* of the Greeks, and not the Place of Torments, for it could not agree with their Piety to think that the Souls of the Patriarchs and other good Persons were detained in that Place of Horror

Afterwards it was the common Notion that Christ went to Hades *to storm Hell Gates, and to triumph over the Devil*

But towards the latter end of the fourth Century, several of the Divines seem to have taken a new turn of Thought, and to have asserted, that Christ went into the very Mansions of the damned, not to suffer there, but to triumph over the Devil, and rescued many Souls which had lain long in Pain 'Tis possible that this Notion might first make its Entrance by reason of Poetical Expression, when an ordinary Meaning might be contained under high Words I think *Prudentius* was one of the first who makes Christ to have entered into *Tartarus*, which he does in these Verses

Quin & ipsum ne solutis inferi expertes forent
Tartarum benignus intrat fracta cedit janua,
Vectibus cadit revulsis cardo dissolubilis.
Illa prompta ad irruentes, ad revertentes tenax,
Obice extrorsum repulso, porta reddit mortuos
Lege versa, & limen atrum jam recalcandum patet.

That Hell and Tartarus *might share*
His Bounty too, he enters there
The Bars and Hinges broke, down flat
Before him fell th' infernal Gate.
The Passage open'd now, in sholes
Out fled the long imprison'd Souls.
Their Doom is chang'd, they Leave obtain
The black Paths to tread back again
Prudent Cathem Hymn ix

But perhaps his Opinion was not, that the Devils and all impenitent Souls were released But only he used *Tartarus* to signifie the ordinary *Hades* Indeed others after him will have Christ to have gone and stormed the Gates of Hell, and enter'd into the very Regions of the damned, and vanquished the Devil there For this I take to be the Meaning of S *Chrysostom* Ἐννόησον γὰρ ἡλίκον ἐστὶν ἀκοῦσαι, ὅτι ὁ ... *Think how great a thing this is, that Christ being God should rise up from his Royal Throne in Heaven, and should not only come down upon Earth, but take a leap into Hell, and put himself in order of Battel there*, Hom ii in Mat And when elsewere he says, Σήμερον γὰρ περὶ ᾅδου ... *It was to day that our Saviour made his search all over Hell it was to day that he broke the brazen Gates, and shiver'd into pieces the Iron Bars* Hom lxxxi Tom 5 And afterwards more particularly ... *He made his way to Hell, he cleared the Prison, brought away the Jailor himself in Chains, and so returned hither ... The Tyrant himself was led Captive, the strong Man was bound, and Death himself throwing away his Arms, ran naked at the King's feet* ibid Of the same Opinion was the Commentator on S *Paul's* Epistles, under the Name of S *Ambrose* *Triumphato ergo Diabolo descendit in cor terræ, ut ostentio ejus prædicatio esset mortuorum ---tertio die resurgens ante omnes mortales, ascendit super cunctos cælos, ut illusam mortem ostenderet creaturæ* Triumphing over the Devil he descend, *descends into the Heart of the Earth, that the shewing himself there might be a preaching to the dead ——And the third day rising again, before all others he ascended into Heaven, displaying his Triumph over Death* in Eph iv S *Austin* says plainly, *Christi animam venisse usque ad ea loca, in quibus peccatores cruciantur, ut eos solveret a tormentis quos esse solvendos occulta nobis sua justitia judicabat, non immerito credimus We do on good grounds believe, that Christ's Soul came even to those Places, where Sinners are tormented, that he might free those from their Torments, whom his hidden Justice had decreed should be freed* Aug in Gen ad lit So *Cassian Christus inferna penetrans, inextricabiles Tartari tenebras coruscatione sui splendoris extinxit, portasque ejus ferreas effringens, ac seras ferreas conterens, captivitatem sanctorum, quæ clausa tenebris immitis tenebatur inferni salubriter captam transvexit secum ad cœlos, Christ going to Hell put out the inextricable darkness of Tartarus by his light, he breaking the brazen Gates, splintering the Iron Bars, and spoiling the Locks, brought away the Captive Saints from Hell to Heaven* Cass de Inst Cœnob Lib iii The same Doctrine was taught by *Fulgentius Restabat tamen ad plenum nostræ Redemptionis effectum, ut illuc usque homo sine peccato a Deo peccati merito recessisset, id est ad infernum, ubi solebat peccatoris anima torqueri,* &c *There remained yet for the finishing our Redemption, that the Man without Sin should go as deep, as Man separated from God by Sin had fallen, i e to Hell, where Sinners Souls are tormented* Fulgent Lib iii ad Trasimund

In the Seventh Century Hell divided into Limbus's.

In the Seventh Century some new Notions were vented by Divines, concerning the different Degrees of Punishment in Hell, and different Receptacles assigned to Souls, according to their different Deserts, the higher of which, that were only attended with the Punishment of Loss, or privation of eternal Happiness, were assigned to the Fathers that were there before Christ's Descent For thus Pope *Gregory* writes *Esse superiora inferni loca, esse alia inferiora credenda sunt ut et justi in superioribus justi requiescerent, et in inferioribus injusti cruciarentur It must be believed, that there are some Places of Hell higher and other lower so that the just did rest in the higher, and the wicked were punished in the lower* Greg Expos Mor Lib xii cap 6 Upon the ground of this Divinity, Hell was supposed to be marked out into several Circles, at a higher or remoter Distance from the Central Fire The nearest was the Place of Devils and damned Spirits, and the most remote was presumed to be the Place of the good Souls which had departed before the coming of Christ The Spaces or Rooms between these Circles were called *Limbi* or Borders, and the outward Border or Receptacle was called *Limbus Patrum* This Name seems to have been common enough in the time of *Anselm*, from this Expression of his, *Tunc magnum fuit gaudium factum in Limbo quando anima Christi in ipsum descendit, et patres inde liberavit, et Limbum destruxit Then there was great joy in* Limbus, *when the Soul of Christ descended thither, and delivered the Fathers, and destroyed that* Limbus Ansel de Pass Dom *Lucas Tudensis*, a Writer of the Twelfth Century, calls them *Ollæ inferni, the several Pots of Hell*, and, *Quod ignis putei inferni inferioris causa sit incendii superioris inferni —ut non absone diversa judicentur diversarum ollarum incendia infernalia, That the higher parts of Hell were heated by the Fire of the lower ----so that the Heats of the several Pots of Hell may be truly said to be different* Bibl Patr Mag Tom iv par.ii p. 360 and then divides the Place into the Seat of the Damned, Purgatory, the Place for unbaptized Infants and the *Limbus* of the Fathers *ibid p* 631 What other Niceties the Schoolmen added to this Infernal Geography, is needless to relate

Different Notions of the first Reformers, concerning Hell or Hades

At the time of the Reformation, those who took in Hand the rectifying the Abuses of Religion, very justly laid aside these Notions which had been taken up by the Divines of the middle Ages, and particularly the Doctrine of Purgatory, which had been the occasion of so great Scandals in the Church But still they all retained the Catholick Doctrine of Christ's Descent into Hell, though it must be confessed there was less Agreement among them than might be expected in a matter of this Nature Mr *Calvin* invented a new Explication of this Article, making Christ's descending into Hell to be the bearing *diros in anima cruciatus damnati & perditi hominis*, during his Agony and suffering on the Cross, *Inst Lib* ii c 16 *Sect* 10 that was the *formidabilis Abyssus sentire se a Deo derelictum* ibid But the Novelty and forced Allegory of this Exposition is a full Confutation thereof. *Beza* was not satisfied with his Master *Calvin's* Explication, and therefore is for having *Hell* to signify no more than the Grave, and for this Reason in the first Edition of his Testament, translated the famous Text *Non derelinques cadaver meum in sepulchro Peter Martyr* maintained a different Opinion from both For he took *HADES* to denote the common State of the dead, both good, and bad, allowing that Christ extended his Redemption to the most wicked Spirits even in the Place of Torment *Descendit ad inferos nihil aliud indicat, nisi quod eundem subiit statum, quem reliquæ animæ a Corpore separatæ experiuntur, quæ aut in Sanctorum societatem cooptantur aut cum damnatorum spiritibus in æternum exitium detruduntur* He descended into Hell, *denotes nothing else, but that he underwent the same State, which other Souls separated from the Body experience, which either are joined to the Society of Saints, or else are thrust down into Hell*, Pet Mart Loc Com Class ii c 18 Nay, he owned his going to the Regions of the damned to Preach to them, grounding this upon the famous Passage of S *Peter*, *Alii etiam Spiritus, æternæ damnationi addicti, animæ Christi adventum persenserunt Nam, ut habetur apud Pet* 1 *Ep cap* iii *Illis spiritibus Christi prædicavit quod eo sensu positum intelligo, ut improbitatem exprobraret obstinationem atque incredulitatem, qua obdurati essent, adversus Dei verbum, sanctasque admonitiones quæ illis dum viverent, sæpe inde fuerant propositæ [illegible] quod hunc et ante [illegible] verbum illud [illegible], idemque [illegible] quod cum semper similes pertinaciter [illegible] tam in morte quam vivi incredulitatem retinuerint, justissimum suæ condemnationis aptissimum sibi ipsis testimonium [illegible], maxime cum nullam amplius ignorantiam possent prætexere Other Spirits being doomed to eternal Damnation, were sensible of Christ's coming For as it is written in the first Epistle of* S Peter, *cap* iii *The Spirit of Christ preached unto them, which may be understood in this Sense, viz that he might thereby upbraid their Obstinacy and Incredulity, with which they were hardened against the Word of God and his holy Admonitions, which, whilst they were alive, were proposed to them, which when they being always like themselves had pertinaciously rejected and retained the same Unbelief, as well dead as alive, they gave a most ample testimony of their Condemnation against themselves, especially when they could no longer pretend Ignorance*, ibid It is generally, and not without probability, said that *Peter Martyr* had no small share in drawing up King *Edward* VI Articles and that may be one Reason, why that Text of S *Peter* was cited in this third Article as Explanatory of the End of Christ's Descent into Hell, according to the Opinion of *Peter Martyr*, who therein plainly differed from some other of the Reformed Divines with whom in most other Points he agreed At the Review of the Articles 1562 this Clause was expunged, either because it might be thought by some to give a handle to the Popish Doctrines of Purgatory and *Limbus*, or because some of the Divines being long abroad had imbibed Mr *Calvin's* Notion of suffering Hell Torments upon the Cross, or because the Members of the Convocation had different Notions of this Point, and therefore they chose to express it only in such general Terms as all of them might subscribe to It would seem to me that Mr *Calvin*'s Notion did pretty much prevail then, tho' it was never the general Opinion of the Clergy of this Nation, who always took the Liberty the Article gave them of maintaining a Local or Virtual Descent as a Theological Point, according to their own Judgment For Mr *Rogers*, who wrote his Exposition upon the Articles near the middle of Queen *Elizabeth*'s Reign says, *in the Interpretation of this Article there is not that Consent as were to be wished* And it otherways appears there was not, by that remarkable Relation set down by Bishop *Montague* in his *Apparatus* The Substance whereof is this In the Month of *July* 1559 one Mr *House* of Queens College keeping an Act, under Dr *Overall* the Regius Professor the Respondent maintaining that Christ did not descend to the Seat of the damned, opened his *Thesis* so, as to explain Christ's Descent into Hell to be an Ascent into Heaven to the Souls of the Patriarchs The Professor, at that Disputation, declared his Judgment, That it was a thing uncertain whether the Souls of the Just, who died before Christ, were in Heaven or no, That there was no Constat for this Opinion in Scripture, and That any Dispute thereof was more curious than necessary Some zealous Calvinists of the University hearing of this, and thinking that by a side Wind it bore against some of their Systematical Doctrines, raised a great Noise thereupon, giving out

ARTICLE IV.

IV Of the Resurrection of Christ

Christ did truly rise again from Death, and took again his Body, with Flesh, Bones, and all things appertaining to the Perfection of Man's Nature, wherewith

Of the Resurrection of Christ.

Christ did [a] truly * rise again from Death, and took again his Body, with Flesh, Bones and all things, appertaining to the Perfection of Man's Nature,

IV De Resurrectione Christi

Christus verè a mortuis resurrexit, suumque corpus cum carne, ossibus, omnibusque ad integritatem humanæ naturæ pertinentibus, rece-

* *Arise again*, MS. CCCC. 1571

out that the Professor had maintained publickly the Popish *Limbus* The Professor explained himself more fully in several following Disputations, shewing the antient Doctrine of the Catholick Fathers in this Point, and withal the Novelty of the Romish Doctrine The Calvinists were so far from being satisfied therewith, that they would bring on the same Question again next Year at the publick Commencement, though the Professor pressed hard that it might be laid aside, as an uncertain and useless Question But their Importunity and Violence carried it, that the Question should be again disputed In the Dispute Dr *Overall* was scandalously reflected upon, by one *Playfer* the *Margaret* Professor, as an Abettor of Popery, and one ignorant or prevaricating in the chief Articles of Faith, that this Doctrine with its Author ought to be banished out of the University. Soon after the learned Professor drew up an incomparable State of this Question, the Substance whereof is contained in the *Apparatus* from p 51 to p 75 The same Doctrine being maintained more than twenty Years afterwards, by Mr *Mountague* in his *Gagg*, and his *Appello Cæsarem*, he was furiously fallen upon by Mr *Yates* in his *Ibis ad Cæsarem*, and by other Puritans Dr *Hammond* some Years afterwards publishing his Practical Catechism, avoiding all Disputes concerning the Ends of Christ's Descent, explained the Word *Hell* by the common State or Place of the Dead, so that in a few Years his Opinion gaining much Ground, Bishop *Pearson*, in his Exposition of the Creed, followed Dr *Hammond* therein, and these Books being in the Hands of most of our Clergy has made this Opinion now to be almost universally received in our Church I have kept my self, in my Notes upon this Article, from closing with any Opinion, giving only an Historical Relation of the different Doctrines, which in the several Ages have been delivered, concerning it, for since the Church, for wise Reasons, has left the Sense of the Article undetermined, I must not pretend to fix any particular Sense upon it

---

a *Truly Rise*] This being an Assertion of our Saviour's Resurrection, for the explaining thereof it will be necessary, to shew,

Of the Resurrection of Christ

Predictions concerning Christ's Resurrection

I It was predicted that our Saviour should rise again from the dead There is an eminent Prophesie of this in the *second* Psalm, which is not only allowed by the Christians to be a Prophesie of the Messiah, but was reckoned to be the same also by the antient Jews *Rabbi Solomon Jarchi* fairly Confesses, *Our Doctors explained this Psalm of King Messiah, but the better to manage the Controversy with the Minæim, i e the Christians, it is better to interpret* of David In which Psalm it is prophesied concerning the Messias, *Thou art my Son, this Day have I begotten thee*, by which Passage is foretold his Resurrection, which is the beginning as it were of another Life, the Grave being the Womb in which for some time he had been inclosed Another Prophesie concerning our Saviour's Resurrection is in the *sixteenth* Psalm *My flesh shall rest in hope, for thou wilt not leave my Soul in Hell, neither wilt thou suffer thy holy one to see corruption*, Psal xvi 10 Which Passage S *Peter* argues cannot belong to *David*, but must be understood as the Jews generally interpreted of Christ, or the Messiah *As for the Patriarch David, he is both dead and buried*, &c *therefore being a Prophet and knowing that God had sworn an Oath to him, that of the fruit of his Loyns, according to the flesh, he would raise up Christ to sit upon his Throne, he seeing this before, spake of the Resurrection of Christ, that his Soul was not left in Hell, neither his flesh did see Corruption* Acts ii 31 The same was prefigured by the Sacrifice which *Abraham*, according to the divine Command, intended to make of his Son *Isaac* which the Apostle intimates in these Words, *accounting that God was able to raise him up from the dead, from whence also he received him in a figure*, Heb xi 19 This the Antients generally make a Type of our Saviour's Resurrection For this *Gregory Nyssen* Οὕτως γὰρ τὸ ἅγιον πνεῦμα τὸ μέγα μυστήριο ... ἀμφοτέροις ... τῷ ἠγαπημένῳ ... τῷ προβάτῳ ... θάνατον ... μονογενεῖ ... ζωὴν ... μὴ διακοπτομένην τῷ θανάτῳ *Thus the holy Spirit does Typically divide a great Mystery, both by the beloved Son and the Beast that was prepared by the Beast is signified Death, and by the beloved Son Life not cut off by Death*, Greg Nyss Or 1. in Resur And so *Prosper* *Ideo Isaac immolatus non est, quia resurrectio Filio servata est* *Therefore Isaac was not sacrificed, because the Resurrection was reserved for Christ.* Prosper de Prom &c

Truth of Christ's Resurrection

II There is the most certain Evidence of the Truth of our Saviour's Resurrection

This proved from the Testimony, 1 Of the Holy Scriptures

1 And for this we have as good Testimony as any reasonable Man can expect, for the Proof of a matter of fact of this Nature (1) For we have an *Historical Relation* of it, containing all the remarkable Circumstances relating to it, in Books written immediately after the time when that Fact happened, by those who were either Eye-witnesses of the same, or constantly conversed with those that were, I mean the History of the Gospels Where it is related, that he appeared to the pious Women who came to anoint his Body, *Mat.* xxviii 1 to the Disciples going to *Emaus*, *Luke* xxiv 13 to *Peter*, *Luke* xxiv 34 to the eleven, *Luke* xxiv 36 at the fishing, *John* xxi 4 to the five hundred Brethren, 1 *Cor* xv. 6

2. Of the Apostles.

(2) Next we have the Testimony of the Apostles themselves, who were in every re-

spect

spect very well qualified to witness what they related They were undoubtedly very pious and good Men. It was a principal Part of their Doctrine to exhort Men to Truth and Fidelity, *Eph* iv 25 *Rom* xii. 1 2 *Cor* vii 19 vi 31 *Gal* i 20 *Col* iii 9 1 *Tim* i 10 *Mat.* xii 26 *John* viii 44 They made it their Business to persuade Men to lead good and holy Lives, to leave off Idolatry, not to put their Trust in outward and ceremonious Actions, being themselves never taxed with Vice and Wickedness, but remarkable for Devotion, Mortification and Self-denyal Now this is a Character, which is wont in all other Matters to enforce Belief And 'tis not so incredible, upon their Testimony, to think that our Saviour rose from the Dead, as to think such honest and good Men should all of a sudden turn Cheats and Impostors Besides the Relators of this matter of Fact were plain and simple Men, not used to the Arts of Prevarication and Sophistry, nor capable of making a Falshood appear with the specious Colours of Truth, and therefore their Testimony is the more to be credited, since it is not to be suspected that they could ever relate an Action with such an Air of Verisimilitude and Truth if it had not been really what they reported it *Origen* speaks very well upon this Head, tho' with particular Regard to the Apostolical Writings Ὁ μαι γὰρ ὅτι ... Ἰησοῦ διὰ τοῦτο ... διδασκάλοις τοῦ δόγματος χρήσασθαι ... ἵνα μηδεμίαν μὲν ἔχῃ χώραν ὑπόνοια ... πιθανῶν σοφισμάτων ... τοῖς ... δυναμένοις ... ὅτι τὸ ἄδολον ... ἀφελέσι ... δυνάμεως, πολλῷ μᾶλλον ... περιβολῇ λόγων, καὶ λέξεων συνθέσεις, καὶ μετὰ διαιρέσεως καὶ τεχνολογίας Ἑλληνικῆς ἀκολουθία 'Tis my Opinion, that our Saviour chose such plain Men to be the Propagators of his Doctrines, that Men might have no suspicion that they were imposed upon by the Sophistry of Men who had been educated in the Arts of Persuasion but that it might be plainly understood, that no Deceit could lye hid under such a Plainness (if I may so call it) of the Writers, which with the assistance of the divine Spirit, was more efficacious, than any fine Composition of Words or Ornaments of Speech, Partition or Method, or any other part of the Grecian Institution.* Orig cont. Cels Lib iii Lastly, for the sake of this Testimony, they not only forfeited all the Advantages and Expectations of the World, but they exposed themselves to continual Persecutions and Sufferings, and even to Death it self For thus *Origen* Οἶμαι γὰρ ὅτι ... πράγματα ... ταύτης ἑαυτοὺς ... βίῳ ... Ἰησοῦ διδασκαλίας, χωρὶς τινὸς μεγάλης πίστεως ... αὐτοῖς, διδάσκων ... κατὰ τὰ μαθήματα αὐτοῦ, ἀλλὰ καὶ ἄλλους διατίθεσθαι ... ὡς τοὺς τῶν ἀνθρώπων βίοι ... τῇ καινότομα ... ἀνθρώπων ... τοῖς ... δόγμασι καὶ ἔθεσι, φίλον ... *'Tis my Opinion, that no one who weighs Matters, will assert, that the Apostles should enter upon a wandring Life, for the sake of the Gospel of Christ, unless they were verily persuaded that they ought not only to learn it themselves but to teach it to others When at the same time Danger every where threatned them for teaching new Opinions, and where they were sure not to have any one Friend left among those who kept to their antient Opinions and Customs* Orig cont Cels Lib i

Truth of Christ's Resurrection proved from the Circumstances which attended it

2 The Circumstances which attended our Saviour's appearing after his Crucifixion, do clearly evince the Truth of his Resurrection (1) His not rising immediately from the Grave, but lying there such a length of time as no one could think that a Person in Health, much less one whose Body was full of Wounds, could stay there without dying, was a demonstrative Proof both of his dying and rising again Which *Athanasius* thus remarks ... *He might have immediately raised up his Body from the dead, and shewed it alive But our Saviour foreseeing very good Reasons to the contrary would not do it For then persons some one would have said, that he did not die at all, or that he was not throughly dead, if immediately after his Death he had evidenced his Resurrection.* Athan de Incarn (2) Another Circumstance, which evidenced the Truth of his Resurrection, was his subjecting his Body, not only to the view but to the touch of those who doubted of it, as in the Case of S *Thomas* Whereupon S *Cyril* says, Ἡ ἀπιστία τοῦ μαθητοῦ τῆς ἡμετέρας πίστεως ... γέγονεν *The Unbelief of that Disciple was the Mother of our Faith.* Cyr Alex de Trin (3) His eating and drinking with his Disciples after his rising again, was another Circumstantial Evidence of the Truth of our Saviour's Resurrection For as a Spectre or an Aereal Body could not stand in need of such Reparations, so our Saviour could not without Collusion have so frequently used Food, if he had had a Body which did not properly Eat and Drink And thus S *Austin* reasons *Sciat, Christum post Resurrectionem cicatrices non vulnera demonstrasse dubitantibus, propter quos etiam Cibum & Potum sumere voluit, non semel sed sæpius, ne illud non Corpus sed Spiritum esse arbitrarentur, & sibi non solide sed imaginaliter apparere Let him know, that Christ after his Resurrection did not shew Wounds to those who doubted but Scars for whose sake likewise he was pleased to take meat and drink, not once but often, that they might know he was a Body and not a Spirit, and that he appeared to them really and not only in Imagination* Aug Ep xxxix ad Deo grat

The frivolous Objections against the Truth of Christ's Resurrection examined.

3 The Truth of our Saviour's Resurrection does further appear from the frivolousness of the Objections, which are raised against it. The Sum of these are contained in this Relation of the Evangelist, *And when the Chief Priests were assembled with the Elders, and had taken Counsel they gave large Money unto the Soldiers, saying, say ye his Disciples came by Night, and stole him away while we slept* Mat xxviii 12 But this is crowded with such a heap of ridiculous improbabilities that no reasonable Person can admit For (1) This supposes to the Disciples such a Degree of Courage as it is clear they were not, at least at that time, Masters of For how can it be supposed, that they who were afraid to stand by their Master when alive, should venture so much for him when he was dead? that they who fled away at the sight of the Chief Priest's Officers, when they had some probability of saving him alive, should, to recover his dead Carcase, venture through the *Roman* Guards which were set to keep it? S *Chrysostom* thus exposes the ridiculousness of this Assertion Πῶς ... εἰπέ μοι, οἱ μαθηταὶ ... ἄνθρωποι πτωχοὶ καὶ ἰδιῶται καὶ οὐδὲ φαίνεσθαι τολμῶντες, ... γὰρ ἐκ ... σφραγὶς ... ; μὴ γὰρ ... φύλακες, καὶ στρατιῶται, καὶ Ἰουδαῖοι; μὴ γὰρ ... αὐτοῖς, καὶ ... *Tell me, I pray you, how was it possible for his Disciples to steal his Body away, that were poor and ordinary Men, and at that time had not Courage to shew their Heads? Was not there a Seal set upon the Sepulchre? were not here Watchmen, Soldiers and Jews that sat by? Had not they Suspicions upon them, did not they watch, and carefully look about them?* Chrys Hom xc in Mat (2) The like Improbability is in the Disciples rolling away the great Stone that covered the Mouth of the Sepulchre, which it was impossible to do in the dead time of the Night so as not to be heard by the Guards, and not to waken them if they had been asleep, which likewise argues a great Improbability that they should be This Stone was a great flat Stone which the Hebrews call *Golal*, vid *Abr ab* ... This *Bitenon* will have sometimes to be bound ... another great Stone on the Top which is called *Dopek Dopakim* vid *Mischn* ... *Syrahrsi* ... p 162 Now it is not easy to imagine, that two or three fearful Men should either enterprize or finish, such a laborious piece of Work as this was in the Neighbourhood of an armed Guard. (3) Neither is it credible, that they had by an unheard of Success, made their way into our Saviour's Sepulchre, so as to be able to convey away his Body, that they would have employ'd their time in the midst of such Danger, upon so needless a curiosity as to strip off his Grave Clothes, and unwind all the Bandage which the viscous Gummins had made stick so close to his Body, that it would require a great deal of time to pull them off, and not only so but that they should lay them up carefully in order For when ... came to the Sepulchre, *he saw the linnen Clothes lye, and the Napkin that was about his Head, not lying with the linnen Clothes, but wrapped together in a place by it self,* John xx 6, 7 ... Improbabilities S *Chrysostom* thus exposes ... τὰ ... τὰ ... ταῦτα γὰρ ... ὁ Πέτρος ... τὸ σῶμα ... διὰ τὸ μὴ ... ἀλλὰ ... μέλλει. καὶ ... διὰ ... καὶ κατὰ ... ὅτι ... τῷ σώματι καὶ τοῖς ἱματίοις, ... τὰ ἱμάτια τοῦ σώματος, ...

he ascended into Heaven, and there sitteth till he re-	wherewith he [b] ascended into Heaven, and there [c] sitteth, un-	*pit cum quibus in cælum ascendit, ibique residet, quoad ex-*

[illegible] τὸ ἀυτὸ ἐσ[illegible] *What account can be given of the Linnen that was stiff with the Myrrh?* Peter *saw these lying Now if they had a mind to steal the Body, would they not have taken it away as it was, not only to avoid being laughed at for an unnecessary Action, but because it would take up so much time, and give the Guard an Opportunity of awaking and apprehending them? Because Myrrh is a Drug, which is of so sticky a nature and clings so close both to the Body and the Clothes, that it would not be easy to pull away such Clothes from a Body, especially when the Men that did this were in a fright* Chrys Hom xc in Mat

Of the Ascension of Christ

b *Ascended into Heaven*] It must be observed, that whereas the Belief of the Ascension of our Saviour is a principal Article of our Faith, so is it both predicted in the Old Testament, and express Testimony is given thereof in the New

Predictions of Christ's Ascension

I The Ascension of Christ is predicted in the Old Testament And this (1) Typically, by the High-Priest's annual entring into the Holy of Holies *The Lord said unto* Moses, *speak unto* Aaron *thy Brother, that he come not at all times into the Holy place within the vail before the Mercy Seat,* &c Lev xvi 2 Which the Apostle makes to be a Typical Representation of Christ's Ascension into Heaven *The High Priest of the good things to come, by a greater and more perfect Tabernacle not made with Hands was to enter into the Holy Place, having obtained eternal Redemption for us,* Heb ix 11, 12 (2) Prophetically. There are two principal Texts of the Old Testament which do Predict the Ascension of our Lord The first is that of the lxviiith *Psalm Thou hast ascended up on high, thou hast led captivity captive, thou hast received Gifts of Men,* Psal lxviii 18 This Text is applied to this purpose by the Apostle S *Paul, Eph* iv 9 intimating that thereby was foretold that Christ should conquer Sin, Death and Hell, and triumphing over them should obtain for us all the advantageous Gifts of God's holy Spirit *Rabbi Solomon* indeed explains this of *Moses,* and *Aben Ezra* of *David,* but it can with no Propriety of Speech be said that they *ascended up on high,* for as *Shobah le marom, return on high,* is attributed in another *Psalm* to God as a peculiar Property of his, *Psal* vii 8 so this is never ascribed to any human Conqueror Another Prophesie of our Saviour's Ascension is that of *Micah* ii 13 *The breaker is come up before them they have broken up and passed through the gate, and are gone out by it, and their King shall pass before them, and the Lord at the Head of them* This the *Bereshith Rabba* explains of the Messiah For on those Words of the lxxxth *Psalm,* the *Vineyard which thy right hand hath planted,* he has these Words, *The plantation from beneath is of Abraham, the plantation from above is of the Messiah, as it is written,* Mic ii 13 And on *Genesis* xiv 18 speaks thus *Lemathi amon,* &c *When shall we rejoice? when the feet of the Divinity shall stand in the mount of Olives, which is Eastward before Jerusalem* vid Raim und Pug Fid p 695

Truth of Christ's Ascension

II The Ascension of Christ is proved by the joint Testimony of the Apostles, who were all Witnesses of that wonderful matter of Fact For they were all there, when S *Mark* says, *so then after the Lord had spoken to them he was received up into Heaven,* Mark xvi 19 And when S *Luke* relates the same, *and he led them out as far as to Bethany, and he lift up his hands and blessed them And it came to pass, when he blessed them he was parted from them and carried up into Heaven,* Luke xxiv 50, 51 and so in that more particular Relation of the Ascension, Acts i 9 *And when he had spoken these things, while they beheld, he was taken up, and a Cloud received him out of their sight* S *Chrysostome* makes a handsome Remark concerning what the Apostles saw with relation to Christ's Resurrection, and what they saw with relation to his Ascension, it being sufficient for a Ground of their Testimony to have seen him risen, but that it was necessary, for a certainty of their Evidence that they should see him actually ascend [illegible] ἐκ εἶδεν, ϐλεπόντων ἢ αὐτῶν [illegible] ὅλως [illegible] τῆς ἀναστάσεως τὸ μ[illegible] τέλ@ εἶδο, τὴν ἢ ἀρχὴν ἐκέτι Καὶ ἢ ἀναλήψεως τὴν μ[illegible] ἀρχὴν εἶδον, τὸ ἢ τέλ@ ἐκέτ. περιττὸν γὰρ ἐκεῖνο τὸ τὴν ἀρχὴν ἰδεῖν. αὐτὸ ταῦτα φθεγγόμενε παρόντ@, ἢ τῷ μνήματ@ δηλοῦντ@, ὅτι [illegible] ἐστιν [illegible] ἀλλὰ τὸ μετὰ τοῦτο λόγω ἔδει μαθεῖν ἐπειδὴ γὰρ ἐκ ἀρκοῦσιν οἱ ὀφθαλμοὶ δεῖξαι τὸ ὕψ@ ἐδὲ παιδεῦσαι πότερον εἰς τὸν ὀρανὸν ἀνῆλθεν, &c *He did not rise again in the sight of his Disciples, but he was taken up as they looked on They saw the end of his Resurrection, but not the beginning They saw the beginning of his Ascension, but not the end It was unnecessary for them to see the beginning, because he being yet present with them could inform them of it, the Sepulchre it self being an Evidence that he was not there. But what followed after this they must learn by Word For their Eyes would not serve them to look to that hight, nor to inform them of that Heaven to which he went,* Chrys in Act Hom ii

Heretical Errors concerning it

III Our Saviour ascended into the highest Heaven, the immediate Seat of the Divine Glory and Presence There were some of the antient Hereticks, who by misunderstanding that Passage in the xixth *Psalm* according to the Septuagint Translation, ἐν τῷ ἡλίῳ ἔθετο τὸ σκήνωμα αὐτῦ: *he has placed his Tabernacle in the Sun,* would have our Saviour only to have ascended thither This was the Opinion of the Manichees and some other Hereticks For thus *Nazianzen* Οὐ [illegible] τῶν Μανιχαίων λῆρος [illegible] ἀποτεθῆναι [illegible] διὰ τὴν ἀτιμίας *For Christ's Body was not, according to the Dreams of the Manichees, lodged in the Sun, to be honoured with Dishonour* Epist. i. ad Cled The Dishonour he mentions is more particularly expressed by S *Austin,* who likewise relates this foolish Notion of those Hereticks, further adding, that they believed the Sun to be Christ *Manichæi solem istum carneis oculis visibilem, expositum & publicum, non tantum hominibus, sed etiam pecoribus ad videndum, Christum Dominum esse putarunt The Manichees did believe the Sun, which is visible by these fleshly Eyes, and open to the view, not only of Men but of Beasts, to be Christ* Tract xxxiv in Joh. But the holy Scriptures inform us that he ascended into the highest Heaven For the Apostle says expresly of him, *he that descended is the same also that ascended up far above all heavens,* Eph iv 10 that *he went into the holy place, even into Heaven it self to appear in the presence of God,* Heb ix 12 And 'tis this which our Saviour himself meaned, when he said, *What and if ye shall see the Son of Man ascend up, where he was before?*

Of Christ's Session on the right Hand of God

c *There sitteth*] For the Explication of this Clause of the Article, it will be requisite to observe the following Particulars

Christ's Session at God's right hand predicted in the Old Testament

I That our Saviour's being exalted to sit on the right Hand of God, was what was predicted in the Old Testament The most remarkable Passage for this purpose is that of the cxth Psal v 1 *The Lord said unto my Lord, sit thou on my right hand until I make thine enemies thy footstool* That this is a Prophesie of the Messiah we have the Testimony of Christ himself, the force of which operated so strong upon the Jews of that time that they were perfectly silenced by it *What think ye of Christ* (says he to the Pharisees) *whose Son is he? they say unto him the Son of David He said unto them, how then doth David in Spirit call him Lord, saying, The Lord said unto my Lord sit thou on my right hand, until I make thine enemies thy footstool If David then call him Lord, how is he his Son? and no man was able to answer him a Word,* Mat xxii 43, &c The Jewish Doctors do explain the same *Psalm* of the Messiah In the *Midrash Tehillim,* or Commentary on the *Psalms* they have this Traditionary Explication *Amar Rabbi Joden,* &c *Rabbi Joden in the name of Rabbi Chama said, that in future times God shall place King Messiah at his right hand as it is written, The Lord said unto my Lord sit thou,* &c And *Rabbi Moses Hadarsan* on *Gen.* xviii makes the same Conclusion from the forementioned Verse of this *Psalm* vid Raimund Pug Fid p 684 Besides the Targum explains the same *Psalm* of the Messiah For in interpreting these Words,

turn to judge all Men at the Last Day | til he return to * d judge all Men at the Last Day. | *tremo die ad judicandos homines ? ever futurus sit.*

* *Judge all Men* MSS CCC 1571.

Words, *The Lord said*, &c he explains, *Amar Jehovah le meirah The Lord said unto his Word.*

Christ's Session at God's right hand expresly declared in the New Testament

II. That our Saviour in the New Testament is expresly declared to be set at the right hand of God For *Mark* xvi 13 he is said *to be received up into Heaven, and to sit on the right hand of God* And by S *Luke*, *Hereafter shall the Son of Man sit on the right hand of the power of God*, Luke xxii 69. S *Peter* argues from the forementioned Passage of the Fulfilment, *David is not ascended into the Heavens, but he saith himself, The Lord said unto my Lord, Sit thou on my right hand*, &c Acts ii 34 The like is argued by the Author to the *Hebrews*, *To which of the Angels said he at any time, Sit on my right hand, until I make thine enemies thy footstool?* Heb i. 13 And S *Peter* says expresly, *Christ is gone into Heaven, and is on the right hand of God*, 1 Pet iii 22

His Session at God's right hand denotes a high degree of Exaltation

III. That this going, to sit on the right hand of God, does denote a high degree of Exaltation This is clear from the import of the Hebrew Phrase, which is used to signify any Person's being highly honoured For when *Solomon* was minded to afford his Mother a distinguishing mark of Honour, he placed her on his right hand *He sat down on his Throne, and caused a Seat to be set for the King's Mother, and she sate on his right hand*, 1 Kings ii. 19 So the Queen in the xlvth *Psalm* is said to stand on *the King's right hand in Gold of Ophir*, Psal xlv 9 And the Writers of the New Testament, when they mention this Session on God's right hand, do intimate thereby that he is exalted to a mighty degree of Majesty and Power This our Saviour himself intends, when he says, *Hereafter ye shall see the Son of man sitting on the right hand of power*, Mat xxvii 64 And so the Author to the *Hebrews*, *When he had by himself purged our Sins, he sate down on the right hand of* the Majesty *on high*, Heb i 3 And elsewhere, *We have an high Priest who is set on the right hand of* the Majesty *in the Heavens*, Heb viii 1 Agreeable to this Custom, among the Heathens, *Tiridates* was placed on the Emperor's right hand *Suet in Nerone* So *Pindar* describes *Minerva*, δεξιὰν κατὰ χεῖρα πατρὸς καθεζομένην *sitting on the right hand of* Jupiter *her Father*, cited by *Aristides*, which *Horace* thus imitates

Proximos illi tamen occupavit
Pallas honores

Christ's sitting on God's right hand does imply his Intercession for us

IV Christ's sitting at the right hand of God does imply his Intercession for us there That Christ does intercede for us to his Father, and plead his Merits to him on our behalf, in that exalted State, to which he is now advanced, is the clear Doctrine of the holy Scriptures For S *John* tells us, *That we have an Advocate with the Father, Jesus Christ the righteous*, 1 John ii 1. S *Paul* informs us, that Christ does *intercede for us at the right hand of God*, Rom viii 34 And the Author to the *Hebrews* says expresly, that Christ *is entered into Heaven it self now to appear in the presence of God for us*, Heb ix 24 This Office of his Intercession is discharged in the Performance of these Particulars

Christ intercedes for us by presenting our Prayers to the Father

(1) In presenting our Prayers to the Father to make them more effectual through his Merits And this the Holy Scripture teaches us when it says, that *through him we both have access to the Father*, Eph ii 18 *and by him we have access to this grace*, Rom v 2 This act of his Intercession is thus expressed by *Origen* [illegible] λόγον καὶ εἰκόνα [illegible] σέβομεν, προσάγοντες [illegible] μονογενοῦς αὐτοῦ [illegible] ἱλασμοῦ [illegible] εὐχὰς καὶ τὰς θυσίας [illegible] Θεῷ *We worship one God, and his Son the Word and his Image with all the Supplications and Postulations we can, offering Prayers to the God of all, through his only begotten to whom we first offer them, beseeching him, as he is the Propitiation for our Sins, that he, as our high Priest, would present our Prayers, Sacrifices and Intercessions, to the supreme God* Orig contr Cels Lib viii 2) In praying for us himself, (i.e.) by using his Intreaties and Intercessions on our behalf For that seems to be the meaning of that Expression *he ever lives to make Intercession for us*, (i e) to pray God to be reconciled to us For it must be observed that [illegible] bears that Sense among the Writers of the New Testament The true original Sense of the Word ἐντυγχάνω is to make an earnest Complaint against any one to a Judge, for redress for an injury done. For *Hesychius* explains [illegible] to be [illegible] *Gregory Nazianzen* observes that ἐντυγχάνειν, or to make Intercession in Scripture, is different from the common or Heathen Notion of the Word [illegible] *The Word [illegible] does not signify here, what is vulgarly [illegible] to seek revenge or redress*, Greg Naz Or xxvi [illegible] for as far as I can observe this Word is used by S *Paul* (for 'tis used no where in the New Testament but in his Epistles) is a Word of a middle Signification, [illegible] It always implies a [illegible] and earnest Prayer or Supplication, tho' it may be applied either to the [illegible] ing for the Benefit or the Suffering of any Person S *Paul* uses the Word once in the vulgar Sense, [illegible] *what the Scripture saith of Elias? how he [illegible] to God against Israel?* Rom xi 2 [illegible] signifies to put in a Plea, or to lay a Charge against which is not properly to *intercede*, and therefore should have been otherways translated In the other Places it signifies, to put in an earnest Plea for, or heartily to intreat for some Benefit for another S *Austin* looks upon Prayer to be so necessary a part of Christ's Intercession, that he cannot imagine it can consist without it *Nam de ipso Domino ut dictum est, quod interpellat pro nobis Num quid interpellat & non etiam postulat? Imo vero quia postulat pro eo positum est interpellat It is said of our Lord that he intercedes for us Does he intercede for us, and not pray for us? Rather, because he prays for us, he is said to intercede* [illegible] Aug Ep [illegible] But then we must not think that this Prayer of our Saviour on our behalf is performed by way of formal Petition, Genuflexion, Prostration, or any other of the ordinary Circumstances of our Devotions here upon Earth *Gregory Nazianzen* very well guards against any such Notion [illegible] *Christ does not [illegible] that in order to intercede for us, to fall down before his Father, and [illegible] in a [illegible] manner Away with the [illegible] of such a dejected Posture, and [illegible] the Spirit For this does not become the Father [illegible]*, Greg Naz Orat xxxvi (3) Lastly, Christ's Intercession is performed by presenting his sacrificed Body to his Father, thereby inclining him by the Intuition of his Merits towards our Pardon, and obtaining all needful Gifts and Graces for us This seems to be intimated, when Christ is said in Scripture, *to appear before God on our behalf*, and to make Intercession for us For thus *Theophylact*, in Rom cap viii [illegible] οὕτως [illegible] ὡς οἱ Μανιχαῖοι [illegible] Πατρὶ [illegible] Πατὴρ [illegible] *Some think that, by Christ's Intercession for us, is meant this, That the Body which he is clothed with (for he has not laid aside his Body as the doting Manichees pretend) is a sort of an Embassage or Petition to the Father. For the Father looking upon this, remembers his dear love to Men which inclined his Son to take upon him a Body, and this inclines him to Mercy and Pity*

Of Christ's Judging the World

d *Until he return to judge* &c] Being to explain this Branch of the Article which relates to the final Judgment, it will be requisite to take Notice, of the following Particulars

Christ's coming to Judgment predicted in the Old Testament

I That Christ's coming to judge the World was predicted, before the appearing of Christ That Traditionary Prophesie of *Enoch*, referred to by the Apostle S. *Jude*, seems to relate to this *Enoch the seventh from Adam prophesied of his coming, saying, behold the Lord cometh with ten thousand of his Angels*, Jude 14 But this is more expresly predicted by *Daniel*, when he said, *I saw in the night Visions, and behold one like the Son of Man, came with the Clouds of Heaven, and came to the antient of days, and they brought him before him And there was given him dominion and glory, and a kingdom, that all people, nations and languages should serve him his dominion is an everlasting dominion, which shall not pass away, and his kingdom that which shall not be destroyed*, Dan vii 13, 14 All the Jewish Writers and Commentators do explain this place of the Messiah *Rabbi Solomon Jarchi* on the place, *Enosh hou melek hameshiach this Man is the King Messiah* And the like Explication is given by *Aben Ezrah Amar Rabbi*, &c *R Jeshuah said, that this Person being the Son of Man was the Messiah, and he said well* Ab Ez in locum Indeed the Jewish Writers and the Christians disagree in this, that the Jews will have this place to be understood, of the first coming of the glorious Messiah, which they expected, for some of them think that the Messiah shall come either humble or glorious, according as their Actions do merit. For thus their Book *Sanedrim*, in the Section *Chelek*, speaks *Amar Rabbi Alexandri*, &c *Rabbi Alexander said, Rabbi Joshuah objected, it is written concerning King Messiah*, Behold he shall come like the Son of Man with the Clouds from Heaven *and it is written elsewhere*, Zach. ix 9 *Poor and riding upon an Ass If they deserve well he shall come in the* Clouds of Heaven, *but if they deserve ill*, poor and riding upon an Ass. *vid Gal Pug Fig* p 354

Christ's coming to Judgment expresly declared in the New Testament

II That there is very clear Evidence of the Truth of this Doctrine For as this is one of the principal Articles of Christianity, which the Apostles had down their Lives to propagate, so they have left it in their Writings expressed in the most clear and ample Words This is positively asserted and foretold by our Saviour himself, *Hereafter shall ye see the Son of man sitting on the right hand of Power, and coming in the Clouds of Heaven*, Mat xxvi 64 When our Saviour's Ascension is related, we have an account, that the Angels which attended him declared, *This same Jesus which is taken up from you into Heaven shall so come in like manner as ye have seen him go into Heaven*, Acts i 11 And S *Paul* informs us, *That the Lord himself shall descend from Heaven with a shout, with the voice of the Archangel and the Trump of God*, 1 Thes iv 16 and again, *when the Lord shall be revealed from Heaven with his mighty Angels*, 2 Thes i 7

III The Circumstances of this future Judgment, are very particularly related in Scripture

Who to be the Judge

1. It is expresly declared, that this judiciary Power is now vested in, and shall hereafter be exercised by our blessed Saviour For this is declared by our blessed Lord himself, *All power is given unto me both in heaven and in earth*, Mat xxviii 18 *The Father judgeth no man, but hath committed all judgment unto the Son*, John v 22 *And he commanded us to preach unto the people, and to testify that it is he, that was ordained of God to be the judge of quick and dead*, Acts x 42 *He hath appointed a day in which he will judge the world in righteousness, by that man whom he hath ordained*, Acts xvii 31 Not but that this will be an Act of the whole blessed Trinity, only the human Nature of the Son visibly appearing therein, it is ascribed more particularly to him Upon this account *Gregory Nyssen* speaks thus. Ἀκούσαντες ὅτι Πατὴρ κρίνει οὐδένα, ἀκ[illegible] ἡγούμεθα μαχέσθαι πρὸς [illegible] τὸ γεγραμμένον· Ὁ γὰρ κρίνων πᾶσαν τὴν γῆν διὰ τοῦ υἱοῦ, ὧ πάσας δέδωκε τῆς κρίσιν, τοῦτο ποιεῖ· καὶ πᾶν τὸ παρὰ τοῦ μονογενοῦς γινόμενον εἰς τὸν πατέρα τὴν ἀναφορὰν ἔχει, ὥστε καὶ κριτὴς αὐτὸς τῶν πάντων [illegible], καὶ κρίνειν μηδένα διὰ τὸ πᾶσαν, ὡς εἴρηται, τὴν κρίσιν τῷ υἱῷ δεδωκέναι, καὶ πᾶσαν τὴν τοῦ υἱοῦ κρίσιν τῷ πατρικῷ μὴ ἀπᾳδειν θελήματος. *When we hear that the Father judges no Man, we must not think that the Scriptures clash For he that judgeth the World by his Son, to whom he hath given judgment, judgeth it himself, and whatever is done by the unbegotten hath relation to the Father, so that he is the Judge of all things and yet judges no one, because as it is said he hath given all judgment to the Son, and the judgment of the Son is not different from the judgment of the Father* Greg Nyss Tract *Quod non tres sint Dii*

The Persons to be judged.

2 The Persons who are to be judged are expresly likewise declared, *viz* all Men *Before him shall be gathered all nations, and he shall separate them one from another, as a Shepherd divideth his Sheep from his Goats*, Mat xxv 32 *We must all appear before the judgment Seat of Christ, that every one may receive the things done in his body, according to that he hath done, whether it be good or bad*, 2 Cor v 10. *And the Sea gave up the dead that were in it, and death and hell delivered up the dead that were in them, and they were judged every man according to their works*, Rev xx 13. *We shall all stand before the judgment seat of Christ*, Rom xiv 10 *It is he that is ordained of God to be the Judge of quick and dead*, Acts x 42 By the *quick and the dead* in this last Passage, some of the Ancients understood Body and Soul As *Isidore Pelusiot* Τὸ κρίνεσθαι ζῶντας καὶ νεκροὺς, [illegible] τὸ καὶ ψυχὴν καὶ σῶμα εἰς κρίσιν ἐλεύσεσθαι *Isid Pel. Ep.* cxxii For the same Opinion *Methodius* is quoted by *Theophylact* in 1 *Thess* iv. But *Theodoret* more truly explains this Expression Νεκρῶν καὶ ζώντων κριτὴν [illegible] κέκληκεν, ἐπειδὴ καὶ τοὺς νεκροὺς ἀνίστησι, καὶ εἰς τὸ κριτήριον ἄγει, καὶ τοὺς κατὰ τὸν τῆς συντελείας καιρὸν [illegible] [illegible] τὴν ἀφθαρσίαν, ἀπαιτεῖ τὰς εὐθύνας *He calls Christ the judge of the quick and the dead, because he raises up the dead and brings them to judgment, and of those, that shall be found at the time of the Consummation, clothing them with incorruption, he shall require of them an account of their actions*, Theod ad 2 Tim iv 1

The form of the judicial procedure.

3 The form of this judicial Procedure is yet further described in Scripture *When the Son of man shall come in his glory, and all the Angels with him, then shall he sit upon the Throne of his glory*, Mat. xxv 31 *The Lord himself shall appear from heaven with a shout, with the voice of the Archangel, and with the Trump of God and the dead shall rise first*, &c 1 Thess iv 16 S *Austin* is of Opinion, that Christ shall be visible, only as to his human Nature to the wicked whom he shall judge *Visio filii hominis exhibebitur & malis Nam visio formae Dei, non nisi mundis corde, quia ipsi Deum videbunt, et eis solis piis exhibebitur, quorum dilectioni hoc ipsum promittit, quia seipsum ostendet illis* *The vision of the Son of Man shall be exhibited even to the wicked But the vision of the form of God only to the pure in heart, for they only shall see God* i. e. *only to the pious, to whose love he has promised this, because he has shewn himself to them*, Aug de Trin Lib. 1 c 13.

ARTICLE

ARTICLE V.

V *The Doctrine of the holy Scripture is sufficient to Salvation*

Of the Holy Ghost.

V De Spiritu Sancto.

Holy Scripture containeth all things necessary to Salvation

The [a] Holy Ghost, [b] proceeding from the Father and the Son,

Spiritus Sanctus, a Patre & Filio procedens, ejusdem est

Personality of the Holy Ghost.

a *Holy Ghost*] The Word *Ghost* is a *Saxon* Word that signifies Spirit, and having the Word *Holy* added to it, is generally used to denote the third Person of the Blessed Trinity Much Opposition has been made to this Article of our Faith, by several Hereticks both Antient and Modern some have denied his Personality, allowing him only to be a Quality or Operation, whilst others, that have acknowledged him to be a Person, have denied his Godhead, contending that he was only a created Being or Spirit But in Opposition to the first of these Opinions, we assert that the whole Phraseology of the Holy Scripture does directly contradict this Notion, all Expressions therein concerning the Holy Ghost being so worded as to denote him to be a Person For with what Propriety of Speech can an Accident or Quality be called the *Comforter*? How can a Quality be said to be *grieved*, Eph iv 30 If the Holy Ghost were not a Person, how could he be said to *Search all things*, 1 Cor ii 10 this being inconsistent with a mere Quality? Can an Accident be said to speak? as when the *Spirit said unto Peter, behold three men seek thee*, Acts x. 19 and when *the Holy Ghost said separate me Barnabas and Saul*, &c Acts xiii. 2 The like is to be said of other Actions ascribed to the Holy Ghost, which are altogether Personal As his making *Intercession for the Saints*, Rom viii 22 For 'tis impossible that an Operation or Quality can intercede or make an interest for any And so of the *speaking* and *hearing*, that is attributed to the Holy Ghost *When he the Spirit of Truth is come he will guide you into all Truth, for he shall not speak of himself, but whatsoever he shall hear, that shall he speak*, John xvi 13.

b *Proceeding from Father and Son*] This Truth being denied by the Greek Church, and thereby an unhappy Schism having arisen between the Greek and the Latin Churches, it may be of Use to consider a little the Rise and Progress of this unlucky Controversie

An Account of the Controversie concerning the Procession

The Church was never troubled with this Dispute till after the Year CCCCXXX The first rise thereof was owing to *Theodoret*, who in his Dispute with *Cyril* gave occasion thereunto. For *Cyril* writing against *Nestorius*, asserted, That Christ did not make use of the Holy Ghost to work his Miracles, as a borrowed Assistance, and That the Holy Ghost was a *Property of the Son* To this *Theodoret* answers, That if he meant by this, that the Holy Ghost was ὁμοφυὲς proceeding from the same Original with the Son, *viz* the Father, the Proposition was true εἰ δὲ ὡς ἐξ υἱοῦ ἢ δι' υἱοῦ τὴν ὕπαρξιν ἔχον, ὡς βλάσφημον τοῦτο καὶ ὡς δυσσεβὲς ἀποκηρύττομεν, *but if he meant, he has his original from the Son, we detest this as blasphemous and impious* Theod in Conf Anath 9 Cyr But the Controversie then died, with those Writers About the Year DCCLXXVII the Dispute was revived under the Emperor *Constantinus Copronymus* And again it was ventilated in the Council of *Aquisgrane*, between *Adelmus* and *John* a Monk of *Jerusalem* *Adonis* Chron Anno DCCCIX But in the Year DCCCLVIII it broke out again more furiously, by the means of *Photius*, who got into the See of *Constantinople*, by the Ejection of *Ignatius* For this and other Practices Pope *Nicholas* excommunicates *Photius*, and *Photius* in his turn excommunicates *Nicholas*, alledging Heresie against him, particularly that he and the Latin Church acknowledged, *That the Holy Ghost did proceed from the Father and the Son* Pope *Nicholas* writes to *Hincmar* Bishop of *Remes* for his Opinion concerning this Controversie Pope *Nicholas* dying, and *Basilius Macedo* being Emperor of *Constantinople*, *Ignatius* is restored, and *Photius* is condemned in the Eighth General Council according to the Latins An DCCCLXIX Many were the bickerings between the two Churches, in private Disputes, for a long time ensuing, but in the Council of *Bari* MXCVII it more was publickly ventilated, where *Anselm* Archbishop of *Canterbury* gained great Honour in defending the cause of the Latin Church, *vid. Will Malmsbur ad an* In the Council of the Lateran under *Innocent* the Third, matters seem to have been brought to a Compromise between the two Churches, but sometime after, under *Johannes Duca* the Emperor, the Disputes burst out into the old Flame again, *Niceph Greg. Lib v* In the Year MCCLXXIV was held the Council of *Lyons*, to which *Michael Palæologus* Emperor of *Constantinople* sent several of his Bishops, who agreed with the Latin Bishops in acknowledging the *Filioque*, Act Syn Lugd But soon after the Flame broke out anew, for *Michael* dying, his Body was not suffered to have Christian Burial, by reason of his Heretical Compliance with the Latins *Nic Greg Lib. vi* In the Year MCCCCXXXIX was held the Council of *Florence* wherein this Controversie was more nicely debated, where great number of the Greeks at first were present, but being tired out with long Disputes most of them withdrew before the Determination, and most of those that remained agreed with the Latins, others refused to subscribe to the Canons of that Council. And being got home again they espoused their old Doctrines, as they continue to do to this Day

The Filioque *proved from Scripture.*

But though this Doctrine of the Latin Church, which we profess, be not in express Terms asserted in Scripture, *viz* That the Holy Ghost proceedeth from the Father and the Son, yet there are several Passages of Holy Writ which do virtually contain this Truth For since the Holy Ghost is called the *Spirit of the Father*, and in other Places the *Spirit of the Son*, it is plain that he proceedeth from both First he is called the Spirit of the Father *It is not ye that speak, but the Spirit of your Father which speaketh in you*, Mat x 20 *The things of God knoweth no Man but the Spirit of God*, 1 Cor xi 12 He is likewise called the Spirit of the Son *God hath sent forth the Spirit of his Son into our hearts*, Gal iv 6 *If any man have not the Spirit of Christ, he is none of his*, Rom viii 9 *The Spirit of Christ which was in the Prophets*, 1 Pet i. 11 The like is proved by the common Mission of the Holy Ghost both by the Father and the Son As *the Holy Ghost whom the Father will send*, John xiv 26 *when the Comforter is come whom I will send unto you*

The Filioque *proved from the Writings of the antient Fathers of the Greek Church*

As fond and tenacious as the later Greeks are of their Opinion, concerning the Procession of the Holy Ghost from the Father alone, their Predecessors in that Church were clearly of a different Opinion To omit Authorities, which are more obscure and Consequential, these following seem to carry positive Clearness with them

EPIPHANIUS in *Ancor. Num* 71 has this express Passage Πνεῦμα ἅγιον πνεῦμα ἀληθείας φῶς τρίτον παρὰ πατρὸς καὶ υἱοῦ *The Holy Ghost is the third Light, proceeding from the Father and the Son* And in his Book of Heresies, *Her* 74 Τὸ δὲ ἅγιον πνεῦμα παρ' ἀμφοτέρων, πνεῦμα ἐκ πνεύματος, πνεῦμα γὰρ ὁ Θεὸς

P

The

The Holy Ghost proceedeth both from the Father and the Son, Spirit from Spirit for God is a Spirit And again, *Hær* 62 Οὐκ ἀλλότριον πατρὸς καὶ υἱοῦ, ἀλλ' ἐκ τῆς αὐτῆς οὐσίας, ἐκ τῆς αὐτῆς θεότητος ἐκ πατρὸς καὶ υἱοῦ, σὺν πατρὶ καὶ υἱῷ ἐνυπόστατον ἀεὶ ὑπάρχον ἅγιον *The Holy Ghost is not of a different Nature from the Father and the Son, but of the same Essence, of the same Godhead with the Father and the Son, always subsisting with the Father and the Son*

GREG NYSSEN, in his second Book against *Eunomius*, makes the Holy Ghost to proceed from the Son as a Principle, as well as from the Father Ὡς γὰρ συνάπτεται τῷ πατρὶ ὁ υἱὸς, καὶ τὸ ἐξ αὐτοῦ εἶναι ἔχων, οὐχ ὑστερίζει κατὰ τὴν ὕπαρξιν, οὕτω πάλιν καὶ τοῦ μονογενοῦς ἔχεται τὸ πνεῦμα τὸ ἅγιον, ἐπινοίᾳ μόνῃ κατὰ τὸν τῆς αἰτίας λόγον, προθεωρουμένου τοῦ πνεύματος [illegible] *As the Son is united to the Father and receives his Essence from him, and is not later than him as to Existence so the Holy Ghost has the Spirit of the unbegotten only by Cogitation, according to the Nature of a Principle, is considered as before*

DIDYMUS in his *de Spiritu Sancto*, translated by *S Jerom*, has this remarkable Expression concerning the Procession *Non enim loquetur de semetipso*] *Hoc est non sine me, & patris arbitrio quia inseparabilis est mea & Patris est voluntate Quia non ex se, ex Patre & me est Hoc enim ipsum, quod subsistit a Patre & me illi est* He shall not speak of himself] *That is, not without me and the Will of my Father because he is inseparable from my Will and that of the Father Because he is not of himself, but of the Father and me For he has his Subsistence from the Father and me* And again in his Comment on the 16th Verse of the same Chapter, he expresses himself thus *Spiritum Sanctum a Filio accipere id quod suæ naturæ fuerat, cognoscendum est It ought to be known, that the Holy Ghost does receive his Nature from the Son*

CYRIL abounds with Testimonies to the support of this Truth Of many which are produced by the Controvertists on the side of the Latins, these are a few Τρεπτὸν γὰρ οὐδαμῶς τὸ πνεῦμα ἐστὶν (ἦ γὰρ ἂν ἡ τῆς τροπῆς νόσος ἐπ' αὐτὸν ὁ μῶμος ἀναδράμοιτο τὴν θείαν φύσιν) ἔστι γὰρ ἐκ τοῦ θεοῦ, καὶ πατρὸς, ἀλλὰ μὴν καὶ τοῦ υἱοῦ τὸ οὐσιωδῶς ἐξ ἀμφοῖν, ἤγουν ἐκ πατρὸς δι' υἱοῦ προχεόμενον πνεῦμα *The Holy Ghost is by no means mutable, for if he were subject to this Infirmity, this would have an influence upon his Divinity For he is of God the Father and the Son, and proceeds essentially from both, viz of the Father by the Son* Cyr de Ador Lib I Again Ἡ γὰρ θεὸς, ἐστι κατὰ φύσιν ὁ υἱὸς (γεγέννηται γὰρ ἐκ θεοῦ καὶ πατρὸς) ἴδιον αὐτοῦ ἐστι, καὶ ἐν αὐτῷ, καὶ ἐξ αὐτοῦ τὸ πνεῦμα ἐστὶ, καθάπερ ἀμέλει καὶ τοῦ αὐτοῦ ὄντος τοῦ θεοῦ καὶ πατρὸς *For as the Son is God, and of God according to his Nature (for he is born of God and the Father) he is his* [ἴδιον] *Property* [or true Off-spring] *and in him and from him the Holy Ghost, who is as much his as God the Father's* Cyr. in Ire [illegible] cap II. In his *Thesaurus*, he has this remarkable Passage, insisted on much by *Beccus*, *Caleccas* and the other old Writers in this Controversie. "Ὅτε τοίνυν τὸ πνεῦμα τὸ ἅγιον ἐν ἡμῖν γινόμενον συμμόρφους θεοῦ ἀποτελεῖ ἡμᾶς, πρόεισι δὲ ἐκ πατρὸς καὶ υἱοῦ, πρόδηλον ὅτι τῆς θείας ἐστὶν οὐσίας, οὐσιωδῶς ἐν αὐτῇ, καὶ ἐξ αὐτῆς προϊὸν, ὥσπερ ἂν ἀμέλει καὶ τὸ ἐκ ἀνθρωπίνου στόματος ἐκτρέχον φύσημα *Whereas the Holy Ghost in us makes us conformable to God, proceedeth from the Father and the Son, it is manifest that he is of the divine Essence, substantially in it, and proceeding from it ; as the Breath which proceedeth from Man's Mouth* Cyr Thes Lib XXXIV.

S BASIL in his third Book against *Eunomius*, has a remarkable Passage upon this Head. Τίς γὰρ ἀνάγκη εἰ τῷ ἀξιώματι, καὶ τῇ τάξει τρίτον ὑπάρχει τὸ πνεῦμα, τρίτον εἶναι καὶ τῇ φύσει, Ἀξιώματι γὰρ δεύτερον τοῦ υἱοῦ [τὸ εἶναι] παρ' αὐτοῦ ἔχον, καὶ παρ' αὐτοῦ λαμβάνον, καὶ ἀναγγέλλον ἡμῖν, καὶ ὅλως ἐκ τῆς αἰτίας [illegible] παραδίδωσιν ὁ τῆς εὐσεβείας λόγος. *What necessity is there that the Holy Ghost, by being third in dignity and order, should be lest in Nature For to be next in dignity after the Son [as having his Essence from him, and receiving Revelation to us and depending upon him as a Principle] as the Holy Scripture informs us* The Words within the Hooks were excepted against by *Marcus Ephesius*, the Champion for the Greek cause, in the Council of *Florence* but *John*, who maintained the *Filioque*, averred, that he had consulted four or five Copies of *S Basil*, that were in *Constantinople*, where the Clause was, and that there were many more Copies which had it, one of which was written before the Controversie was started, *Vid Conc Flor. Sess* XX

The Latin Fathers likewise, who flourished before this unhappy Controversie began, assert the same Doctrine

The Filioque proved from the Testimonies of the Latin Fathers, who lived before the Controversie.

S HILARY in his second Book of the Trinity has these Words *Loqui de eo* [i e Spiritu Sancto] *non necesse est, quia de Patre & Filio Auctoribus confitendus est There is no occasion to speak of the Holy Ghost, because he is acknowledged to proceed from the Father and the Son* And in his Eighth Book thus *A Filio igitur accipit, qui & ab eo mittitur, & a Patre procedit & interrogo utrum id ipsum sit a Filio accipere, quod a Patre procedere Quod si nihil differre credetur, inter accipere a Filio, & a Patre procedere certè idipsum, atque unum esse existimabitur a Filio accipere, quod sit accipere a Patre Ipse autem Dominus ait, Quoniam de meo accipiat, &c He therefore receives from the Son, because he is sent by him, and proceedeth from the Father and I ask, whether it be the same thing to receive from the Son, as to proceed from the Father certainly it is the same, for the Lord saith He shall receive of mine*, &c

S AMBROSE in his first Book of the Holy Ghost, speaks thus *Spiritus quoque Sanctus, cum procedit a Patre & Filio, non separatur a Patre, non separatur a Filio Whereas the Holy Ghost proceedeth from the Father and the Son, he is not separated from the Father, nor from the Son*

S AUSTIN in his fourth Book of the Trinity does very clearly assert the Procession of the Holy Ghost both from Father and Son *Non possumus dicere, quod Spiritus Sanctus & a Filio non procedat neque enim frustra idem Spiritus & Patris, & Filii Spiritus dicitur We cannot say, that the Holy Ghost does not proceed from the Son: for otherways he could not be called the Spirit of the Father, and the Spirit of the Son* And again in his fifteenth Book, having asserted that the Holy Ghost does proceed originally from the Father, he adds, *Ideo autem addidi, principaliter, quia & de Filio Spiritus Sanctus procedere reperitur I therefore add the word* principally, *because the Holy Ghost is likewise said to proceed from the Son.*

LEO in his xciiid Epistle lays down the same Doctrine, and says, *alium esse qui genuit, alium qui genitus est, alium qui de utroque processit He that begat is one, he that is begotten is another, and different yet is he that proceeds from both*

PRUDENTIUS likewise asserts the Procession from the Son, as well as from the Father who speaking of the Son writes thus

Qui noster Dominus, qui tuus unicus,
Spirat de patrio corde Paraclitum.

Our blessed Lord, thy only Son,
Does from his Father's Bosom breath
The Paraclet ———

Prud Cathemer. v

So *PAULINUS* on the Birth-day of *S Felix*.

— — *Et in servos cælesti a dona profudit*
Spiritum ab Unigena Sanctum & Patre procedentem.

——*On us his Spirit he bestows*
That both from Son and Father flows

But before this, in the Year CCCC, the first Council of *Toledo* drew up a Confession of Faith, wherein they thus assert the Procession of the Holy Ghost from the Father and the Son *Credimus Spiritum quoque esse Paraclitum, qui nec Pater sit ipse, nec Filius, sed a Patre Filioque procedens Est ergo ingenitus Pater, genitus Filius, non genitus Paraclitus, sed a Patre Filioque procedens. We believe also that the Holy Ghost is the Comforter, who neither is the Father himself, nor the Son, but proceeding from Father and Son Therefore the Father is unbegotten, the Son begotten, the Comforter not begotten, but proceeding from Father and Son* This indeed was but a Provincial Council, but however it shew'd the Faith of the Church in that Age A few Years after A D CCCCXI the same was confirmed by the Council of *Bracara*, by the third Council of *Toledo*, A D CCCCLXXXIX, by the fourth Council of *Toledo*, A D DCXXXIII, by the eighth Council of *Toledo*, A. D. DCLIII, by the eleventh Council of the same Place, A D DCC, all held before the time the Greeks formally separated from the Latins

So that whatsoever is neither read therein, nor may be proved thereby, altho' it be sometime received of the Faithful as godly and profitable for an order and comeliness, yet no Man ought to be constrained to believe it as an Article of Faith, or reputed requisite to the necessity of Salvation

[c] is of one Substance, Majesty and Glory with the Father and the Son, very and Eternal God.

cum Patre & Filio essentiæ, majestatis & gloriæ, verus ac æternus Deus.

Holy Ghost the true God

c *Of one Substance*, &c *very and Eternal God*] These Words are here added to shew, that the Holy Ghost is not a nominal and titular God, a Creature of extraordinary Excellence, which is advanced to the Divine Honours, but the Real, True and Eternal God Now for establishing the Truth of this Assertion, it will be requisite shortly to mention the Arguments which Divines both Antient and Modern have made use of, which do clearly make out what is here laid down

Because called God in Scripture

I The Holy Ghost is very and true God, Because he is expresly called so in the Holy Scriptures For when *Peter* said, *Ananias, Why hath Satan filled thine Heart to lie to the Holy Ghost*, he shewing the grievousness of his Offence saith, *Why hast thou conceived this thing in thine Heart, thou hast not lied unto Men but unto God?* From whence it is plain that the Person whom he had lied unto, *viz* the Holy Ghost, was God From which Passage of Scripture *Epiphanius* very well concludes the Deity of the Holy Ghost Ἄρα θεὸς ἐκ θεοῦ, καὶ θεὸς τὸ πνεῦμα τὸ ἅγιον ᾧ ἐψεύσαντο οἱ τοῦ τιμήματος τοῦ χωρίου νοσφισάμενοι. *The Holy Ghost is God of God, and very God, to whom they who had misapplied the price the Field was sold for, lied* Epiph Hær lxxiv

Because number'd with the Father and Son in Baptism.

II The Holy Ghost is very and true God, Because he is set upon the Level with the Father and Son in the Form prescribed for the Administration of Baptism, *Go therefore and teach all Nations, baptizing them in the name of the Father, and of the Son, and of the Holy Ghost* But if the Holy Ghost were not really God, this would be such a sacrilegious advance of his Dignity, as nothing could warrant For thus *Theodoret* argues upon this subject Εἰ γὰρ κτιστὴν εἶχε φύσιν ὁ υἱὸς ἢ τὸ πνεῦμα τὸ ἅγιον, οὐκ ἂν συνηριθμήθησαν τῷ κεκτικότι θεῷ· κατηγοροῦσι γὰρ οἱ θεῖοι λόγοι τῶν λελατρευκότων τῇ κτίσει παρὰ τὸν κτίσαντα. *If the Son or the Holy Ghost had a created Nature, they would not be set on a Level with the Creator For the Holy Scriptures do blame those who serve the Creature, instead of the Creator* Theod v contr Hær

The like is said by *Athanasius*. Ποία γὰρ κοινωνία τῷ κτίσματι πρὸς κτίστην, ἢ διὰ τί τὸ πεποιημένον συναριθμεῖται τῷ ποιήσαντι εἰς τὴν τῶν πάντων τελείωσιν *What Society or Communion has the Creature with the Creator? how should that which is made be reckoned at the same time with Infinite Perfection?* Athan. Or iii. contr Ar

Because the divine Attributes ascribed to him

III The Holy Ghost is real and true God, Because the divine Attributes, as that of Omniscience or knowing all things, Omnipresence, &c are ascribed to him. For he is said *to dwell in us*, 1 Cor iii 16 and to *search out the hidden things of God*, 1 Cor ii 10 Whereupon *Athanasius* observes, *no Inferior can search out the Secrets of a Superior* Athan Epist ad Serap

The like he argues from his Sanctification Μὴ δὲ μετοχὸν αγιασμοῦ, ἀλλὰ αὐτὸ μεθεκτὸν ὂν καὶ ἐν ᾧ τὰ κτίσματα πάντα ἁγιάζεται πῶς ἂν εἴη ἐν τῶν πάντων, ἢ ἴδιον τῶν μετεχόντων, *Now if that which is not sanctified by another, but does impart Sanctification by which all other Creatures are sanctified, shall that be reduced to the Condition of created beings?* ibid

And so likewise S *Ambrose*. *Divinæ solius est potestatis arcana novisse It belongs to the divine Power to search out hidden things* Ambr de Spir Sanct Lib

Because he is said to dwell in us as a Temple

IV Because we are said in Scripture to be his Temples, which is a plain Allusion to his Deity, Temples being dedicated to none but those, who are Partakers of the divine Nature For thus the Apostle, *Know you not, that your Body is the Temple of the Holy Ghost*, 1 Cor vi 19 And again, *Know ye not that ye are the Temple of the Holy Ghost, and that the Spirit of God dwelleth in you?* 1 Cor iii 16 Upon which Consideration S *Basil* asks the Question Ἆρα τὸ ἐνοικεῖν οὐ τιμίου κατηγορεῖ τοῦ τότε τὸ τῇ ναῷ προσηγορίᾳ τιμήσαι, *Do you think that this Expression imports no more than a servile Inhabitation?* Bas de Sp. Sanct cap 21 And S *Cyril* makes this to be one of the divine Properties, which is ascribed to the Holy Ghost. Οὐδὲν γὰρ τῶν γενητῶν ἢ πεποιημένων, ὡς θεὸς, ἐν ναῷ λέγεται κατοικεῖν, μόνης γὰρ τῆς θείας φύσεως καὶ τὸ ὅτι καὶ τῶν ἄλλων ἐξαίρετον *There is nothing that is born or made which does dwell, as a God, in a Temple, for this with others is a Property only of the divine Nature*, Cyr Thes Lib xxiv

Because the Sin against him is irremissible

V Because the Sin committed against him is irremissible *All manner of Sin and Blasphemy shall be forgiven unto Men, but the Blasphemy against the Holy Ghost shall not be forgiven unto Men*, Mat xii 31 From whence S *Ambrose* thus Reasons *Quomodo igitur inter creaturas audet aliquis Spiritum computare? Aut quis se sic obligat, ut si creaturam lædit, non putet sibi hoc aliqua venia relaxandum? How therefore shall any one dare to reckon the Holy Ghost among Creatures? Or how can any one be bound, for an Offence against a Creature, as never to be released?* Ambr de Spir Sanct Lib i. cap 3.

ARTICLE VI.

VI *The Old Testament is not to be refused*

Of the Sufficiency of the Holy Scriptures for Salvation.

VI. *De Divinis Scripturis, quod sufficiant ad Salutem*

The Old Testament is not to be put away as though it were contrary to the New, but to be kept

Holy Scripture containeth [a] all things necessary to Salvation: So that whatsoever is

Scriptura Sacra continet omnia, quæ ad salutem sunt necessaria, ita ut quicquid in ea nec legitur,

a *All things Necessary*] The Compilers of our Articles, having in the foregoing Articles laid down the main Branches of the Christian Faith, proceed now to establish the Rule thereof And here begins our avowed Difference with the Church of *Rome* They assert, that the Books of Holy Scripture, though divinely inspired, were occasionally only written, and do not contain the whole Rule of Faith, many other Doctrines of the Apostles being delivered by Word of Mouth were conveyed down to us by Oral Tradition We on the contrary assert, that the Holy Scriptures are a compleat Rule of Faith, and whatever is not contained therein is not necessary to be believed by any Christian Man

That the Holy Scriptures are a compleat Rule of Faith

This Truth is proved,

I By the Authority of the Holy Scriptures themselves And this is so plainly laid down therein, that nothing but strange Prejudice, and Resolution to support a Cause, could contradict it. Those words of S *Paul* are very full to this purpose *All Scripture is given by inspiration of God, and is profitable for doctrine, for reproof, for correction, for instruction in righteousness, that the Man of God may be perfect, throughly furnished unto all good works*, 2 Tim iii. 16, 17 *Moses* expresly forbids, *That any one should add unto the words that I command you, neither shall ye diminish ought from it*, Deut iv 2 *Whatsoever I command unto you to observe and do it, thou shalt not add thereunto nor diminish from it*, Deut. xii 32 The same Prohibition is given out in the New Testament For S *John* closing his Book of the *Revelation*, and with that our Christian Canon (so that it may not improbably seem to bear relation to the whole New Testament) forbids any Addition or Diminution, with a Cause annexed to it *If any man shall add unto these things, God shall add unto him the plagues that are written in this Book, and if any man shall take away from the words of the Book of this Prophesie, God shall take away his part out of the Book of life, and out of the holy City, and from the things which are written in this Book*, Rev xxii 18, 19 But the Substance of this had been before declared by S. *Paul* *But, though we or an Angel from Heaven preach any other Gospel unto you, than that which we have preached unto you, let him be accursed*, Gal i 8 And as for the endeavour of some to piece out God's written Word by Tradition, our Saviour warns us against this, when he blames the Pharisees for it, *viz* in *teaching for doctrines the Commandments of men*, Mat xv. 9 and *making the Commandment of God of none effect by their Traditions*, v 3

Scriptures a compleat Rule of Faith, proved by Scripture.

II By Reason, drawn from the Nature of the thing, and the whole Order of the gracious Dispensation of the Gospel, which God hath been pleased to bless Mankind with, this is no more than we might expect For our Saviour having first made known the Gospel to the World by his own Preaching and Suffering, and propagated it throughout the several Parts thereof by the Preaching of his Apostles, in order to be convey'd down to successive Generations, this could not well be effected without a written Word For to have delivered down the Gospel Truths by Word of Mouth, or Oral Tradition, would have made it subject to as many Errors, as the Prejudices, Fancies and Mistakes of the several Relaters could have given it Now since God has been pleased to make use of this Method to convey those Truths which he has revealed to us, it is but reasonable to think, that all the Truth, which he has judged necessary for our Salvation, and which he has required of us to believe, are contained in this written Word, for why God should leave some of the Gospel Truths to be conveyed in a purer, and others in a more corrupt Channel, some by Scripture and others by Tradition, is unaccountable Why, since he designed the Scriptures to be in some Measure the Rule of Faith, he should not at the same time render it a compleat one, why this Divine Law of God must be eked out by Human Traditions, which have been uncertain in the best Times, and pernicious in some, and which strangely vary according to different Countries and Ages These Notions do highly reflect upon the Divine Wisdom and Goodness, and are taken up only to defend the corrupt Practices of the Roman Church, which they are resolved to maintain at any rate rather than to part with

By Reason

III The like Reasons are alledged by the antient Divines of the Church, which they reduce to these general Topicks (1.) The first is drawn from the Excellency of God's Word, which is so contrived as to be useful to Men of all Capacities and Conditions For thus S *Basil* Πᾶσα γραφὴ θεόπνευστος καὶ ὠφέλιμος, διὰ τοῦτο συγγραφεῖσα παρὰ τοῦ πνεύματος, ἵν' ὥσπερ ἐν κοινῷ τῶν ψυχῶν ἰατρείῳ πάντες ἄνθρωποι τὸ ἴαμα τοῦ οἰκείου πάθους ἕκαστος ἐκλεγώμεθα *Every part of the Holy Scripture is divinely inspired, and profitable, it being for this end written by the Spirit, that it might be as it were a common Shop of Physick, for every one to fetch what Medicine is most proper for the Disease of his Soul* Bas Pref in Psal (2.) The Compleatness of this Rule is not to be taken from any particular part of the Holy Scripture, but from the whole Canon or Collection of sacred Books For thus S *Basil* Ἄλλα μὲν οὖν προφῆται παιδεύουσι, καὶ ἄλλα ἱστορικοί, καὶ ὁ νόμος ἕτερα, καὶ ἄλλο τι εἶδος ἡ παροιμιακὴ παραίνεσις *Some things we are instructed in by the Apostles, in others by the Historians some things the Law informs of, and other Admonitions we have from the Proverbs* Bas ibid (3.) They argue from the great Crime of adding to, or detracting any thing from Holy Scripture For upon this Consideration is grounded that Argument of *Tertullian* *Scriptum esse doceat Hermogenis officina Si non est Scriptum, timeat væ illud adjicientibus, aut detrahentibus destinatum* Let Hermogenes his Shop *shew that this is written But if it be not written, let him be afraid of that Curse, that is denounced against those that add any thing to, or detract any thing from God's Word* Tert adv Hermog cap xxii. S *Cyprian* argues against a pretended Tradition from the same Topick *Unde est ista Traditio? utrumne de Dominica & Evangelica authoritate descendens, an de Apostolorum mandatis, atque Epistolis veniens? Ea enim facienda esse, quæ scripta sunt, Deus testatur & ponit ad Jesum plane dicens, Non recedet Liber legis hujus ex ore tuo, sed meditaberis in eo die ac nocte, ut observes facere omnia quæ scripta sunt in eo. From whence comes this Tradition? Does it depend upon the Authority of Christ*

Reasons assigned by the antient Fathers, for the Scriptures being a compleat Rule of Faith

1 *Because useful for all Capacities.*

2 *The Compleatness to be measured by the whole.*

3 *From the Curse against adding or diminishing*

still; for both in the Old and New Testaments Everlasting Life is offered to Mankind by Christ, who is the only Mediator between God and Man, being both God and Man Wherefore they are not to be heard,

not [b] read therein, nor may be proved thereby, is not be required of any Man, that it should be believed * as an Article of Faith, or be thought † requisite or necessary to Salvation. In the name * of the Holy Scripture we do under-

neque inde probari potest, non sit a quoquam exigendum, ut tanquam Articulus Fidei credatur, aut ad salutis necessitatem requiri putetur. Sacræ Scripturæ nomine, eos Canonicos Libros veteris & novi Testamenti intel-

* *As an Article of the Faith.* MS. CCCC 1571
† *Requisite as necessary to Salvation.* MS CCCC 1571
* *Of Holy Scripture* MS CCCC 1571

Christ or the Gospels, is it grounded on the Precepts or Epistles of the Apostles? For God himself witnesses, that we are to do those things that are written, and he puts it to Joshua *the Son of* Nun *saying, The Book of this Law shall not depart from thy Mouth, but thou shalt meditate therein day and night, &c* Cyr ad Pomp Ep ed Pam lxxiv S *Chrysostom* stands so steadily for the Compleatness of the Scripture as a Rule of Faith and Life, that he reckons him a Thief, that pretends to advance any other Ὁ γὰρ μὴ ταῖς γραφαῖς χρώμενος, καὶ ἀναβαίνων ἀλλαχόθεν, τουτέστιν ἑτέραν ἑαυτῷ καὶ μὴ νενομισμένην τέμνων ὁδὸν, οὗτος κλέπτης ἐστί *He that does not make use of the holy Scriptures, but goes aside into another Road, leaving the common way, the same is a Thief* Chryf in Joh x

b *May not be proved*] These Words likewise are added in Opposition to the Roman Church, which allow Articles of Faith to be founded upon Tradition, but we on the contrary assert that all Doctrines of Faith and Life, and whatsoever is taught in the Church as a Divine Doctrine, ought to be founded upon the Holy Scriptures This Opinion of ours we ground upon the Doctrine of the Holy Scriptures themselves.

All Doctrines to be proved by Scripture

This proved out of God's Word

I Our Saviour informs us, that the end of enditing the Sacred Books was to lay down the Foundation of Christians Faith. *These things are written that ye might believe, &c and that in believing ye might have life through his name,* John xx 31 Which if true of the Books of the Old Testament, are much more so of the New For these were written by those Apostles who were the Friends and Associates of our Blessed Saviour, whom he fully informed of his Will, of whom our Saviour thus speaks, *I have called you friends, because all things which I have heard of my Father I have made known unto you,* John xv 15 They were written by Persons who had not only the Advantage of this Information, but were under the immediate Direction of the unerring Spirit of God *But the Comforter which is the Holy Ghost, whom the Father will send in my name, he shall teach you all things, and bring all things to your remembrance, whatsoever I have said unto you,* John xiv. 26

By Reason.

II We have very good Reason to believe, that all things necessary to Salvation should be contained in Scripture, for as these are but few in number, so is it but reasonable to think they are contained some where or other in the Holy Scriptures. For whereas there are several things mixed in those Sacred Books, which are not plainly necessary to Salvation, but are only useful Truths, which the Holy Spirit has thought proper for our Spiritual Improvement, that we should be informed of, we cannot think, that any things, which are absolutely necessary for our Salvation, should be omitted.

Arguments of the Fathers
1 From the Conviction which the Holy Scriptures carry

III. The antient Divines of the Church were of the same Opinion. Which they confirm by arguing some several very excellent Topicks (1) Because the Doctrines which are confirmed by the Holy Scriptures carry the greatest force of Persuasion with them, and which all Believers cannot but assent to. For thus *Origen* upon the Third of the *Romans. Post hæc vero, ut ei moris est,* &c *After this S. Paul according to his Custom, proves what he said out of the Holy Scriptures thereby giving an example to the Doctors of the Church, that those things which they teach the People, should not be built upon their own Opinions, but should depend upon the divine Testimonies For if so great an Apostle does not think it fit, that Men should relie upon his Words, unless he prove what he said to be written in the Law and the Prophets how much rather ought we little Persons to observe this, that, when we teach, we do not deliver our own Opinions, but those of the Holy Ghost?* To like purpose S *Basil.* Δεῖ πᾶν ῥῆμα ἢ πρᾶγμα πιστοῦσθαι τῇ μαρτυρίᾳ τῆς θεοπνεύστου γραφῆς εἰς πληροφορίαν μὲν τῶν ἀγαθῶν, ἐντροπὴν δὲ τῶν πονηρῶν *Every thing that is done or said ought to be confirmed by the Testimony of the Holy Scripture · as well to the full and perfect Persuasion of good Men, as the Confusion of ill Men* Bas. Eth Def xxvi So likewise *Clement* of *Alexandria.* Οὐ γὰρ ἁπλῶς ἀποφαινομένοις ἀνθρώποις προσέχοιμεν, οἷς καὶ ἀνταποφαίνεσθαι ἐπ' ἴσης ἔξεστιν εἰ δ' οὐκ ἀρκεῖ μόνον ἁπλῶς εἰπεῖν τὸ δόξαν, ἀλλὰ πιστώσασθαι δεῖ τὸ λεχθὲν, οὐ τὴν ἐξ ἀνθρώπων ἀναμένομεν μαρτυρίαν, ἀλλὰ τῇ τοῦ Κυρίου φωνῇ πιστούμεθα τὸ ζητούμενον, ἣ πασῶν ἀποδείξεων ἐχεγγυωτέρα, μᾶλλον δὲ ἡ μόνη ἀπόδειξις οὖσα τυγχάνει. *It is not reasonable that we should assent to Mens simple Words against which we may justly oppose our Assertion. But if it be not sufficient only to say that which is barely probable, but we ought likewise to gain assent to what we say, let us not content our selves with Testimonies from Men, but let us confirm that which comes into Question by the Word of God, which is the most certain of all Demonstrations, nay which only is Demonstration* Clem Alex Strom vii

2 Because Hereticks, are best confuted by them

(2) Because this is the best way of confuting any Heretical Opinions which arise For thus *Tertullian* reasons *Aufer Hereticis, quæ cum Ethnicis sapiunt, ut de Scripturis solis quæstiones suas sistant, & stare non poterunt. Take away from the Hereticks their Pagan Doctrines, and let them state their Doctrines according to the Holy Scriptures, and they will not be able to stand.* Tertul. de Resur Carn cap iii S *Basil* having declared the former Unfruitfulness of his Labours in opposing the Hereticks by Arguments drawn from Reason, declares, for the future, his Resolution in attacking them with Scripture Νῦν δὲ πρὸς τὸν κοινὸν ἡμῶν τε καὶ ὑμῶν σκοπὸν ἁρμόζον ἐλογισάμην ἐν ἁπλότητι τῆς ὑγιαινούσης πίστεως τὸ ἐπίταγμα τῆς ὑμετέρας ἐν Χριστῷ ἀγάπης πληρῶσαι, εἰπὼν ἃ ἐδιδάχθην παρὰ τῆς θεοπνεύστου γραφῆς φειδόμενος μὲν καὶ τῶν ὀνομάτων καὶ ῥημάτων ἐκείνων ἃ λέξεσι μὲν αὐταῖς οὐκ ἐμφέρεται τῇ θείᾳ γραφῇ, διάνοιαν γε μὴν ἐκείνην τὴν ἐγκειμένην τῇ γραφῇ διασώζει ὅσα δὲ πρὸς τῷ ξένῳ τῆς λέξεως, ἔτι καὶ τὸν νοῦν ξένον ἡμῖν ἐπεισάγει καὶ οὐκ ἔστιν ὑπὸ τῶν ἁγίων κηρυσσόμενα εὑρεῖν, ταῦτα ὡς ξένα καὶ ἀλλότρια τῆς εὐσεβοῦς πίστεως παντάπασι παραιτούμενος *Now accommodating my self to my own and your Profession, I have resolved in the Simplicity of the Faith, to fulfil the command of your love in Christ, to speak those things which I have learned from the Holy Scriptures abstaining from those Names and Words which are not contained in Scripture, although they retain the Sense of Scriptures For those, besides the novelty of the Expression, are apt to induce a new Meaning, and are not found to be preached by the Apostles, therefore I will avoid these as foreign Words,*

and

which feign that the Old Fathers did look only for transitory Promises

stand those [c] Canonical Books of the Old and New Testament, of whose Authority was never any doubt in the Church.

ligimus, de quorum authoritate, in Ecclesiâ nunquam dubitatum est

Of the Names and Number of the Canonical Books.

De nominibus & numero Librorum Sacræ Canonicæ Scripturæ veteris Testamenti

[d] *Genesis.*

Genesis.

and distant from the Holy Faith. Bas Hom de fide (3) Because all other Testimonies are fallible And thus S *Cyril* of *Jerusalem* argues Μὴ τοῖς ἐμαῖς εὑρεσιλογίαις πρόσεχε ... δεῖ γὰρ περὶ τῶν θείων ... μηδὲ τὸ τυχὸν ἄνευ τῶν θείων παραδίδοσθαι γραφῶν ... *Do not give heed to my Words, for you may be deceived nay unless I bring my vouchers for every thing I say, do not believe me unless you have Proof out of Scripture of the Virgin, of the Place, of the Time and the Manner, do not admit the Testimony of Man.* Cyr. Catech xii

3 *Because all other Testimonies are fallible*

(4) Because this is the best way of ending Controversies S *Austin* sets the Authority of these above that of the greatest Councils *Sed nunc nec ego Nicænum, nec tu debes Ariminense, tanquam præjudicaturus proferre Concilium Neque ego hujus authoritate, neque tu illius detineris Scripturarum authoritatibus, non quorumcunque propriis, sed utrisque communibus testibus, res cum re, causa cum causa, ratio cum ratione concertet* *I ought not to appeal to the Nicene Council, nor you to that of* Ariminum, *as being prejudiced in favour of that I am not swayed by the Authority of the one, nor you of the other Making use of the Authority of the Scriptures, which are common Witnesses to us both, let us set Controversie against Controversie, Cause against Cause, Reason against Reason* Aug contr Maxim Lib iii. cap 14. The Great Emperor *Constantine* proposed these as the best Rule for Faith, in the Council of *Nice* Εὐαγγελικαὶ γὰρ βίβλοι καὶ ἀποστολικαὶ καὶ τῶν παλαιῶν προφητῶν τὰ θεσπίσματα, σαφῶς ἡμᾶς ἃ χρὴ περὶ τοῦ θείου φρονεῖν ἐκπαιδεύουσι *The Gospels and the Books of the Apostles, and the Oracles of the antient Prophets, can best instruct us what we ought to believe of the divine Nature.* Thiod Hist Eccl Lib i cap 7

4 *Because this is the best way of ending Controversies.*

c *Canonical Books*] They are called Canonical Books from the Greek word κανών, which signifies in the Church Language a Catalogue For among the Ecclesiastical Writers, sometimes κανών signifies the Catalogue or Roll of the Clergy, whose Names were entered, at their Ordination, into the Church Books Thus in the xviith Canon of the Council of *Nice*, Οἱ ἐν τῷ κανόνι ἐξεταζόμενοι *They who are reckoned up in the Catalogue of the Clergy* In like manner the Catalogue of the Sacred Books, which were reckoned of undoubted Authority in the Church, was called the Κανὼν or the Canon The most antient of these Catalogues or Canons now extant is that of *Melito* Bishop of *Sardis* in the second Century, recorded in the fourth Book of *Eusebius*'s Ecclesiastical History, who writ it to *Onesimus*, who had desired him to give him Information concerning the number and order of the Books of the Old Testament, as he had learned from the Churches of the East With which agrees the Catalogue given in the lixth Canon of the Council of *Laodicea* Another in the xxxixth Epistle of *Athanasius* one in *Cyril* of *Jerusalem*, Catech iv.

d GENESIS] This Book, in Conjunction with the other four following, is called by the Name of the *Pentateuch*, which Word in the Greek Tongue signifies the five Volumes That they were written by *Moses*, whose Name they bear, is agreed upon by the universal Consent, not only of Jewish and Christian, but even of Heathen Writers. For these are owned as *Moses* his Books by *Manetho*, who wrote a Greek History of *Ægypt*, as he is cited by *Josephus*, contr Ap. Lib i which Author lived under *Ptolomy Philadelphus*, 250 Years before Christ They are attributed to *Moses* by *Philochorus Atheniensis*, cited by *Justin Martyr*, Exhor ad Gen which Writer lived under *Ptol Philopator*, 180 Years before Christ *Apollonius Molo*, another ancient Greek Author, quoted by *Josephus*, cont. Ap. as also *Alexander Polyhistor*, in *Eusebius*, Præp E vang ascribe these Books to him. So likewise do *Strabo*, Lib. xvi *Pliny*, Nat Hist Lib xxx c 2 *Tacitus*, Hist Lib v *Juvenal*, Sat 14 And when *Longinus* says of *Moses*, for the Sublimity of his Expression, that he was οὐχ ὁ τυχὼν ἀνήρ, *a Man not of the ordinary size of Understanding*, and also when *Numenius* stiles *Plato*, *Atticizing Moses*, they did most undoubtedly attribute these Books to *Moses* To say nothing of the constant Reception of these Books, as the Mosaical, in the Jewish Church and Nation, or of the *Samaritan Pentateuch*, which is written in Characters which have not been used since the Jewish Captivity, in which these Books bear the Name of *Moses* Nor lastly, to insist upon the Septuagint Translation, which Version was made 250 Years before Christ, and which renders these into Greek, as *Moses*'s Books For, though there were none of these Authorities to vouch for this ancient Writer the bare Testimony of our Saviour were sufficient *If ye believed Moses you would have believed me, for he wrote of me*, John v. 46 To which we may add that of *Philip* to *Nathaniel*, *We have found him of whom Moses in the Law, and the Prophets, did write*, John i 45 So S *Luke*, in his relation of our Saviour's Discourse in the Journey to *Emmaus* says, *Luke* xxiv 27 that *beginning at Moses*, &c i e. the *Pentateuch*, or Books writ by *Moses* So that, without bringing to the account the constant and uninterrupted Consent, in this Matter, of the Jewish and Christian Churches, for so many thousand Years, hardly a Book in the World was, with more universal Agreement, attributed to the Author, whose Name it bears, than those Books of *Moses* It must be owned that some small Additions have been made to them since *Moses*'s Time, as for Instance, the Passage in the close of the Book of *Deuteronomy*, concerning the Death of *Moses*, which is generally thought to be added by *Joshua*, who succeeded him in the Prophesie, as well as the Government And possibly some marginal Annotations, formerly affixed to the sides of a very ancient Copy, have since got into the Text, as *Gen* xiv 10 *Dan* is put for *Lais*, as also a few other Modern, and more known Names, may be put for the Ancient and more obscure Which has given occasion to some irreligious Persons, to question *Moses*'s being the Author of the Book Which Objections, as they are frivolous, so they have been over and over again answered by learned Men The first of these Books is, in the Hebrew Copies, called *Bereshith*, (i e) *In the beginning*, so named from the first Word of the Book, in the Greek, Latin, and most other Translations, it is called *Genesis*, or the Book of the Generation, because it gives an account of the *Genesis*, or Formation of the World, as also of the Succession of the first Families of Mankind

Some are of Opinion that *Moses* wrote this Book, when he was an Exile in *Midian*, *Exod* ii 15 to raise up the dejected Spirit of the Jews, under *Pharaoh*'s Oppression But 'tis most probable, that he wrote it in the Wilderness of *Sinai*, whilst, under the Divine Directions, he was forming that Sacred Commonwealth Nor is it probable, that every part of the History was revealed to him as a Matter perfectly New, and that *Moses* was the first Writer that ever was,

[e] *Exodus.* [f] *Leviticus.* [g] *Numbers.* [h] *Deuteronomy.* [i] *Josuah.* [k] *Judges. Ruth.* [l] *The first Book of Samuel. The second Book of Samuel.* [m] *The first Book of Kings. The second Book of Kings. The first Book of Chronicles. The second Book of Chronicles.*	*Exodus. Leviticus. Numeri. Deuteronomium. Josuæ. Judicum. Ruth. Prior Liber Samuelis. Secundus Liber Samuelis. Prior Liber Regum. Secundus Liber Regum. Prior Liber Paralipom. Secundus Liber Paralipom.*

was, it is more just to think, that he made use of some short Memoirs written before his Time, probably contained in ancient Hymns and Genealogical Tables, kept among the principal Families of the Jews, which he inserted into his History, the whole Work being carried on, under the particular Conduct and Direction of the Holy Spirit of God. It is certain, this is, by far, the most antient Book in the World now extant. It was written near 1500 Years before Christ, and almost 600 Years before *Homer*, the most ancient of all the Greek Writers now remaining. For, as for the Pieces ascribed to *Trismegistus*, *Orpheus*, *Musæus*, &c. they are but Forgeries of later Ages, nor were the Authors themselves, which they were ascribed to, by much so ancient as *Moses*.

e *EXODUS*] This Book is called so from the Greek Word ἔξοδος, which signifies the *Going out*; because it chiefly Treats of the *Israelites* going out of *Ægypt*, and therefore in the Scriptural Catalogue in the Council of *Laodicea*, it is more expresly called, Ἔξοδος ἐξ Αἰγύπτου. That this Book was written by *Moses* at the positive Command of God is clear from these Passages in this Book. *Write this for a memorial in a Book*, &c. Exod. xvii. 14. *And Moses wrote all the words of the Lord*, &c. Exod. xxiv. 4. *And the Lord said unto Moses, write thou these words*, &c. Exod. xxxiv. 27. Besides there is further weight added to the Authority of this Book, because several Passages thereof are cited by our Saviour himself in the fifth of S. *Matthew*.

f *LEVITICUS*] This Book was written by *Moses*, soon after the rearing of the Tabernacle, which was the first Month of *the second Year* after the going out of *Ægypt*, Exod. xl. 17. for then God began to speak to *Moses*, not out of Mount *Sinai*, as when the Tables of the Law were given, but *out of the Tabernacle of the Congregation*, Lev. i. 1. several Passages of this Book are cited in the New Testament. The Law concerning the Leprous Person, *Lev.* xiii. 14. is mentioned *Luk.* v. 14. The *Lex Talionis*, *Lev.* xxiv. 20. is referred to *Mat.* v. 38.

g *NUMBERS*] This Book contains the History of the Israelitish Affairs, from the second Year of their going out of *Ægypt* to the last Year of *Moses* his Life, that is about 38 Years of the 40, which they travelled about in the Wilderness. For in *the eleventh month of the fortieth year* the Book of *Deuteronomy* was begun to be written, *Deut.* i. 3. Passages out of this Book are mentioned in the New Testament. As the Brazen Serpent, *Num.* xxi. is mentioned by our Saviour, *John* iii. 14. and by S. *Paul*, 1 Cor. x. 9.

h *DEUTERONOMY*] This Book was written by *Moses* in the last Year of his Life. It was first delivered to the *Israelites* by Word of Mouth, and afterwards put into writing by him, as we learn *Deut.* xxxi. 9. *And Moses wrote this Law, and delivered it to the Priests the Sons of Levi*, &c. It is a Compendium, or shorter Explanation of the Law, which had been delivered in the former Books, and for that Reason is called by the Greeks Δευτερονόμιον or the *second Law*. Passages out of it are cited, *Mat.* xii. 11. *Mat.* xviii. 16. *Luke* x. 26. *Mark* xii. 19. The last Chapter, which treats of *Moses* his Death, is supposed to be written by *Joshuah*, who was Successor to *Moses* in the Prophesies.

i *JOSUAH*] That this Book was written by *Josuah* is expresly attested, *Jos.* xxiv. 26. *And Joshuah wrote these words in the Book of the Law of God*, &c. i. e. he joyned the History of his Time to the Transactions formerly written by *Moses*. The Author of the Book of *Ecclesiasticus* attributes this Book to him. *Jesus the Son of Nave was valiant in the Wars, and Successor of Moses in the Prophesies*, Eccl. xlvi. 1. A Passage of this Book is quoted by the Writer of the Book of *Kings*, 1 Kings xvi. 34. *In his days did Hiel the Bethelite build Jericho: he laid the foundation thereof in Abiram his first born, and set up the gates thereof in his youngest Son Segub, according to the word of the Lord, which he spake by Joshua the Son of Nun.* Which manifestly refers to the saying of *Joshuah*, *Cursed be the man before the Lord, that riseth up and buildeth this City Jericho: he shall lay the foundation thereof in his first born, and in his youngest Son he shall set up the gates of it*, Jos. vi. 26. The History of *Rahab* recorded in this Book is referred to *Heb.* xi. 30. and *Jam.* ii. 25.

k *JUDGES. RUTH*] The Book of *Judges*, to which the Book of *Ruth* is a little Appendix, is not without probability attributed by the Jews to *Samuel*. For, whereas he was for many Years at the Head of the Jewish Affairs, and settled their Church and Common-wealth which had long lay in disorder, 'tis not likely that he should neglect to gather together their History from their first Settlement in *Canaan*, out of antient and dispersed Memoirs. However that the Book of *Judges* is very antient is clear, because it is alluded to in a *Psalm of David*, which he made upon removing the Ark. *When thou wentest forth before the People, when thou didst march through the wilderness; the earth shook, the heavens also dropped at the presence of God.* Which Words are an exact Imitation of *Judges* v. 4. *Lord, when thou wentest out of Seir, when thou marchedst out of the field of Edom, the earth trembled, the heavens dropped, the clouds also dropped water.* Immediately after the Psalmist says, That *the mountain of Sinai was moved at the presence of the God of Israel.* Which Words are likewise copied from the Words which follow, in the foresaid Chapter of *Judges*. *The mountains melted from before the Lord, even that Sinai from before the God of Jacob.*

l *SAMUEL*] It is not certain who the Author of these Books were. But it is not without Probability asserted by the Jewish Writers, that the first twenty four Chapters were written by *Samuel* himself, and the rest by the Prophets *Nathan* and *Gad*. But there do not want evident Marks of the Antiquity of these Books. For they are referred to *Psal.* cxiii. 7. where a Passage of *Hannah's* Song is transcribed. *He raiseth up the poor out of the dust, and lifteth up the needy out of the dunghil, that he may set him with Princes, even the Princes of his People.* Which passage in 1 *Sam.* ii. 8. is thus: *He raiseth the poor out of the dust, and lifteth up the beggar from the dunghil, to set them among Princes, and to make them inherit the throne of Glory.* The History of these Books is likewise referred to 1 *Kings* ii. 27. *So Solomon thrust out Abiathar from being Priest unto the Lord, that he might fulfil the word of the Lord, which he spake concerning the house of Eli in Shilo.* See 1 Sam. ii. 31.

m *KINGS. CHRONICLES*] It is uncertain whether the Books of *Kings* and *Chronicles* were put into the Form, they now stand in, before, or after the Captivity. It is probable they were collected after the Return, out of Memoirs that were written before, *Esdras* himself either performing or supervising the Compilation. Now the Books being at first written by Men of a Prophetick Spirit, they were not less the Word of God, by being put into another Form, especially by one

who

[n] The first Book of Esdras. The second Book of Esdras. [o] The Book of Hester. [p] The Book of Job. [q] The Psalms. [r] The Proverbs. Ecclesiastes or Preacher. Cantica or Song of Solomon.

Primus Liber Esdræ Secundus Liber Esdræ Liber Hester. Liber Job. Psalmi Proverbia. Ecclesiastes vel Concionator. Cantica Solomonis.

who was a Prophet himself, as *Esdras* was Nay, so over scrupulous this Compilator, whoever he was, seems to be, that he takes the very Words of the antient Prophets, out of whose Memoirs he composed these Books, as is evident from 2 *Chron* v 5 where the Introduction of the Ark into the Oracle is thus described, and it is said, *There it is unto this Day* Now either the Books of the *Chronicles* were written before the Captivity, under the first Temple, when the Ark was there, or else *Esdras*, or whoever the Compilator was, made use of the very words of the antienter Prophet, out of whom he transcribed this Work Either of which Suppositions give sufficient Authority to these Books For if the Author lived before the Captivity, he was an Eye-witness of many of the Matters of Fact he relates, and if he lived after, we see he is so just to his Original Authors, as not to vary a tittle from their Words All that *Esdras* (or whoever else the Compiler was) added of his own, were some Genealogical Observations at the beginning of the *Chronicles*, and some other Passages of little Moment, which relate to the times after the Captivity The Authority of these Books is established, by being cited in the New Testament The History of *Elijah* and the Woman of *Sarepta*, 1 *Kings* xvii is mentioned *Luke* iv 25 that of *Naaman* the *Assyrian*, 2 *Kings* v 14 is referred to *Luke* v 25 And 1 *Pet* i 17 is taken out of 2 *Chron* xix 7

n *First Book of* ESDRAS] This is what we call in our English Bibles (according to the Hebrew Copies) the Book of *Ezra* And this Book all but the first six Chapters, was composed by him For *Ezra* speaks expresly in his own Person, as Chap vii ver 27 *Blessed be the Lord God of our Fathers, which has put such a thing into the Kings heart, to beautify the house of the Lord, which is in Jerusalem*, &c

The second Book of ESDRAS, as it is called in some Copies, was written by *Nehemiah*, whose Name it bears in the Hebrew, and the Jewish Church has always attributed it to him The Son of *Sirach* mentions his building the Walls of *Jerusalem*, recited in that History *And among the elect was Nehemias, whose renown was great, who raised up for us the Walls that were fallen, and set up the Gates and the Bars, and raised up our ruins again*, Eccl xlix 13 And 'tis plain that the Book of *Nehemiah* was not only received into the Jewish Canon, but went under *Nehemiah* his Name, when the Books of the *Maccabees* were written, as is evident from 2 *Mac* ii 13 *The same things were also reported in the Writings and Commentaries of Nehemias, and how he founding a Library, gathered together the Acts of the Kings and the Prophets, and of David, and the Epistles of the Kings concerning the holy Gifts*

o HESTER] This Book was received into the Jewish, and into most of the Christian Canons, though it be not contained in the Catalogues of *Melito*, *Athanasius*, or that of *Nazianzen* Some of the Jews ascribe it to no certain Author, but will have it to be drawn up by Order of the Synagogue, to which *Mordechai* wrote, cap ix some will have it to be written by *Mordechai* himself, which seems most probable, from these words, *And Mordecai wrote these things*, ver 20

p JOB] The Author of the Book of *Job* is uncertain, but being received into the Jewish Canon, it must be supposed to be written by an inspired Writer The Author of it, whoever he be, is very antient, and lived, as is most probable, before the Promulgation of the Jewish Law, for there are not any Traces to be found of the Mosaical Precepts in the whole Book, nay we may find some things contrary to them, as particularly *Job's* offering Sacrifice himself, after the Patriarchal manner, which was allowed only to the Priests under the Judaical Law. It is not improbable, which some conjecture, that it was written by *Moses* during his abode in *Egypt*, or in his flight into the Land of *Midian*, before he had promulged the Judaical Law and his design might be to hearten up the Jews under the Severities of the *Egyptian* Bondage, by shewing the gracious Designs of God's Providence, and that he oftentimes lays his sharpest Afflictions upon his best Servants That the whole Story is an Allegorical Fable must in no wise be allowed for the Testimonies of *Ezechiel* and S *James*, who mention *Job* as a real Person, prove the contrary of this Opinion Nay, from hence it appears, that the Book of *Job* was generally read among the Jews in *Ezechiel*'s time, which was before the composing of *Esdras* his Canon

q PSALMS.] The *Psalms* are no late Compositions, most of them being written before the Captivity Indeed we ought not, as some do, to attribute them all to *David*, when their several Titles do allot them to other Authors, although a great share of them are owing to that inspired Prince It is certain that in the antientest Times, both after and before the Deluge, holy Men were wont to sing the Praises of God, for singular Mercies received, in Hymns, the care of composing which, Persons of good Parts and a Prophetick Spirit, were pleased to take upon themselves, as is plain in the Instances of *Moses* and *Miriam*, *Deborah*, *David*, *Solomon*, &c The Hymns were wont, not only to be learned by pious People, as helps to their Devotion, but were delivered to the *Levites*, to be laid up in the Archives of the Temple, as *Josephus* writes, *Antiq Lib* iii *cap* 1 and out of these the *Levites* made their Choice to sing in the Temple, upon set Occasions Of these there was a vast number gathered together (composed by the Prophets of so many preceding Ages) in the Temple of *Jerusalem*, before the burning of it by the *Chaldeans*, for *Solomon* himself is recorded to have composed above a thousand Of these Hymns a great many were carried into the Captivity by some devout Men, and brought back with them upon their Restoration; which, together with some others composed at *Babylon*, were by *Esdras* and the Great Synagogue formed into this Book of *Psalms*, which we now have. Besides, 'tis evident, that many of them were known to the antient Prophets, before the Captivity, by their making use of the Words of them For a part of the first *Psalm*, is thus in a manner transcribed by *Jeremiah*, *Jer* xvii 7 *Blessed is the man that trusteth in the Lord, and whose hope the Lord is, for he shall be as a Tree planted by the Waters, and that spreadeth out her Roots by the River, and shall not see when heat cometh, but her leaf shall be green, and shall not be careful in the year of draught, neither shall cease from yielding fruit.* These words in the xcviiith *Psalm*, *With his right hand and holy arm hath he gotten him the victory, and all the ends of the earth have seen the Salvation of our God*, are used by the Prophet, *Is* lii. 10. That of *Jeremiah*, Lam v. 19. *Thou Lord remainest for ever, and thy Throne from Generation to Generation*, is taken out of *Psalm* cii. That of *Is* li 6 *They all shall wax old as a Garment*, is taken out of the cist *Psalm* likewise From whence we may gather, that most of the *Psalms* are not only very antient Compositions, but were used very early in the Service of the Temple, which occasioned the Prophets in their Writings to make use of their Phraseology

r PROVERBS] There is no doubt to be made, but that the Book of *Proverbs* (except perhaps the xxxth Chapter) was written by the King, whose Name it bears. The first twenty four Chapters seem to be the Original Collection, made by *Solomon* himself, and to be the beginning of a greater Work, which was destroyed with the Temple at the Captivity And the following Chapters are a Collection made by others, as appears by the beginning

Four Prophets the Greater. 4 *Prophetæ majores*
Twelve Prophets the Less. 12 *Prophetæ minores.*

ning of the twenty fifth Chapter *The Proverbs of Solomon, which the men of Hezekiah, King of Judah, copped out.* By the Men of *Hezekiah* are meant some Persons, whom the King employed for this purpose They were probably *Eliakim* the Son of *Hilkiah*, and *Shebna* the Scribe, and *Joash* the Recorder, who were Secretaries to *Hezekiah*, and who might probably likewise have the Assistance of the Prophet *Isaiah* This Collection holds to the thirtieth Chapter, which has the Title of *Agur*, but who this *Agur* was is uncertain, he does not seem to be *Solomon*, from the mean Character he gives of himself *Surely I am more brutish than any man, and have not the understanding of a man I have neither learned wisdom, nor have the knowledge of the Holy*, Prov xxx 10 Which is no ways agreeable to the great Wisdom God gave to *Solomon*, 1 *King* iv 29 nor indeed to that Character, which *Solomon*, in *Ecclesiastes*, gives of himself. *I have gotten more wisdom than all they that have been before me in Jerusalem, yea my heart hath great experience of wisdom and knowledge*, Eccl 1 16 The last Chapter, which bears the Name of *Lemuel*, must likewise be written by King *Solomon*, who either was so called by his Mother in his Childhood, or that Prince on purpose took this disguised Name This Chapter seems to be made up of some wise Instructions, which his Mother *Bathsheba* had taught him, when he was a Child.

ECCLESIASTES is likewise, upon good grounds, ascribed to the same Royal Author. *Grotius* indeed would have it to be written by *Zerubbabel*, because of some *Syriack* and *Chaldee* words which are found therein But it is possible that these words might have crept into the Hebrew Tongue in *Solomon*'s time, or at least *Solomon*, by his Conversation with so many strange Women, might have learned them from them. But the great Character of Wisdom, which this Author lays claim to, his building Houses and planting Vineyards, his making Gardens and Fishpools, his gathering so much Silver and Gold, *&c* which he speaks of Chap 1 is the peculiar Character of *Solomon*, which such a poor Prince as *Zerubbabel* could never pretend to

THE SONG of *Solomon* is the Composition of the same Prince, the Title of this Poem declaring the same. And though some Hereticks of old, and Anabaptists of late, have looked upon it only as an ordinary Love Song, yet the Pious in all Ages have esteemed it an Allegorical Dialogue, between God and his Church

[*Four Prophets the Greater*] The four Greater Prophets are, *Isaiah*, *Jeremiah*, *Ezekiel*, *Daniel*

ISAIAH was certainly the Writer of the Prophesie which goes under his Name because his Name is set in the beginning of the Book Some will have him to be of Royal Extraction and to be the Son of that *Amos* who was Brother of *Azariah*, which noble Education gave him a turn of Thought above the rest of the Prophets That this Prophesie is older than many Parts of Scripture is evident, because almost two Chapters of it, Chap xxxvii and xxxviii, are well nigh verbatim transcribed in the second Book of *Kings*, Chap xix and some Expressions made use of by *Jeremiah*, *Jer* l. 2 xlv ii. 4 The Passages of his Prophesie are frequently cited in the New Testament, *Luke* iv 18 *Mark* i 3 *Acts* vii 32.

JEREMIAH began his Prophesies very Young, *viz* under the 13th Year of *Josiah*, and continued them under the Reigns of *Jehoazah*, *Joachim*, *Jechoniah* and *Zedekiah*, throughout the Course of 40 Years, prophesying the Evil and Destruction of the City which happened in the last Year of *Zedekiah* His Prophesie is referred to by several of the succeeding Prophets, by *Ezechiel* cap xviii 3,4 xxxi 29, 30 by *Daniel* cap ix 2 by the Author of the *Chronicles*, *Chron* xxxvi 22 by *Zechary*, cap i 4 As likewise by the Authors of the Books of the New Testament, *Mat* xvi 14 *Mat* xi 26 *Mark* xi 7

EZECHIEL was of the House of *Levi*, the Son of *Buzi* a Priest, he was carried with King *Jechoniah* into *Chaldea* and prophesied on the Banks of the River *Chebar*, for about 20 Years His Prophesie is so obscure and full of Mystery, that the Jews will not allow their Rabbins to explain some Parts thereof, till they are above thirty Years old His Prophesie seems to be referred to by *Daniel* cap x 13 and by *Zechary*, cap xiii 2 cited likewise by the Authors of the New Testament, *Mat* xxiv.29 *Joh*. x 11

DANIEL is the Author of that Book which bears his Name, and the antient Jews did acknowledge the same, and that withal that he was an inspired Prophet, (though some of the Modern ones, among other of their Fooleries, now deny it) is evident from this Passage of *Josephus* *Whatsoever Books* Daniel *left written by him the same are read this Day with us, and we do believe from them, that* Daniel *had a Communication with God* And as for the Arguments which the modern Jews use, to prove that he was not properly a Prophet, they are Fond and Silly, for let God communicate himself to him how he will, yet still he is a Prophet, because he Predicts future things, and those in so plain and express a Manner, as few of the other Prophets are herein comparable to him And this *Josephus* was conscious of, and affirms the like *For, says he, he does not only predict future things, but limits the time in which they are to happen And when other Prophets predict evil things, and for this reason raised the hatred of the common People against them*, Daniel *was the Foreteller to them of good things*.

[*Twelve Prophets the Less*] It is evident that the twelve Prophets were received into the Jewish Canon, when the Book of *Ecclesiasticus* was written, by this remarkable Passage Where after Praises bestowed on *Ezechiel*, and other Prophets and Worthies of *Israel*, there are these words *And of the twelve Prophets let the Memorial be blessed, let their Bones flourish again out of their place, for they comforted Jacob, and delivered them by assured hope*, Ecclus xlix. 10 Of these *HOSEAH* prophesied in the Reigns of *Uzziah*, *Jotham* and *Hezekiah* Kings of *Judah* He is cited in the New Testament, *Mat* ii 15 *Mat* ix 13 1 *Cor* xv 4 Contemporary with him was *JOEL*, who was of the Tribe of *Reuben*, and exercised his Prophetic quality in *Bethoron* Passages out of his Prophesie are referred to *Mat* xxiv 29 *Mark* xiii 24 *Acts* ii 17 *Rom* x 13 *AMOS* was a Person of ordinary Extraction, being a Shepherd of *Tekoa*, a Village belonging to the Tribe of *Judah*, and prophesied in the time of *Uzziah* King of *Judah* His Prophesie is referred to *Luke* vi 24 *Rom* v 9 *Acts* vii 43 *OBADIAH* is thought by some to be a *Sichemite*, *Isid. de Vit Sanct.* cap 44. *Epiphan de Vit Sanct cap* 15 Others think him to be that Steward of *Ahab*, who hid the hundred Prophets and fed them His Prophesie is cited by S *Paul*. 1 *Cor* i 19 *JONAH* was the Son of *Amittai*, who was likewise a Prophet of the City of *Gath* belonging to the Tribe of *Zebulum* in *Galilee* He was sent to preach Repentance to the City of *Nineveh*, and his Book is the relation of his Journey and other Occurrences which fell in with it This Book is quoted by *Tob* xiv 3 and by our Saviour himself, *Mat* xii 40 *MICAH* prophesied under the Reigns of *Jotham*, *Ahaz* and *Hezekiah* His Prophesie was extant before *Jeremiah* prophesied, who mentions a Passage out of *Micah*'s Prophecy, *Jer* xxvi *NAHUM* prophesied in the Reign of *Hezekiah* and *Manasses* He followed *Jonah* the Prophet in his Prophetick Denunciations against the *Ninivites* *HABAKKUK* prophesied in the Reign of *Manasses* His Aphorism, *The Just shall live by Faith*, Hab ii 4 is famous for being several times cited by the Writers of the New Testament, *Rom* i 17 *Gal* iii 11 *Heb* x 38 *ZEPHANIAH*, as the beginning of his Prophesie witnesseth, prophesied under the Reign of *Josiah*, but most probably he exercised his Prophesie towards the beginning of his Government, before he had made a Reformation in the Church, and abolished those Idolatrous Rites which had been introduced by his Father *Manasses*, for he exclaims against those, Cap i 4, 5, 9 *HAGGAI* prophesied about the second Year of *Darius Histaspes*, some little time before *Zechary* began to exercise his Prophesie He prophesied to the Jews after their Return from the Captivity, exhorting them to build the Temple, notwithstanding the Opposition which was made against it *ZECHARY* seconded *Haggai* in his Prophesie, pursuing mostly the same Argument, exhorting his Countrymen to the rebuilding of the Temple But many obscure Prophesies are mixed in his Book concerning future Events, which have exercised the Wits both of the Jewish and Christian Wr-

And [u] the other Books (as *Hierom* faith) the Church doth read for Example of Life, and Instruction of Manners; * but yet it doth not apply them to establish any Doctrine. Such are these following.

Alios autem Libros (ut ait Hieronymus) legit quidem Ecclesia, ad exempla vitæ, & formandos mores illos autem ad dogmata confirmanda, non adhibet ut sunt,

[w] *The third Book of Esdras. The fourth Book of Esdras.* [x] *The Book of Tobias.* [y] *The Book of Judith.* [z] *The rest of the Book of Esther.* [aa] *The Book of Wisdom. Jesus the Son of Syrach.* [bb] † *Baruch the Prophet. The Song of the three Children.*

Tertius Liber Esdræ Quartus Liber Esdræ Liber Tobiæ Liber Judith Reliquum Libri Hester. Liber Sapientiæ Liber Jesu filii Sirach. Baruch propheta Canticum trium puerorum

* *But yet doth it not apply*, MS CCCC 1571.
† *Baruch*, MS. CCCC. 1571.

ters The Parts of his Prophesie are frequently cited in the New Testament, as *Mat* xxi 4 *Mar.* xiv 27 *John* xix 37 *Luke* i. 78 MALACHY, the last of the Prophets, lived in the same time with *Haggai* and *Zachary*, tho' a much younger Person, and exercised his Prophesie after their Decease His famous Prophesie concerning the Forerunner of the Messias, is cited by S *Matthew* xi 10 S *Mark* i 2 and S *Luke* i 17.

Of the Apocryphal Books

u *The other Books, as* Hierom *saith*, &c] The Place of S *Jerom*, here referred to, is in his Preface to the Book of *Proverbs Sicut ergo Judith & Tobiæ & Maccabæorum libros legit quidem Ecclesia, sed eas inter canonicas Scripturas non recipit sic & hæc duo volumina legat ad ædificationem plebis, non ad authoritatem ecclesiasticorum dogmatum confirmandam As the Church reads the Books of* Judith, Tobit *and the* Maccabees, *but doth not receive them among the Canonical Scriptures, so she may read these two Volumes, for the Edification of the People, but not for the Confirmation of Ecclesiastical Doctrines*, Hier Op. Tom iii ed Frob p 25 *Ruffinus* was of the same Opinion *Sciendum tamen, quod & alii libri sunt, qui non Canonici, sed Ecclesiastici a majoribus appellati sunt----Quæ omnia legi quidem in Ecclesiis voluerunt, non tamen proferri ad authoritatem ex his fidei confirmandam Cæteras vero Apocryphas nominaverunt, quas in Ecclesiis legi noluerunt. It must be known that there are other Books, which are not called Canonical but Ecclesiastical, by our Ancestors --Both which ads they would have read in the Churches, but would not have them produced for the Confirmation of Faith But as for the other Apocryphal Books, they would not have them read in the Churches* Ruf Expos Symb And here it must be noted, that *Ruffinus* calls those Books Ecclesiastical, which we now call Apocryphal So that according to the Language of those Times, there were three Ranks of the Books The *first* were those which were received in the Canon, and were undoubtedly of Divine Inspiration The *second* were the Books we now call the *Apocrypha*, but the Antients called them the Ecclesiastical Books, as the Books of *Judith, Tobit*, &c The *third* were called the Apocryphal, such as the Gospel of S *Thomas*, of the Nazarens, &c

w *Third and fourth Book of Esdras*] The third Book is found in no antient Catalogue, but is in the Greek, the fourth is only in the Latin The third is mostly a Repetition of what is related in the two first Books, (viz *Esdra* and *Nehemiah*) and the fourth filled with insignificant Dreams and Visions

x *Tobias*] The Book of *Tobit* is wanting in all the old Catalogues, but is cited as a pious Book by many of the Antients, *Orig Hom* xxvii in *Num Isid. Lib* iii. *cap* 34 *Hil* in *Psal* cxxix

y *Judith*] The Book of *Judith* is but little cited by the Antients Tho' *Clement Romanus* refers to her History, in his Epistle to the *Corinthians*. *Tertullian*, Lib i contr Marc and *Clement* of *Alexandria*, Strom Lib iv recommend her Action as Heroick, which shews that the Antients had an Esteem for this Book.

z *Rest of the Book of Esther*] The Six last Chapters of that Book are not in the Hebrew, nor were they so in *Origen*'s Time And as they contain several things of a more Modern date, appear to be the Work of some later Hellenistical Jew

aa *Wisdom Son of Syrach*] These Books are wanting in all the old Catalogues, and several of the Antients reject them, as having no Title to be owned as Canonical Scripture Thus do *Origen*, S *Jerom* and *Hilary* S *Basil* on the *Proverbs* looks on them as uncanonical Books, and *Theodoret*, in his Preface to the *Canticles*, declares himself of the same Opinion Notwithstanding they are quoted with respect by S *Barnabas, Clemens Romanus*, and the other of *Alexandria*, by *Tertullian*, S *Cyprian* and S *Austin*

bb *Baruch*] This Book is rejected out of the Number of the Canonical Books, by S *Jerom* in his Commentary on *Jeremiah*. Nor is it to be found in the Catalogues of *Melito, Origen, Nazianzen* or *Epiphanius* It takes a place indeed in the Catalogue of the Council of *Laodicea*, and is quoted by *Clement* of *Alexandria*, S. *Cyprian* and some others of the Antients, under the name of *Jeremiah*, the Supposition of its being written by him, gaining it that Authority with them

Song of the three Children] Tho' this was not owned by the Antients for Canonical Scripture, yet they had such an Esteem for this Composition, as to use it very antiently in their publick Service of the Church As *Ruffinus*, Lib 2 contr Hier witnesseth S *Austin*, Aug Hom 35. Tom 10 and the Council of *Toledo*, Conc Tol iv can 3

cc *The*

cc *The History of Susanna. Of Bell and the Dragon.* dd *The Prayer of Manasses.* ee *The first Book of Maccabees. The second Book of Maccabees.*

Historiæ Susannæ. De Bel & Dracone. Oratio Manasses Prior Liber Machabæorum. Secundus Liber Machabæorum.

ff All the Books of the New Testament as they are commonly received, we do receive, * and account them Canonical.

Novi Testamenti omnes Libros (ut vulgo recepti sunt) recipimus, & habemus pro Canonicis

* *And account them for Canonical*, MS CCCC 1571

cc *The Story of Susannah, of Bell and the Dragon*] These Histories are rejected as fabulous by many of the Antients, particularly by *Africanus* and *Eusebius* And S *Jerom* in his Preface upon *Daniel* is of the same Opinion And *Theodoret*, who has commented upon *Daniel*, speaks nothing of these last Chapters, which relate these Stories However it is plain, that these Histories were not unknown to many of the antient Writers For *Clement* of *Alexandria* not only refers to, but commends the Action of *Susanna*, Strom Lib iv and so does *Tertullian*, de Cor Lib iv as likewise S *Cyprian*, Ep 4 S. *Austin*, Serm cxviii and S *Basil*, de Spir Sanct cap 7

dd *The Prayer of Manasses*] This is a serious piece of Devotion, but is of no Authority. It is neither in Hebrew nor Greek.

ee *Maccabees*] The Books of the *Maccabees* are not found in any of the antient Catalogues, and are rejected from being Canonical by the best Criticks of Antiquity *Eusebius* in his Chronicon excludes them from any Title of being Canonical Scripture And so does S *Jerom* in several Places S *Ambrose*, *Chrysostom* and others indeed quote them, but only as secular History

Of the Books of the New Testament.

ff *All the Books of the New Testament*] The Authority of the Books of the New Testament does not depend upon the Decree or Determination of any Council or Assembly, but upon the universal Consent of the Christians of all Ages and Nations since the Apostolical Times, which they have agreed to receive, as Books written by the first inspired Propagators of Christianity, and particularly by those whose Name they bear For the four Gospels, and the fourteen Epistles of S *Paul* were universally acknowledged Some of the other Epistles indeed were controverted, because some particular Churches did not admit them, but after the matter was fairly debated these were likewise accepted as Genuine Now since all Churches did receive these Books as the Works of the inspired Apostles, it is very clear Evidence that they were written by them For what could move such different Bodies of Men of different Nations to afford this extraordinary Esteem to these Books above others, if they had not been written by these extraordinary Men? Men of different Persuasions would not have quitted their Country Religion which they had been educated in, and have been contented to have been governed by the Rules of the Institution which these Books deliver. And thus *Origen* well argues Πᾶσα [illegible] καὶ [illegible] τὴν οἰκουμένην ζηλωτὰς ἔχει μυρίας κατα[illegible] τοὺς τῆς πατρῴους νόμους καὶ νομιζομένους θεοὺς, [illegible] Μωσέως νόμων. καὶ τῆς μαθητείας τῶν Ἰησοῦ Χριστοῦ λόγων [illegible] μισούμενοι ὑπὸ τῶν τὰ ἀγάλματα προσκυνούντων [illegible] Μωσέως νόμον προσιέμενοι καὶ τὸν ἐπὶ θανάτῳ [illegible] κινδυνεύοντες [illegible] Χριστοῦ λόγον παραδεξάμενοι *Both Greece, and the Barbarous all over the World, have innumerable Proselytes who, having abandoned their Country, Laws and Gods, have professed Obedience to the Laws* of Moses *and the Discipline of Jesus Christ Tho' the fulfilling the Laws of* Moses *subjects them to the most inveterate hatred of those that worship Idols, and to profess Christianity, besides being hated, exposes Men to the danger of their Lives*, Orig Philocal Cap 1

Besides, the very Originals of the Books were extant, and to be seen by any Persons whose Curiosity enquired after them, in the several Churches where they were lodged This is evident from that remarkable Passage of *Tertullian* *Age jam qui voles curiositatem melius exercere in negotio salutis tuæ, percurre Ecclesias Apostolicas, apud quas ipsæ adhuc cathedræ Apostolorum suis locis præsident, apud quas ipsæ authenticæ literæ eorum recitantur* *You that have a mind to exercise your Curiosity, in the matter of your Salvation, run through the Apostolick Churches, where the Sees of the Apostles are still remaining, and there you shall find, that their very Authentick Letters are recited* Tert de Prescript

The first of these Books is the Gospel according to S *MATTHEW*, which, according to the Testimony of the most antient in the Christian Church, viz *Papias*, *Irenæus* &c that Apostle wrote in Hebrew There are Authorities brought out of this Gospel by *Clemens Romanus*, by *Barnabas* in his Epistle, by *Ignatius* and *Polycarp*, by *Justin Martyr* and *Irenæus* nay, this Gospel was owned by the Heretick *Cerinthus*, who lived in the Apostolical times, and who rejected all the rest, because they contradicted his Heresie It was very early translated out of the Hebrew or Syriack into the Greek, in the Apostolick time, and S *Jerom* certifies, that in his time he saw a Copy of it in the Library of *Cæsarea*

The Gospel according to S *MARK* was written by a Disciple of S *Peter*, who was a different Person from that *Mark* mentioned in the Epistles of S *Paul* *Irenæus* says, he composed this Gospel out of the Sermons of S *Peter*, and others that S *Peter* approved of it, wherefore some have called it the Gospel of S *Peter*, as *Tertullian* writes

The Gospel of S *LUKE* was written by a Disciple of S *Paul*, of that Name, a Physician by Profession, of the City of *Antioch*, and one who was well skilled in the Greek Tongue 'Tis probable, that he was no immediate Disciple of Christ, as some contend, because he says, what he wrote he learned from others 'Tis plain from his Preface to [illegible], that there were several other Gospels extant in his time, and probably some spurious ones which made him, as *Eusebius* says, undertake the Evangelick History, to rescue it out of bad Hands, having been informed of the particular Circumstances of those Transactions by Eye witnesses, and particularly being aided by the assistance of his Tutor S *Paul* Therefore it is supposed, that S *Paul* means this History, when he says, *according to my Gospel*, and for this reason he gives S *Luke* this Elogium, *whose praise is in the Gospel* This Gospel is quoted by *Clemens Romanus*, and the Epistle of *Barnabas* has something out of it *Irenæus* owns it, and so do the Hereticks *Cerdo* and *Marcion*, who admit of none else The same S *Luke* wrote *THE ACTS OF THE APOSTLES*, as appears from his Preface to *Theophilus* Besides the Antiquity of this Book is sufficiently proved, because it was rejected by the Heretick *Cerinthus*, who lived in the Apostles time

That S *JOHN's GOSPEL* was written by the Apostle of that Name, is the joint Voice of Antiquity It is quoted by *Justin Martyr* who lived in the next

Age

ARTICLE VII.

VI *The Old Testament is not to be refused.*	*Of the Old Testament.*	VII. De veteri Testamento.
The Old Testament is not to be put away	[a] The Old Testament is not	* *Testamentum vetus novo contrarium*

* Only the words, *Testamentum vetus novo contrarium non est, quandoquidem*, &c in MS. CCC 1562

Age after S. *John*, as Authentick Scripture, and Authorities out of the same are made use of by *Irenæus* *Clement* of *Alexandria* writes, that it was a Tradition he had received from his Predecessors, that S *John* last of all wrote his Gospel Nay, the Copies of that Gospel were so common as to be viewed by the Heathens of that Age for *Amelius* the Platonick Philosopher, cites the beginning of the Gospel of S *John*, whom he calls *That Barbarian*, and he lived not above threescore or fourscore Years after S *John*. He was likewise the Author of the Epistles, which go under his Name The first of the Epistles is unanimously, by all Antiquity, allowed for Canonical Scripture, and ascribed to S *John* the Apostle, and the two last were never disputed, whether they were Divine Writings, or no, but whether they were written by S. *John* the Apostle. Whether the *Apocalypse* was written by this Apostle, or by another S *John*, has been a Question among some, but the general Consent of Christians has carried it for the Apostle, *Vid Just Mart. Dial cum Tryph. Tertul adv Marc. Lib* iii. *Clem. Alex apud Euseb Lib* iii *Orig* in *Mat*

The Epistles of S *PAUL* were ever received with the unanimous Consent of all Christians, they were read in the Churches very early in the Apostolick times, as appears by that of S *Peter*, in his second Epistle, where he mentions S *Paul*'s Epistles, and says, *In which some things are hard to be understood, which they that are unlearned and unstable wrest, as they do also the other Scriptures, unto their Destruction* *Clemens Romanus* takes many Expressions out of these The Epistles to the *Galatians* and *Philippians* are quoted by *Polycarp*, the Scholar of S *John*, and some Places out of those, and others, are cited by *Athenagoras*, *Clemens Alexandrinus* and *Tertullian* Only some have doubted, whether or no S. *Paul* wrote the Epistle to the *Hebrews*, but the best Judges of Antiquity, *Clemens Alexandrinus*, *Origen*, *Eusebius* and S *Jerom*, attribute it to S *Paul* However this Epistle was taken so antiently for Scripture, that *Clement* of *Rome*, who was Contemporary with S *Paul*, cites some Passages *verbatim* out of it And S *Jerom* writes, that this Epistle was always attributed to S *Paul*, in the Eastern Church, though it was for some time excepted against in the Latin

The Epistle of S *JAMES* is quoted by as antient Authors as *Clemens Alexandrinus*, *Origen*, *Cyprian* and *Tertullian*, and though, as *Eusebius* relates, it was for some time doubted by some, yet it is plain that, upon better weighing the Matter, at last all received it

The first of S *PETER* was universally received as of undubitable Authority The second (as *Origen* *Eusebius* and S *Jerom* write) was some time doubted, *i. e.* whether it were S *Peter*'s, but the same Writers who relate this do themselves adjudge it to him, and it is mentioned in the Catalogues of Canonical Books, *viz* of *Clement* of *Alexandria*, S *Athanasius* and *Nazianzen*

The Epistle of S *JUDE* is quoted as Canonical Scripture, by *Tertullian* and S *Cyprian*, and is in all the Catalogues of the Sacred Books Indeed it was sometime doubted, like the second of S *Peter*, by some Churches, but upon more mature Consideration it was universally received It seems to be written upon the same Occasion as the second of S *Peter*, *viz* to warn the Faithful, against the Pretences of the Gnosticks, or some other very antient Hereticks

The Purport and Design of the Article, from Bishop Burnet

a *The Old Testament is not contrary to the New*] I The learned Bishop of *Sarum* has made the following excellent Remark, which is very necessary for a due stating of the Sense and Tendency of this Article. "This Article is "made up of the Sixth and Nineteenth of King *Edward*'s "Articles laid together Only the Nineteenth of King *Edward*'s has these words after *Moral* *Wherefore they* "*are not to be heard, which teach that the holy Scriptures* "*were given to none but to the weak and brag continually* "*of the Spirit, by which they do pretend, that all whatsoever they preach is suggested to them, though manifestly* "*contrary to the holy Scriptures* This whole Article re"lates to the *Antinomians* As these last words were "added by reason of the Extravagance of some Enthusiasts "at that time, but that Madness having ceased in Queen "*Elizabeth*'s time, it seems it was thought that there "was no more occasion for those Words.

This Heresie first broached by the Marcionites *and* Manichees

II This pestilent Doctrine of the *Antinomians*, in making the Old Testament contrary to the New, was but a part of the *Manichean* and *Marcionian* Heresies, revived For thus *Theodoret* relates of *Marcion* Τὸν νόμον καὶ τοὺς προφήτας, καὶ τὴν παλαιὰν πᾶσαν ἐξέβαλλεν, ὡς ἀπ' ἀλλοτρίου δεδομένην θεοῦ *He rejected the Law and the Prophets, and all the old Testament, as given by another God.* Theod. Hær Fab Lib I cap 24 And so *Epiphanius* of the same Heretick. Τὸν νόμον ἀποβάλλει καὶ πάντας προφήτας, λέγων ὅτι τοῦ ἄρχοντος τοῦ τὸν κόσμον πεποιηκότος τοὺς τοιούτους προφητευκέναι *He rejected the Law and all the Prophets, saying that they did not predict future things, from the Instinct of that Archon who made this World.* Epiphn Hær xlii The same Impiety *Socrates* relates of the Heretick *Manes* Καὶ νόμον καὶ προφήτας ἀθετεῖ *He rejects the Law and the Prophets* Socr Hist. Eccl Lib. 1 ed Steph. p 185 And so does *Theophylact* mention him, as maintaining the same Opinion, in common with *Marcion* Εἷς δὲ αὐτὸς ὁ νομοθέτης παλαιᾶς τε καὶ νέας διαθήκης, κἂν Μαρκίων καὶ Μάνης, καὶ ὁ λοιπὸς τῶν πάντων αἱρετικῶν κατάλογος ἀθετοῦσι τὴν παλαιὰν, τοῦ πονηροῦ δημιουργοῦ λέγοντες αὐτὴν εἶναι νομοθεσίαν *There is one and the same Legislator of the Old and the New Testament, though* Marcion *and* Manes, *and the other like Tribe of Hereticks, do reject the Old Testament, saying that it is the Legislature of an evil Demiurg* Theoph in iii Joh

Revived by Johannes Agricola, *the Founder of the Sect of the* Antinomians

III This wicked and dangerous Opinion was in part revived by *Johannes Agricola*, who was first a Scholar of *Luther*, and afterwards the Founder of the *Antinomian* Sect He was born at *Isleb* in *Saxony*, A D 1442 He accompanied Count *Mansfield*, as a Chaplain to the Diet of *Spire*, 1526 And to that of *Ausburg*, 1530, in the Retinue of the Elector of *Saxony* He was afterwards a Professor and Minister at *Wittenberg*, where he vented his *Antinomian* Doctrines, using very contemptuous Expressions in his Lectures, concerning the Mosaical Law and the Old Testament *Luther* wrote against him with his usual Spirit, and by his Interest with the Protestant Princes obliged him to Recantation, which he submitted to, though with no

great

as tho' it were contrary to the New, but to be kept still; for both in the Old and New Testaments everlasting Life is offered to Mankind by Christ, who is the only Mediator between

contrary to the New. For [b] both in the Old and New Testament everlasting Life is offered to Mankind by Christ, who is the only Mediator between God and Man. Where-

non est, quandoquidem tam in veteri, quam in novo, per Christum, qui unicus est Mediator Dei, & hominum, Deus & Homo, æterna vita humano generi est proposita Quare male

great Sincerity His Opinions took Root among many of the more negligent sort of the common People who had left Popery, which was no little Scandal to the Reformation, and which occasioned *Luther*, and the other Protestants, vigorously to attack the Founder of them. His Opinions are reported to be, That Men are not obliged by the Law of Works, *i e* the Moral Law, That 'tis against Mens Conscience to endeavour to be Righteous, That if a Man be an Adulterer, a Whoremonger, or Covetous, if he does but believe he shall be saved *Luther. Lu de Conc l Prateol Elench H[illegible] voce Antinomi* His Opinions were afterwards espoused by *Paulus Crellius*, in his Book de *Libertate Christiana*, with an unparallel ed degree of Impudence and blasphemous Buffoonery, he calling the Moral Law of the Old Testament, *old Bottles, & calceos a angulo derelictos*, and *Shoos thrown into a Hole*, and saying that to look for Salvation from thence, was, *Pediculum in scabie quærere, to look for a Louse in a Scab* Some of the *Gospellers*, as they were called in King *Edward* the Sixth's time (*i e* those who pretended a further Reformation than the Laws allowed) were tainted with these Opinions which was the occasion of the compiling this Article, or at least of the wording it so, as it stood in the Edition of King *Edward*.

The Antinomian Doctrine contrary to Scripture

IV But the Doctrine of these Hereticks is directly contrary to that of the holy Scriptures For our Saviour plainly tells us, that he came *not to destroy the Law and the Prophets, but to fulfill*, Mat v 17 And the Apostle puts the Question, as a very great Absurdity in the Christian Religion, *do we then make void the Law through Faith? God forbid, yea* (says he) *we establish the Law*, Rom iii 31 And again *What shall we say then? is the Law Sin? God forbid Nay I had not known Sin, but by the Law, for I had not known Lust, except the Law had said, Thou shalt not covet*, Rom. vii 7

As for those Passages of Scripture, which the *Antinomians* ground their Opinion upon, viz *By the deeds of the Law no flesh shall be justified*, Rom iii 20 *Ye are become dead to the Law by the body of Christ*, Rom vii. 4 *Now we are delivered from the Law*, &c. Rom vii. 6 *When we were Children, we were in bondage under the elements of the world*, Gal iv 3 *Stand fast in the Liberty wherewith Christ hath made us free, and be not entangled again with the yoke of bondage*, Eph v 1 These are to be understood only of the Jewish Ceremonial Law, which was abolished by Christianity, but not of the Moral which was taken in to be a part of it Or if any of them have a regard to the old Moral Law, they are to be understood of the Rigor of it, which entailed a Curse upon all Offenders, and allowed no Satisfaction for wilful Sins, whereas the Gospel allows of the Repentance of all Offenders, and accepts of an imperfect, when sincere, instead of a unsinning Obedience

That the New Testament is not contrary to the old, the Doctrine of the antient Church

V. And that there is no Contrariety between the Old and the New Testament, as these Persons do pretend, the Divines of the antient Church do testify. For thus S *Chrysostom* [illegible Greek] *The two Testaments differ only in words, but there is no Opposition or Contrariety between them But this does not argue any Opposition or Contrariety, but only a difference in the wording* Chrys Hom lvi edit Sav Tom v pag 376. And elsewhere. [illegible Greek] *There is nothing omitted in the Writings both of the Old and the New Testament; the Old said the same thing first, and the New interpreted the Old I have often said there are two Testaments, two Handmaids and two Sisters, that like Centinels attend upon our Lord Christ is preached by the Prophets, and Christ is preached in the New Testament. The New indeed is the New, for the Old led the way to it, the Old is not abrogated, but is only explained in the New* Hom. cxi Tom v

In what particulars the Old and New Testament differ.

VI. The only difference between the Old and New Testament is in some few Particulars, which argues rather an Improvement than a Contradiction or Abrogation As (1) In the clearness of the Revelation of the divine Will and the Mysteries of our Redemption, which are set down in express Words in the New Testament, but are darkly shadowed out by Types and Figures under the Old This is well expressed by the *Pseudo-Dionysius*. Ἡ μὲν παλαιὰ διαθήκη ἔφη ... [illegible Greek] *The old Testament spoke of the Actions of Christ to come, but the new Testament has declared them in Perfection, this wrote of the Truth in Figures, but the other has demonstrated it as present, this by its Predictions begets a Faith to the Truth, the other is the very Operation of the divine Words, and the summary of the divine Actions.* Eccl Hier cap iii. The like S *Chrysostom* expresses in a very few words [illegible Greek] *The Dispensations of the new Testament were shadowed out in the Old* Chrys Hom xxiv Tom ed Savil vii (2) The new Testament requires greater Perfection than the Old, extending its Obligation not only to our exterior Actions, but even to the very Thoughts and Desires of our Hearts On which *Isidore Pelusiota* makes this excellent Remark [illegible Greek] *There is one Legislator of both Testaments, but the Jewish Law, being given to a cross and stubborn People, prohibited only Actions but the Gospel delivering Precepts to Persons as it were of a philosophical Genius, forbids Thoughts from which Actions arise, thereby stopping up the Fountain of Evils before they break out, not only forbidding Sins, but carefully providing that they should not be committed* Isid. Pel. Ep. ccix

b *Both in the old and new Testament----- Christ who is the only Mediator*, &c.] That Christ was expected as a Mediator and Saviour by those under the old Law, and his Coming predicted in innumerable places of the old Testament, is evident to all those who will but give themselves the trouble of perusing those sacred Writings

Antient Prophesies concerning Christ's Mediatorship.

I. The first great Prediction of Christ's coming to be a Saviour to the World, is found in the third Chapter of *Genesis*, where it is said, That the *Seed of the Woman* shall *bruise* the *Serpent's Head*, in which words is plainly foretold, that some great and remarkable Person should some time or other proceed

tween God and Man, being both God and Man. Wherefore they are not to be heard, which feign that the old Fathers did look only for transitory Promises

fore [c] they are not to be heard, which feign that the old Fathers did look only for transitory Promisses.

Altho' the Law given from God by *Moses*, as touching Ceremonies and Rites, do not

sentiunt, qui veteres tantum in promissiones temporarias sperasse confingunt Quamquam lex a Deo data per Mosen (quoad Ceremonias & ritus) Christianos non astringat, neque

proceed out of the Stock, which was to be raised from the Body of that Female, that should defeat the Devil's Purposes in procuring the lapse of Mankind, and ruin the Kingdom he thought thereby to establish Another great Prediction and Promise of Christ's Mediatorship was made to *Abraham*, Gen xii 3 *In thee shall all the nations of the earth be blessed* Which Promise can have no other tolerable Sense put upon it, than that Christ who was to be born of the Seed of *Abraham* was to be the Saviour of the whole World, as the Apostle very well observes, *Gal* iii 8 *Jacob's* Prediction, That the *Scepter should not depart from Judah, nor the Lawgiver from between his feet, till Shilo come*, and That the *gathering of the Gentiles should be to him*, Gen xlix 10 is an exact Prediction, not only of the Reality, but of the Time of Christ's coming For till that time the Jews had a Polity, and were governed by their own Laws, but afterwards all their Government and Jurisdiction were destroyed, they enjoyed neither City, Temple, Laws, nor any thing that might entitle them to a Civil or Ecclesiastical Legislature. And the Gentiles were in a true and proper Sense gathered to him for as great part of the Jews fell off from him, so the Gentile World in all Parts came in crowds to embrace the new Religion which he preached *Balaam's* Prophesie of a *Star's coming out of Jacob*, and a *Scepter's arising out of Israel*, which *should smite the corners of Moab*, &c *Num* xxiv 17 was a Prediction of the Messias, as the Jews themselves own, and the pretended Messias, *Barcoceba* (i e) the Son of a Star, took this Name from this Character and the smiting the Corners of *Moab* an Heathen Nation, did aptly denote our Saviour's destroying the Heathen Idolatry In the Psalms, particularly the ii xxii xlv cx cx are many Passages which relate to the Messias as the Jewish Writers themselves own The Prophet *Isaiah* does in many Places predict the Kingdom of the Messias, and in the liii Chapter does very lively describe his Sufferings and Satisfaction The Prophet *Daniel* does foretel the precise time in which the Messias shall be cut off, and the Jewish Oeconomy cease *Dan* ix 24, 25, 26 The Prophet *Micah* does predict his being born at *Bethelem*, *Mic* v 2 The Prophet *Haggai* does foretel the *Glory of the second Temple*, or Dispensation of the Jewish Affairs after the Captivity, *exceeding that of the former*, which in all particulars, excepting the coming of the Messias under it was inferior *Hag* ii 6 And lastly the Prophet *Malachi* foretels, *That the Messenger of the Covenant* (i e *the Messias*) *in whom they delighted, should suddenly come to his Temple*, Mal iv 1 I have dispatched these Particulars with greater Brevity, because I have more largely insisted on them in another Treatise, vid *Conference with a Theist*, Vol III from p 1c. to p 122 From these Passages it is plain, that the Notion of the Mediatorship of the Messias, or his coming into the World to be the Saviour thereof, was well settled in the Minds of the Jews before the coming of Christ For both our Saviour and his Apostles make their Appeals to these Prophecies, as universally understood in this Sense, in their several Sermons and Discourses For thus our blessed Saviour, *Had ye believed Moses, ye would have believed me for he wrote of me*, Joh v 46 So S *Peter* in his Sermon, *Acts* iii 20 *He shall send Jesus Christ, which before was preached unto you whom the heaven must receive, until the time of restitution of all things, which God hath spoken by the mouth of all his holy Prophets, since the world began For Moses truly said unto the Fathers, a Prophet shall the Lord your God raise up unto you, of your Brethren, like unto me, him ye shall hear in all things whatsoever he shall say unto you, &c Yea, and all the Prophets from Samuel, and those that follow after, as many as have spoken, have likewise foretold of these days.* S *Paul* in his Speech to *Agrippa* asserts the same *Having therefore obtained help of God, I continue unto this day, witnessing both to small and great, saying none other things, than those which the Prophets and Moses did say should come, that Christ should suffer*, &c *Acts* xxvi 22, 23 And so S *Peter* in his first Epistle, cap i 10. *Of which Salvation the Prophets have inquired, and searched diligently, who prophesied of the grace that should come unto you, searching what or what manner of time the Spirit of Christ that was in them did signifie, when it was testified before hand the sufferings of Christ, and the glory that should follow*

II Upon this account many of the Antients looked upon the old Patriarchs, and other good People before the coming of Christ, to be saved by their belief in Christ to come, as Christians are by their believing in him as already come, and thereby to have been Members of the same Christian Church, and Professors of the same Christian Religion For thus *Eusebius* Τί δὴ ἐν λοιπὸν ἐμποδὼν ἂν εἴη, μὴ οὐχὶ ενα καὶ τὸν αὐτὸν βίον τε καὶ τρόπον εὐσεβείας ἡμῖν τε καὶ τοῖς ἀπὸ Χριστοῦ καὶ τοῖς πρὸ πάλαι θεοφιλέσιν ὁμολογεῖν, ὡς τε μὴ νέαν καὶ ξένην ἀλλ᾽ εἰ δεῖ φάναι ἀληθεύοντα, πρώτην ὑπάρχειν καὶ μόνην καὶ ἀληθῆ κατορθώσιν εὐσεβείας, τὴν διὰ τῆς τοῦ Χριστοῦ διδασκαλίας παραδοθεῖσαν ἡμῖν ἀποδείκνυσθαι *What should hinder but to say, that the good People who were before Christ made Profession of the same Religion with us so that the Christian is not a new and strange Religion, but, to speak the Truth, is the antient discipline of Godliness which the Patriarchs professed* Euseb Hist Eccl Lib i ed Step cap iv S *Chrysostom* on the same Argument expresses himself thus Οἱ γὰρ τοῦ θεοῦ φίλοι, οἱ θαυμαστοὶ πάντες, Χριστὸν ἐπεγνώσαν καὶ πρὸ τῆς εἰσόδου τῆς παρουσίας *The Friends of God, admirable Persons in former times were acquainted with Christ before his coming in the Flesh* Chrys Hom viii in Joh And so again upon those words, *One Lord, one faith*, &c he has these remarkable words Τί δ᾽ ὅσοι ἐν σώματι, οἱ πανταχοῦ τῆς οἰκουμένης πιστοὶ, οἱ ὄντες καὶ γενόμενοι καὶ ἐσόμενοι, πάλιν δὲ οἱ πρὸ τῆς τοῦ Χριστοῦ παρουσίας εὐηρεστηκότες, εἷς σῶμά εἰσι Πῶς; ὅτι κἀκεῖνοι τὸν Χριστὸν ᾔδεσαν Πόθεν δῆλον, Ἀβραὰμ ὁ πατὴρ ὑμῶν &c *What is one Body? The Believers of all Countries which have been and which shall be, nay those who were pleasing to God before Christ's coming are one Body But how so? because they knew or believed in Christ How does this appear? from that of our Saviour*, your Father *Abraham* rejoiced to see my Day, &c Chrys Hom x in Eph The same Doctrine was yet more expresly taught by *Nazianzen* Ἀλλὰ μυστικὸς τις ὁ ἀπόρρητος οὗτος ὁ λόγος, ἀλλ᾽ ἔδοξεν πιθανὸς ἐμοί γε, καὶ πᾶσι τοῖς φιλοθέοις, μηδένα τῶν πρὸ τῆς Χριστοῦ παρουσίας τελειωθέντων, δίχα τῆς εἰς Χριστὸν πίστεως ταύτης τυχεῖν Ὁ γὰρ λόγος, ἐπαρρησιάσθη μὲν ὕστερον καιροῖς ἰδίοις, ἐγινώσκετο δὲ καὶ πρότερον τοῖς καθαροῖς τὴν διάνοιαν *This is a secret and hidden Doctrine, but yet what seems probable to me and pious Persons, that none of those who went to Happiness before the coming of, did obtain it without Faith in Christ For although the Word was freely divulged in time, yet he was known to those good People long before* Greg Naz. Orat xxii

c *They are not to be heard, which feign that the old Fathers did look only for transitory Promises*] *Moses* being, by God's Order, to erect the frame of a sacred Commonwealth among the Jews, doth, in the Books, which he hath written, and the several Tables of the Laws which he

bind Christian Men, nor the Civil Precepts thereof ought of necessity to be received in any Commonwealth, yet notwithstanding, [d] no Christian Man whatsoever is free from the Obedience of the Commandments which are called Moral.

civilia ejus præcepta in aliqua repub. necessario recipi debeant, nihilominus tamen ab obedientia mandatorum (quæ moralia vocantur) nullus (quantumvis Christianus) est solutus.

he promulgated, excite the Jews to the Observance of them from Temporal Promises and Threatnings, both because these were the most likely to engage the Affections of a carnal People, that had been long used to Meanness and Slavery and because God's Covenant with that Nation being National, publick and visible Blessings upon the Observation of the Terms of it, and national Miseries upon the Violation thereof, were the most proper Means to engage that Nation to a Compliance therewith But besides these general Promises of Temporal Blessings, and the Denunciation of publick Miseries, which do most frequently occur in the Writings of the old Testament, there are many Places which do evidently shew, that tho this was the ordinary Tenour of the National Covenant, yet particular Persons had Encouragement from the divine Revelation to expect even Spiritual Rewards, or Blessings in another Life after this For what else could be the meaning of the Faith of *Abraham* being so highly magnified in Scripture, in believing that in his *Seed all the Nations of the earth should be blessed*, Gen xii 18 but that he expected a Saviour to descend from his Body, whose happy Influences should extend not only to his Posterity, but to all the World besides? Which Blessings could not be Temporal Ones, for the Temporal Successes of one Nation are, for the most part, rather prejudicial than beneficial to others And the Apostle elsewhere declares plainly, that his Faith was grounded chiefly upon such Spiritual Blessings *He looked for a city which hath foundations, whose builder and maker is God*, (i e another unchangeable Life or State of Happiness, which God had prepared for his pious Servants) *Hebr* x 10. To this *Isaiah* refers, when he speaks of *an everlasting Covenant, which if they heard their Souls should live*, Is lv 3 It is to this that holy *Job* refers, when he said, *I know that my Redeemer liveth, and that he shall stand at the later day upon the earth And tho' after my skin worms destroy this Body, yet in my flesh I shall see God Whom I shall see for my self, and mine eyes shall behold and not another, though my reins be consumed within me* Job xxix 25, 26, &c And tis this that the Psalmist means, *Thou wilt not leave my Soul in Hell, neither wilt thou suffer thy holy one to see corruption Thou wilt shew me the path of life in thy presence is fulness of joy, at thy hand there are pleasures for evermore* Psal xvi 10, 11 The like is to be understood of that Passage in the next Psalm Where having declared that wicked Men have their *portion in this life*, he says, *As for me I will behold thy face in righteousness I shall be satisfied, when I awake, with thy likeness* Psal xvii 15 which is a clear Description of the Resurrection Which is yet more fully described in that remarkable Passage of the Prophet *Daniel. At that time thy people shall be delivered, every one that shall be found written in the book And many of them that sleep in the dust of the earth shall awake, some to everlasting life, and some to shame and everlasting contempt And they that be wise shall shine as the brightness of the firmament, and they that turn many to righteousness, as the stars for ever and ever*, Dan xii 1, 2, 3

d *No Christian Man*] vid. Note a, § iv

ARTICLE

ARTICLE VIII.

VII *The three Creeds.* — **Of the three [a] Creeds.** — VIII De tribus Symbolis.

a *Creeds*] Our English word *Creed* comes from the Latin Verb *Creao*, and is a kind of Contraction of *Credendum*, as being a Summary of what is to be believed by every Christian Man It was called Σύμβολον or *Symbolum* by the generallity of the Writers of the Greek and Latin Church, but of what Antiquity that Appellation is, and what was the ground of its being called so, is not so universally agreed

The Creed not generally call'd Symbolum *by the most primitive antiquity*

I It is certain that the most antient Writers of Christianity do not call it *Symbolum*, when they have occasion to speak of the Christian Summary or publick Confession of Faith, but *Regulam Veritatis, the Rule of Truth*, Iren Lib. I c 19 and *Regulam Fidei, the Rule of Faith*, Tertul de Virg vel Nov de Trin But it is called *Symbolum* by S *Cyprian*, Ep lxxvi And S *Ambrose* in his xxxviiith Epistle, Lib v speaks thus. *Sequenti die, erat autem Dominica, post lectiones, atque tractatum, dimissis Catechumenis SYMBOLUM aliquibus Competentibus in baptisteriis tradebam Basilicæ The next day, being Sunday, after the Lessons and the Sermon, having sent away the Catechumens, I delivered the SYMBOL to some of the Competents, in the Baptistery of the Church*

Some will have it to be called Symbolum, *because the Apostles singly contributed to frame it.*

II But as to the Reason why it was called the Symbol, the Writers of Antiquity are divided Those of the Antients who were of Opinion that the Apostles, in a joint Assembly of all their number, framed the Creed, each of them contributing to put in an Article, would have the word to take its Signification from the Greek συμβάλλειν which signifies *to contribute* Hence that of *Terence*, *Symbolum* (or as others read it) *Symbolam dedit He has sent in his Club, or Share for the Entertainment*. Ter. Andr. Act I And that of Gellius, *Ne omnino immunes & asymboli veniremus, conjectabamus ad cœnulam*, &c *Least we should come on free cost and without our Symbol, we have thrown in something towards the Supper*, &c A. Gell Lib. vi c 16 From this Sense of the word I say, those, who thought the Apostles clubbed together to make the Creed, would have it to be called the *Symbol* Upon which account *Ruffinus* writes thus *Symbolum dici potuit collatio, hoc est quod plures in unum conferunt, id enim fecerunt Apostoli in his sermonibus in unum conferendo quod unusquisque sensit It may be called a Symbol, because it is a Collation, i e which many contribute to make up, which the Apostles did in this Composition (i e the Creed by bringing together into one what each of them thought.* Ruff Expos Symb § 2 And after him *Cassian* says it is called *Symbolum*, ex collatione, *quia in unum ab Apostolis Domini quicquid per universorum divinorum voluminum corpus immensa funditur copia, totum in Symboli colligitur brevitate. It is called a Symbol from Collection because whatsoever lies diffused in the large Volumes of the Scriptures, was put together by the Apostles of our Lord in a short Symbol or Creed* Cass de Incar Dom Lib. v But this Criticism must stand or fall, by the Authority which is vouched, for such a Combination of the Apostles in framing the Creed, of which more hereafter

Others from the Symbolum *or Watchword of the Soldiers*

III Others will have it to be called a Symbol, from the *Symbolum* or Watchword of the Soldiers, by which they were wont to distinguish those of their own Party from the Enemy Which is another Reason assigned by *Ruffinus*, for this Name being given to the Creed, *Idcirco istud indicium posuere, per quod agnosceretur is, qui Christum verè secundum Apostolicas regulas prædicaret Denique & in bellis civilibus hoc observari ferunt, quoniam & armorum habitus par, & sonus vocis idem & mos unus est, atque eadem instituta bellandi, ne qua doli surreptio fiat, symbola discreta unusquisque dux suis militibus tradit, quæ Latinè vel signa, vel indicia nominantur, ut si forte occurrerit quis de quo dubitetur, interrogatus symbolum, prodat an sit hostis vel socius The Christians use this as a Token to distinguish him by, who should hold Doctrines truly according to the Apostolical Rules For this is wont to be observed in Civil Wars, because their Armor is alike, there is the same Tone of their Voice, and the same Method of fighting, therefore least any deceit should take Place, every General gives out among his Soldiers some distinct Symbols, which the Latins call SIGNA and INDICIA that when any suspicious Person is met with, being asked the Symbol, he may discover himself either to be an Enemy or a Friend* After him *Maximus Taurinensis* makes the same Observation, *Symbolum Tessera est & signaculum, quo inter fideles perfidosque secernitur A Symbol is a Token or Sign, by which Friends and Enemies may be distinguished* Max Taur. de Trad Symb.

Others from the Heathen Sacra

IV. Others will have this Denomination of the Creed to have taken its rise, from the *Symbola*, made use of in the idolatrous *Sacra* of the Heathen For these are termed *Symbola* Τῆς Θέμιδος τὰ ἀπόῤῥητα σύμβολα, ὀρίγανον λύχνος, ξίφος, &c. *The hidden Symbols of* Themis *are the Fiddle, the Candle, the Sword.* Clem Alex Protrept *Ipsa denique symbola, quæ rogata sacrorum in acceptionibus respondetis Jejunavi atque ebibi Cyceonem, ex cista sumpsi, & in Calathum misi accepi rursus in cistulam transtuli These are the Symbols which you answer to in your Initiation into the Sacra of Ceres I have fasted and drunk* Cyceon. *I have taken out of the Chest and put into the Basket I took again out of the Basket and put into the little Chest* Arnob. cont. Gent Lib v Now though some wanton Critiques to shew their Skill and Learning have given out, that the Christians gave the name of *Symbolum* to their Creed, because they held it as much an ἀπόῤῥητον as the Heathens did their Mysteries, yet any one of a less form of Learning, that understands the cursed Lewdness and Villany of the Heathen Symbols or Rites, and withal the Piety of the first Christians, will think that they would have sooner embraced Martyrdom, than to have prophaned their Religion with such a scandalous Imitation of the Heathen *Sacra*

Most probably from the general Signification of the word, which denotes a Badge.

V. It is most probable, that this Name was given to the Creed, not with relation to any appropriate Sense of the Word used by any Body of Men, either Soldiers or Mysticks, but from the general Signification of the Word σύμβολον, which signifies a Badge or Note of Distinction For *Hesychius* explains σύμβολον by σημεῖον, *a Sign*, and so does *Suidas*, and *Ruffinus* as before mentioned, interprets *Symbolum* by *Indicium*, a Badge or Token For Christians having learned this Orthodox Confession of Faith in their Baptism, and solemnly promised therein to make a constant Profession of, whenever they changed their Aboad, or travelled into Foreign Parts, upon this Declaration of their Faith, they were admitted to the Communion of the Churches which they came among.

The three Creeds, *Nicene* Creed, *Athanasius*'s Creed, and that which is com-

The three Creeds, [b] *Nice* Creed, [c] *Athanasius* Creed, and ** that which is called the *Apostles*

Symbola tria, Nicænum, Athanasii, & quod vulgo Apostolorum appellatur, om-

** *That which is called the Apostles Creed*] This was called the Apostles Creed, because for many Ages together an Opinion prevailed in the Church, That the Apostles, before their separating from *Jerusalem*, drew up this Form as an unchangeable Rule of Faith, to be delivered to all the new Converts to Christianity, not in the least to be varied from by themselves or their Successors, and particularly that each of them added a Clause, the Sum of which made up this Formulary This Opinion did in some measure take its Rise, from some very antient Writers of the Church, but was improved to the height by a Sermon supposed to be written by St *Austin*, from whom the Schoolmen and the generality of the Writers of the *Roman* Writers, who maintain the same, received it *Petrus dixit, Credo in Deum Patrem*, &c Peter said, *I believe in God the Father Almighty*, John, *Maker of Heaven and Earth*, James, *And in Jesus Christ his only Son our Lord*, Andrew, *Who was conceived by the Holy Ghost, born of the Virgin Mary*, Philip, *Suffered under Pontius Pilate, was dead and buried*, Thomas, *He descended into Hell, the third day he rose again from the dead*, Bartholomew, *He ascended into Heaven, sitteth at the right hand of God the Father Almighty*, Matthew, *From thence he shall come to judge the quick and the dead*, James the Son of Alphæus, *I believe in the Holy Ghost, the Holy Catholick Church*, Simon Zelotes, *The Communion of Saints, the forgiveness of Sins*, Jude the Brother of James, *The Resurrection of the Body*, Matthias, *Life everlasting Amen* Aug Serm de Temp 115 But possibly this Opinion was older than the Writer of this Homily, for it seems not obscurely to be hinted at in that Passage of *Leo* the Great *Ipsius Catholici symboli brevis & perfecta confessio, quæ duodecim Apostolorum totidem est signata sententiis, tam instructa sit munitione cælesti, ut omnes Hæreticorum opiniones solo possint gladio detruncari* *This short and perfect Confession of the Catholick Creed, which is composed of the twelve Sentences of the twelve Apostles, is such heavenly Armour, that all the Opinions of the Hereticks may be dispatched by this Sword alone* Leo. Ep xcvi.

Improbability of every Apostle his contributing an Article.

VII But to speak freely, this is a fond Opinion grounded upon no Reason, but only a Tradition of late date, and, when it comes to be examined, is pressed with insuperable Difficulties For 1 Had the Apostles engaged themselves in a matter of this Importance, especially in this formal and solemn Manner as in this Story is related, it could hardly have escaped the being mentioned by St *Luke*, who wrote the History of the Time this is supposed to have been done in, especially when that Historian has descended to the Relation of other Matters of Fact, seemingly of less Moment 2 Or if it had escaped the Pen of S *Luke*, it could hardly have avoided being mentioned by *Eusebius*, *Socrates*, and other Ecclesiastical Historians, who supply many Matters from Tradition and antient Annals, which the Scriptures have passed over especially when they relate the Errors of so many Hereticks, and so frequently have a fair Opportunity of declaring, how they oppose the Creed, which was thus solemnly agreed upon by the Apostles. 3 If this Creed had been generally esteemed to have been drawn up by the Apostles, it can't be supposed that so many several Creeds should have been drawn up, about the fourth Century, and Persons by publick Authority enjoyned to be baptized by the *Nicene* Creed *Evag. Hist Eccl. Lib* iii *c* 4 4 Nor lastly, if the Apostles had drawn up the Form of this Creed, in the manner as is related, it cannot be supposed, that there should be so great difference found in the Forms used by the several Churches, hardly any of which do agree, but if it had been composed, as is by this account pretended, it would undoubtedly have been kept as inviolable in all Churches, as the Scriptures themselves, and no private Hand or publick Authority would have been suffered to have made the least Variation therein

Its Rise from the antient Baptismal Interrogatories

VIII However, this Creed, tho' it did not appear exactly in the same Form we have it now in, in the most antient Ages of the Church, yet the Substance thereof and, for the main, the very Expressions were used, from the very beginning of Christianity It seems at first to have been a short Catechism, consisting of the Baptismal Interrogatories, with their Answers And the present Creed is but a Sum of all the Answers, without the Interrogatories, put together This is evident from many Passages of Antiquity As particularly from that of *Irenæus* Οὕτω δὲ καὶ ὁ τὸν κανόνα τῆς ἀληθείας ἀκλινῆ ἐν ἑαυτῷ κατέχων, ὃν διὰ τοῦ βαπτίσματος εἴληφε *So preserving the unmoveable Rule of Faith, which he received in Baptism*. Iren Lib i cap i and then presently after relates the substance of the Apostles Creed, almost in the same Words we now have it Πιστεύων εἰς ἕνα Θεὸν πατέρα παντοκράτορα, τὸν πεποιηκότα τὸν οὐρανὸν καὶ τὴν γῆν, &c *I believe in God the Father Almighty, maker of Heaven and Earth*, &c ib cap ii The same is further evinced by that of S. *Cyprian* *Quod si aliquis illud opponit, ut dicat eundem Novatianum legem tenere, quam Catholica Ecclesia teneat, eodem symbolo, quo & nos, baptizare, eundem nosse Deum, Patrem, eundem Filium Christum, eundem Spiritum Sanctum, ac propter hoc usurpare eum potestatem baptizandi posse, quod non discrepare videatur in interrogatione Baptismi, a nobis non discrepare sciat quisquis hoc opponendum putat, primum, non esse unam nobis & Schismaticis symboli legem, neque eandem interrogationem Jam cum dicunt Credis Remissionem peccatorum & vitam æternam per sanctam Ecclesiam, mentiuntur in interrogatione, quando non habeant Ecclesiam* *But if any one shall object and say, that* Novatianus *holds the same Rule which the Catholick Church holds, that he baptizes with the same Creed that we do, that he acknowledges the same God the Father, the same Christ his Son, and the same Holy Ghost, and that therefore he has the power of baptizing, because he does not seem to differ from us in the Baptismal Interrogatories but let him who objects this know, that we have not the same Rule of the Creed in common with the Schismaticks, nor the same Interrogatories. For when they say, Do you believe the Forgiveness of Sins, and Life everlasting by the Holy Church, they falsifie in the Interrogation, since they have no Church*, &c Cypr ed Pam Ep lxxvi

Antient Creeds not very different.

IX It is true indeed that the Forms we have in *Tertullian*, *Irenæus*, &c are somewhat different, but that may be in some Measure owing to their citing the Words by Memory, and varying the Phrases, according to the Rules of Rhetorick But when the Answers to the Baptismal Interrogatories were joyned together, in one continued Series, without the Questions, we find very little difference between them, as appears by the Copies of the several Creeds of Oriental Churches, and those of *Rome* and *Aquileia* in the West That Creed which *Marcellus* sent to *Julius* Bishop of *Rome*, was an antient Oriental Creed, and is but very little different from the Roman and Aquileian Πιστεύω εἰς Θεὸν παντοκράτορα, &c *I believe in God Almighty, and in Jesus Christ his only begotten Son our Lord, who was born of the Holy Ghost and the Virgin Mary, crucified under Pontius Pilate, and buried and rose the third day again from the dead, who ascended into Heaven, and sitteth at the right hand of the Father from whence he shall come to judge the quick and the dead* Καὶ εἰς τὸ ἅγιον πνεῦμα &c *And in the holy Ghost, the holy Church, the forgiveness of Sins, the Resurrection of the Flesh, and Life everlasting* Epiph Hær Lib iii § 3 The Article of the *Descent into Hell*, was wanting in the old Creeds, both Greek and Latin, and was first taken from the Creed of *Aquileia* into the Roman The words *Life everlasting*, were wanting in most of the Western Creeds For S *Jerom* says, *Omne Christiani dogmatis sacramentum carnis Resurrectione concluditur* *The Creed is concluded by the words the Resurrection of the flesh* Hier Ep. lxi ad Pammach The Creed of *Aquileia*, besides the Article of the Descent into Hell, was particular in the words, *hujus carnis resurrectionem*, *the Resurrection of this very Body* and

monly called the Apostles Creed, ought thorowly to be received. for they may be proved by most certain Warrants of Holy Scripture	Creed, ought thoroughly to be received and believed; for they may be proved * by most certain Warrants of Holy Scripture.	*nino recipienda sunt, & credenda nam firmissimis Scripturarum Testimoniis probari possunt.*

* *By most certain Warrantes of Holy Scripture* MS. CCCC 1571

in adding after the words, *Father Almighty, Invisible and Impassible*, vid Ruff. in Symb.

The Interrogatories, out of which the Creed was formed, had their rise from the Apostles

X Now this uniform Consent of the several Churches, so very distant from each other, both in Time and Place, does seem very probably to infer that these Baptismal Interrogatories, which afterwards collectively taken formed the Symbol, were delivered down from the Apostles, by uninterrupted Tradition, and affords good ground for that Assertion of *Irenæus*, Ἡ μὲν γὰρ ἐκκλησία, καίπερ καθ' ὅλης τῆς οἰκουμένης, ἕως περάτων τῆς γῆς διεσπαρμένη, παρὰ δὲ τῶν Ἀποστόλων, καὶ τῶν ἐκείνων μαθητῶν παραλαβοῦσα τὴν Εἰς ἕνα θεὸν πατέρα παντοκράτορα, &c *For the Church throughout the whole World, dispersed to the utmost bounds of the earth, has received from the Apostles and their Scholars*, I believe in God the Father Almighty, *&c Iren. Lib* 1 *cap.* 2.

b *Nice Creed*] It was so called, because it was framed at *Nice*, a City of *Bithynia*, in the great general Council, which was held there, *A D* 325, to quiet the disturbance which the Heretic of *Arius* had given to the Church, by denying the Divinity of our Saviour Now their design being to secure the Orthodox Faith against the Poison of this Heretic, they did not intend to make a new Creed, but only to explain the Articles of the old one, so as that they might not be perverted to an Heterodox Sense And therefore the Confessions of Faith which the Fathers of that Council subscribed to, contained only those Articles which related to the Trinity

The first draught of the Nicene *Creed*

The first form of a Creed, or Confession of Faith, which this Council agreed unto, was that delivered into the Council by *Eusebius* of *Cæsarea* and it run thus Πιστεύομεν εἰς ἕνα θεὸν, &c We *believe in one God the Father Almighty, Maker of all things* visible and invisible. *And in* one Lord *Jesus Christ, the Word of God*, God of God, Light of Light, *Life of Life, the only* begotten *Son, the first born of every Creature*, begotten of his Father before all Worlds, by whom all things were made, who was crucified for our Salvation, *dwelt among men, and suffered, and rose again the third day, and ascended unto the Father, and shall come again* in Glory *to judge both the quick and the dead We believe in one holy Ghost* Socr Hist Eccl. Lib. 1. ad. Steph c. 5 Act Conc. Nic. par III From hence we may observe, that the θεὸς ἐκ θεοῦ, φῶς ἐκ φωτὸς, *God of God, light of light*, the πρὸ πάντων τῶν αἰώνων ἐκ τοῦ πατρὸς γεγεννημένον, δι' οὗ καὶ ἐγένετο πάντα, *who was begotten of the Father before all Worlds, by whom all things were made*. the ἥξοντα πάλιν ἐν δόξῃ, *shall come again in glory* (which Passages stand in the common *Nicene* Creed now used among us) were owing to this first draught of it

The second draught of the Nicene Creed, and the Additions therein made.

Afterwards they made some other Additions, to prevent the Subterfuges of the *Arians*, who maintained an Heterodox Sense, under the Covert of some more general words in the former Confession, and that second draught was this Πιστεύομεν εἰς ἕνα θεὸν, &c *I believe in one God the Father Almighty, Maker of all things visible and invisible, and in one Lord Jesus Christ* the *Son of God*, the only begotten Son of the Father, i e. *of the substance of the Father God of God, light of light*, very God of very God, begotten not made, of the same substance with the Father, *by whom all things were made* Who for us Men and for our Salvation came down, was incarnate and made Man, *who suffered and rose again the third day, ascended into Heaven, and shall come to judge the quick and the dead And in the Holy Ghost* To this Edition are owing these several Passages in our present *Nicene* Creed. The ἐκ πατρὸς μονογενῆ, *the only begotten Son of God* the θεὸν ἀληθινὸν ἐκ θεοῦ ἀληθινοῦ γεννηθέντα, οὐ ποιηθέντα, ὁμοούσιον τῷ πατρί, *very God of very God, begotten not made, being of one substance with the Father* the δι' ἡμᾶς τοὺς ἀνθρώπους καὶ διὰ τὴν ἡμετέραν σωτηρίαν κατελθόντα καὶ σαρκωθέντα καὶ ἐνανθρωπήσαντα *who for us Men and our Salvation came down, was incarnate and was made Man* It should seem before their breaking up that they made some other few Additions. For *Epiphanius* in his account has given us a Copy of the *Nicene* Creed, which was used in the Eastern Churches, in which there are some new Clauses, which were in neither of the former For after the words, *judge the quick and the dead*, that Creed concludes thus, οὗ τῆς βασιλείας οὐκ ἔσται τέλος. Καὶ εἰς πνεῦμα τὸ ἅγιον, τὸ κύριον καὶ ζωοποιὸν, τὸ ἐκ τοῦ πατρὸς ἐκπορευόμενον, τὸ σὺν πατρὶ καὶ υἱῷ συμπροσκυνούμενον καὶ συνδοξαζόμενον, τὸ λαλῆσαν διὰ τῶν προφητῶν Εἰς μίαν ἁγίαν καθολικὴν καὶ ἀποστολικὴν ἐκκλησίαν Ὁμολογοῦμεν ἓν βάπτισμα εἰς ἄφεσιν ἁμαρτιῶν, Προσδοκῶμεν ἀνάστασιν νεκρῶν καὶ ζωὴν τοῦ μέλλοντος αἰῶνος. Ἀμήν, *Whose kingdom shall have no end And in the Holy Ghost*, the Lord *and giver of Life, who proceedeth from the Father, who with the Father and the Son together is worshipped and glorified, who spake by the Prophets We acknowledge one Baptism for the Remission of Sins We look for the Resurrection of the dead, and the life of the World to come.* Amen Whether this were a new draught of the Creed, or whether it were a part of the former, the first part thereof relating to the Trinity only being made use of, as a Test upon the Hereticks, I leave others to judge. There remains only the *Filioque*, which was afterwards added, *vid. Note on the* Nicene *Creed, in the Comment on the Common Prayer.*

c *Athanasius's Creed*] Of the Antiquity of this Creed, and the Exceptions against it, *see Note on the* Athanasian *Creed, in the Comment on the Common Prayer.*

ARTICLE

ARTICLE IX.

VIII *Of Original or Birth-sin*

Of Original or Birth-sin.

IX. De peccato originali.

Original Sin standeth not in the following of *Adam*, (as the Pelagians do vainly

[a] **Original Sin [b] standeth not in the following of *Adam* (as the ** Pelagians do vainly talk)**

Peccatum originis non est (ut fabulantur Pelagiani) in imitatione Adami si-

** *Pelagians*] The Pelagian Heresie was so called from *Pelagius*, who about the Year of Christ 405, disseminated the same. He was a Native of *Great Britain* as all agree, St *Austin*, Ep 106 *Prosper* in Chronic and *Marius Mercator* calling him *Britannus*, and *Brito* That he was a Monk by Profession, S *Chrysostom* does testifie, who condoling his lapse into Heresie, in an Epistle which he wrote in his Exile, says, Σφόδρα ἀλγῶ ὑπὲρ Πελαγίου τοῦ μονάζοντος, &c *I am very much grieved on account of* Pelagius *the Monk*, &c. *Chrys Ep* iv *ad Olymp* But it must be understood that he was a Monk only, according to the Usage of those Times, *i e* one who having no publick Cure in the Church, retired to some solitary dwelling for the greater convenience of Devotion and Study, they oftentimes living in the Families of some honourably or wealthy Person, where they were Tutors to their Sons, or performed divine Offices in their Families Our Monkish Historians will have him to have been a Monk of *Bangor* and afterwards Abbot, but that is a wild Fancy without Ground Some will have him to be born in that part of *Great Britain* called *Scotland*, from that Passage of S *Jerom* where he says of him, that he was *Scotorum pultibus prægravatus*, *Grown fat with* Scotch *Flummery*, Hier Præf in Hier but others will have the *Scots* here to denote the *Irish*, vid Ush de prim Whilst he was a Student in the East, he had vented some Heterodox Notions which made him frequently change his College or Monastery (as they called it) *i e* the Place where the Students lodged, either the better to diffuse his Heresie, or to avoid the Reproach and Opposition he fell under for it *Isidore Pelusiot* says, the Occasion was his running in Debt by his intemperate way of living, *Isid Pelus Ep* cccxiv but that seems to be a groundless Scandal, for all who were acquainted with him, do acknowledge him to have been a vertuous and pious Person, for S *Chrysostom* in the forementioned Epistle commends him for his Piety, and so does S *Austin*, Retract. *Lib* ii *c* 33 Coming afterwards to *Rome*, he got acquainted with *Ruffinus*, who had before espoused the like Notions, which he had learned from the Origenian Books, particularly that περὶ ἀρχῶν which he had translated, and communicated other Notions to *Pelagius*, which he was a Stranger to before Upon which account S *Jerom* calls *Ruffinus* his Forerunner, *Precursor ejus Grunnius*, *Grunnius* (*i e* the Nick Name he gave *Ruffinus*) *his Forerunner* Hier Præf in Hier The like Notions had been vented before by *Jovinian*, and condemned in a Council at *Carthage*, which occasioned S *Jerom* to say, *Non erubescis explosam atque damnatam Jovinianam sententiam sequi*, *you are not ashamed to follow the exploded and condemned Opinion of Jovinian*, Hier Lib ii contr Pelag The like had been broached by *Evagrius Ponticus*, in his Book περὶ ἀπαθείας, which *Ruffinus* had translated into Latin *Hier Ep ad Ctesiphon* His Principal Errors were, his denying Original Sin, and the necessity of divine Grace, and his asserting that Men might arrive to a State of Impeccability in this Life His Doctrines were vigorously defended by his Scholars *Celestius* and *Julianus*, and as strenuously opposed by S *Jerom*, *Austin*, *Fulgentius* and *Prosper*, with many others His Errors were condemned by several Provincial Councils, as that of *Diospolis* in *Palestine*, that of *Milevis* in *Numidia*, the Council of *Africa* under *Zozimus*, the General Council of *Africa*, and that of *Ephesus* The Books of *Pelagius* himself were written with more Cunning and Caution than those of his Scholars, he chusing to vent his Doctrine chiefly by their Books Which occasioned that Expression of S *Jerom* spoken of *Pelagius* *O te felicem! cujus præter discipulos nemo conscribit libros, ut quicquid videris displicere, non tuum, sed alienum esse contendas* *O happy Man! all whose Books are written by his Scholars*, so that *whatsoever does not please you, you contend, that it is not yours, but anothers*, Hier contr Pel Lib iv.

Original Sin formerly called by other Names before S Austin.

a *Original Sin*] The Denomination of *Original Sin*, to denote the Corruption or Depravation of human Nature, derived from the lapse of our first Parents, is not of very early use in the Church S. *Austin* is esteemed first to have used it But, however, the Doctrine is as early as Christianity it self, and the Writers of the first Centuries do express very clearly the thing it self, though under different Names. For they call it παλαιὰ δυσσέβεια, *the old guilt*, *antiqua plaga*, *the antient wound*, κοινὴ ἀρά, *the common curse*, ἀρχαία ἁμαρτία, *the old Sin*, &c But after the Pelagian Controversie was set on foot, the Divines of the Church generally used *Originale Peccatum*, to signifie the corruption of Nature and Proneness to Sin, which was transmitted down from the first Parents to their Posterity; following therein S *Austin*, who thought this the most significant Expression to denote that Depravation of Nature, which the Pelagians denied

Now that there is such an Original warping of our Nature, which renders us unapt to Good and prone to Sin, and for that reason places us in our natural State, out of Favour with God, is the constant Doctrine of the Holy Scriptures

Scripture account of Original Sin.

God saw that every imagination of the thoughts of mens hearts were only evil continually, Gen. vi 5 *The imagination of man's heart is evil from his youth*, Gen viii. 25 'Tis with relation to this general Corruption of Nature, which accompanies us from our Birth, that *Job* asks the question, *Who can bring a clean thing out of an unclean*, Job xiv. 4 To the same purpose the Psalmist speaks, *Behold I was shapen in iniquity, and in sin did my Mother conceive me*, Psal li. 1 Our Saviour says, *That which is born of flesh is flesh*, Joh iii 5 The Apostle tells us, that both Jews and Gentiles are equally born Children of Wrath, *Were by nature the Children of wrath even as others*, Eph. iii 4 *Wherefore, as by one man sin entered into the world, and death by Sin, and so death passed upon all men, for that all have sinned*, Rom v 12

Doctrine of the Fathers who wrote before the Pelagian Controversie, concerning Original Sin.

These express Passages of holy Scripture, together with ordinary Experience, occasioned the antient Writers of the Church, even before the Pelagian Heresie sprung up, to assert in their Writings this general Depravation of human Nature and proneness to Sin, caused by the Fall of our first Progenitors But they contented themselves with the Doctrine in general, without descending to those nice Speculations, and particular ways of explaining the Modes of it, which later Divines, in opposing this Heresie, have filled their Books with.

IGNATIUS owns that this old Crime of our first Parents brought an Impurity upon our Nature, which was only *to be cleansed by Christ's blood* Δὺς ἑαυτὸν ὑπὲρ ἡμῶν λύτρον, ἵνα τῷ αἵματι αὐτοῦ καθάρῃ ἡμᾶς παλαιᾶς δυσσεβείας, *giving himself a ransom for us, that with his blood he might purge us from the old Transgression* Ign Ep ad Trall

JUSTIN Martyr owns our proneness to Sin, and our giving way to the Wiles of the Devil, and our Subjection to Death, to proceed from the lapse of our first Parents. Οὐ γὰρ ὡς ἐνδεὴς τοῦ γεννηθῆναι καὶ σταυρωθῆναι ὡς ἐνδεὴς τούτων, ὑπέμεινεν, ἀλλ' ὑπὲρ τοῦ γένους τῶν ἀνθρώπων ὃ ἀπὸ τοῦ Ἀδὰμ ὑπὸ θάνατον καὶ πλάνην τὴν τοῦ ὄφεως ἐπεπτώκει. *He was not born and crucified for his own sake, as having no need of any of these things, but for the sake of Mankind, which on account of* Adam *had fallen into Death and the Temptation of the Serpent* Just Mart Dial cum Tryph

TATIAN, Orat contr Gent owns, that by reason of this Sin of our first Parents all Mankind are not only subject to Death, but deprived of the Commerce with the *Logos*, which they would have all otherways have had. Τότε ἡ τοῦ λόγου δύναμις τούτε ἀρξάντα τῆς τοιαύτης καὶ τοὺς συνακολουθήσαντας αὐτῷ ... καὶ ὁ μὲν κατ' εἰκόνα τοῦ Θεοῦ γεγονὼς χωρισθέντος ἀπὸ αὐτοῦ τοῦ πνεύματος τοῦ δυνατωτέρου θνητὸς γίνεται *Then the Power of the* Logos *deprived the Author of the Sin, and those who obey him of his Commerce. And Man who was made according to the Image of God, being divested of his more powerful Spirit was made Mortal.* And again, Πτέρωσις γὰρ ἡ τῆς ψυχῆς τὸ πνεῦμα, τὸ τέλειον, ὅπερ ἀπορρίψασα διὰ τὴν ἁμαρτίαν, ἔπτη ὥσπερ νεοσσὸς καὶ χαμαιπετὴς ἐγένετο, μεταβᾶσα δὲ τῆς οὐρανίου συνουσίας *At first the Soul was lift up on the Wings of a perfect Spirit which being lost by Sin, she flew like a young Bird close to the ground, and lost its divine Conversation*, ibid

IRENÆUS says, that this old Wound given by the Serpent is only healed by Faith in Christ. *Non aliter salvantur homines ab antiqua serpentis plaga, nisi credant in eum qui secundum similitudinem carnis peccati in ligno martyrii exaltatus a terra, & omnia trahit ad se & vivificavit mortuos. Men cannot otherways be saved from the old Wound of the Serpent, unless they believe in him, who according to the similitude of the Sin of the Flesh, being lifted from Earth in the Martyrial Wood, draws all things after him, and quickens the dead.* Iren adv Hæres Lib iv cap. 5

ORIGEN, contr Cels Lib iv. says, that the Curse of *Adam* and *Eve* was common to all their Posterity. Ἡ γὰρ τοῦ Ἀδὰμ κοινὴ πάντων ἐστὶ καὶ τὰ κατὰ τῆς γυναικὸς οὐκ ἔστι καθ' ἧς οὐ λέγεται. *The Curse of* Adam *is common to all Men, and there is no Woman of which the same things may not be said, as are said of* Eve

TERTULLIAN will have, that the Sin of *Adam* involved all his Posterity in the same Condemnation. *Satanam dicimus per quem homo a primordio circumventus, ut præceptum Dei excederet, & propterea in mortem datus, exinde totum genus de suo semine infectum suæ etiam damnationis traducem fecit. We say Satan, by whom Man at the beginning was circumvented to violate the command of God, from whence his whole Race which proceeded from his Seed being infected, made them liable to his Condemnation.* Tert de An

S *CYPRIAN* asserts, That in Baptism the old Adamical Sin is remitted. *A Baptismo prohiberi non debet infans, qui recens natus nihil peccavit, nisi quod secundum Adam carnaliter natus, contagium mortis antiquæ prima nativitate contraxit qui ad remissionem peccatorum accipendum hoc ipso facilius accedit, quod illi remittuntur non propria sed aliena. An Infant ought not to be repelled from Baptism, who being newly born has committed no Sin, but only being born carnally according to* Adam, *by his first Nativity has contracted the Contagion of the old Death who for this Reason is more readily admitted to Baptism, he has not his own Sins, but those of another remitted.* Cypr Ep ad Fid

S *ATHANASIUS*, Orat ii speaks of the Traduction of *Adam's* Guilt upon all Men. Ὥσπερ τοῦ Ἀδὰμ παραβάντος εἰς πάντας τοὺς ἀνθρώπους ἡ ἁμαρτία διῆλθεν, οὕτω τοῦ κυρίου ἰσχύσαντος ἡ τοιαύτη ἰσχὺς λοιπὸν εἰς ἡμᾶς διαβήσεται. *As through* Adam's *Fall Sin came upon all Mankind, so the Lord having conquered the Serpent, his Power shall have effect upon us all.* And again, Ἀρχαίαν ἁμαρτίαν τὴν διὰ τοῦ Ἀδὰμ εἰς ἅπαντας γινομένην *That old Sin which by* Adam *came upon all.* Syn Sacr Script.

S. *BASIL* speaks of the Spiritual Weakness which has befallen all Mankind by reason of the Fall. Καλὸς μὲν γὰρ ἤμην κατὰ τὴν φύσιν, ἀσθενὴς δὲ διὰ τὸ ἐκ τῆς ἐπιβουλῆς τοῦ ὄφεως τεθνάναι τῷ παραπτώματι. *I was beautiful according to Nature, but now am weak, because I am dead through the wiles of the Serpent.* Bas in Psal xxix

NAZIANZEN says, that all of us were dead in Sin through *Adam*. Πάντες δὲ οἱ τοῦ αὐτοῦ Ἀδὰμ μεταχόντες, καὶ ὑπὸ τοῦ ὄφεως παραλογισθέντες, ἐν τῇ ἁμαρτίᾳ θανατωθέντες, καὶ διὰ τοῦ οὐρανίου Ἀδὰμ ἀνασωθέντες, καὶ πρὸς τὸ ξύλον τῆς ζωῆς ἐπαναχθέντες, διὰ τοῦ ξύλου τῆς ἀτιμίας ὅθεν ἀπεπέσαμεν. *All that have participated of the same* Adam, *and have been beguiled by the Serpent, are dead by Sin, and are restored to health by the heavenly* Adam, *are restored to that Tree of Life, from which Men were cut off.* Naz Orat xxv. And elsewhere Ἔχειν γὰρ ὅλον με σώζεσθαι, ὅλον πλήσσοντα καὶ κατακριθέντα διὰ τὴν τοῦ πρωτοπλάστου παρακοήν, καὶ λοιπὸν τοῦ ἀντικειμένου. *There was a necessity of my being saved on every part, because in every part I fell, and was condemned through the disobedience of my first Parent, and the fraud of the Devil.* Id Orat iii

S *CHRYSOSTOM*, That the Predominancy of our sensual Appetites was owing to *Adam's* Sin. Τὸ σῶμα ἡμῶν πρὸ μὲν τῆς τοῦ Χριστοῦ παρουσίας εὐχείρωτον ἦν τῇ ἁμαρτίᾳ. μετὰ γὰρ τὸν θάνατον καὶ πολὺς παθῶν εἰσῆλθεν ἑσμός. *Our Body before the coming of Christ was easily attacked, for after Death there entered a swarm of Passions.* Chrys in Rom. cap vi Hom 11. And again. Ὅτι γὰρ ἥμαρτεν ὁ Ἀδὰμ καὶ τὸ σῶμα αὐτοῦ γέγονε θνητὸν καὶ παθητόν, καὶ πολλὰ ἐλαττώματα ἐδέξατο φυσικά, καὶ βαρύτερος καὶ δυσήνιος ὁ ἵππος κατέστη. *After Adam had sinned, and his Body was made Mortal and Passible, he then admitted many natural Vices, and the Horse was rendered more untameable.* Id in Rom vii

From these and many other Passages, of these more early Christian Writers, it is manifest, that they all admitted that there was a general Corruption of human Nature, a great warping from the Original Rectitude of the first Creation, and a mighty proneness to Sin (which necessarily required a Renovation in Christ) were owing to the Fall of our first Parents.

Several doctrines relating to Original Sin, particularly insisted on after the rise of the Pelagian Heresie

These most essential Truths of Christianity being denied by the Pelagians, those who opposed that Heresie, insisted upon some other Doctrines, which the former Writers had not so commonly touched upon. (1) And then much stress was laid upon the Doctrine of the Imputation of *Adam's* Sin to all his Posterity, asserting that he sinned as it were in our stead, as the common Representative of our human Nature, and therefore all his Posterity are involved, not only in the Guilt, but in the Punishment of his Crime.

1. The Doctrine of the Imputation of Adam's personal Guilt

This is the Doctrine which S *Austin* on all Occasions inculcates, and from him the Schoolmen received it. *Nascuntur non proprie, sed originaliter Peccatores. Men are born Sinners, not upon their own account, but on account of their Original.* De Civ Dei Lib xvi cap 18. And again. *Parvuli, non secundum vitæ suæ proprietatem, sed secundum communem generis humani originem, omnes in illo uno testamentum Dei dissipaverunt. Children, not upon the proper account of the Actions of their Life, but upon account of the common Original of their Nature, have lost their title in the divine Testament* ibid cap 27. Which he understands, not only of the loss of Reward, but of the Obligation to Punishment. *Peccatum eos ex Adam dicimus originaliter trahere, id est reatu eos implicatos & ob hoc pœnæ obnoxios detineri. We understand by contracting Sin originally from* Adam, *that they are involved in the Guilt, and for that reason are obnoxious to Punishment.* Aug Retract Lib 1. cap 15. And, when he was pressed by his Adversaries Argument drawn from the Goodness of God, which cannot incline him to punish one Man for another's Faults especially, since he is so gracious to Pardon Sins committed by Mens own selves, he cannot be so hard to punish them for those, committed by other Persons. To this S *Austin* answers, that the Sins of our first Parents are not the Sins of others. *Imputat vero [Deus] non jam aliena sed propria.*

Aliena

Aliena quippe erant, quando his qui ea propagata portarent, nondum erant, nunc vero carnali generatione jam eorum sunt, quibus nondum spirituali regeneratione dimissa sunt No, God does not, in this Case, impute other Persons Sins, but our own They were other Persons Sins, when they, who bear them now by Propagation, were not in being but now by carnal Generation they are Their Sins, to whom they are not forgiven by a spiritual Regeneration Aug de Remiss Pecc Lib iii After him, other Writers of his and the following Ages speak the like As particularly *Orosius*, who writes thus on the same Subject *Omnes peccaverunt, sive in Adam sive in seipsis, & egent glor a Dei. Universa igitur massa pœnas debet Et, si omnibus debitum damnationis supplicium redderetur, non injuste proculdubio redderetur* All have sinned, either in Adam or in themselves, and fall short of the Glory of God. Therefore the whole Mass stands obliged to Punishment. And if the Punishment of Damnation were inflicted on all, undoubtedly it would not be unjustly inflicted Orof Apol de arbitr Libert (2) Another Doctrine, which was particularly insisted on by many of the Divines, after the rise of the Pelagian Heresie, was That Children who died without Baptism were damned The Orthodox urged the Truth of Original Sin, from the Necessity of Baptism. The Pelagians answered, that the Necessity thereof was not altogether and in every case absolute, because some Children died unbaptized, whom to consign over, for that reason, to everlasting Misery, was highly Uncharitable The Managers of the Orthodox side replied, That by the Terms of the Gospel they had no right to Salvation, and consequently that they must be damned Thus S *Austin*, *Sed nos dicimus, eos aliter salutem & vitam æternam non habit eros, nisi baptizentur in Christo* But we say that they (*i. e.* unbaptized Children) can have no Salvation or eternal Life, unless they be baptized in Christ Aug de verb Apost Ser. xiv *Noli credere, noli dicere, noli docere, infantes antequam baptizentur morte preventos, pervenire posse ad originalium indulgentiam peccatorum, si vis esse Catholicus* Do not you believe, do not you say, do not you teach, That Children who die before Baptism, can ever attain to the Pardon of their Original Sins, if you would be a Catholick Aust Lib iii de orig in Indeed this Father, when he is in a milder Temper, makes their Damnation pretty tolerable. *Ego non dico parvulos sine baptismate Christi morientes tanta pœna esse plectendos, ut eis non nasci potius expediret* I do not say, that Children who die without Baptism suffer so great a Punishment, that it were better for them they had not been born Aug contr Jul Lib v c 8 And in another place, *Potest proinde recte dici parvulos sine baptismo de corpore exeuntes, in damnatione omnium mitissima futuros* It may very truly be asserted, that Children who go out of the Body before Baptism, shall be in the gentlest Damnation of all Aug de pecc mer & remiss Lib i c 16. And in this harsh Doctrine he is followed by a great number of Divines who succeeded him As by *Orosius* *Qui non per illam gratiam liberantur, sive qui audire nondum potuerunt, sive cum per ætatem audire non possent, lavacrum regenerationis quod accipere possent, per quod salvi fierent, non acceperunt, juste utique damnatur quia sine peccato non sunt, vel quod originaliter traxerunt, vel quod malis moribus addiderunt* They who are not delivered by that Grace (*i e.* of Baptism) who as yet could not hear it, or being of Age, or when by their Age they could not hear it, have not received the Baptism of Regeneration, which is necessary to Salvation, as they ought to have done, are justly damned because they are not without Sin, either which they have originally contracted, or which they have brought upon them by their ill living Orof in Apol L b Arb vid Prosp. contr Coll cap 19 Isid Hisp Eccl Off Lib ii c 24 The same Opinion being entertained by most of the School Divines, when they came to divide Hell into *Limbus's*, the unbaptized Children had one set aside for them But before the Pelagian Controversie was set a-foot, the Divines of the Church maintained a more moderate and charitable Opinion, concerning unbaptized Infants The antient Commentator on the Epistles of S *Paul*, under the name of S. *Ambrose*, would allow Hell Torments to be due only to actual Sinners For he writes thus *Est & alia mors, quæ secunda dicitur in gehenna, quam non peccato Adæ patimur, sed ejus occasione propriis peccatis acquiritur* There is another Death which is called the second in Hell, which we do not suffer for the Sin of Adam, but is acquired, through occasion of that, by our own Sins in Cap v ad Rom *Gregory Nazianzen* allows a sort of a middle State to them, neither in Heaven, nor in Hell Τὰς δὲ μήτε δοξασθήσεσθαι, μήτε κολασθήσεσθαι παρὰ τοῦ δικαίου κριτοῦ, ὡς ἀσφραγίστους μὲν, ἀπονήρους δὲ, ἀλλὰ παθόντας μᾶλλον τὴν ζημίαν, ἢ δράσαντας· οὐ γὰρ ὅστις οὐ κολάσεως ἄξιος, ἤδη καὶ τιμῆς· ὥσπερ οὐδὲ ὅστις οὐ τιμῆς ἤδη καὶ κολάσεως These (*i. e.* unbaptized Children) shall neither have allotted them celestial Glory, nor yet Punishment by the just Judge as those, who though they were not baptized, yet have not committed ill, suffering rather loss than bringing it on themselves For every one that does not deserve Punishment, does not deserve Honour: as whosoever is not worthy of Honour, does not deserve Punishment Greg Naz Or de Bapt The same Opinion was maintained by the Author of the Questions *ad Antiochum*, under the name of *Athanasius* Τὰ δὲ ἀβάπτιστα, καὶ τὰ ἔθνικα, οὔτε εἰς βασιλείαν εἰσέρχονται ἀλλ' οὔτε πάλιν εἰς κόλασιν· ἁμαρτίαν γὰρ οὐκ ἔπραξαν Unbaptized Children do not enter into the Kingdom, nor yet into Punishment, because they have not committed Sin Neither does S *Austin* himself seem to have been of a different Opinion, when he wrote his Book of Free-Will. For there he thus speaks *Non enim metuendum est, ne vita potuerit esse media quædam inter recte factum atque peccatum & sententia judicis media esse non possit, inter præmium atque supplicium* There is no reason to fear, but that there may be a middle Life between Virtue and Sin, and that the Sentence of the Judge may go the middle way between Reward and Punishment Aug de Lib Arb Lib iii cap. 23 (3) Other Disputes have arisen, since this Pelagian Controversie began, whether Original Sin be something positive or a mere Privation, whether it be propagated with the Soul, or the Body, *&c* which as they are curious and useless Questions, I shall forbear to speak further of them.

2 The Doctrine of the Damnation of unbaptized Children

The contrary Doctrine taught by the more early Divines of the Church.

Latter Disputes concerning Original Sin.

b *Standeth not in the following of* Adam] That the Pelagians did acknowledge, the Corruption of human Nature to proceed only from the Imitation of *Adam*'s Sins, is evident from the many Passages produced out of their Writings by St *Austin*, and others of their Opposers S *Austin* quotes this Passage out of *Pelagius*'s own Book of *Nature* wherein that Doctrine is couched *In Adamo peccasse omnes, non propter peccatum nascendi origine contractum, sed propter imitationem, dictum est* It is said, that in Adam all have sinned, not by reason of Sin contracted by our Birth, but by reason of Imitation Aug de Nat. & Gr c 9 The same Doctrine is delivered by *Julianus* *Apostolus Paulus nullam erroris occasionem præbuit, quia nihil dixit improprium, si pronunciavit, peccatorem primum hominem, sequentibus exemplum fuisse* The Apostle gave occasion to no mistake, because he said nothing improperly, when he pronounced that the first Man by sinning set an example to the rest Aug contr Jul Lib ii c 53 And again, *Per unum hominem peccatum in hunc mundum transiit. Hic autem unus præbenda imitationi sufficit, generationi implendæ non sufficit* By one Man Sin came into the World Now this one sufficed for to afford Imitation of Sin, but not to propagate by Generation, id c 56. But this erroneous Doctrine the Orthodox opposed, by several very demonstrative Arguments, drawn from the Places of Scripture before mentioned, as also from the two following Topicks (1) From the change of our Nature, from that primitive Rectitude and Subordination to the Soul, which *Adam* possessed it in, and its Subjection to those disorderly Appetites and Passions, which now domineer over it On this head S *Austin* thus argues *Natura humana duorum primorum hominum prævaricat one mutata est, at tanta corruptione, quantam videmus atque sentimus, & per hanc subjaceret morti, ac tot ac tantis, tamque inter se contrariis perturbaretur & fluctuaret affectibus qualis in paradiso, ante peccatum, licet in corpore esset animali, utique non fuit.* Human Nature was changed by the sin of the first Pair, so as to be subject to a gradual decay, as we plainly see and perceive, and by reason of this to Death, and besides this to be disturbed and tossed about by so many boisterous and contrary Passions the State of which was different in Paradise before the Fall, though in an animal Body likewise Aug de Civ Dei Lib xiii c 3 (2) From the great Ignorance and Error, human Nature is involved in And thus S *Austin* reasons *Quid aliud indicat horrenda profunditas ignorantiæ, ex qua om-*

1 Argument of the Antients for original Sin from the change of our Nature

2 From our present Ignorance and Error

nis

talk, which also the Anabaptists do now adays renew) but it is the fault and corruption of the Nature of every Man, that naturally is ingendred of the Off-spring of *Adam*, whereby Man is very far gone from his former Righteousness which he had at his Creation, and is of his own Nature given to Evil; so that the Flesh desireth always contrary to the

* but is the Fault or Corruption of the Nature of every Man that naturally is engendred of the Off-spring of *Adam*, whereby Man is very † far gone from c Original Righteousness, and is of his own Nature inclined to Evil, so that the Flesh lusteth always contary to the Spirit, and therefore in every Person born into the World, it d deserveth God's Wrath and

tum, sed est vitium & depravatio naturæ, cujuslibet hominis ex Adamo naturaliter propagati, qua fit, ut ab originali justitia quam longissime distet, ad malum sua natura propendeat, & caro semper adversus spiritum concupiscat, unde in unoquoque nascentium iram Dei atque damnationem meretur. Manet

* *But it is the Fault*, MS CCCC 1571
† *From his original Righteousness*, MS CCCC 1571.

nis error existit, qui omnes filios Adam tenebroso quodam sinu suscipit, ut homo ab illo liberari, sine labore, dolore, et more non possit? What else, besides original Sin, doth betoken, that horrid depth of Ignorance, from whence proceed all our mistakes, that include all the Sons of Adam *as in a dark dungeon, so that Men cannot be delivered from them, without much Labour and Grief and Fear?* Aug. de Civ D Lib xxii c 22 Now since all Men, from the lapse of our first Parents, have been involved in so much disorderly Passion and Ignorance, which came upon them in their Birth, before they can imitate *Adam*'s Transgression, it necessarily follows, that there must be some other Sin which is punished by these Misfortunes, besides the Imitation of a bad Example.

What is meant by Original Righteousness

c *Whereby Man is very far gone from original Righteousness*, &c] By original Righteousness the Divines of the Church do understand, a primitive Rectitude of Nature which our first Parents were born with, and which, if they had not sinned, would have been traduced down to all their Posterity This would have been such a Bridle to their Affections and Passions, as they could not easily have rebelled against their Reason, so that they might without any Reluctancy have obeyed all the Commands, which God had been pleased to lay upon them It has been a dispute among Divines, whether this original Righteousness was a natural Habit, or whether it were a supernatural, and superabundant Infusion of the divine Grace The antient Divines seem to be of the later Opinion, because they make the Death and Sickness of the Soul, to consist in the withdrawing the divine Grace *Quomodo si anima deserat, moritur Corpus, sic anima moritur, si deserat Deus Ipsa est gratia ejus, ut resuscitet & sit nobiscum In the same manner as when the Soul leaves us the Body dies, so the Soul dies when God leaves it It is his Grace, that makes us rise again, and which is present with us* Aug de ver rel. cap x Now that Man after the Fall lost this Bridle of his Affections, and from thenceforward run precipitately into Error and Vice, is the doctrine of the Antients For thus the Author of the Book *de vocatione Gentium*, under the Name of S *Ambrose Humana natura in prima hominis prævaricatione vitiata, etiam inter beneficia, inter præcepta & auxilia Dei, semper in deteriorem est proclivior voluntatem, cui committi non est aliud, quam amitti Human Nature was vitiated by the first Sin of Man, even in the midst of the Benefits, the Commands and the Aid of God, his Will is always bent to the worse side, so that God, whilst he gives him Talents, is forced to forgive him*, c 3 The like he elsewhere asserts *Fuit in Adam natura sine vitio, qui per voluntatis inobedientiam mala multa contraxit, & in posteros magis magisque multiplicanda transfudit* Adam *had a Nature without Fault, who by the disobedience of his Will contracted many Evils, and traduced them more in number down to Posterity* Id cap 8 The same is more fully and expresly laid down by *Petrus Diaconus*, in his Treatise of the Incarnation *Atque ser-pentis astutia*, &c *Man being depraved by the wiles of the Serpent, and being become a voluntary Transgressor of the divine Law, according as was predicted, by the just Judgment of God, he has the penalty of Death inflicted upon him, being both as to Body and Soul wholly changed for the worse, losing his proper Liberty he is sold under Sin After this there is no Man, who is not born bound with this band of Sin, besides him who came to loose the bond of Sin, being born after a new Manner of Generation, the Mediator between God and Man, the Man Christ Jesus.* Petr Diac de Incar cap vi

What meant by God's Wrath and Damnation

d *Deserveth God's Wrath and Damnation*] It may be thought that our Church here teacheth, That all Persons, whose Original Guilt is not washed away by Baptism, but who happen to die before they can partake of that Sacrament, are, by the just Judgment of God, consigned over to God's eternal Wrath and Damnation in Hell, as a Punishment which by their Original Guilt they deserve But that these words do not bear this Sense, is evident from those two Passages of Scripture which they refer to That concerning *God's Wrath* is, Eph ii. 3. *were by nature the Children of Wrath even as others* That concerning *Damnation* is, Rom v. 16 *For the judgment was by one εἰς κατάκριμα to Condemnation.* Now there is neither of these Passages which do necessarily imply eternal Damnation, but contrariwise a temporal Judgment or Condemnation. In the first Passage, by the *Children of Wrath*, is not understood Persons doomed to God's eternal Vengeance, but only in general, Persons who have some Penalty adjudged upon them. For ὀργὴ, Wrath, in Scriptural Language, signifies Punishment So the *Day of Wrath*, Rom ii 5 is the Day of Judgment or Punishment *The Law worketh Wrath*, *i e.* exposeth to Punishment And τέκνα, *Children*, does denote a Society, Number or Rank of Persons: so τέκνα σοφίας, *Wisdom's Children*, Luk vii 35 that is the Number of those who apply themselves to the study of Wisdom And in the like manner τέκνα φωτὸς, *Children of Light*, Eph v 8 *i.e* the number of those who have Hearts illuminated by divine Truths, or those who endeavour to attain the *Light* of the other World. On the like account the τέκνα ὀργῆς, the *Children of Wrath* or Punishment, does signifie the Number of those, whom God has or shall inflict Punishment upon, and seems to be a Hebrew Phrase, to denote *condemned Persons*, or those upon whom judicial Sentence has passed So that, if this Passage of the Apostle to the *Ephesians* refers to Mens actual Sins, which they were in under their Natural, *i e* Jewish or Heathen State before their Conversion to Christianity (as is most probable from the words, *our Conversation in times past in the Lusts of our Flesh*) then *Children of Wrath* signifies those, who, if they continue in their wicked Course, God will put under Sentence of eternal Death, at the general Judgment But if it relates to Original Sin (as S *Austin*, *Prosper* and other antient Writers in the Pelagian Controversie will have it) then

Spirit; and therefore in every Person born into this World, it deserveth God's Wrath and Damnation; and this Infection of Nature doth remain, yea in them that are baptized, whereby the Lust of the Flesh, called in Greek φρόνημα σαρκὸς, which some do expound the Wisdom, some the Sensuality, some the Affection, some the Desire of the Flesh, is not subject to the Law of God. And

Damnation: And this [e] Infection of Nature doth remain in * them that are regenerated, whereby [f] the Lust of the Flesh, called in Greek, φρόνημα σαρκὸς, which some do expound the Wisdom, some Sensuality, some the Affection, some the Desire of the Flesh, is not subject to the Law of God. And though there is no Condemnation for them that believe and are baptized, yet the A-

etiam in renatis hæc naturæ depravatio. Qua fit ut affectus carnis Græcè φρόνημα σαρκὸς, quod alii sapientiam, alii sensum, alii affectum, alii studium carnis interpretantur, legi Dei non subjiciatur Et quamquam renatis & credentibus nulla propter Christum est condemnatio, peccati tamen in sese rationem habere concupiscentiam, fatetur Apostolus.

* *Them that be Regenerated*, MS CCCC 1571.

then by *Children of Wrath* must be denoted the number of those who are sentenced *to die*, by reason of *Adam*'s Transgression, *i e* all Mankind, who as being descended from him must share his Punishment, and, during their *natural State*, can have no hopes of being freed from it In the second Passage, *viz the judgment was by one to Condemnation*, Rom v 16 the word κατάκριμα does not signifie eternal Damnation or Condemnation, but only the Sentence or Condemnation of Temporal Death For the meaning of this is explained in the next verse, *For if by one Mans offence Death reigned by one, much more they which receive abundance of Grace and of the gift of Righteousness, shall reign in life by one Jesus Christ* Wherein the Resurrection to Life is opposed to the Sentence to Death, inflicted upon *Adam* and his Posterity Which Opposition the Apostle makes use of in other Places, as 1 Cor. xv 22 *As in Adam all die, so in Christ shall all be made alive.*

e *Infection of Nature doth remain*]

Pelagians objected that the Orthodox invalidated the force of Baptism

I It was a Calumny raised by the Pelagians against the Orthodox, that they did invalidate the Efficacy of Baptism, by asserting that any Sin or Stain in the Soul remained after it For thus S *Austin* reports their Objection *Nec omnia dicitis peccata remitti in Baptismo, si aliquid in baptizatis conjugibus remanet, ex quo regenerantur* [forte generantur] *mali You say that all Sins are not remitted in Baptism, if there remains any in married Persons baptized, by whom evil Persons are generated* Lib. ii. contr Julian And again, *Dicunt etiam, baptisma non dare omnium indulgentiam peccatorum · nec auferre crimina, sed radere, ut omnium peccatorum radices in mala carne teneantur They* (*i e* the Catholicks) *pretend that Baptism does not afford us pardon for all Sins, nor does it so much take away Crimes as shave them, so that all the Roots of all Sins are yet preserved in the evil Flesh.* Aug Lib 1 ad Bonif c 13.

The Catholicks taught that the Infection was left for a Trial of Faith

II But for all these Scoffs of the Pelagians, the Orthodox maintained, That the Infection of Nature does remain after Baptism, and particularly that these Struggles and Rebellions of the Animal Nature are purposely left in us by God, for an exercise of our Faith, and to excite our Vigilance and Constancy in guarding against them For thus S *Austin* *Evacuatur per Baptismum caro peccati, non ut in ipsa vivente carne concupiscentia conspersa, & innata repente absumatur & non sit sed ne obsit mortuo, quæ inerat nato Nam si post Baptismum vixerit, atque ad ætatem capacem præcepti pervenire potuerit, ibi habet cum qua pugnet, eamque, adjuvante Deo, superat, si non in vacuum gratiam ejus susceperit, si reprobus esse noluerit The sinful Flesh is purged in Baptism* [illegible] *that the Concupiscence which is mixed and born with it is totally consumed, so as no longer to have any being, but that that which was in a Man alive may prejudice him when dead For if the party lives after Baptism, and comes to an Age, as to be capable of obeying the Precept, he has something wherewith he may combat, and by the assistance of God overcome, if he does not receive the Grace of God in vain, and be not a Reprobate* Aug de Peccat mer. &c. Lib. 1 cap 39 And presently afterwards speaking of Concupiscence he has this Expression. *Ipsa soluto reatus vinculo, quo illam Diabolus animam retinebat, & interclusione destructa, quæ hominem a suo creatore separabat, manet in certamine, quo corpus nostrum castigamus, & servituti subjicimus, vel ea ipsis licitis, & necessariis relaxanda, vel continentia cohibenda That* (*i e* Concupiscence) *the bond of the Guilt being loosed, by which the Devil held the Soul fast, and the partition wall being thrown down, which separated Man from his Creator, it remains for an Exercise to us, to chasten our Body and to get the mastery over it, either by gratifying it in lawful and necessary Uses, or exercising our Continence* ibid.

Concupiscence after Baptism proved from Scripture

III Nor is this Doctrine grounded only upon the Opinion and Reason of the Catholicks, but upon the express Assertions of the holy Scriptures For the Apostle says, *The Flesh lusteth against the Spirit, and the Spirit against the Flesh and these are contrary the one to the other, so that ye cannot do the things that ye would*, Gal v 17. S *James* excepts no Person from being subject to the Temptation of his Lust *Every man is tempted, when he is drawn away of his own lust, and enticed*, Jam 1 14. And the Spiritual Combat of the Soul with its Lusts, is thus described by S *Peter*. *Dearly beloved, I beseech you as Strangers and Pilgrims, abstain from fleshly Lusts, which war against the Soul*, 1 Pet ii 4

f *Lust of the Flesh*] The Place of Scripture here referred to, is *Rom* viii. 7 *The carnal mind is enmity against God for it is not subject to the Law of God, nor indeed can be* Here our Translators have rendred φρόνημα σαρκὸς *carnal mind*, and in the verse before *carnally minded* neither of which Versions, if they are just, are literal enough, for as φρονέω signifies *to think*, so φρόνημα signifies *Thought*, and whereas the Hebrews and Hellenists express an Adjective by a second Substantive, so φρόνημα σαρκὸς signifies the same as φρόνημα σαρκικὸν, *fleshly thoughts, or carnal Desire* The vulgar renders it by *sapientia*, and *prudentia carnis*, the *Wisdom of the Flesh*, but that is to restrain φρόνημα to too narrow a Sense S *Chrysostom* explains it by [illegible], *a gross Imp*[illegible] *of Thought*, Chrys. in loc and *Theodoret* by [illegible], and [illegible] *gross and material thoughts, and an impetus of thought that tends to the ground* Theod. in *Rom.* [illegible]

although there is no Condemnation for them that believe and are baptized, yet the Apoſtle doth confeſs, that Concupiſcence and Luſt hath of it ſelf the nature of Sin.

poſtle doth confeſs, that [g] Concupiſcence and Luſt hath of it ſelf the nature of Sin.

How Concupiſcence is Sin

g *Concupiſcence and Luſt hath of its ſelf the Nature of Sin.*] It is obſervable here, that the Compilers of our Articles here, do not ſay, That Concupiſcence has only then the Nature of Sin, when it is ripened into outward Act, or has the Will conſenting to it, but that it has the Nature of Sin *of it ſelf*, antecedently to the Compliance of the Will, and before it is reduced into Act And moreover it's obſervable that they do not ſay, That Concupiſcence is a Sin properly ſo called, as when Men voluntarily comply with a Temptation, or do an unlawful Action, but only that it hath *the Nature of Sin* Now a thing may have the Nature of Sin, or be deemed a Sin in a large and figurative Senſe, to which no Act of the Will is conſenting Now the Nature of Sin does partly conſiſt, in a Deflection from the Rectitude of the divine Rule, which muſt make it for that Reaſon diſagreeable to the Divine Wiſdom and Goodneſs, and conſequently render the Perſons, who are the Subject of this Deflection or Depravation, out of favour with God For no one can ſay, that the Luſts and Paſſions of our animal Nature, and thoſe Tendencies to Vice which we all of us feel within our ſelves, are as pleaſing to God, as if all our Appetites were perfectly calm and quiet, and were continually in that exact Obedience and Conformity to our Reaſon, and the Rules which God has preſcribed, as they would have been, if Man had continued in his unlapſed State

Concupiſcence not a Sin properly ſo called, unleſs conſented to, the Doctrine of S Auſtin

And this Doctrine was maintained by S. *Auſtin* himſelf, in the midſt of his moſt vigorous Oppoſition to the Pelagian Tenets For he does not look upon it as a Sin properly ſo called, unleſs the Conſent of the Will go along with it For explaining thoſe words of S *James*, *Every one is tempted when he is drawn aſide by his own Luſts*, &c he ſpeaks thus, *Pariens enim eſt concupiſcentia, partus peccatum Sed concupiſcentia non parit, niſi conceperit, non concipit niſi illexerit hoc eſt ad malum perpetrandum obtinuerit voluntatis aſſenſum. The Mother is Concupiſcence, the Child Sin But Concupiſcence does not bring forth unleſs it conceive, and it does not conceive unleſs it draw aſide, i e has gained the Conſent of the Will to an evil Action* Lib vi cont Jul cap 3 And ſo in his Letter to *Aſellicus* *Quamvis in ſint, dum ſimus in corpore mortis hujus, deſideria peccati, ſi nulli eorum adhiberemus aſſenſum, non eſſet unde diceremus Patri noſtro, qui eſt in Cœlis Demitte nobis debita noſtra Although there be in this Body of Death deſires of ſinning, if we give our aſſent to none of them, we could not ſay to our Father which is in Heaven, Forgive us our treſpaſſes* Aug. Ep cc ad Aſell From whence it is plain, that S *Auſtin* did not look upon Concupiſcence, to be among the number of thoſe Sins, which being proper and voluntary, Forgiveneſs is prayed for them, in the Lord's Prayer

1. Concupiſcence a Sin, becauſe it rebels againſt the Superior Faculties.

But yet in a large and figurative Senſe, he looked upon Concupiſcence (as we do) to have the Nature of Sin (1.) Upon account of its Rebellion and Diſobedience to Reaſon and the ſuperior Faculties *Concupiſcentia carnis, adverſus quam bonus concupiſcit ſpiritus, & peccatum eſt, quia ineſt ei inobedientia contra dominatum mentis*, &c *The Luſt of the Fleſh againſt which the Spirit luſteth, is therefore a Sin, becauſe it is a Rebellion againſt the Government of Reaſon*, &c Aug Lib v in Jul c. 3. And ſo again, *Neque enim nulla eſt iniquitas, ſi in uno homine vel ſuperiora inferioribus turpiter ſerviant, vel inferiora ſuperioribus contumaciter rebellentur, etiamſi vincere non ſinantur Nor is it no Sin that in Man the ſuperior Faculties baſely ſerve the Inferior, or the Inferior contumaciouſly rebel againſt the Superior, though they are not ſuffered to Conquer them.* Aug Lib vi contr Jul cap 8 (2)

2 Becauſe the Temptation is received with delight

It has the Nature of Sin, Becauſe the Temptation is ſuggeſted with ſome degree of Delight *Quia peccandi delectatione movetur, eſſe ei vincente delectatione juſtitiæ non conſentiatur Becauſe it is moved with a delight of ſinning, although it be not conſented to, by the Superior force of the delight in Goodneſs.* Aug cont 2. Pelag. Ep Lib iii c 13 (3) Becauſe Concupiſcence expoſes us to the Hatred of God For ſpeaking of this, S *Auſtin* ſays. *Non ergo Deus quædam peccata damnat, quædam juſtificat & laudat. nulli laudat ſed odit omnia God does not condemn ſome Sins, and juſtifie and commend others he praiſes none, but hates all* And of Concupiſcence in particular he ſays, *Deus odit & curando agit, ut conſumatur. God hates it, and therefore provides a Cure, that it may be leſſened* Lib ii cont. Jul

3 Becauſe it expoſes us to the Hatred of God

ARTICLE X.

IX *Of Free-will*

* *Of Free-will.*

X *De libero arbitrio*

We have no Power to do good Works pleasant and acceptable to God, with-

The [a] Condition of Man, after the Fall of *Adam*, is such, that he cannot [b] turn and pre-

Ea est hominis post lapsum Adæ conditio, ut sese naturalibus suis viribus, & bo-

* *Good Will and working in us* MS CCCC. 1571

That the Liberty of the Will was impaired by the Fall, the Doctrine of holy Scripture

a *The Condition of Man after the Fall is such*, &c] I. It has been shewn before, by what has been said upon the former Article, that it has been the Doctrine of the holy Scriptures and of the antient Church, That a very great Corruption has befallen human Nature since the Fall, That our Bodies have not only been subject to Diseases and Mortality, but That our Souls, having lost that divine Grace, which was habitually or naturally planted in our first Parents, (and which, had they not sinned, would have descended down to their Posterity) are now more exposed to Temptations, and have a greater Proneness to Sin, than to Goodness. This happy State of our first Parents, we before said, was called by the name of *Original Rectitude or Righteousness* That they were endowed with such a noble Quality, the Scripture does attest *God hath made man upright*, Eccl vii 29 and the same is not obscurely proved from those words, in the History of the Creation, *God made man after his own image and likeness*, Gen i 27 Indeed the Socinians, and their Followers, will have the Resemblance, or Image of God, which Man was created after, to consist only in Dominion over the Creatures, but this is a jejune Interpretation And S *Paul*, who understood Scripture as well as they, took it in another Sense, as is plain by these Passages *Ye have put off the old man with his deeds, and have put on the new man, which is renewed in knowledge, after the image of him that created him*, Col iii 10 *Be renewed in the spirit of your mind and that ye may put on the new man, which after God is created in righteousness, and true holiness*, Eph iv 23, 29 In this Comparison between Christ and *Adam*, the Benefits conferred by the one, and the Miseries entailed upon us by the other, such express mention being made of the *Image of God* being renewed by the one, as it was depraved by the other, it must necessarily follow, that the first Man was created with original Knowledge, Righteousness and Holiness Therefore, as Man's Knowledge and intellectual Capacities were impaired by the Fall, so was the Liberty of his Will and its natural Indifferency, to do Good or Evil at his Pleasure, weakened, and for the future all his Byass lay on the worse side This the holy Scripture asserts, when it says, tho' with particular relation to the *Antediluvians*, that *God saw the wickedness of man was great upon the earth, and that every imagination of the thoughts of his heart was only evil continually*, Gen vi 5.

The same the Doctrine of the antient Divines of the Church before the Pelagian Controversie.

II The like was the Doctrine of the antient Divines of the Christian Church, as well before, as after the Pelagian Controversie

IRENÆUS says, that one of the main ends of Christ's coming into the World was, to redeem us from this Captivity, which this Misfortune had laid our Souls under *Verbum potens & homo verus, sanguine suo rationabiliter redimens nos redemptionem semetipsum dedit, pro his qui in captivitatem ducti sunt. Christ the powerful Word, and true Man, reasonably redeeming us by his Blood, has given himself for those who were led into Captivity* Iren Lib v. c. 1.

TERTULLIAN says, that in Mens natural State, and without the Grace of God assisting, there is a Perverseness in their Nature, which hinders them from doing Good *Nihil verum in his, qui Deum nesciunt, præsidem & magistrum veritatis Perversa sunt omnia, quæ a Deo non sunt There is nothing true in them, who are ignorant of God's Being, the President and the Master of Truth. For all which is not from God must be cross and perverse.* Tert de cult. fœm.

S *AMBROSE* very lively describes the Blindness and Captivity of the Will, since the Fall, in these words. *Inde tracta mortalitas, & non minor miser ærum multitudo quam criminum Fide perdita, spe relicta, intelligentia obcæcata, voluntate captiva, nemo in se unde repararetur invenit Sine cultu veri Dei, etiam quod virtus videtur esse peccatum est nec placere ullus Deo, sine Deo potest Qui vero Deo non placet, cui nisi sibi & Diabolo placet? Quæ ergo natura erat bona, qualitate facta est mala Homo non rediret, nisi Deus eum converteret From thence came Mortality, and not a smaller number of Miseries than of Crimes Faith being lost, Hope being left, the Understanding being darkened, the WILL CAPTIVATED, no one found any means by which he might be repaired Without the worship of the true God, that which seems to be Virtue is Sin, neither can any one please God, without God But he that does not please God, whom does he please but himself and the Devil? That Nature which was once Good, by habit is made Evil And Man would never return, unless God turned him* Ambr de voc gent Lib 1. cap 3

S *CHRYSOSTOM*, Hom xxix in Gen expresses the Weakness of the Will, since the Fall, in these words Ἐπειδὴ δὲ εἰσῆλθεν ἡ ἁμαρτία, ἐλυμήνατο τὴν ἐλευθερίαν, καὶ διέφθειρε τὴν ἀπὸ τῆς φύσεως δεδομένην ἐξουσίαν [forte ἀξίαν] καὶ τὴν δουλείαν ἐπεισήγαγεν *After Sin entered it destroyed Liberty, corrupted the Strength or Power* [or Dignity] *of the Soul given by Nature, and brought upon her Slavery.*

S *JEROM* denies that there is such a freedom of Will in Mens Actions to do Acts of Virtue, but that they are beholding to God's Grace, for Assistance therein *Ubi sunt ergo, qui dicunt hominem proprio posse regi arbitrio, & sic datam Liberi arbitrii potestatem, ut Dei Misericordia tollatur atque Justitia? Where now are they, who say that Man is so governed by a Free Will, as to leave no room for the Mercy and Righteousness of God?* Hier in Jerem cap ix

b *Cannot turn and prepare*, &c *without the Grace of God preventing us*, &c] These words are added, in Opposition to the Opinion of those, who denied God's *preventing* Grace, tho' they owned his *concurring* or *assisting* The latter being only denied by the Pelagians, the former by those whom they called formerly Semipelagians

Of the Semipelagians

The Rise, Progress and Doctrine of the Semipelagians

I And here it will be requisite to speak something, concerning the Persons who went under that Name It must be observed, that S *Austin*, who had undertaken to be the greatest Champion against the Pelagian Heresie managed every Ar-

X gument

out the Grace of God by Christ preventing us, that we may have a Good Will, and working in us when we have that Will.

pare himself, by his own natural Strength and good Works to Faith, and calling upon God; wherefore we have no power to do good Works, pleasant and acceptable to God,

nis operibus, ad fidem & invocationem Dei convertere ac præparare non possit. Quare absque gratia Dei (quæ per Christum est) nos præveniente, ut velimus,

gument that he urged against it with a Force and Vehemence, that he thought would bear the hardest upon his Adversary, and run the most contrary to them As *Pelagius* had asserted the intire Liberty of Man's Will since the Fall, S *Austin* brought the Infirmity of it to the lowest Degree, ascribing every part of a good Action perfectly to God's Grace, as particularly in his Epistle to *Sixtus*, his Book *de Libero Arbitrio, de Correptione & Gratia* Some Expressions therein gave Offence to some learned Bishops and Presbyters of the Provinces of *Lyons* and *Arles* in *France*, particularly those of *Marseils* The chief of these were *Johannes Cassianus*, who lived at *Marseils*, a Monk renowned for Learning and Sanctity *Faustus Riensis*, a *Britain* by Birth, and Abbot of the Abby of *Lier*, *Hilary* Bishop of *Arles*, and the famous *Vincentius Lirinensis* Their chief Error was, that they asserted the Beginning of Righteousness or Salvation was from our own selves, and that we had a Will and a Faith antecedent to any Influx of God's Grace, and which did incline him to bestow it They maintained some other Points against S *Austin* and his Scholars, as particularly Universal Grace, That there is no absolute Predestination, That Men may fall from Grace, and That Grace is not irresistible But none of these Doctrines entituled them to be stiled Hereticks, nor to have their Opinions condemned by publick Authority, during the course of many Years When S *Austin* managed the Dispute with them himself, he calls them, *Fratres & Dilectores nostros, my Brethren and loving Friends*, Aug Lib de don Persev Afterwards when *Prosper* came to take up the Controversie, he calls them Catholicks *Quis hæc prædicari a Catholicis inter Catholicos crederet? Who can believe that such Doctrines should be taught by Catholicks, and among Catholicks?* Prosp contr Collat cap 33 And the hardest word he gives them is that of Calumniators, because they found fault with his Master S *Austin*'s Doctrine This Book of *Prosper*'s, however, gave Offence to the Semipelagians, who published fifteen absurd and erroneous Propositions drawn out of it, to which *Prosper* replied in his Treatise, intituled, *Responsio ad Capitula Gallorum* Not long after, *Vincentius Lirinensis* published an Index of sixteen blasphemous Propositions, which those, who maintained S *Austin*'s Doctrines, were guilty of These were likewise answered by *Prosper* in a Treatise, intituled, *Ad Capitula objectionum Vincentiarum Responsiones* These Controversies not being ended by Writing, Superior Power was at last called in to put a Period to them The Tenets of the Semipelagians were condemned by a Synod of the *African* Bishops, who were then under Banishment in *Sardinia*, and *Fulgentius* was ordered to write against them *Isid. Hisp c.* 14. *Cæsarius* Bishop of *Arles* not only wrote against them, but engaged *Felix* III Bishop of *Rome*, to condemn their Opinions, and to get them to be anathematized in the second Council of *Aurange* A D DXXIX They were likewise condemned by the Council of *Valentia*, and the Decrees of both Councils were confirmed by Pope *Boniface* II *Ep Bonif* A D 530

II As to the Doctrine of preventing Grace, the Denial whereof was their chiefest Error, this is grounded upon the express Words and frequent Attestation of holy Scripture *No man*, saith our Saviour, *can come unto me, except the Father, which hath sent me, draw him*, John vi 44 *Who maketh thee*, saith St *Paul to differ from another? and what hast thou that didst not receive? now if thou didst receive it, why dost thou glory, as if thou hadst not received it?* 1 Cor iv 7 This Passage of Scripture seemed so forcible to S *Austin* for the support of Preventing Grace, that whereas he in his younger Days was inclinable to the Semipelagian Doctrine in this Point, this perfectly convinced him of his Error. *Quo præcipuo testimonio ipse convictus sum, cum similiter errorem, putans fidem qua in Deum credimus non esse donum Dei, sed a nobis esse in nobis, & per illam nos impetrare Dei dona, quibus temperanter & justè & pie vivamus in hoc seculo* By which Testimony chiefly, I my self was convicted, *when I was in the same Error, thinking that Faith by which we believe in God, is not the Gift of God, but is in us from our selves, and that by this we desire the Gifts of God, to live Soberly, Righteously and Godly in this present World.* Aug de Prædest. Sanct c 3 S *Paul* declares, concerning his Conversion to the Gospel, *That he obtained mercy of the Lord to be faithful*, 1 Cor vii. 25 Upon which Words S *Austin* well remarks. *Non, dixit misericordiam consecutus sum, quia fidelis eram, sed ut fidelis essem hinc ostendens etiam ipsam fidem haberi, nisi Deo miserante non posse, & esse donum Dei He does not say he obtained Mercy, because he was Faithful, but that he might be Faithful shewing from hence, that Faith it self cannot be obtained, but only by the Mercy of God, and that this is the Gift of God* Aug. de grat & lib. arb c 7 The same Apostle declares in favour of this Truth, in these Words. *By grace ye are saved, thro' faith, and that not of your selves, it is the gift of God*, Eph ii 8 And elsewhere *Not that we are sufficient of our selves, to think any thing as of our selves, but our sufficiency is of God*, 2 Cor iii 5 With these Words, S *Austin* presses home upon the Adversaries of this Truth *Attendant hic & verba ista perpendant, qui putant ex nobis esse fidei cæptum, & ex Deo esse fidei supplementum Quis enim non videat prius esse cogitare quam credere? Nullus quippe credit aliquid, nisi prius cogitaverit esse credendum. Let those attend here and weigh these words, who think the beginning of Faith is from our selves, and that the increase of our Faith is from God For who does not see, that Men must think before they believe? For no one can believe, unless he first think what he is to believe* Aug de Prædest Sanct c 2

III Nor is this only the Doctrine of the Scripture, and of those who were engaged against the Pelagian and Semi-pelagian Doctrines, but even of those antient Fathers, who wrote before these Controversies began It is true indeed, that in some Places of their Writings, when they are opposing the *Manichean* and Stoical Doctrines, or enforcing the Duties of Christian Watchfulness and Assiduity, they may let fall some Expressions, in which they may seem to lay more Stress upon Mens Freedom of Will and natural Strength, than will bear the nicest Scanning But when they speak of Grace and the Divine Assistance, they attribute as much thereunto as those, who wrote professedly against them, that were tainted with the Pelagian Tenets

Preventing Grace asserted in Scripture.

The Doctrine of the Fathers before the Pelagian Controversie.

JUSTIN Martyr acknowledges, that the Power of understanding the Truth, does proceed from the divine Assistance Εὔχου δὲ σοι πρὸ πάντων φωτὸς ἀνοιχθῆναι πύλας· Οὐ γὰρ σύνοπτα οὐδὲ συνιητὰ πᾶσιν ἐστὶν, εἰ μὴ τῷ Θεὸς δῷ συνιέναι, καὶ ὁ Χριστὸς αὐτοῦ *Do you pray, that before all things the Gates of Light may be opened For they are not perceiveable or intelligible by any, but to him, to whom God and his Christ shall give to understand.* Just Mart Dial. cum Tryph

CLEMENT of Alexandria, Strom Lib vii asserts, that God gives his Grace before we ask it Ἑκούσιος ἡ τῶν ἀγαθῶν μεταδόσις αὐτοῦ, κἂν προλαμβάνῃ τὴν αἴτησιν *His voluntary Gift anticipates our Petition*

MACARIUS in his Homilies says, that God, by the Gift of his holy Spirit, prevents our Petitions Προλαβὼν ἡμῖ τὰ χαρίσματα, καὶ τὰ τοῦ ἁγίου πνεύματος δωρήματα. Mac Hom xxix

S *CHRYSOSTOM* asserts, that Faith, by which we assent to the Gospel Truths, doth not proceed from our selves, but from God Μηδὲν ἡμέτερον εἶναι νομίζωμεν· οὔτε

without the Grace of God by Christ preventing us, that we may have * a good Will, and

& cooperante dum volumus, ad pietatis opera facienda, quæ Deo grata sunt &

* *This Article not in,* MS CCCC 1562.

πάγε κ̓ αὐτὴ ἡ πίστις, ἐχ' ἡμετέρα, ἀλλὰ τὸ πλέον τε̃ θεε̃ ἄκυε Παύλε λέγοντος κ̓ τε̃το ἐκ ἐξ ὑμω̃ν, Θεε̃ τὸ δω̃ρον. Let us think nothing to be our own, forasmuch as Faith it self is not our Work For that it is not our Work, but rather that of God, let us hear S. Paul saying, it is not of our selves, it is the Gift of God Chrys Hom xxx in Act

ISIDORE Pelusiot, his excellent Scholar, follows his Master S *Chrysostom*, in delivering the like Doctrine for thus he speaks of God's Grace Ἡ γὰρ τὰς καθεύδοντας διεγείρεσα, κ̓ τὰς μὴ βελομένας, προτρέπεσα, ἐκ ἂν τὰς ἀφ' ἑαυτω̃ν ἑλομένες τὴν ἀρετὴν ἐγκαταλείψει, ἀλλὰ κ̓ συμπράξει κ̓ εἰς τέλος αἴσιον τὸ κατόρθωμα ἄξει *That which rouses up those who sleep, and spurs on those who are unwilling, will never be wanting to those, who voluntarily seek after Virtue, but will rather assist them, and bring them to a happy End, and Perfection* Isid Lib iv Ep 13

S AMBROSE in his Book *de Fuga Seculi* says, *Non est in potestate cor nostrum, & nostræ cogitationes Our Hearts and our Thoughts are not in our Power* And in his Comment upon S *Luke*'s Preface to his Gospel, *It seemed good to me*, he has these words *Potest non soli visum esse, quod sibi visum esse declarat, non enim voluntate tantum humana visum est, sed sicut placuit ei, qui in me loquitur Christus, qui ut id quod bonum est, nobis quoque videri bonum possit, operatur That may not seem good to him only, which he declares seems good to him for it seemed good not only by human Will, but as it pleased Christ who speaks in me who works in us that that may seem good to us, which seems good to him*

The general Topicks of the Antients, by which they proved preventing Grace

IV But those Divines, who wrote professedly in defence of Preventive Grace, against the Pelagians and Semipelagians, have argued in behalf of it from these following Heads 1. From the Nature of Grace, which, as the Word imports, denotes a Freedom of Gift, without any regard to preceding Merit For thus S *Austin* argues against this Opinion *Videte, si aliud agitur isto modo, nisi ut gratia Dei secundum merita nostra detur quolibet modo, ac si gratia jam non sit gratia Redditur namque hoc pacto debita, non donatur gratis See now what else this Opinion* (viz of God's Grace coming after Mens pious Desires) *infers, but only that the Grace of God is given according to Merit, and so Grace shall not be Grace For according to this Notion, it is a Debt paid, and not a Gift conferred* Aug de Præd Sanct c. 2

So *Prosper* in his Poem *de Ingratis*

Usque adeo donum est quod credimus, & data gratis
Gratia, non merita dicit mercede vocatos

Faith is the Gift of God, 'tis Grace bestow'd
Freely, without regard to previous Good

(2) Another Argument for preventing Grace they draw from the Nature of Faith, which being the Beginning and Foundation of Salvation, as Salvation cannot be obtained without Grace, so neither can Faith, the Foundation and Ground of it, be attained without the same Thus S. *Austin*, having cited some Passages of Scripture for God's Grace in bringing to Faith, thus argues *Nolens ergo his tam claris testimoniis repugnare, & tamen volens a seipso sibi esse quod credit, quasi componit homo cum Deo, ut partem fidei sibi vendicet, atque illi partem relinquat, &, quod est elatius, primam tollit ipse, sequentem dat illi & in eo quod dicit esse amborum, priorem se facit, posteriorem Deum The Pelagian is unwilling to deny these express Testimonies of Scripture, and yet he is willing to think that 'tis from himself that he believes as if Man compounded with God challenging part to himself, and leaving part to God nay, what is the more arrogant, takes the first himself, and leaves the remaining to him and, by saying that both have a share, he makes himself the first and God the last* Aug ibid (3) Another Argument for preventing Grace, they draw from the Divine Promises made in Scripture to Faith the making good of which Promises, does not depend upon the Will of Man, for then God would be beholding to Man to make good his Promises. For thus S *Austin* argues upon the Promise made to *Abraham Dicit Apostolus ideo ex fide, ut secundum gratiam firma sit promissio omni semini, non de nostra voluntatis potestate, sed de sua prædestinatione promisit. Promisit enim quod ipse facturus fuerat, non quod homines The Apostle saith of Faith, that according to Grace the promise might be firm to every Seed he did not promise, according to the Power of our will, but according to what he had purposed For he promised what he himself would do, not what Men would do.* Aug ib. c 10 (4) Another Argument for preventing Grace was drawn from the Prayers of the Church for Conversion of Infidels, for Men pray to God for what is in his Power, not that of Men For thus S *Austin* reasons with great Smartness against the Pelagian *Exere contra orationes Ecclesiæ disputationes tuas, & quando audis sacerdotem Dei ad altare exhortantem populum Dei, orare pro incredulis, ut eos Deus convertat ad fidem, & pro Catechumenis, ut eis desiderium regenerationis inspiret, & pro fidelibus, ut in eo quod esse cœperunt, ejus munere perseverent, subsanna pias voces, & dic te non facere quod hortatur, id est, Deum pro infidelibus, ut eos fideles faciat, non rogare, eo quod non sint ista divinæ miserationis beneficia, sed humanæ officia voluntatis And now set your Disputations against the Prayers of the Church, and when you hear the Priest of God at the Altar exhorting the People to pray for the Unbelievers, that God would convert them to the Faith and for the Faithful, that they may persevere in what they have begun, do, laugh at the pious Prayers, and say that you will not do as he exhorts you, i. e that you will not pray to God, that he would make Believers of the Infidels, because this is not a Benefit of the Divine Mercy, but is owing to the Courtesie of human Will* Aug Ep cvii. ad Vitalem

The Doctrine of Preventing Grace particularly inculcated by our Church

V It is farther to be observed, that the Doctrine of preventing Grace is more inculcated in the publick Service of our Church, than any one Doctrine besides, it being so eminently Necessary to beget in Men an Earnestness and Humility in their Devotion This Doctrine we have recommended in the ordinary Service for the Evening, every Day throughout the Year *O God, from whom all holy* DESIRES, *all good Counsels, and just Works do proceed.* Second Col. for Ev Prayer The same Doctrine is taught in the Communion Service of our Church PREVENT *us, O Lord, in all our Doings-- that in all our Works* BEGUN, *continued*, &c Fourth Collect after the Offertory The Collects for the Sundays and Saints Days, throughout the Year, do abound with Passages, which set forth the same Doctrine *We humbly beseech thee, that, as by thy special* GRACE PREVENTING *us thou dost put into our Minds good desires, so by thy continual help* &c. Collect for *Easter-day Grant to us thy humble Servants, that by thy holy Inspiration we may* THINK *those things that be good*, &c Fifth Sund aft East *Grant that we to whom thou hast granted an hearty* DESIRE *to pray*, &c Third Sund aft Trin *Grant to us Lord, we beseech thee, the Spirit to* THINK *and do such things as be rightful*, &c Ninth Sund aft Trin *Lord, we pray thee, that thy Grace may always* PREVENT *and follow us*, &c. Seventeenth Sund aft Trin *Mercifully grant that thy holy Spirit may in all things direct and rule our* HEARTS, &c Nineteenth Sund aft Trin *Stir up, we beseech thee, the* WILLS *of thy faithful people* &c Twenty fifth Sund aft Trin So that, upon the whole, no Doctrine can be more expresly the Doctrine of any Church, than that of preventing Grace is of ours.

c *Without the Grace of God----working in us*, &c]

Of Assisting Grace

Assisting Grace denied by the Pelagians

I. As the Doctrine of *preventing Grace* was denied by the Semipelagians, so the Doctrine of *assisting Grace*, and indeed all Grace in general, was denied by the Pelagians That this was their Tenet, ap-

pears,

working with us when we have that good Will.

accepta, nihil valemus.

peals, not only by the Writings of those Divines of the Church who wrote against them, and charge it home upon them from their own Books, but also from the Decrees of the Councils which condemned them For thus S *Jerom* speaks concerning them *Ita Dei gratiam ponunt, ut non per singula opera ejus nitamur & regamur auxilio, sed ad liberum referant arbitrium They so lay down the Grace of God, that we do rely upon, and are governed by his Assistance in all our Actions, but attribute this to Man's Free-will* Hier ad Ctesiph *Ipsum liberum (ut diximus) arbitrium Dei innititur auxilio, illiusq; per singula ope indiget, quod vos non vultis, sed id vultis, ut qui semel habet liberum arbitrium, Deo adjutore non egeat Our Free-will (as we before said) depends upon the Assistance of God, so that it wants his help in every Action, which you Pelagians will not own, but this you own, that he that has once Free-will does not stand in need of God for his Helper.* Hier ibid The same is imputed to them by the Fathers of the Second Council of *Carthage*, who condemned their Errors *Persuadere non cessant ad operandam perficiendamque justitiam, & Dei mandata complenda, solam sibi humanam posse sufficere naturam, non attendentes, quod Scriptum est, Spiritus adjuvat infirmitatem nostram Et non est volentis neque currentis, sed miserentis Dei They do not forbear to teach, that for the working and perfecting Righteousness, and for the fulfilling the Law of God, human Nature is sufficient not attending to what is written* The Spirit helpeth our Infirmities It is not of him that willeth or runneth, but of God that sheweth Mercy

A Doctrine delivered in the Holy Scriptures

II. But, as this Doctrine was denied by these Hereticks, so it is expressly asserted by the Holy Scriptures That there was a certain Influx or Blessing of God, which assisted Men in transacting of Goodness, and quickened their good Desires or Resolutions, was a Doctrine received in the Jewish Church, and clearly set down in many Places of the old Testament The Devotional Books of Scripture are full of this. *Turn thou us unto thee* (saith the Author of the *Lamentations*) *and so shall be we turned*, Lam v 21 The holy Psalmist begs of God, that he would *open his Eyes to behold the wonderous things of the Law*, Psal cxix 18 *to make him understand the way of God's Precepts*, v 27 *to incline his heart to God's Testimonies*, v 36 *to create in him a clean heart*, Psal li 1 But this is a Truth more clearly revealed in the new Testament Our Saviour promises, *that his heavenly Father would give the holy Spirit to them that ask him*, Luke xi 13 And declares, *that without him we can do nothing*, John xv 5. The Apostles inform us, that, in our Spiritual Concerns, *God worketh all in all*, 1 Cor xii 6 that *God, who hath begun in us a good work, will perform it*, Phil. i 6 and that *God worketh in us, to will and to do, of his good pleasure*, Phil. ii 13. S *James* reads us the same Lesson. *Every good gift and every perfect gift is from above, and cometh down from the Father of lights*, Jam i 17

Assisting Grace, the Doctrine of the Greek Fathers, before Pelagius

III The same was the Doctrine of the most antient Fathers of the Church. For though some of the Favourers of Pelagianism have asserted, that the Notion of Grace was first set up by those Fathers who wrote against *Pelagius*, whereas the Fathers who lived before, do ascribe as much to Free-will as *Pelagius* did, yet that this Assertion is false and groundless will appear by the following Testimonies

JUSTIN in Dial cum Tryph declares, that the outward reading of the Scripture is not sufficient, but that there is moreover required the inward Illumination of God's Grace Ἐγὼ δὲ αὐ εἶπον, οἴεσθε ἄν ἡμᾶς ποτε, ὦ ἄνδρες, νοῆσαι δυνηθῆναι ἐν ταῖς γραφαῖς ταῦτα, εἰ μὴ θελήματι τοῦ θελήσαντος αὐτὰ ἐλάβομεν χάριν τοῦ νοῆσαι *I answered, do you think, Sirs, that we could ever understand these things in the Scriptures, unless we had received GRACE by the Will of God to understand them?*

IRENÆUS, Lib iii c 22 writes thus *Paulus infirmitatem hominis annuncians, ait, Scio enim, quoniam non habitat in carne mea bonum, significans quoniam non a nobis, sed a Deo est bonum salutis nostræ* S Paul *declaring* *Weakness of Man, saith*, I know that no good thing dwelleth in my Flesh, *signifying, that the good of our Salvation does not depend upon us, but upon God*

CLEMENS Alexandrinus, Strom Lib v speaks thus. Δεῖ δὴ καὶ τῆς γνώμης ὑγιοῦς ἀκλινῶς, ... *We ought to have a sound Mind, unwearied in the Prosecution of Virtue, for which we stand in need of the divine GRACE, right Doctrine, chast and clean Affections, and the Father's drawing us to him*

ORIGEN, contr Cell Lib iv. asserts, that God's Grace is requisite for the understanding of the Divine Truths Ταῦτα τὰ πράγματα μὴ δύναται χωρεῖν ἐπὶ τὸν νοῦ κρείττονος καὶ θειοτέρας δυνάμεως θεωρηθῆναι *These things cannot become the subject of human Contemplation, without a better and more divine Inspiration.* And elsewhere, Χάριτι θεοῦ φωτίζοντος τὸ ἡγεμονικὸν *the GRACE of God enlightening our Understanding* Id contr Cels Lib v

ATHANASIUS in Pass & Cruc Dom Διὰ τοῦτο πέπονθεν ὡς ἄνθρωπος, ἵνα τοῖς ἀνθρώποις τὰ ὑπὲρ ἄνθρωπον καὶ θεῖα χαρίσηται ... *For this reason he suffered as Man, that for Man he might procure things Divine and above Man For all that is done well by Man is his Work* For if S *Paul* says, *that there is no other that speaketh in his but Christ, so when Man does great and remarkable Actions, it is the Grace of Christ which worketh these.*

S *BASIL*, Hom in Psal xxxiii delivers this Doctrine concerning Grace Οὐ ἐν δυνάμει ἀνθρώπων ἢ ἐν σοφίᾳ, ἀλλ' ἐν χάριτι τῇ θεοῦ ἐστιν ἡ σωτηρία *Salvation does depend, not on any Power or Wisdom of Men, but on the Grace of God* On the xlviiith *Psalm* he says, Δύναμιν τῆς ψυχῆς οὐκ αὐτοτελῶς εἶναι πρὸς σωτηρίαν *the Powers of the Soul are not sufficient for Salvation* And on *Psal* cxv. Πίστις οὐχ ἡ γεωμετρικαῖς ἀνάγκαις ἀλλ' ἡ ταῖς τοῦ πνεύματος ἐνεργείαις ἐγγινομένη *Faith doth not depend upon Geometrical Demonstrations, which they call Necessities, but insinuates it self into our Souls by an efficacious Operation*

GREG NAZIANZEN, Orat xxxi highly blames those who do, Τὸ πᾶν ἑαυτοῖς διδόναι, καὶ μηδὲν τῷ ποιήσαντι καὶ σοφίσαντι, καὶ χορηγῷ τῶν καλῶν, *impute all things to themselves, and nothing to him who gives us our Being and Wisdom, and is the Giver of all good things* The same Father, in his Poem on human Virtue, has these remarkable Verses

Ἔρχομαι ἐκ ἀγέρως ἐν ἅλμασι κῶλα τιταίνων,
Κεῖνον ἔχων πνοιήν, χεῖρα τε Θεὸν, ὄλβον ἀγητὸν,
Ὅς μὴ καὶ ... τίθησι
Κεῖνος δ' ... παίγνια θεητος,
Καὶ νεκύες, ζώοντες, ... ἀμπλακίησιν

I walk to purpose, every step I stride,
Whilst Christ inspires, and is my Strength and Guide,
And in my Race does Eyes and Limbs provide,
Without him Mankind is a foolish Toy,
A Carkase which does all around annoy

S *CHRYSOSTOM*, in Cor xvi Hom xii. speaking upon those Words of the Apostle, *what hast thou which thou hast not received?* says Διὰ τοῦτο ... *For this reason we ought not to be exalted, for 'tis not thine which is given thee but that of the Giver. But if thou receive it from another, thou dost not receive thine own. And, if thou dost not receive thy own, why dost thou boast thy self, as if thou wert in Possession of thine own? therefore he adds, if thou hast received, why dost thou boast, as if thou hadst not received?*

IV The

ARTICLE XI.

XI *Of the Justification of Man*

Of the Justification of Man.

XI De hominis Justificatione.

Justification by only Faith in Jesus

We are [a] accounted righteous

Tantum propter meritum Domini ac

The same was the Doctrine of the most antient Latin Fathers

IV The more antient Latin Fathers write in the same Strain

TERTULLIAN, in support of the same Truth says, *Non dabit enim arbor mala bonos fructus, si non inseratur, & bona malos dabit, si non colatur. Et lapides filii Abrahæ fient, si in fidem Abrahæ formentur Et genimina viperarum, fructum pœnitentiæ facient, si venena malignitatis expuerint Hæc erit vis divinæ Gratiæ, potentior utique natura, habens in nobis subjacentem sibi liberi arbitrii potestatem, quod αὐτεξούσιον dicitur An evil Tree will not bring forth good Fruit, unless it be ingrafted, and a good Tree will give evil Fruit, unless it be cultivated So Stones shall become the Children of* Abraham, *if they be formed after the Faith of* Abraham , *and the Generation of Vipers shall bring forth Fruits meet for Repentance, if they throw off their venomous Malignity For, this is the force of Divine GRACE, a more powerful sort of Nature, having the Freedom of Will subject to it, which is called the* αὐτεξούσιον. Tert de An cap 31

S *CYPRIAN* in Pr Dom says, *Hoc diebus & noctibus postulamus, ut sanctificatio & vivificatio, quæ Dei gratia sumitur, ipsius protectione servetur This we beg day and night, that our Sanctification and enlivening, which took its beginning from the Grace of God, may be preserved by his Protection* And again, *Oramus, ut fiat in nobis voluntas Dei, quæ ut fiat in nobis, opus est Dei voluntate, i. e. ope ejus & protectione, quia nemo suis viribus fortis est, sed Dei indulgentia & misericordia tutus est We pray, that the Will of God may be done in us, to do which in us there is need of the Will of God, i e his Assistance and Protection, because no one is mighty by his own Strength, but is safe by the Indulgence and Mercy of God.* Ibid.

ARNOBIUS, Lib. ii contr gent declares this as the Doctrine of the Christians *At vero nos nobis nihil de nostra infirmitate promittimus, naturam intuentes nostram esse virium nullarum, & ab suis affectibus in omni rerum contentione superari We do not promise any thing of our own Infirmity, looking upon our Nature to be of no Force, but that in every combat we are overcome by our Passions*

S *HILARY* in Psal cxviii delivers the like Doctrine *Infirmi per naturam nostram erimus, adjuvandi igitur per gratiam ejus dirigendique sumus ut præceptarum ordinem justificationum consequamur We are weak of our own Nature, and therefore we are to be assisted and directed by his Grace, to perform the whole course of God's Precepts.*

S *AMBROSE* has much upon this Head, as he is cited by S *Austin*, Lib I de Grat Chr But particularly this *Nec ab initio immaculata* (i e Hominis voluntas) *humanæ enim hoc impossibile naturæ sed per Dei gratiam & qualitatem sui, quia jam non peccat, fit ut immaculata videatur Man's Will was not without fault from the beginning, for that was impossible for human Nature, but because now by the Grace of God, and his own quality Sin is not imputed to him, it seems as it were without fault* Ambr in Luc cit ab August

I have spent perhaps more time in these Testimonies, than was absolutely necessary, but however I have done it to shew, that the Doctrine of Divine Grace is so essential a Doctrine of Christianity, that not only the holy Scriptures and the primitive Fathers assert it, but likewise to shew that the Christians could not in any Age maintain their Religion without it, it being necessary, not only for the discharge of Christian Duties, but for the Performance of our ordinary Devotions

[a] *Accounted righteous before God*]

The rise of the Questions concerning Justification

I The Question concerning Justification, which is shortly determined in this Article, is not only the oldest, but, by the Wrangles and Disputes of Divines about it, is become one of the most intricate Questions, in Divinity It began in St *Paul's* Time, when many of the Jewish Converts stickled for the Observation of the Mosaical Law, being carried down, (though sometimes pretty silently) through the several following Ages, but at the time of the Reformation it broke out again with great fierceness, and is not yet wholly allayed, either between Protestants and Papists, or among Protestants themselves. But the main Reason of all this Quarrel has been, because Men have had different Notions of being *justified*, different Notions of *Faith*, and so likewise of *Works*, some meaning one thing by these Words and some another; disputing in the Dark, fastening upon their Adversaries what they never affirmed, and themselves affirming things sometimes False, sometimes Obscure or Uncertain, whereby has been occasioned, that what has been generally written upon this Subject, has not been intelligible either to the Readers, or the Writers themselves It will be requisite therefore to shew, what is the Meaning of these Words, as they are used in Scripture, which will be the best Key to resolve all the Difficulties, which may be started concerning these Points for all the contending Parties do agree, that the Sense they themselves put upon the Words (whatever it be) is the Scriptural Sense

What is meant in Scripture by the word justified

II To begin with the Words *justified*, or *Justication*. The Greek word, which the Writers of the New Testament make use of to denote this, is δικαιόω, which signifies to absolve, to acquit, or to declare any one a righteous Person, notwithstanding any Imputation, or Accusation which may be laid against him And so it is used by the Writers of the Gospels ἐδικαιώθη ἡ σοφία ἀπὸ τῶν τέκνων *Wisdom is justified of her Children*, *i e* the good Lives of the sincere Professors of the true Religion, will acquit it of the Imputations, that are raised against it *Mat* xi 19 So the Publican went out of the Temple, δεδικαιωμένος, *justified*, *i e* acquitted of the Crimes of his Life which he repented of, *Luke* xviii 14 And so innumerable times in St *Paul's* Epistles *By the works of the Law*, οὐ δικαιωθήσεται πᾶσα σάρξ *no flesh shall be justified*, *i e* no Man can have his Sins pardoned by performing the Mosaical Ordinances, *Rom* iii. 28 So again, *we conclude*, πίστει δικαιοῦσθαι ἄνθρωπον, *that by faith a man is justified*, &c. *Rom* iii 28. And so δικαιωθέντες ἐκ πίστεως, *being justified by faith*, *Rom* v 1 Indeed the use of the Word in this Signification seems to be peculiar to the Hellenistical Greeks, for the Classical Authors generally use it, to denote *Condemnation* or *Punishment* For *Suidas* explains, δικαιοῦν by τὸ κολάζειν to *Punish*. And *Hesychius* explains the same by μαστιγοῦν, to *scourge* and ἐυθύνειν to *correct* But the Hellenists take the Signification of the Word from the import of the Hebrew Verb *Zadak* which the Septuagint translate by δικαιόω, *Gen* xxxviii 26 *Exod* xxiii 7 *Psal.* li 5 in which and many more Places the Word signifies to *aquit* or *absolve*, or to deem one *righteous* or *innocent* The Jews seem to have taken the Original use of the Word, from the Notion they had of their *Zadik*, or righteous Man for their *Zadikim*, or righteous Persons, were those, who were in favour with God for their strict Performance of the Law, and were contradistinguished to the *Reshangim*, who were out of God's favour, for their neglect and transgression of his Laws And thus we see them frequently opposed to one another, throughout the whole Book of the *Psalms* and *Proverbs* As the Jewish Church began to be corrupted by Pharisaical Traditions, and the greatest stress was laid upon the nice Performance of the Ceremonial Parts of the Law, they divided their *Zadikim*, or righteous Persons, into two ranks One were the *barely righteous*, such as performed only the common or Moral Parts of Religion, but, besides these, were the *Zadikim gemorim*, or the *perfectly just*, otherwise called *anshi mongashi*, *Men of Works*, i e such as were nice in observing every Punctilio of the Jewish Law Of such an one the *Talmud* relates, *that he never committed a trespass all the days of his Life, but only once he put on the Phylacteries for his Forehead, before the Phylacteries for his Arms*, vid Lightfoot. Talm Exerc in xv *Luke* And 'tis probable, that the rich young Man, who told our Saviour, *All these things have I kept from my youth up, what want I yet?* Mat xix 20 was one who aspired to this Perfection And so likewise that Lawyer, who having enumerated to our Saviour the main Points of the Moral Law, our Saviour bid him, *this do and thou shalt live* But the Man was willing to shew that he reached after some greater Perfection than this, and therefore he enlarges his Discourse into further Questions *But he willing to justifie himself, said unto Jesus, and who is my neighbour?* That is, he had a mind to appear to be a *Zadik gamor* a *perfectly righteous Man*, or a *Man of Works* i e one in the highest State of Justification, and nearest favour with God. This may be sufficient, to settle the precise Sense of the word Justification, &c as used in Scripture, and among the Jews

What is meant, in Scripture, by the word Faith

III. As to the word *Faith*, besides the general Purport thereof, to denote the believing in the Gospel of Jesus Christ, in many Places of Scripture, particularly in St *Paul*'s Epistles, it is used to signifie the Gospel it self, or the whole Oeconomy of the Christian Religion Thus *Acts* vi 7 *A great number of the Priests*, ὑπήκουον τῇ πίστει, *were obedient to the FAITH*, i e professed Christianity So *Acts* xiii 8 *Elymas the Sorcerer sought*, διαστρέψαι τὸν ἀνθύπατον ἀπὸ τῆς πίστεως, *to turn away the Deputy from the FAITH*, i e to make him renounce Christianity And so likewise, in those many Places of St *Paul*'s Epistles, where mention is made of the νόμος πίστεως, *the Law of FAITH*, Rom iii 27 δικαιοσύνη πίστεως, *the righteousness of FAITH*, Rom iv. 13 ix. 30. x 6 And so likewise in all those Places, where mention is made of Justification by Faith, the word Faith signifies the Christian Religion, in Opposition to the Jewish, as is plain by the several Contexts, where the Jewish Religion is signified by the words *Circumcision*, *Law*, *Works*, &c in Contradistinction to Christianity, which the Apostle calls *Faith* *But now the righteousness of God without the Law is manifested*, &c *which is by the FAITH of Jesus Christ*, Rom iii 21, 22 *Where is boasting then? it is excluded By what Law? of Works? nay but by the Law of FAITH*, v. 27 *Therefore we conclude that a Man is justified by FAITH, without the deeds of the Law*, v 28 *Do we then make void the Law through FAITH? God forbid yea we establish the Law*, v 31. So *Gal.* iii 2. the ἔργα τοῦ νόμου, the *Works of the Law*, and the ἀκοὴ πίστεως, the *hearing of Faith*, are contradistinguished, the one denoting Judaism, the other Christianity *Received ye the Spirit by the Works of the Law, or by the hearing of FAITH?* Again, *The Scripture foreseeing that God would justifie the Heathen thro' FAITH*, Gal iii 8. *But before FAITH came, we were kept under the Law, shut up unto the Faith*, v 23.

What is meant, in Scripture, by the word Works

IV By the word *Works*, when this Question of Justification is debated, is understood the Mosaical Law, or the whole Oeconomy of the Jewish Dispensation, in Opposition to the new Dispensation of Christianity *Where is boasting then? it is excluded By what Law? of WORKS?* i e. the Jewish Dispensation *Nay but by the Law of FAITH*, i e the Christian Dispensation *Rom* iii. 27 *Therefore we conclude, that a Man is justified by FAITH*, i e the Christian Religion, χωρὶς ἔργων νόμου, *without the DEEDS* or Works *of the Law*, v. 28 If the Election or Call to the Gospel *be of Grace, it is no more of WORKS*, Rom xi. 6. *Knowing that a man is not justified by the WORKS of the Law*, i e the Jewish Dispensation, *but by the FAITH* of Jesus Christ, i e. the Gospel Dispensation, *Gal.* ii. 16. *Received ye the Spirit by the WORKS of the Law, or by the hearing of FAITH?* Gal iii. 2

The Controversie, when S Paul *wrote concerning Justification*

V The first great Question which was raised among the Christians, and was for some time very earnestly debated on both sides, was concerning Justification by Faith, i e whether or no a Man might be in Favour with God, and be entituled to his Promises, only by performing the Duties which FAITH or Christianity enjoyns, without those WORKS, or operose Performances, which the Jewish Religion obliges to The Apostle S *Paul*, in the several Passages before mentioned, declares his Opinion, in favour of Christianity, as likewise in several other Places of the Epistles to the *Romans* and *Galatians* So that all his Expressions concerning *Justification by Faith*, are to be understood, that Men may be saved only by performing Christian Precepts, exclusive of the Judaical Law, i e such part thereof as was not taken into Christianity This Question the Apostle debated with great force of Argument, and by several demonstrative Reasons, drawn from the Excellence of the Gospel above the Law, *Rom* iii from the Temporal Continuance of the Law, *Rom* vii. *Gal* iv. from the Extent of Christian Liberty, &c. *Gal* v shews that Men were justified by Faith without Works, i e by Christianity, without any mixture of Judaism And afterwards the matter was fully determined, by the Council of the Apostles, at *Jerusalem*, Acts xv

The Controversie, when S James *wrote his Epistle, concerning Justification.*

VI By the time that S *James* wrote his Epistle, another Question was raised, concerning *Justification by Faith*, which, though alike in Terms, was very different in Substance For S *Paul* having expressed the Terms of the Question in a Metaphorical manner, using FAITH to signifie Christianity, and WORKS to signifie the Law of *Moses*, some ill-principled Christians of that time perverted his Meaning, and explained his Words so, that, when he said in the Affirmative Men were *justified by Faith*, as if he meant by Faith, a bare act of Credence; and when he said in the Negative, that Men were *not justified by Works*, they would have his Meaning to be, that, under the Christian Dispensation, there was no need of performing any outward Acts of Piety, they taking WORKS, in his Language, to denote the Moral *Law*, and not the Ceremonial, or the whole bulk of the Jewish Oeconomy. And this S *Peter* seems to refer to, when he speaks of the δυσνόητά τινα, in S *Paul*'s Epistles *In which are some things hard to be understood, which they that are unlearned and unstable wrest, as they do also other Scriptures, to their own destruction*, 2 Pet iii. 16 This was to introduce into Christianity a Solifidian Doctrine, contrary to the tenor of the Gospel, and to the great scandal of our common Religion To set this matter right, S *James* labours the Point with very earnest and prudent Application declaring that *Abraham was justified by works, when he had offered Isaac his Son upon the Altar*, Jam ii. 21 that *faith wrought with his works, and by works was faith made perfect*, v 22 that *by works a man is justified, and not by faith only*, v 24 So that by the wise Determination of this Apostle, this second Question was likewise settled, and the Christian Doctrine declared to be, That a good Life, as well as a firm Belief, was absolutely necessary to Salvation, or Justification.

What the Fathers of the first four Centuries wrote concerning Justification

VII. The Christians, of the three or four first Centuries, acquiesced in this settling of the Question, and added little more thereunto, but only upon occasion to press the Dignity of Faith, and to quel Mens Pride, when they saw them lay too much stress upon outward Actions, though good and honourable, and to value themselves too much upon them. For, before the Popish Doctrine of Merits began, Men were in all Ages apt to value themselves too highly upon their good Actions, and not have the justest regard to God's Grace, which quickened their good Resolutions, and ripened them into Action For thus S *Basil* upon this Point Αὕτη ἡ τελεία καὶ ὁλόκληρος καύχησις ἐν Θεῷ, ὅτε μήτε ἐπὶ δικαιοσύνῃ τις ἐπαίρεται τῇ ἑαυτοῦ, ἀλλ' ἔγνω μὲν ἐνδεῆ ὄντα ἑαυτὸν δικαιοσύνης ἀληθοῦς, πίστει δὲ μόνῃ τῇ εἰς Χριστὸν δεδικαιωμένον *That is the perfect and compleat boasting in God, when a Man is not elated on account of his own Righteousness, but acknowledges that he is destitute of all true Righteousness, and is justified only by his faith in Christ* Basil Hom xxii The like is taught by *Macarius*, Αἱ πιστεύουσαι ψυχαὶ μόνῳ τῷ ἐλέει ἐλπίζουσι αἳ πᾶσαν δικαιοσύνην αὐτῶν ἀποβάλλονται ὥσπερ γὰρ χωρὶς τῆς ἀμπέλου τὸ κλῆμα ψύγεται οὕτως καὶ ὁ ἄνευ Χριστοῦ δικαιοῦ-

ϑαι

Jesus Christ, in that Sense as it is declared in the Homily of Justification, is a most certain and wholesome Doctrine for Christian Men

before God, only [b] for the Merit of our Lord and Saviour Jesus Christ by Faith, and not for our own works, or deserving. Wherefore, that we are

servatoris nostris Jesu Christi, per fidem, non propter opera, & merita nostra, justi coram Deo reputamur Quarè solâ fide nos justificari do-

σαι θελω *Faithful Souls do always hope in Christ, ascribing all righteousness unto him For as the Branch withers without the Vine, so does he, that is willing to be justified, without Christ* Mac. Hom xxiii To the like purport speaks S. *Chrysostom.* Κακῶνοι (i e those who are liberal to the Poor) στεφανοῦνται κατὰ χάριν κἂν γὰρ μυρία ὦσι πεποιηκότες, χάριτός ἐστιν ἡ φιλοτιμία, τὸ ἀντὶ μικρῶν οὕτω καὶ εὐτελῶν ἔργων τοσοῦτον καὶ βασιλείαν καὶ τηλικαύτην αὐτοῖς δοῦναι τιμὴν *These are crowned by Grace, for tho' they perform myriads of such like Actions, all the glory of their Reward proceeds from Grace, that for such little things such a glorious Heaven and a Kingdom, and so great Honour should be given* Chrys Hom lxxix in Mat

How the Question was managed, after the Pelagian Controversie

VIII After the Pelagian Controversie was set on foot, the Question about Justification began to be ventilated afresh, and the State of it to be something altered For as the Predestinarian Controversies had then started up, so the Question concerning Justification was brought in, as an Appendage of them For then the words of S *Paul, Whom he did foreknow them he did predestinate,* &c *whom he called them he also justified,* &c were improved into a sort of Systematical Scale of the divine Decrees, of which Justification was esteemed to be a considerable Step So that whereas the more antient Writers of the Church had only a general Notion of Justification, as Mens being in such a State of favour with God, as would entitle them to Heaven, when God should think fit to call them out of this World, it was then made to be a solemn Declaration or Pronunciation of the Divine Purpose, that such a Person was acquitted of all Guilt, and thereby entituled to the everlasting Rewards, which were from all Eternity decreed him And in this Sense S *Austin,* and others after him, frequently use it For in his Comment on those words of the Psalmist, *For thou O Lord wilt bless the righteous,* &c. Psal v 12 he speaks thus *Hæc est Benedictio gloriari in deo, & inhabitari a Deo Ista Sanctificatio conceditur justis, sed ut justificetur, præcedit vocatio quæ non est meritorum sed gratiæ Dei This is his blessing to glory in God, and to be inhabited by God This Sanctification is granted to the Just. But Calling comes before Justification, which is not from Merit, but from the Grace of God* Aug Enar in Psal. v And elsewhere, *Nisi vocando præcedat miser cordia Dei, nec credere quisquam potest, ut ex hoc incipiat justificari, & accipiat facultatem bene operandi Unless the Mercy of God begins by Calling, no one can believe, so that from hence he begins to be justified, and receives a power of doing good Works* Aug Lib 1 ad Simpl qu. 2.

What was added therein by the School Divines

IX. The School Divines, who built, for the main, upon S *Austin's* Doctrine, added several more curious Speculations, to this Question They taught, That, in carrying on the Work of Justification, it was necessary there should be an infused habit of Grace or Righteousness, *Aqu* 1 2 *Q* 113 *Art* 7 That there should be a Motion of Free-will, antecedent to Justification, *Id* 1 2. *Q*. 133 *Art* 3. That Justification is performed, not by any Dispositions or successive Acts, but in an Instant *Id* 1 2 *Q*. 113. *Art* 7. That the Justification of a wicked Person is greater than Creation, or any other Act of the divine Power *Id*. 1. 2 *Q* 113 *Art* 9 That the Sacraments of the Church are the instrumental cause of Justification. *Id* 3 *Q* 64 others added the Merit of Good Works, not only *ex congruo,* but *ex condigno,* of which more hereafter

The Renewing of the Question, at the time of the Reformation

X When the Reformation came on, those who undertook to animadvert upon the intolerable Abuses of the Romish Church, brought on the Dispute of Justification afresh. They observed, How scandalously the Doctrine of Merits and Good Works was cried up by the Divines of that Church, and how much the Grace of God was undervalued in respect thereof, That the Good Works, which they pretended to ground Justification upon, were chiefly, going of Pilgrimages, offering at Shrines, and giving Mony for Masses to deliver Souls out of Purgatory, &c. and therefore they took Advantage of the Scriptural Expressions of being *justified by Faith only,* to give a check to these external *Works,* which were less commendable than any of the Jewish Ceremonies, which the Apostles had formerly opposed Some things, perhaps, might be said with too great a Warmth, in the Ventilation of this Controversie, on the Protestant side, but as these matters have been since more cautiously expressed, so the vigorousness of the Attack has made the Papists, in some Measure, to mend their Divinity, and to ascribe less to Good Works, and more to Grace, than formerly they did.

The Popish Doctrine of Merits very modern, and grounded upon the Signification of the word Meritum, in the Declension of the Latin Tongue

b *Only for the Merit of our Lord,* &c. *and not for our own Works or Deservings*] I Our Church here, in Opposition to the Church of *Rome,* asserts, that we are justified only by the Merits of Christ, and not by our own Works For they assert, that Mens inherent Righteousness is the meritorious cause of their Justification, that these Works are truly meritorious, or as the Council of *Trent* expresses it, they do *ad vitam æternam consequendam vere promereri are truly meritorious in obtaining eternal Life.* Conc Trid de Bon. Oper Cap 11 As this Doctrine of the Merits of Good Works is one of the most arrogant, and scandalous, of the Corruptions in the Romish Church, so it is one of the most Modern, occasioned partly by the Corruption of the Latin Tongue and the Ignorance of the School Divines, they not understanding the true Import of the Latin word *Meritum,* which signifies properly the Duty or Service which any one is to do *Mereri* is to do Duty or Service, as for Instance, that of a Soldier under his Captain, and *Merces,* qu *Mereces,* is the Pay or Reward which is given for that Duty or Service Now, whereas Christianity is a sort of Spiritual Warfare, and the several Branches thereof do bear some Analogy to the antient Militia, some of the Military Terms were used by the Fathers in speaking of Religion, as particularly *Sacramentum, Symbolum,* &c. And so in like manner *Mereri* and *Meritum* were used, to denote the Service which a Christian was obliged to perform, in his Spiritual Exercise But when this was first used, it had no relation to the modern Sense of the word, in which *Mereri* signifies to deserve But the word being commonly used in that Sense when the Schoolmen wrote, they adapted their Divinity to this Notion, and by what the Antients understood Duty, they understood Merit or Desert It was some time before this Doctrine was hammered out, their Divines holding different Opinions concerning it Some held that Good Works were *ex condigno,* meritorious of eternal Life, in their own Nature, though God had made no Stipulation with Men concerning it, which is the Opinion of *Cajetan* Others, that they are Meritorious only, with regard to the divine Compact by which they are promised, which is the Opinion of *Scotus* Others, that they are *ex condigno,* meritorious, *ratione pacti & operis simul,* both upon account of the Stipulation and the Dignity of the Work it self likewise This last Opinion *Bellarmin* will have, to be the Doctrine of the Council of *Trent.*

Popish Doctrine of Merits contrary to Scripture.

II But let whatever Sanction be given to this Doctrine by that Convention, it is contrary to the Doctrine of the holy Scriptures, which declare, that we are so far from meriting of God, that *when we have done all those things which are commanded us, we are to say we are unprofitable Servants,* Luke xvii 12 We are therein

is informed, that *every good gift and every perfect gift is from above, and cometh down from the father of lights*, Jam i 17 that *God worketh in us to will and to do of his good pleasure*, Phil ii. 13 The same holy Scriptures instruct us, that all our very best Actions are mixed with very great Failures and Imperfections *For the flesh lusteth against the spirit, and the spirit against the flesh, so that ye cannot do the things that ye would*, Gal v 17 That there is no Proportion between the things of this World, and the infinite Joys of the other, so that there can be any ground for a Parity of the Duty with the Recompense *For I reckon* (says the Apostle) *that the sufferings of this present time are not worthy to be compared with the glory, which shall be revealed in us*, Rom viii 18 And again, *For our light affliction, which is but for a moment, worketh for us a far more exceeding and eternal weight of glory*, 2 Cor iv 17

Contrary to the Doctrine of the antient Fathers, who argued against Merits

(1) Because the reward of our labour is owing to the Free Grace of God

III. And the current Doctrine of Antiquity is consonant to these great Oracles of Truth And this they most demonstratively shew, from the following general Topicks (1) Because everlasting Life, which is the Reward of our Christian Labours, does depend upon the Free Grace of God For thus S *Basil* reasons upon this Head Πρόκειται γὰρ ἀνάπαυσις αἰώνια τοῖς νομίμως τὸν ἐνταῦθα ἀθλήσασι βίον οὐ κατ' ὀφείλημα τῶν ἔργων ἀποδιδομένη, ἀλλὰ κατὰ χάριν τοῦ μεγαλοδώρου Θεοῦ τοῖς εἰς αὐτὸν ἠλπικόσι παρεχομένη *Eternal Rest remains for those, who have combated as they ought to do in this Life, not given for the debt of their Works, but on account of a munificent God, in whom they have put their Trust* Bas in Psal cxiv S *Chrysostom* likewise argues, from the same Head For, speaking upon those words of the Apostle, *hath made us meet to be partakers of the inheritance of the saints in light*, Col i 12 he says Διὰ τί κλῆρον λαλεῖ, δείκνυς ὅτι οὐδεὶς ἀπὸ κατορθωμάτων οἰκείων βασιλείας τυγχάνει ἀλλ' ὥσπερ ὁ κλῆρος ἐπιτυχίας μᾶλλόν ἐστι, οὕτω δὴ καὶ ἐνταῦθα οὐδεὶς γὰρ τοιαύτην ἐπιδείκνυται πολιτείαν, ὥστε βασιλείας ἀξιωθῆναι, ἀλλὰ τὸ πᾶν δωρεᾶς ἐστὶ τοῦ Θεοῦ *Why doth he call it an inheritance? shewing, that no one can attain this Kingdom, by his own Actions and good Deeds But as a κλῆρος, i e an Inheritance by Lot betokens good Fortune, so it is here No one can square his Life so well, as to be worthy of the Kingdom, therefore whatever he receives is the Gift of God* Chrys in Col Hom ii To the like purport S *Hierom* *Si humiliaveris te sub potenti manu Dei, & scriptum semper memineris, superbis Deus resistit, humilibus vero dat gratiam Ubi autem gratia, non operum retributio, sed donantis est largitas, ut impleatur dictum Apostoli Non est volentis, neque currentis, sed Dei miserentis*. *If you humble your self under the mighty hand of God, and always have in mind that Passage of Scripture*, God resisteth the proud, but giveth Grace to the humble *But where there is Grace there is not a reward of Works, but the munificence of the Giver, that that saying of the Apostle may be fulfilled*, It is not of him that willeth, or of him that runneth, but of God who sheweth Mercy. *Hier ad Demetr* So likewise S *Austin* *Tua peccata sunt, merita Dei sunt Supplicium tibi debetur, & cum praemium venerit, sua dona coronabit, non merita tua* *The Sins belong to you, the Merits to God* *To you Punishment is owed, and when the Reward comes, God shall crown his Gifts, not your Merits* Aug in Psal lxx conc 2

(2) Because all our good Works are imperfect

(2) Because all our good Works are imperfect and full of Failure, so that they rather stand in need of Pardon, than merit Reward Which Argument is urged by S *Hilary* in these words *Spes in misericordia Dei in seculum, & in seculum seculi est Nec ipsa illa justitia opera sufficient ad perfectae beatitudinis meritum, nisi misericordia Dei etiam in hac justitiae voluntate, humanarum demutationum & motuum vitia non reputet. Hope in the Mercy of God is for ever and ever For Works of Righteousness will not suffice to merit the perfect Beatitude, unless the Mercy of God in this will of Justice shall not bring to account the Faults and Irregularities of our Passions* Hil in Psal li To the like purport S *Cyril* of Alexandria Αὐτὸ ἡμῖν τὸ ὀρθῶς ἔχειν δοκοῦν, μομφῆς ἢ αἰτίας ἀμοιρεῖ οὐκ ἄν, εἴπερ ἀκριβῶς ἐξετάζοιτο [illegible] *That which seems to be rightly done by us, cannot avoid Reprehension and Blame, if God shall, at any time, strictly and rigidly call us to an account for it* Cyr Alex de Ador Lib iv

(3) Because there is no Proportion between the Works and the Reward.

(3) Because there is no Proportion between the best of our good Actions, and the everlasting Rewards of the other Life, so that there cannot be any the least Pretence, that the one should be merited by the other Which Argument is thus pursued by S *Chrysostom* Κἂν μυρία κατορθώσωσι, χάριτος ἐστὶ τὸ στεφανοῦσθαι [illegible] χάριτος ἐστὶν ἡ φιλοτιμία, τὸ ἀντὶ μικρῶν οὕτω καὶ εὐτελῶν ἔργων τοσούτων καὶ τηλικαύτην αὐτοῖς δοθῆναι τιμήν *Those that do well are crowned by* Grace *for if they had done infinite of such Actions, the glory of them must all be ascribed to Grace, that Heaven and a Kingdom, and so great Honour is given for such mean and little Actions* Chrys. Hom lxxix in Mat. And in like manner *Theodoret*. Τὸ δὲ χάρισμα τοῦ Θεοῦ ζωὴ αἰώνιος ἐν Ἰησοῦ Χριστῷ, &c Ἐνταῦθα οὐκ ἔφη μισθὸν ἀλλὰ χάρισμα Θεοῦ γὰρ δῶρον ἡ ζωὴ ἡ αἰώνιος, κἂν γὰρ πᾶσαν τις κατορθώσῃ δικαιοσύνην, οὐκ ἀντιταλαντεύεται τοῖς προσκαίροις πόνοις τὰ αἰώνια ἀγαθά *The Grace of God is eternal Life in Christ Jesus*, &c *He does not call it here a Reward but Grace For eternal Life is the Gift of God For, if any should perform the highest and most perfect Righteousness, eternal Happiness would never be counterballanced by temporal Labours* Theod in cap vi ad Rom

The Doctrine of Merits not fully acknowledged by the Church of Rome, *before the Council of* Trent.

V This Doctrine of Merits was never generally received, in the Roman Church it self, before it was settled by the Council of *Trent* *Peter Lombard*, the Founder of the School Divinity, in his famous Book of the Sentences, has nothing of the Merit *ex condigno*, or the Proportion of our Works to the Reward, but on the contrary says, that *they are God's Gifts, and that the Reward it self is from the Grace of God* Lomb Sent Lib 2 dist 27 *Thomas Aquinas* denies, *that there can be any simple Merit, with respect to God, because that cannot be any where, where there is so great an inequality* Aq 1 2 Q 114 Art 1. Pope *Adrian* declares, *That our Merits are a broken Reed, which pierce the Hand of him that leans upon them, That they are a menstruous Cloth, and our best Actions mixed with Impurities, and That, when we have done all that we can, we are unprofitable Servants* Adr de Sacr Euch. *Petrus de Alliaco*, in his Comment upon the Sentences, saith, *That the Reward is not to be attributed to any Virtue in them, but to the Will of the Giver* Petr. de Alliac. in 4 Lib. Sent Qu 1 Art 1 *Gabriel Biel* ascribes the *Merits of good Works, not to any intrinsick Goodness in them, but to God's Acceptation* Biel in Lib 2. Sent. Qu 1 Ar 1 But we need not go any further for an Authentick Testimony for the Truth of this, than to the publick Offices of the Roman Church which they used before the Reformation, though forbidden to be used afterward For in their *Office of visiting the Sick*, which was supposed to be drawn up by S *Anselm*, and always, after his time, used in the Latin Church, there are these Expressions, which perfectly cut the Throat of the Doctrine of Merits *Credis te non posse, nisi per mortem Christi, salvari?* Respondet infirmus, *Etiam* Tunc illi dicitur. *Age ergo, dum superest, in te anima, in hac sola morte fiduciam tuam constitue, in nulla alia re fiduciam habe, huic morti te totum committe, hac sola te totum contege*, &c *Do you believe, that you cannot be saved, but only by the Death of Christ?* The sick Person answers, *Yes*. *Then it shall be said to him Go on therefore, whilst your Soul remains in you, and place your whole Confidence in his Death only, have Confidence in nothing else, and wrap your self wholly up in this*, &c Now can any one think, that the Drawers up of this Form had any Notion of the modern Notion of Merits? Their antient Form for Baptism was yet more express against Merits *Credis non propriis meritis, sed passionis Domini nostri Jesu Christi, virtute & merito ad gloriam pervenire* Credo *Credis quod Dominus noster Jesus Christus, pro salute nostra mortuus sit, & quod ex propriis meritis, vel alio modo nullus possit salvari, nisi in merito passionis ejus?* Credo *Dost thou believe that thou shalt come to Glory, not by thy own Merits, but by the Virtue and Merits of our Lord Jesus Christ?* This I do believe *Dost thou believe that our Lord Jesus Christ died for our Salvation, and that no one can be saved by his own Merits, or by any other way than by the Merits of his Passion?* This I do believe *Sacerd Rom Ven* 1575 Tho' this be since expurged by the *Indices Expurgatorii*, which were ordered to be made by the Council of *Trent*, yet we have still enough of their Offices, both in Print and

juſtified by Faith only, [c] is a moſt wholſome Doctrine, and very full of Comfort, as more largely is expreſſed in the Homily of Juſtification.

Doctrina eſt ſaluberrima, ac conſolationis pleniſſima, ut in homilia, de juſtificatione hominis, fuſius explicatur

in MSS, to ſtare the Church of *Rome* in the face, and to demonſtrate to them the Novelty of their Doctrine of Merits, even among themſelves.

c *Is a moſt wholſome Doctrine, and very full of Comfort, as more largely is expreſſed in the Homily of Juſtification*] The Homily of Juſtification here meant is not expreſſly ſo called, in our Book of Homilies, but is intituled there, A Sermon of the SALVATION of Mankind, by only Jeſus Chriſt our Saviour, from Sin and Death everlaſting, and divided into three Parts It is called here the Homily of Juſtification, becauſe the chief Points of that Doctrine are treated of therein Now it muſt be obſerved, that the Moderation of our Church is very remarkable, that, whereas the World was blown up into ſo much Flame among the contending Parties, concerning the Speculative Points which were raiſed about this Doctrine, at the time of the Compoſing the Articles and Homilies of our Church, neither in the Article it ſelf, nor in the Homily to which the Article refers, any of thoſe nice Matters are inſiſted on, but only the plain Chriſtian Doctrine in general is ſet down, and little more of Controverſie touched upon than what the groſs Errors of the *Roman* Church, concerning Merits, made abſolutely neceſſary Here are no Diſputes whether Juſtification be made in Time, or from all Eternity? Whether it be an Indiviſible Act, or be performed all together? Whether there be one Juſtification of all the Righteous, or whether every good Perſon have a particular Juſtification? Whether it be neceſſary to Salvation, that every Man be certain of his Juſtification? Whether God juſtifies Men being Holy, or ſanctifies them being juſtified? &c Diſputes which, for a Century and an half, have perplexed the Churches abroad, and the Minds of ſome among our ſelves who have been pleaſed officiouſly to take them up, here at home, to very little Edification and much Contention Since therefore the Article points out to the Homily for a further Explication of the Doctrine of Juſtification, as maintained by our Church, it will be requiſite to give a ſhort account of the main Points contained in that Homily.

The Doctrine of the Homily of Salvation, concerning Juſtification.

Now, I The Homily, in oppoſition to the Errors of the Church of *Rome*, teaches, That *Good Works are not the meritorious Cauſe of our Juſtification* Firſt Becauſe all Men be Sinners and Offenders againſt God, and breakers of his Laws and Commandments, therefore can no Man by his own Acts, Works and Deeds (ſeem they never ſo good) be juſtifyed and made righteous before God · but every Man of neceſſity is conſtrained to ſeek for another righteouſneſs or juſtifycation, to be received at Gods own Hands Hom of Salv P 1. Secondly, Becauſe all our good Works are imperfect, and none of them good enough to juſtify us before God For our own imperfection is ſo great, through the corruption of Original Sin, that all is imperfect that is within us, Faith, Charity, Hope, Dread, Thoughts, Words and Works, and therefore not apt to merit and deſerve any part of our Juſtifycation for us, Hom of Salv P 3. And again, Although we fear Gods Word and believe it, although we have Faith, Hope, Charity, Repentance, Dread, and the fear of God within us, and do never ſo many good Works thereunto, yet we muſt renounce the Merit of all our ſaid Vertues, of Faith, Hope, Charity, and all other Vertues and good Deeds, which we either have done, ſhall do, or can do, as things that be far too weak and inſufficient, and imperfect to deſerve Remiſſion of our Sins, and our Juſtifycation, and therefore we muſt only truſt in Gods Mercy, and that Sacrifice which our High Prieſt and Saviour Chriſt Jeſus, the Son of God, once offered for us upon the Croſs, to obtain thereby Gods Grace and Remiſſion, as well of our Original Sin in Baptiſm, as of all Actual Sin committed by us after our Baptiſm, if we truly Repent, and unfeignedly turn unto him again Hom of Salv P 2

The Homily teaches that good works are not the meritorious cauſe of Juſtification

II. The Homily teaches, That tho' theſe Works are neceſſary to be done, We may not do them to this intent, to be made good by the doing of them For all the good Works we can do be imperfect, and therefore not able to deſerve Juſtifycation · but our Juſtifycation doth come freely, by the meer Mercy of God, and of ſo great and free Mercy, that whereas all the World was not able of their ſelves to pay any part towards their Ranſome, it pleaſed our Heavenly Father, of his infinite Mercy, without any our deſert or deſerving, to prepare for us the moſt precious jewels of Chriſt's Body and Blood, whereby our Ranſome might be fully payd, and his Juſtice fully ſatisfyed Hom of Salv P 1

That however there is a neceſſity of performing them

III The Homily teaches, That Chriſt is the only meritorious Cauſe of our Juſtification This Juſtifycation or Righteouſneſs, which we ſo receive of God's Mercy, and Chriſt's Merits, embraced by Faith, is taken, accepted and allowed of God, for our perfect and full Juſtifycation For it is our Parts and Dutys ever to remember the great Mercy of God, how that (all the World being wrapped in Sin by breaking of the Law) God ſent his only Son our Saviour Chriſt into the World to fulfill the Law for us, and by ſhedding of his moſt precious Blood, to make a Sacrifice and Satisfaction, or (as it may be called) amends to his Father for our Sins, to aſſwage his Wrath and Indignation conceived againſt us for the ſame Hom of Salv P 1 And this both by his Active as well as Paſſive Obedience So that Chriſt is now the Righteouſneſs of all them that truly do believe in him. He for them payd their Ranſom by his Death He for them fulfilled the Law in his Life. So that now in him, and by him, every true Chriſtian Man may be a fulfiller of the Law, foraſmuch as that which their infirmity lacked, Chriſt's juſtice hath ſupplyed. ibid

That Chriſt is the only meritorious cauſe of Juſtification

IV The Homily teaches, That Faith is the inſtrumental Cauſe of our Juſtification Becauſe Faith doth directly ſend us to Chriſt for the Remiſſion of our Sins, and that by Faith given us of God, we embrace the promiſe of Gods mercy, and of the Remiſſion of our Sins (which thing none other of our Vertues properly doth) therefore the Scripture uſeth to ſay, that Faith without Works doth juſtify. Hom of Salv P 3

That Faith is the inſtrumental cauſe of Juſtification

V The Homily ſhews the *Comfortableneſs* (as the Article particularly Remarks) of this Doctrine, in ſetting forth, that thereby is plainly expreſſed the weakneſs of Man, and the goodneſs of God, the great infirmity of ourſelves, and the might and power of God, the imperfectneſs of our own Works, and the moſt abundant Grace of our Saviour Chriſt, and therefore wholly to aſcribe the Merit and Deſerving of our Juſtifycation unto Chriſt only, and his moſt precious Bloodſhedding. This faith the Holy Scripture teaches us, this is the ſtrong Rock and Foundation of Chriſtian Religion this Doctrine all old and ancient Authors of Chriſt's Church do approve, this Doctrine advanceth and ſetteth forth the true glory of Chriſt, and beateth down the vain glory of Man, this whoſoever denyeth is not to be accounted for a Chriſtian Man, nor for a ſetter forth of Chriſt's glory, but for an Adverſary to Chriſt and his Goſpel, and for a ſetter forth of Man's vain glory.

That this is a Comfortable Doctrine

A R T I C L E XII.

Of Good Works.

XII De bonis operibus

Albeit that good Works, which are the fruits of Faith, and follow after Justification, cannot put away our Sins, and [a] endure the severity of God's Judg-

Bona opera quæ sunt fructus Fidei, & justificatos sequuntur, quamquam peccata nostra expiare & divini judicii severitatem ferre non

The difference between the Papists and Protestants, concerning the Perfection of good Works.

a *Cannot endure the Severity of God's Judgment*] I The Popish Doctrine of Merits was so highly reflecting upon the Honour of God, and offensive to all Christian Ears, that had a Zeal for the true Worship and Dignity of their Creator, that the first Reformers set themselves with particular Earnestness to oppose it. Whilst the Popish Divines on the one side cried up the Sufficiency of Good Works, asserting that they were truly just without Culpability or Blame, and that Men might not only do their Duty as they ought, but that they might do more than they were obliged to, the Protestant Divines denied all this, and *Luther* in his warm way of Expression said, *bona opera totidem esse venialia peccata*, *that all good Works were only so many Sins, which we were beholden to God's Mercy for the Pardon of. And, æque nobis impossibilia sunt omnia præcepta atque illud unum non concupisces All the Commandments are equally impossible, as that Thou shall not covet.* Luth de Lib Christ *Calvin* expresses himself in as high Terms *Nec unum a sanctis exit opus quod non mereatur justi opprobrii mercedem No one Action is committed by Good Men, which they are not to be reproached for* Inst. Lib III c 14 *Non sunt tantopere exagitandi qui dixerunt qualibet bona opera, si exacto rigore censeantur, æterna potius damnatione, quam vitæ præmio digna esse They are not so much to be blamed, who have asserted, that good Works if they be scanned with exact rigor, do rather deserve eternal Damnation, than the reward of eternal Life.* Calv in Antid Conc But the Protestants, in their Publick and Authentick Papers, bated much of the Heat and Ruggedness of these Expressions For in the *Wirtemberg* Confession of Faith, which was delivered into the Council of *Trent*, 24 *Jan* MDLII some little time before our Articles were set forth, the very words of our Article are used *Omnia enim bona opera, quæ nos facimus, sunt imperfecta, nec possunt severitatem divini judicii ferre. All the good Actions which we do are imperfect*, and cannot bear the Severity of God's Judgment. Against this Doctrine of the Protestants, the Tridentine Fathers thunder out their *Anathema Siquis in qualibet opere justum saltem venialiter peccare dixerit, aut quod intolerabilius est, mortaliter, atque ideo pœnas æternas mereri, tantumque ob id non damnari, quia Deus ea opera non imputet ad damnationem, Anathema sit. If any one shall say, that a righteous Person in every good Work, does at least Sin venially, or, what is more intolerable, mortally, and for this Reason does deserve eternal Punishment, and is not damned, only because God does not impute it to Damnation, let him be* Anathema Conc. Trid Sess vi. cap 25

It is none of my Business to vindicate the several harsh Expressions enumerated in this Canon, our Church having nothing to do therewith, nor being answerable for them, but only to shew that this moderate Expression, *that good Works cannot endure the Severity of God's Judgment*, is a most true and Christian Assertion, for which the Holy Scriptures, and the Writers of the purest Ages of Antiquity, will vouch.

The Imperfection of good Works proved from Scripture

II The Holy Scriptures, in this Particular, are incontestibly on the Protestant side, for we find nothing there, but what tends to quell human Pride, and to bear down any pretended Abilities of Nature We are there told, That *there is not a just man upon earth that doth good, and sinneth not*, Eccl vii 20 That *all our righteousnesses are as filthy rags*, If lxiv 6. That *a corrupt tree bringeth forth evil fruit*, Mat vii 18 That *the flesh lusteth against the spirit, and the spirit against the flesh, and these are contrary the one to the other, so that ye cannot do the things that ye would*, Gal v 17 And lastly, That this Imperfection of our Natures is acknowledged by the most pious Men, whose Characters are recorded in holy Writ. For thus holy *Job* professes *How should a man be just with God?* Job ix 2. *What is man that he should be clean? and he which is born of a woman that he should be righteous? behold he putteth no trust in his Saints, and the Heavens are not clean in his sight*, Job xv 15. So holy *David*, *If thou, Lord, shouldest mark iniquities, who should stand?* Psal cxxx. 3 And again, *Enter not into judgment with thy servant, for in thy sight shall no man living be justified*, Psal cxliii 2 So likewise *Daniel*, *O Lord righteousness belongeth unto thee, but to us confusion of faces*, Dan ix 7 And again, *We do not present our supplications before thee, for our righteousnesses, but for thy great mercies*, v. 18 S. *Paul* affirms of himself, that he had not *already attained or was already perfect*, Phil. iii. 12 S *James* declares, That *in many things we offend all*, Jam iii. 2. And S *John*, *If we say that we have no sin, we deceive our selves and the truth is not in us*, 1 Joh i 8

The Imperfection of good Works proved from the Writings of the antient Fathers.

III And, if we look into the Writers of the antient Church, we shall find their Doctrine to be the same S *CHRISOSTOM* commenting on 1 Cor i 1. *By the will of God*, &c. says, Διὰ θελήματος Θεοῦ. Ὁ γὰρ Θεὸς τοῦτο ἠθέλησε τὸ οὕτως ἡμᾶς σωθῆναι. οὐδὲν γὰρ ἡμεῖς κατωρθώσαμεν, ἀλλὰ διὰ τοῦ θελήματος τοῦ Θεοῦ τὴν σωτηρίαν εὑράμεθα *By the Will of God.*] *For God willed that you should thus be saved. For we do nothing right, but by the will of God we find our Salvation*

S *CYRIL* writes, Αὐτὸ ἡμῶν τὸ ὀρθῶς ἐργάζεσθαι δοκοῦν, μωμοῦς καὶ αἰτίας ἀμοιρήσειεν ἂν οὐ τι που περιεργαζόμενόν τε καὶ βασανίζοντος Θεοῦ *That which seems to be done well by us, cannot escape Reprehension and Blame, if it be narrowly searched into by God* Cyr de Ador Lib iv N B. these are almost the very words of our Article. And not long after, Καθαρὸς οὐδεὶς ἀπὸ ῥύπου, κἂν εἰ σφόδρα τις εἴη τῶν εὐδοκιμούντων εἶναι δοκούντων· τετήρηται γὰρ τὸ τελείως ἅγιον εἰς αἰῶνα τὸν μέλλοντα *There is no one pure from defilement, although he be of the number of them, who are esteemed the most excellent Persons for perfect holiness is reserved for the other World*, ibid

THEOPHY-

ment, yet [b] are they pleasing and acceptable to God in Christ, and do spring out necessarily of a true and lively Faith, insomuch that by them a lively Faith may be as evidently known, as a Tree discerned by the Fruit.

possunt; Deo tamen grata sunt, & accepta in Christo, atque ex vera & viva fide, necessario profluunt, ut planè ex illis, æquè fides viva cognosci possit, atque arbor ex fructu judicari.

THEOPHYLACT, ad Eph ii 5 writes thus, Χάριτί ἐστε σεσωσμένοι· οὐ καμάτοις καὶ ἔργοις ἰδίοις ἐσώθητε, ἀλλὰ χάριτι μόνῃ· ὅσον γὰρ ἐκ τῶν ἔργων, κολάσεως καὶ ὀργῆς ἄξιοι *By Grace ye are saved*] *not saved by your own Labours and Virtues, but by Grace only. for, as for Works, they are worthy of God's Punishment and Anger* Which Expression, by the way, seems to run as high, as any of those of *Luther* and *Calvin*

S *AUSTIN*, Ep. xxix. ad Hier. writes, *Virtus est charitas, qua id quod diligendum est, diligitur hæc aliis major, in aliis minor, in aliis nulla est plenissima vero, quæ jam non possit augeri, quamdiu hic homo vivit, est in nemine - quamdiu autem augeri potest, profecto illud quod minus est, quam debet, ex vitio est Virtue is a Charity, by which that is loved which ought to be loved this is greater in some, lesser in others, in some none at all but the fullest which admits of no increase, as long as this World lasts, is in no Man Now as long as it can be increased, and is less than it ought to be, it is blameable.*

S *GREGORY*, Moral. ix. cap 2 says, *Sanctus vir, quia omne virtutis nostræ meritum esse vitium conspicit, si ab interno arbitrio districte judicetur, rectè subjungit, si voluerit contendere cum eo, non poterit respondere ei unum pro mille The holy Man, because he sees that all the merit of our Virtue is Vice, if he be strictly judged by his inward Will, doth rightly add, if he will contend with him he cannot answer him one of a thousand* And again, ibid cap 11 *Quictium si habuero quippiam justum non respondebo, sed meum judicem deprecabor Ut enim sæpe diximus, omnis humana justitia injustitia esse convincitur, si districte judicetur Prece ergo post justitiam indiget, ut quæ succumbere discussa poterat, ex sola judicis potestate coalescat If I have any thing that is just I will not answer,* [i e plead it,] but *I will ask my judge pardon for it. For, as we have often said, all human justice is convicted of injustice, if it be strictly judged Therefore after justice it stands in need of Prayer, that that, which might be cast in being judged, might come off by the mercy of the judge* Now since this Protestant Doctrine was taught by this antient Bishop of *Rome*, methinks the Council of *Trent* should have been more cautious, in the heat of their Fulminations, how they had anathematized the Ashes and Writings of one of their greatest and most famous Popes

The Protestants calumniated by the Papists, for denying the necessity of good Works.

b *Yet they are pleasing and acceptable unto God*] I It was a frequent Calumny raised by the Papists against the Protestants from the beginning of the Reformation, that the whole of their Religion consisted in Faith, and that they did reject good Works as unnecessary things Nay, this Calumny, false and scandalous as it is, is not only objected to the Protestants by the private Writers of the Roman Church, but even by the Council of *Trent* it self, tho' at the same time they had the several Protestant Confessions, which had been delivered in to them, lying before them For this Imputation is plainly enough objected in the *xxth Can Siquis hominem justificatum & quantumlibet perfectum dixerit non teneri ad observantiam mandatorum Dei & Ecclesiæ, sed tantum ad credendum, quasi vero Evangelium sit nuda & absoluta promissio vitæ æternæ sine conditione Observationis mandatorum, Anathema sit. If any one shall say, that a Man justified and every way perfect, is not obliged to observe the Commandments of God and the Church, but only to believe, as if the Gospel were only a naked and absolute promise of eternal Life, without the Condition of observing God's Commandments, let him be* Anathema

The Protestants industriously vindicate themselves from this Calumny in their several Confessions

II Therefore the Protestants in all their Apologies and Confessions do strenuously disavow this Principle, which the Papists had so unjustly fasten'd upon them, and take all occasion to assert the Necessity of good Works Thus the *Augustan* Confession *Additur & doctrina de bonis operibus quod viz necessaria sit in reconciliatis obedientia erga legem Dei. We add moreover the doctrine of good Works because an obedience to the Law of God is necessary in all regenerate Persons* Aug Conf cap. *de bon op.* So in that of *Wirtemberg Docemus bona opera divinitus præcepta necessariò facienda esse Good Works commanded by God are absolutely Necessary* Conf Wirtemberg cap *de bon. op.* So in that of *Saxony*, which comes nigher to our Articles *Obedientiam & bonam conscientiam, quamquam abest a perfectione legis, tamen in reconciliatis placere Deo. Obedience and a good Conscience, altho' they come far short of the Perfection of the Law, yet in regenerate Persons they are pleasing to God* Conf Sax cap 9

The necessity of good Works, the Doctrine of the holy Scriptures.

III. For this is a Doctrine which is every where inculcated in the holy Scriptures, as the main design of Religion, and without which Christianity would only be an empty speculative Science For the Exhortations and Commands for the Performance of good Works are as express in Scripture as Words can make them. *God hath not called us to Uncleanness, but to Sanctification*, 1 Thes. iv 7. *What then, shall we sin because we are not under the Law, but under Grace? God forbid*, Rom vi. 15 *Teaching us that denying all ungodliness and worldly Lusts, we should live soberly, righteously and godly in this present world*, Tit ii 12 And again, *Who gave himself for us, that he might redeem us from all iniquity, and purifie unto himself a peculiar people, zealous of good works*, Tit ii. 14 They elsewhere inform us, that no Faith is true or genuine, unless it draw after it good Works as a Consequent of it. For *Faith worketh by Love*, Gal v. 6 And *this is the Love of God that we keep his Commandments*, 1 Joh v 2. And *S. James* informs us, that *Faith if it have not works is dead being alone*, Jam ii 17. Besides, God denounces the severest Punishment, against those who neglect or violate his Commands *God is the avenger of all such*, 1 Thes iv 6 *If ye live after the flesh ye shall die*, Rom. viii 13 *For which things sake the wrath of God cometh upon the Children of disobedience*, Col iii. 6. *For this ye know, that no whoremonger, nor unclean person, nor covetous man, who is an Idolater, hath any inheritance in the kingdom of Christ, or of God*, Eph v 5

The Doctrine of the antient Fathers

IV. The Writers of the antient Church do exactly agree with the holy Scriptures in this Doctrine For though they set the highest value upon God's Grace, and a sincere Faith, as to the Point of Justification, yet they always require the Concomitancy or Presence of good Works

IGNATIUS makes the Conjunction of Faith and Works to be the Perfection of a Christian, and uses the very same Similitude which our Articles do, of the Fruit and the Tree, making good Works to be the natural Fruit or Produce of a true Faith For thus speaks that most antient Father Ἀρχὴ ζωῆς πίστις, τέλος δὲ ἀγάπη, τὰ δὲ δύο ἐν ἑνότητι γενόμενα Θεοῦ ἄνθρωπον ἀποτελεῖ *The beginning of life is Faith the perfection Love. but these*

ARTICLE XIII.

XIII *Works before Justification*

Of Works before Justification.

XIII De operibus ante Justificationem

Works done before the Grace of Christ, and the Inspiration of his Spirit, are not pleasant to God, forasmuch as they spring not of Faith in Jesu Christ, neither do

Works done before the Grace of Christ, and the Inspiration of his Spirit, [a] are not pleasant to God, forasmuch as they spring not of Faith in Jesu

Opera quæ fiunt ante gratiam Christi, & spiritus ejus afflatum, cum ex fide Jesu Christi non prodeant, minime Deo grata sunt, neque gratiam (ut multi

these two, when they are joyned together perfect the man of God Ignat Ep ad Eph And a little after thus, Οἱ ἐπαγγελλόμενοι Χριστοῦ εἶναι [illegible] πράττουσι, [illegible] *They who profess themselves Christians, are known, not by what they say, but by what they do For the Tree is known by its Fruit It is better to say nothing and to be, than to talk and not to be* Ibid

CLEMENT of *Alexandria* says, that true Faith is necessarily productive of good Works, and that Men ought to use their utmost Diligence in performing them Ἡ πίστις, εἰ καὶ ἑκούσιος [illegible] ἐργάτις ἀγαθῶν, καὶ δικαιοπραγίας θεμέλιος *Faith, although it be a voluntary assent of the Mind, is yet a Worker of good Actions, and the Foundation of righteous doing* Clem. Strom. Lib v And elsewhere, [illegible] *By Grace we are saved, but not without good Works but we ought to be rightly disposed to Good, and employ all our Diligence in performing it For we ought to have a sound Mind, and to be constant and unalterable in our Pursuit after Virtue* Ibid

GREGORY Nazianzen, Orat xxviii requires the Presence of good Works with Faith [illegible] *As well doing, if it be destitute of Faith, deserves no Praise, (for some Men embrace Virtue, out of a love of Honour or from natural Disposition) so Faith without Works is dead*

ISIDORE Pelusiot says, in favour of good Works, Τὴν πίστιν τὰ ἔργα μᾶλλον ἢ οἱ λόγοι [illegible] *Good Works shew forth Faith, more than Words* Isid Pelus clviii

THEODORET, Qu. 63 in Exod writes, Οὐκ ἀρκεῖ ἡ πίστις εἰς σωτηρίαν, ἀλλὰ δεῖται τῶν ἔργων εἰς τελειότητα *Faith is not sufficient for Salvation, but it wants Works to perfect it*

PHOTIUS expresses the Orthodox Doctrine very accurately upon this Head. [illegible] *It is necessary that good Works should be joyned to Faith, and that by both of them the good Man be perfected and compleated For a sound Faith produces good Actions, and the pureness of the Actions do shew that the Faith is Divine Now these two are often separated and torn from each other, but they cannot subsist separately in Mens Minds* Phot Ep 1.

S *AMBROSE*, or the Writer of the *Comment* on the *Epistle* to the *Hebrews*, among his Works, on the ivth Chapter writes thus *Festinemus ingredi in illam requiem, festinemus inquit, quia non sufficit fides, sed debet ad hanc & vitæ fidei congrua [illegible] coelum possidere, fidem operibus bonis ornare* *Let us make haste to enter into that rest I say, let us make haste, because Faith alone is not sufficient, but there ought to be added a suitable Life For it is necessary for every one who would possess himself of Heaven, to adorn Faith with good Works*

S. *JEROM* in his Comment on the xxvith of *Isaiah*, speaks thus for the necessity of good Works being joyned with Faith *Murus & ante-murale ponetur in ea Murus (inquit) bonorum operum, & ante murale fidei Non enim sufficit habere murum fidei, nisi ipsa fides bonis operibus confirmetur* *A Wall and a Bulwark shall be placed in her A Wall, says he, of good Works and a Bulwark of Faith For it is not sufficient to have a Wall of Faith, unless Faith be confirmed by Works*

S *AUSTIN* teaches the like Doctrine *Jam illud videamus, quod excutiendum est a cordibus religiosis, ne mala securitate, salutem suam perdant, si ad eam obtinendam, sufficere solam fidem putaverint* *Let us therefore look out for that, which is to be shaken off from all pious Hearts, that they do not miss of their Salvation by an evil Security, if they think that Faith alone is sufficient to obtain it* De fid & op cap 18

FULGENTIUS speaks thus in behalf of good Works, and against the Solifidian Doctrines *Vita bona non veraciter dicitur, quæ perversa credulitatis vitio depravatur neque sufficit ad salutem fides recta cui [illegible] conversatio moribus atque operibus turpetur obscenis* *That is not truly called a good Life, which is polluted with the fault of a perverse Credulity for the Faith of a right Believer is not sufficient for Salvation if his Conversation be defiled by ill Morals and Actions* Fulg Lib ii de Remiss pecc cap 1

The Popish Writers, it is true, would draw these and the like Passages, with which the Writings of the Antients abound, to prove a *Necessity of Efficiency*, as if they were the immediate Cause of Justification, which Doctrine the Antients, (as has been shewn before) so vigorously oppose, but any one who impartially views the Places may see, that they meant only a *Necessity of Presence*, or that it was necessary in order to Salvation, that a good Life should always go along with a sound Faith

---

a *Are not pleasant to God*] I. This Article is designed partly against an Error of the Pelagians, who contended that the good Actions of the Heathens were acceptable to God, and to another of the Papists, who in some measure have closed with them, in their fond Distinction of good Works into Merits *ex congruo* and *ex condigno*.

What Errors this Article opposes

condigno. The *Pelagians* in their Disputes against the Necessity of Grace, were used frequently to instance in some of the more noble and splendid Actions of the Heathens, who tho' they were unassisted by Grace, yet no one could deny but they were very laudable in the Eyes of Men, and therefore they concluded that God Almighty likewise must look upon them with a very favourable Aspect, and if heathen Men could do such good Actions without Grace, it was in no ways necessary that Christians should be beholding to this supernatural Assistance for all the good Actions they do. But the Orthodox deny'd the Force of this Argument, and on the contrary asserted, that their good Actions were unacceptable to God, as not proceeding from Faith in Christ, and the Motives of the Christian Religion, to which only God had promised his Acceptance, and had allotted a Reward to them by the Charter of the Gospel

Now that the Actions of such Persons cannot be acceptable or pleasant to God, is evident from the particular Reason here assigned in this Article

Good Works before Justification do not please God, because they spring not from Faith

II Because they *spring not of Faith in Jesus Christ.* i e because the Doers of them are not instructed in the Principles of Christianity, and do not act upon those Rules which God has prescribed, how he will be worshipped, and how he will have an acceptable Service paid unto him For whatsoever Men do of their own Heads, without a Command of God for it, however plausible it may be in its own Nature, the Apostle calls it ἐθελοθρησκεία, a *Will-worship*, Col ii. 13. and our Saviour condemns any such Practice, saying, *In vain do they worship God, teaching for Doctrines the Commandments of Men*, Mat xv 9 Besides, we see, how that, when Men were left to themselves to regulate and direct their religious Worship as they pleas'd, what gross and stupid Idolatry they fell into, which began in the most early Ages of the World, and overspread the whole Face of the Earth, the Nation of the *Jews* only excepted, to whom God himself was pleased to prescribe a Form of Worship Now there are hardly any Actions which Men are more sincere and serious in, than the Honours and Respects which they ascribe to the Divine Nature, but yet the Heathen Nations, by paying a Worship which God had not prescribed, or directing it to an Object inferior to the great Creator of all Things, were so far from being acceptable in the Eyes of God, that they became hateful in his Sight This provoked God to withdraw his particular Countenance and Favour from all the idolatrous Nations, and confine it only to the *Jews*, who worshipped him according to his Will

Because they do not proceed from the Love and Honour of God

III The good Actions of unjustified Persons, or Unbelievers, are not pleasing to God, because they do not proceed from the Love of God, or from any Tendency to the Advancement of his Glory or Honour, but only from some sensual or worldly Principle, which has no Relation to Piety or Religion. There is no doubt to be made that *Alexander*'s returning back to *Darius*, after he had conquer'd him, all the Court Ladies whom he took Prisoners, without any Violence offered to them, *Plutarch in Alexand.* and *Scipio*'s restoring the beautiful *Spanish* Lady that was brought Captive to him, unto the Gentleman to whom she was espoused, *Liv Hist Lib* xxvi. were brave and gallant Actions, and did betoken a noble and generous Mind, but yet it may be justly questioned, whether they were Actions acceptable in the Eyes of God, as proceeding from Desire of Fame, a Design of gaining an Interest and Respect from the conquered People, or some other Principle which might be quite foreign to Goodness and Piety. And the Case would have been otherwise, had these Actions taken their Rise from Christian or truly Religious Principles Had these great Persons resolved to quell their Passions, and to give up their sensual Satisfactions, in Obedience to the Commands and in Regard to the Honour of their great Creator, or for the Love of their blessed Redeemer, for such religious Considerations only can render an Action acceptable in God's Sight (1) This is the constant Doctrine of the holy Scripture Our Saviour commands, that Mens good Works *should shine before Men* (not in order to vulgar Applause) *but that they may glorifie our Father which is in Heaven*, Mat v 16 The Apostle exhorts us to *do all to the Glory of God*, 1 Cor x 31. and that the *Fruits of Righteousness* (i e good Works) *be by Jesus Christ, unto the Praise and Glory of God*, Phil. i 11. S. *Peter* enjoyns the same, tho' with particular Relation to Works of Charity, *If any Man minister, let him do it, as of the Ability which God giveth that God in all things may be glorified through Jesus Christ*, 1 Pet. iv 11. S *Paul* makes the Love of God to be the great Spring and Principle of all virtuous Actions *Love is the fulfilling of the Law*, Rom xiii 10. We are elsewhere taught, that Mens Hearts are only to be purified by the Christian Faith, *Acts* xv 9 *Unto the pure all things are pure, but unto them that are defiled and unbelieving nothing is pure*, Tit i 15. These are the great Privileges which God Almighty in his holy Word has promised to the Members of his Church, which those that are out of the Pale of it have no Title to (2) The ancient Writers of the Church do maintain the same Doctrine, which the holy Scriptures had laid down before them Indeed it must be acknowledged, that some of the Ecclesiastical Writers, who wrote before the Pelagian Controversie troubled the Church, out of some charitable Motives, were inclined to hope very well of the State of the virtuous Heathens in another World, and in order to that advanced some Principles, whereby they might the better defend their well-natured Opinion, as particularly that their squaring their Lives by the Rules of their Moral Philosophy, was acceptable to God for their Salvation, whilst they were destitute of Revelation. I think *Clement* of *Alexandria*, who was bred up in a Philosophick Sect, and upon that Account must retain some Tenderness for those who had been engaged in the like Studies, was the first who advanced this Notion For thus he speaks, Ἰουδαίοις μὲν νόμος, Ἕλλησι δὲ φιλοσοφία, μέχρι τῆς τοῦ Χριστοῦ παρουσίας· ἐντεῦθεν δὲ ἡ κλῆσις ἡ καθολικὴ εἰς περιούσιον δικαιοσύνης λαὸν, κατὰ τὴν ἐκ πίστεως διδασκαλίαν. *The Law was a Rule to the Jews, and the Philosophy to the Gentiles, unto the coming of Christ. But then the Evangelical Calling raised a People more excellent in vertuous Acts, according to the Doctrine of Faith*, Clem Alex Strom Lib vii. And again, Καθάπερ Ἰουδαίους σώζεσθαι ἐβούλετο ὁ Θεὸς τοὺς Προφήτας διδοὺς, οὕτω καὶ Ἑλλήνων τοὺς δοκιμωτάτους οἰκείους αὐτῶν τῇ διαλέκτῳ προφήτας ἀναστήσας, ὡς οἷοί τε ἦσαν δέχεσθαι τὴν παρὰ Θεοῦ εὐεργεσίαν, τῶν χυδαίων ἀνθρώπων διέκρινε *As God would have the Jews be saved, when he gave them Prophets, so as for the more excellent of the Heathens, by raising them up Prophets in their own Tongue, according as they were able to receive the Benefit, he distinguish'd them from the common Rank of Men*, ibid. He elsewhere positively asserts, Καθ' ἑαυτὴν ἐδικαίου ποτὲ καὶ ἡ φιλοσοφία τοὺς Ἕλληνας *That the Heathens, for a time, were justified by Philosophy*, Stom Lib i The same Opinion is maintained not only by his Scholar *Origen contr Celsum Lib* ii, but also by S *Chrysostom*, who speaks thus, Τὸ εἰς σωτηρίαν ἤρκει, καθάπερ ἔφθην εἰπὼν, τότε τὸ Θεὸν εἰδέναι μόνον· νυνὶ δὲ οὐκέτι, ἀλλὰ δεῖ καὶ τῆς τοῦ Χριστοῦ γνώσεως. *Then it was sufficient for Salvation to know God, but now that does not suffice, but the Knowledge of Christ is likewise necessary*, Hom xxviii. in *Mat* And presently afterwards, Οἱ τὸν Χριστὸν οὐκ ἐγνωκότες πρὸ τῆς ἐνσάρκου παρουσίας, εἰδωλολατρείας δὲ ἀποστάντες καὶ τὸν Θεὸν προσκυνήσαντες μόνον, καὶ τὸν ἄριστον ἐπιδειξάμενοι βίον, πάντων ἀπολαύσονται τῶν ἀγαθῶν *They shall enjoy all the Happiness of eternal Life, who did not know Christ before his Incarnation but only abstaining from Idolatry, adored the true God and lived a good Life*, ibid. But others of the Fathers, who lived before, and after the Pelagian Controversie, affirmed all their Virtues to be false and counterfeit, and not to be acceptable in the Eyes of God S *CYPRIAN*, who was as unprejudiced in this Matter as any one, speaking of the Virtue of Patience, writes thus, *Hanc se sectari Philosophi quoque profitentur, sed tam illic patientia falsa est, quam falsa sapientia est. Unde enim vel sapiens esse, vel patiens possit, qui nec sapientiam, nec potentiam Dei novit: quando ipse de iis, qui sibi sapere in mundo videntur moneat & dicat, perdam sapientiam sapientum prudentiam prudentium reprobabo The Philosophers likewise profess to prosecute this Vertue, but their Patience is as false as their Wisdom For whence can any one be wise, or patient, who neither knows the Wisdom or Power of God, who admonishes of those things of which they think to be wise in the World, I will destroy the Wisdom of the Wise, and bring to nothing the Understanding of the Prudent* Cypr de Con patient. S *HIEROM* speaking of the Words, *The Just shall live by Faith*, writes thus *Faciamus & nos aliquid simile huic, quod dicitur, Justus ex fide vivit, & dicamus, Castus ex fide vivit, sapiens*

they make men meet to receive grace, or (as the Scholl-Authors say) deserve grace of congruity.

Christ, [b] neither do they make men meet to receive grace, or (as the School-Authors say) deserve grace of congruity:

vocant de congruo merentur Immo cum non sunt facta, ut Deus illa fieri vo-

punt ex fide vivit, fortis ex fide vivit · & a cæteris virtutum partibus victuam sententiam profeiamus adversum eos qui in Christum non credentes, fortes & sapientes temperantes sequtant esse, vel justos, nisi aut nullum absque Christo vivere, sine quo omnis virtus in vitio est Let us frame a Sentence like this, The Just liveth by Faith, *and say the chast Man liveth by Faith the wise Man liveth by Faith, the couragious Man liveth by Faith, and pronounce a like Sentence of the other Branches of Virtue against those, who not believing in Christ, think that they are couragious and wise, and temperate, or just, that they may know that no one can live without Christ, without whom all Virtue is Vice* Hier in Gal Cap iii The same Father does elsewhere inculcate the same Doctrine, *Quomodo autem, juxta Apostolum Jacobum, fides absque operibus mortua est, sic absque fide, quamvis bona opera sint, mortua computantur Qui igitur in Christo non credunt, & sunt bonis moribus, aliud quid magis ... quam opera virtutum As according to the Apostle S. James,* Faith without Works is dead, *so without Faith, altho' the Works be good, they are accounted dead Therefore they, who do not believe in Christ, and are of good Morals, have something in them more than the Works of Virtue* Hier Ep. iii S. AMBROSE, or whoever else is the Writer of the Book *de Vocat one Gentium*, says, *Etsi naturali intellectu conatus sit vitiis reluctari, hujus tamen temporis vitam steriliter ornat et ad veras virtutes, æternamque felicitatem non proficit Altho' by our natural Understanding there be an Endeavour to withstand Vice, this only serves for a bare adorning of this Life, but it adds nothing to true Virtue, and eternal Happiness* de voc Gent Lib. i Cap vii S AUSTIN has a great deal upon this Subject, and particularly this *Absit, ut sit in aliquo virtus, nisi fuerit justus, absit, at ... sit justus verè, nisi vivat ex fide, justus enim ex fide vivit Far be it that any one should say, that there is Virtue in any one who is not righteous Far be it that any one should say, that any Man is righteous unless he live by Faith, for the Just shall live by Faith,* Aug contr Jul Lib iv C 3 And elsewhere, *Infidelis, sive abstinent, sive comedat, non sanctè vel justè comedit, vel abstinet, quia pravo ... utrumque facit* The Unbeliever, *whether he abstain or whether he eat, does not eat or abstain holily, or justly because he does both out of an ill View,* cont. Faust Lib xxxi Cap 4 PROSPER in this, as in other Matters writes after his Master S *Austin's* Copy *Natura, etsi excellentissimis artibus & cunctis mortalium eruditionum polleat disciplinis justificari ex se non potest, quia bonis suis malè utitur, in quibus sine cultu veri dei, impietatis immunditiaque convincitur, & unde se defendi existimat, accusatur Nature, altho' it be adorned with all the most excellent Arts and learned Sciences, cannot of it self be justified, because it makes an ill Use of its Goods, in which, without the Worship of the true God it is arraigned of Impiety and Pollution, and is accused by that by which it thinks to defend it self.* Prop contr Collat Cap xxii The same Doctrine he teaches in his Poem *de Ingratis*

Et licet eximias studeat pollere per artes,
Ingeniumque bonum generosis moribus ornet,
Cæca tamen finem ad mortis per devia currit,
Nec vitæ æternæ veros, acquerere fructus
De falsa virtute potest ——

Tho' Nature be adorn'd with all the Art,
Which Wit and Education can impart,
She blindly leads to Death her crooked Ways,
Which downwards tend, will not to Heaven raise,
Nor her false Virtue gain cœlestial Joys.

THEOPHYLACT speaks the Sense of the *Greek* Church in this Point of Doctrine, Τὸ μὲν εἶναι φαύλους Χριστιανοὺς, καὶ αὐτὸς φημὶ, τὸ δὲ Ἕλληνας ἀγαθοὺς εὑρεθῆναι, οὐκ ἂν ποτε φαίην· εἰ δὲ τινες ἔδοξαν ἀγαθοὶ ἀλλὰ πρὸς δόξαν πάντα ἔπραττον. *That there are wicked Christians I freely confess but that there are good Heathens I will not venture to say. For tho' they might seem to be good, yet they did all things for the Sake of Glory* Theoph in Joh iii. 19

b *Neither do they make Men meet to receive Grace, or (as the School-Authors say) deserve Grace of Congruity*] I When the Church of *Rome* had advanced their Doctrine of Merits, they distinguish'd Merit into two Kinds, the one Kind of Merit they called *Meritum ex Congruo*, the other *Meritum ex Condigno* The Merit of Congruity their Writers define to be, *Opus cui ex Justitia non debetur merces sed tantum ex Congruitate quadam, vel ex sola acceptantis liberalitate A Work to which a Reward is not strictly due, but only from its Fitness to receive a Reward, or out of the Liberality of the Donor* But of their *Meritum ex Condigno* they speak more arrogantly. For thus *Cajetan* explains it *Mereri ex condigno, est mereri sic, ut secundum Justitiam sibi debeatur, ita quod injustum esset non reddi mercedem mer to ex condigno To merit ex condigno, is to merit as it would be unjust that a Reward should not be allotted to it* Cajet in 1, 2dæ qu 124 The last Sort of Merit they ascribe to Persons in a State of Belief, the former to Persons *in puris Naturalibus*, or under a State of Nature or Unbelief

The Popish Distinction of Merit into Meritum ex congruo, *and* Meritum ex condigno

II The Arguments which they make use of, to establish their *Merit of Congruity*, are chiefly these The *first* is drawn from some Examples in Scripture of God's kind Acceptance, and rewarding of the good Actions of several Heathen Persons As that of the Midwives in saving the *Hebrew* Children, upon which it is said, *That God dealt well with the Midwives, and that he built them Houses*, Exod i 20, 21 Of *Nebuchadnezzar*, to whom God promised *to give the Land of Ægypt*, because he *caused his Army to serve a great Service against Tyrus*, Ez xxix 18, 19. A *second* is drawn from that Passage of *Zachery*, *Turn ye unto me, saith the Lord, and I will turn unto you*, Zech i 3 A *third* is drawn from the Instance of *Cornelius*, who had an Angel sent to him, because he was a devout Man, &c to whom God declared, *Thy Prayers and Alms are come up for a Memorial before God*, Acts x 2, 4

The Arguments which the School Men use to establish the Doctrine of Merit of Congruity.

III But these are frivolous Arguments to establish this Doctrine upon For in the Instances of the Midwives, and *Nebuchadnezzar*, there is nothing of Merit mentioned in those Places. Besides, the Matter of their Reward are purely temporal, and divine Favours of that Kind none ever pretended to deprive the Heathens of But because God was pleased liberally to reward these Actions to establish a Merit thereupon, when it was owing only to the divine Munificence, is not only a foolish Subtilty, but tends to heighten Human Pride, and to rob God of his Honour As to the Argument drawn from the Passage in *Ezekiel*, *Turn ye*, &c this is not only a Popish, but a Pelagian *Heterodoxy* For thus St *Austin* says of the Pelagians, *Talia ergo de Scripturis colligunt, quale hoc est unum, Convertimini ad me, & ego convertar ad vos, ut secundum meritum Conversionis nostræ ad Deum, detur Gratia ejus, in qua ad nos & ipse convertitur. They are wont to draw such Arguments as these from the Scriptures,* Turn ye unto me, and I will turn unto you · *That according to the Merit of our Conversion to God, his Grace may be given, in which he turns to us,* Aug de Grat & Lib Arb But to the Argument it self, S *Austin* returns this solid Answer *Nec attendunt qui hoc sentiunt*, &c *They who are of this Opinion, do not consider, that unless our Conversion to God were the Gift of God, it would not be*

Their Arguments answered.

said

but because they are not done as God hath willed and commanded them to be done, we doubt not but they have the nature of Sin

yea, rather for that they are not done as God hath willed and commanded them to be done, [c] we doubt not but they have the nature of Sin.

luit & præcepit, peccati rationem habere non dubitamus.

said to him, Turn us O God of our Strength Do thou turn and quicken *us* And turn us O God of our Health, *and many other things, which it is too long here to commemorate For what is it to come to Christ, but only by believing to turn unto him And yet he saith,* No Man can come unto me, unless it be given him of my Father. *ibid* As to the Instance of *Cornelius,* he was not in a pure state of Nature, but was in some measure a Believer And if the Schoolmen of the Church of *Rome* say to the contrary, we have the Authority of one of their most celebrated Popes to confront them, even that of *Gregory* the great *Cornelius Centurio,* &c Cornelius *the Centurion, whose Alms before Baptism, by the testimony of an Angel were praised, did not come by works to faith, but by faith he came to works For it is said to him by an Angel,* Thy Prayers and Alms have come up for a Memorial before God *For if he did not truly believe in God before Baptism, why did he pray? or why did the Almighty God hear him, if he did not ask of him to be perfected in good things? Therefore he knew that God was the Creator of all things but was ignorant that his Almighty Son was incarnate Nor could he do good unless he had been before a Believer For it is written,* without Faith it is impossible to please God *Therefore he must have faith, whose Works and Alms could please God.* Greg Hom in Ezech xix

Merit of Congruity contrary to the Scriptures, and the Catholick doctrine of preventing Grace

IV Besides, this doctrine of *Merit of Congruity* is contrary to the Notion which the holy Scriptures give us of Persons in a State of Unbelief, and likewise to the doctrine of Preventing Grace For (1) the Description which the Scriptures afford us of Unbelievers is, that they are Enemies to God, *When we were Enemies, we were reconciled by the Death of his Son,* Rom v 10 dead in Sins, *Even when we were dead in Sins hath quickened us together with Christ,* Eph ii. 5 Atheists, *having no hope, without God in the world,* Eph ii 12. Now is it reasonable to think that Persons who sustain this vile Character, can be supposed to merit of God? (2) This Doctrine does perfectly overthrow preventing Grace For if there be any previous Work to deserve Grace, Grace can neither make the first step in Conversion, neither can it be free For thus S *Austin* well reasons upon this Head. *Si gratia utique nullis meritis reddita sed gratuita bonitate donata. If it be grace it is not given for merit, but it is freely bestowed,* Aug Ep cv And again, *Percipiendæ hujus gratiæ merita nulla præcedunt quoniam meritis impii non gratia sed pœna debetur nec ipsa esset gratia, si non daretur gratuita, sed debita redderetur No merits go before the reception of Grace, because the wicked does not deserve grace but punishment, nor indeed would it be grace if it were not given* gratis, *paid as a debt* ibid

Virtues of the Heathens sinful

c *We doubt not but that they have the nature of Sin*] The more Antient Writers of the Church, who wrote before the Pelagian Controversie, did not usually express themselves in these Terms, they rather chose to say, that the Virtues of the Heathens were imperfect, and that they made but a false shew, *&c* But when the Pelagians, in Opposition to divine Grace, were wont to aggrandize the Ethnick Virtues to the highest degree, and to make them Heroical and Divine, as if it were in despight to the Christian Morality, St. *Austin,* and the other Managers of the Orthodox Cause, run up Matters as high as they could, and on the contrary asserted, that the good Works of the Heathens were so far from being virtuous that they were sinful And this they proved, because all their most glorious Actions had something of Sin mixed with them For thus S *AUSTIN Si Gentilis nudum operuerit, quia non est ex fide peccatum? Prorsus, quia non est ex fide peccatum est non quia per seipsum factum, quod est nudum operire, peccatum est, sed tali opere non in Domino gloriari, solus impius negat esse peccatum If a Gentile shall clothe the naked, is it Sin, because it is not of Faith? yes, because it is not of Faith it is Sin, not because it is a Sin that he clothes the naked, but because he does not do it for God's honour, which none but a wicked Person can deny not to be a Sin* Aug contr Jul Lib iv cap 3 And in another place *Quantumlibet opera infidelium prædicentur, Apostoli sententiam veram novimus, Omne quod non est ex fide peccatum est Though the Works of the Gentiles be never so much cried up, yet we are acquainted with the true doctrine of the Apostle,* Whatsoever is not of Faith is Sin *Aug de gest Palæst cap* 14. The same doctrine is taught by *LEO Aliud agit sub veritate ratio, aliud sub falsitate deceptio Apud nos fides justificat etiam manducantem, apud illos infidelitas polluit jejunantem, unde? quia extra Ecclesiam Catholicam nihil est integrum nihil castum, dicente Apostolo, Omne quod non est ex fide peccatum est, cum divisis ab unitate corporis Christi, nulla similitudine comparamur nulla communione miscemur Ad virtutem enim continentiæ nihil prius pertinet, quam ab erroribus abstinere, quia tum demum bene ambulatur, cum per viam veritatis inceditur Reason with Truth is one thing, and Deception with Falsity is another. Among us Christians Faith justifies him that eateth, among the Heathens Infidelity polluteth him that fasteth, wherefore because out of the Catholick Church there is nothing good or holy, the Apostle saying, whatsoever is without Faith is Sin, since we have no Similitude and no Communion with those who are divided from the Unity of Christ's Body Now to the vertue of* Continence *nothing more conduces, than to abstain from Error, because we then walk well, when we walk in the way of Truth* Leo Serm ii de jejun Pentec. *PROSPER* delivers the same doctrine *Dicendo omne quod non est ex fide peccatum est, declaravit quod omnia bona, aut ex fide gesta virtutes sunt, quæ profecto justificant, aut si fuerint sine fide, non sunt aliqua bona credenda, sed vitia The Apostle, by saying* whatsoever is not of Faith is Sin, *has declared, that all good Actions or Virtues proceeding from Faith do truly justifie, but if they are not of Faith, they are not to be esteemed good Actions, but Sins* De Vit. Contemp Lib. iii.

ARTICLE

ARTICLE XIV.

XIV Of Works of Supererogation

Voluntary Wo ks besides, over and above God's Commandments, which they call Works of Supererogation, can-

Of Works of Supererogation.

[a] Voluntary Works besides, over and above God's Commandments, which they call Works of Supererogation,

XIV. De operibus Supeierogationis.

Opera quæ supererogationis appellant, non possunt sine arrogantia & impietate predicari Nam illis

a *Voluntary Works, over and above God's Commandments, which they call Works of Supererogation.*]

The difference which the Church of Rome makes between Counsels and Precepts

I The Works here mention d, are called in tle Roman Church likewise by the Name of *Counsels*, and *Evangelical Perfections* They are defined by their Writers to be *good Works, not commanded by Christ, but only shewn and recommended* Bellarm Lib ii. de Mon cap 7 Their Writers make Precepts and Commands to differ in these Particulars *First*, In the Matter, Counsels being difficult, and Precepts more easie *Secondly*, In the Subject, one in common oblige all, the other only, after consent, some few *Thirdly*, As to the Form, Precepts oblige of their own force, Counsels are left to every ones Pleasure *Fourthly*, In the End or Effect, Precepts bringing Rewards to the Observers, and Punishments upon the Neglecters of them, but to the Observers of Counsels, though there be a greater Reward to the Observer, yet there is no Punishment to the Neglecter *Bell* ibid

Some prudential Rules in Scripture proper for the first state of Christianity after misapplied to support the doctrine of Counsels.

II Now it must be owned, that though many of the Points of the doctrine of Supererogation are modern enough, yet some of them are pretty antient, being grounded upon some particular Texts of Scripture wrongly interpreted. For it must be observed, that at the beginning of Christianity, some particular Injunctions were necessary to be laid upon the Members of that spiritual Community, which as their Circumstances were altered, became no longer Obligatory The Communication of Goods, or the laying up of Estates in a publick Fund for the use of the Community, was necessary for the more speedy Propagation of the Gospel, and for the sending out Missionaries to Preach in the distant Parts of the World And so was abstaining from Marriage for a time, during the flagrancy of a Persecution, in all Persons who could bear it And our Saviour in his Sermons did prepare his Disciples for this Doctrine, when it should be expedient *If thou wilt be perfect, go and sell that thou hast and give to the poor, and thou shalt have treasure in heaven*, Mat xix 21 And v 12 *For there are some Eunuchs which were so born from their Mothers womb, and there are some Eunuchs, which were made Eunuchs of men, and there be Eunuchs, which have made themselves Eunuchs for the Kingdom of Heavens sake He that is able to receive it, let him receive it* Now we see that these Rules of our Saviour were put in practice by the first Professors of Christianity, as being necessary for their present Circumstances and Condition. *For as many as were possessors of lands or houses sold them, and brought the prices of the things that were sold, and laid them down at the Apostles feet*, Act. iv 34, 35 And as to the other case of Celibacy, under the then present case of Persecution, the Apostle St. *Paul* delivers his judgment *I suppose therefore, that it is good, for the present distress, I say it is good for a man so to be*, (i.e unmarried) 1 Cor vii 26

These Texts brought by some of the antients, in favour of Celibacy and a Monastick Life.

III But within a few Centuries after the beginning of Christianity, the state of Celibacy and of the Monastick Life gaining vogue among Christians, these Prudential Rules, which at first related only to particular Persons and Circumstances, were advanced into Lessons of sublimer Perfection, which all Persons who aspired to any degree of more elevated Piety, were to come up to. This is clear from the Writings of St *Jerom* and others, who wrote in favour of the state of Celibacy and the Monastick Life

The occasion of the name of Works of Supererogation.

IV Afterwards, the frequent use of the Text in the History of the friendly *Samaritan*, in the Latin Translation, *siquid supererogaveris*, &c *what thou layest out more I will pay thee*, brought for the support of the doctrine of Works of more than ordinary Perfection, occasioned the Denomination of Works of Supererogation For thus S *Austin* *Stabularius autem Apostolus, duo denarii duo praecepta charitatis, quam per spiritum sanctum acceperant Apostoli, ad evangelandum cæteris, quod supererogat illud est quod ait, de Virginibus autem Præceptum Domini non habeo, Concilium autem do. The Apostle is the Host, or Inkeeper, the two pence are the two precepts of Charity, which the Apostles had received by the Spirit, to preach to others, the laying out more, is what he says, As concerning Virgins, I have no command of the Lord, but I give my advice* Aug Lib. ii 4 Evang. c 19 And again *Quæ licita sunt, nec ullo præcepto Domini prohibentur, sed sicut expedit potius tractanda sunt, non præter pto Legis, sed Concilio Charitatis, Hæc quæ amplius* Supererogantur, *saucio qui curandus ad stabulum Samaritani miseratione perductus est These things which are lawful, nor are prohibited by any precept of the Lord, but are to be performed according as it is expedient, not by command of any Law, but by Councel of Charity These are those things which are* [Supererogantur] *laid out over and above, upon the wounded man, who by the pity of the* Samaritan *was brought to the Inn* Aug de Adul Con. Lib ii c 14 The like doctrine is laid down by *Fulgentius*. *Quid est, siquid supererogaveris, nisi quid a me magis acceperis? Nam & ipse quia supererogabat, in eo quod non acceperat præceptum, sed dabat ex charitate Concilium, misericordiam se profitetur utique consecutum. What is the meaning of these words,* what thou layest out more, *but only what thou hast more received of me? For because he laid out more, insomuch that he received no command, but gave Advice out of Charity, he declares that he had recived Mercy.* Fulg Prol Lib. contr Moniinum This doctrine of Supererogating with relation to the state of Celibacy, stood without any further Alteration to the time of *Bede*, who writes thus, upon this Head *Quandocunque supererogaveris, ego cum rediero, reddam tibi, supererogat stabularius, quod in duobus denariis, non accepit, cum dicit Apostolus, De Virginibus autem præceptum Domini non habeo, Concilium autem do If you shall lay out more, I will pay it, when I return, the Innkeeper lays out more than the two pence, which he had received, when the Apostle says,* as concerning Virgins I *have*

not be taught without arrogancy and iniquity For by them Men do declare, that they do not only render to God as much as they are bound to do, but that they do more for his sake than of bounden duty is required: Whereas Christ saith plainly, *When ye have done all that is commanded you, say, We be unprofitable Servants.*

* [b] cannot be taught without arrogancy and impiety. For by them men do declare, That they do not only render unto God as much as they are bound to do, but that they do more for his sake, than of bounden duty is required: whereas Christ saith plainly, when ye have done all that are commanded to you, say, † We are unprofitable Servants.

declarans homines, non tantum Deo se reddere, quæ tenentur, sed plus in ejus gratiam facere, quam deberent, cum aperte Christus, dicat; cum feceritis omnia quæcunque præcepta sunt vobis, dicite, servi inutiles sumus

* *Cannot be taught without Arrogancy and Impiety*, MS CCCC 1571
† *We be unprofitable Servants*, MS CCCC. 1571

have no command of the Lord, but I give my Advice. *Bed in cap* 10 *Luc.*

What the doctrine of Works of Supererogation was in the more corrupt state of the Roman *Church.*

V In succeeding Ages, about the tenth or eleventh Century, as the Corruptions of the *Roman* Church increased, and new Doctrines were brought in of Purgatory, Satisfaction and Indulgences, the Doctrine of Supererogation was advanced to a more scandalous height For then it began to be the current Doctrine of that Church, That there was a temporal Punishment due for every Sin, which Men must satisfie for (as their Phrase is) by remarkable Afflictions, or by Penances in this World, or by Purgatory in the next That the temporal Punishments of some good Persons were so very great, and their Lives so very virtuous, that they bore an Over proportion to the few Sins they had committed, that these Satisfactions were not without their Effect,tho' not to the Souls of those good Persons who they supposed to have no need of them, but to those of greater Sinners who did, That these meritorious Satisfactions of the Saints, whom by fabulous Relations and Legendary Stories, they were wont to multiply to an excessive Degree, were laid up, as it were, in a publick Bank or Treasury of the Church, of which the Pope was the Keeper or Dispenser, That it was in his Power to communicate the Efficacy of these Merits at his Pleasure And this he did not fail to do for many Ages together, in Plenary Pardons, Indulgences, &c which, as for some time it brought in incredible Wealth to the Papacy, so it rose at last to such an intolerable Scandal, that it made a ready way for the Reformation, all good and wise Persons growing impatient under such insupportable Abuses

b *Cannot be taught without arrogancy and impiety*, &c]

The doctrine of Works of Supererogation arrogant and impious.

Our Church does very justly tax the Church of *Rome* with Arrogance and Impiety, for the maintaining this Doctrine For what can be more arrogant and impious, than for sinful Man, whose life, when it is best spent, is full of Failures and Imperfections, to pretend not only to make Satisfaction to God for his own Sins, but to satisfie for the Sins of other Men likewise? Now it will appear, that this Charge may be justly made out against the *Roman* Church, by attending to the two following Considerations

Because every one is obliged to do his best

I. Because every Man is obliged to do all the Good that he can do, so that if he leaves any good Action undone, *which* it is in his Power to do, and which is consistent with his Circumstances and other prudent Considerations, he commits a Sin, and by doing of it he does no more than what his Duty obliges him to, he is so far from meriting either for himself or others by the Performance, that by the Neglect of it he lays himself open to the Divine Justice This is plain from the Text of holy Scripture quoted in this Article, *When ye have done all that is commanded you, say, ye are unprofitable Servants* And this is but consonant to the general Tenour of the holy Scriptures Which command us to *love God, with all our Heart, Soul, Strength and Mind, and our Neighbour as our selves*, Mat xxii 36. *to cleanse our selves from all filthiness, both of flesh and spirit, perfecting holiness in the fear of the Lord*, 2 Cor vii 1 Now how is this consistent with fixing a Period in our Progress of Piety, with making a Stop when we are arrived at a common degree of Sanctity, and looking upon all further Advances to be more than we are oblig'd to?

Because every one has enough to do to work out his Repentance for his own Sins.

II Because every Man has enough to do, to work out his Repentance for own Sins, the best of Men being subject to many For the Apostle S *James*, tells us, that *in many things we offend all*, Jam iii. 2 The holy Psalmist informs us, that in God's *sight shall no man living be justified*, Psal. cxliii 2. And S. *John* says, *If we say that we have no Sin, we deceive our selves, and the Truth is not in us*, 1 John i 8 Now is it reasonable to think, that any Man can over-merit both for himself and others, that has so much to quit upon his own Score? This is as absurd, as to imagine, that one Traytor, who has forfeited his own Life by his Treason, should presume to intercede with his Prince for another Traytor's Pardon.

ARTICLE XV.

XV. *No man is without ſin but Chriſt alone*

Of Chriſt alone without Sin.

XV. De Chriſto qui ſolus eſt ſine peccato.

Chriſt in the truth of our Nature was made like unto us in all things, (ſin only except) from which he was clearly void, both in his Fleſh and in his Spirit He came to be the Lamb without ſpot, who by ſacrifice of himſelf made once for ever, ſhould take away the ſins of the world. and ſin (as St *John* ſaith) was not in him But the reſt, (yea, altho' we be baptized and

Chriſt in the truth of our Nature, was made like unto us in all Things (* a Sin only excepted) from which he was clearly void, both in his Fleſh and his Spirit. He came † to be a Lamb without ſpot, who by Sacrifice of himſelf once made, ſhould take away the Sins of the World: and Sin, as St *John* ſaith, was not in him. * b But all we the reſt (although baptized and born again in

Chriſtus in noſtræ naturæ veritate per omnia ſimilis factus eſt nobis, excepto peccato, a quo prorſus erat immunis, tum in carne, tum in ſpiritu Venit ut agnus abſque macula, qui mundi peccata per immolationem ſui ſemel factam, tolleret, & peccatum (ut inquit Johannes) in eo non erat ſed nos reliqui etiam baptizati, & in Chriſto rege-

* *Sin only except*, MS. CCCC. 1571.
† *To be the Lamb without ſpot*, MS CCCC. 1571
* *But we the reſt, though, baptized and born again in Chriſt, yet we all offend*, MS. CCCC. 1571

What is the Deſign of this Article

The learned Biſhop of *Sarum*, in his Expoſition, is of Opinion, that this Article is placed here as an Appendix of the former concerning Works of Supererogation, which depending upon the ſuppoſed Perfection of the Saints, this latter likewiſe is here oppoſed Which Obſervation may be in ſome meaſure juſt But I humbly conceive, that the Compilers had ſomething farther in view, and that is the old Pelagian Doctrine of the Impeccability of holy Men For the Papiſts never ſay, that their Saints (barring the Controverſie about the bleſſed Virgin) are without Sin Beſides it is plain, that all the Series of Articles from the VIIIth to the XVIIIth are advanced chiefly againſt Pelagianiſm, and againſt the Papiſts only as taking a ſhare with them in their Errors And taking it in this Senſe, I ſhall make my Obſervations thereupon accordingly

Our bleſſed Saviour without Sin

a *(Sin only except) from which he was clearly void*] The Doctrine of the ſinleſs Nature of our bleſſed Saviour, is a Point ſo clear in Scripture, and ſo frequently aſſerted therein, that it is needleſs to inſiſt much upon the Proof thereof The Author to the *Hebrews* argues the great Efficacy of his Sacrifice, and the Superiority of it to any of the Moſaical, from this Head. *For ſuch an high Prieſt became us, who is holy, harmleſs, undefiled, ſeparate from Sinners, and made higher than the Heavens Who needed not daily, as thoſe high Prieſts, to offer up Sacrifices, firſt for his own Sins, and then for the peoples* Heb viii 26, 27 St *Peter* ſays, that we *are redeemed with the precious blood of Chriſt, as of a Lamb without blemiſh, and without ſpot*, 1 Pet i 19 His *going about always doing good*, and making his very Miracles, which atteſted his divine Commiſſion, to be ſo extraordinarily beneficial to Mankind, in curing the Blind, the Lame and the Sick whitherſoever he came, are demonſtrative Proofs of his unſinning Perfection But no more need be inſiſted upon for the Confirmation of this Point, ſince it never was denied by any Chriſtian, the Hereticks of old, who in their ſeveral turns run into all Manner of Errors, concerning almoſt every particular of our Saviour's Humanity, Divinity and other Properties, yet never preſumed to queſtion his unſpotted Purity, and freedom from Sin

The Pelagians aſſerted that Chriſtians might live without Sin.

b *But all we the reſt, although baptized, &c. yet offend, &c*] This Clauſe ſeems to be levelled againſt the Pelagians and their Followers, who aſſerted that Perſons after Baptiſm might live without Sin This was the expreſs Doctrine of *Pelagius*, as S *Auſtin* reports it *Arbitrii libertate qui bene utitur, ita ſe totum tradit Deo, omnemque ſuam mortificat voluntatem, ut cum Apoſtolo poſſit dicere, Vivo autem jam non ego, vivit autem in me Chriſtus*. *He that uſes the Liberty of his Will well, doth ſo give himſelf wholly up to God, and mortifies all his Will, that he may ſay with the Apoſtle, Now I no longer live, but Chriſt liveth in me* Pel ad Demetr citant Aug. Lib de grat. cap xxiii And ſo again in his Book of Nature *Hoc rectè dici poteſt de his, quorum neque bonorum, neque malorum ſcriptura ſit memor De illis vero quorum juſtitiæ meminit & peccatorum ſine dubio meminiſſet, ſi illa eos peccaſſe ſenſiſſet This may be rightly ſpoken of them, of whoſe good or evil Actions the Scripture makes no mention. But of thoſe whoſe Righteouſneſs it takes notice of, it would without all doubt have mentioned their Sins, if they had committed any* Cit Aug Lib de Nat cap 37 *Cœleſtius* the Pelagian in S. *Jerom* aſſerts the like *Eſto ut nullus potuerit omne vitare peccatum in pueritia,*

born again in Christ) yet we offend in many things, and if we say we have no sin, we deceive our selves, and the truth is not in us

Christ) yet [c] offend in many things, and if we say we have no Sin, we deceive our selves, and the Truth is not in us.

nerati, in multis tamen offendimus omnes. Etsi dixerimus quod peccatum non habemus, nos ipsos seducimus, & veritas in nobis non est

p rerit i, adolescent a & juventute ... usque nunc negare potes, plurimos, istos & sanctos viros post vite, omni se al... virtutes animo contulisse, & per has caruisse peccato? Grant that in the Time of Childhood, Nonage, or Youth, no one can avoid all Sin. Can you deny that many just and holy Men after Vice have so wholly applied themselves to Virtue, and for this Reason have altogether been void of Sin? Hier Dial iii adv. Pelag

II But this extravagant Opinion, as it is contrary to the holy Scriptures, as is demonstrated in the former Article, so the ancient Fathers, in their several Ages, have declared their Opinion against it

The ancient Writers of the Church declare themselves against this Opinion

JUSTIN MARTYR directly opposes it, in these Words Πᾶν γένος ἀνθρώπων εὑρεθήσεται ὑπὸ κατάραν ὂν κατὰ τὸν νόμον Μωσέως. Ἐπικατάρατος γὰρ εἴρηται πᾶς ὃς οὐκ ἐμμένει ἐν τοῖς γεγραμμένοις ἐν τῷ βιβλίῳ τοῦ νόμου τοῦ ποιῆσαι αὐτά. καὶ οὐδεὶς ἀκριβῶς πάντα ἐποίησεν, ... ἀλλ' εἰσὶν οἱ μᾶλλον, καὶ ἧττον ἀλλήλων ἐντεταλμένα ἐφύλαξαν. *All humankind will be found obnoxious to the Curse, according to the Law of* Moses *For every one is pronounced accursed, who doth not continue in all those things which are written in the Book of the Law to do them But certainly no Man hath exactly observed them all Nor will any venture to deny this But there are some who observe the Commandments more, and others less* Just Mar Dial cum Tryph

IRENÆUS delivers the same Doctrine *Veniens autem Lex, quæ data est per Mosen, & testificans de peccato, quoniam peccator est, regnum quidem ejus abstulit, latronem & non regem eum detegens, & homicidam eum ostendit Oneravit autem hominem, qui habet peccatum in se, reum mortis ostendens. ... Spiritualis enim cum lex esset, manifestavit tantummodo peccatum, non autem interemit The Law coming which was given by* Moses, *and testifying concerning Sin, that every Man is a Sinner, took away the Devil's Kingdom, and discovering him to be a Thief and not a King, shew'd him a Murderer But it laid a Burden on Man, who had Sin in him, shewing him to be guilty of Death But since the Law is spiritual, it only discovered Sin, but did not kill it* Iren Lib iii cap 30

ORIGEN speaks to the same Purpose. *Quis super justitiâ sua gloriabitur, cum audiat Deum per Prophetam dicentem, Quia omnis justitia vestra, sicut pannus mulieris menstruatæ? Sola igitur justa gloriatio est in fide crucis Christi, quæ excludit omnem illam gloriationem, quæ descendit ex operibus Legis Who can glory in his Righteousness, when he hears God speaking by the Prophet, That all your Righteousnesses like filthy Rags? Therefore the only just glorying is in the Faith of Christ's Cross, which excludes all Boasting which proceeds from performing the Works the Law obliges to* Orig in cap iii Ep ad Rom.

MACARIUS asserts, that tho' sometimes Men may pride themselves in their virtuous Actions, yet upon better Thoughts, they must allow themselves to be great Sinners. Μετὰ γὰρ χρόνον καὶ πεῖραν μεταβάλλεται τὰ πράγματα. ὥστε ἐξ ἀληθείας ὁ τοιοῦτος αὐτὸς ἡγεῖται ἁμαρτωλότερον πάντων ἀνθρώπων *But after Time and Experience things are changed, so that truly such an one comes to think himself the greatest Sinners* Mac Hom xxxviii

S CHRYSOSTOM speaks in the same Tenor. Ὁ δὲ δίκαιος ἐκ πίστεως ζήσεται. τοῦτο γὰρ ὅτι ἐκ πίστεως δείκνυσι δι' αὐτοῦ οὐ μόνον, ἀλλ' ὅτι καὶ διὰ νόμου σωθῆναι οὐκ ἔνι. ... γὰρ νόμος φησίν, οὐδεὶς ἐπλήρωσεν ἀλλὰ πάντες ἦσαν ὑπὸ τὴν ἀράν, διὰ τῆς παραβάσεως, ἐπενοήθη ῥᾳδία τις ὁδὸς ἡ ἀπὸ τῆς πίστεως ὅπερ καὶ σημεῖον μέγιστόν ἐστι τοῦ μὴ δύνασθαι συνοδεῦσαι δικαιωθῆναι ἐκ τοῦ νόμου. ... ὁ δὲ δίκαιος ἐκ νόμου ζήσεται ἀλλ' ἐκ πίστεως ... οὐκ ἔστιν ἐκ πίστεως *He doth not only shew, that Justification is by Faith, but that it cannot be that Salvation is attainable by the Law Afterwards he says, that no one hath kept the Law, but that all by Transgression are subject to the Curse, there is found out an easier Way by Faith, which is an undeniable Argument, that no one can attain at Righteousness by the Law For the Prophet doth not say, that the Just shall live by the Law, but by Faith But the Law is not of Faith* Chrys in Gal cap iii.

St *CYPRIAN* among the *Latins*, asserts the same Truth *Ne quis sibi quasi innocens placeat, & ... extollendo plus pereat, instruitur & docetur, peccare se quotidie, dum quotidie pro peccatis jubetur orare* Cypr de Orat Dom

St *JEROM* upon the same Head writes thus *Omnes peccaverunt, & indigent Gloria Dei Ecclesiastes quoque hanc firmans sententiam Homo non est justus in terra, qui faciat bonum, & non peccet ... quæ & ... Apostoli dictum non solum doceat nec Moysen, nec illustrem aliquem de antiquis virum, apud Deum justificari posse per Legem. All have sinned and fallen short of the Glory of God The Preacher likewise confirming this Doctrine, There is no one righteous upon the Earth, who doth good and sinneth not And this last Saying of the Apostle clearly shews, that neither Moses, nor any other famous Man among the Ancients, could be justified before God by the Law* Hier in cap iii Epist ad Gal

St *AUSTIN*, among many Passages in Support of this Doctrine, has this remarkable one *Virtus est Charitas, qua id quod diligendum est diligitur. Hæc in aliis major, in aliis minor, in aliis nulla est Plenissima vero, quæ jam non possit augeri, quamdiu hic homo vivit, est in nemine Quamdiu autem augeri potest, profecto illud quod minus est, quam debet ex vitio est Ex quo vitio non est justus in terra, qui faciat bonum, & non peccet Virtue is a Charity, by which that is beloved, which ought to be beloved This is greater in some, less in others, in some none at all But the most perfect Virtue, which admits of no Increase, is in no one at all For since it can be increased, that which is less than it ought to be, is from Sin On Account of which Sin, there is no righteous Man upon Earth, who doeth good and sinneth not* Aug Ep xxix ad Hier

[c] *Offend in many things*] This Apostolical Aphorism which the Article uses the Words of, viz that of St. *James*, *in many things we offend all*, Jam iii 2 must be supposed to relate only to Sins of Ignorance and Infirmity, and not to the Habit of any wilful Sin, nor to the single Act of any Sin of a gross and enormous Nature, for the Commission of such Sins do exclude from the Kingdom of God, Gal v 19, &c Now it being too fatally evident, that the best of Men are not freed from Sins of this lesser Nature, they being frequently drawn into them by Passion or Surprise, the *Pelagians* of old not having the Confidence to deny so manifest a Truth, and yet being withal resolved to maintain their Doctrine of Impeccability of the Saints, denied that irregular Actions committed out of Ignorance or Infirmity were Sins at all Upon this Account *Celestius* the *Pelagian* in St. *Austin* plainly declares *Oblivionem, & ignorantiam non subjacere peccato, quoniam non secundum voluntatem eveniunt sed secundum necessitatem Faults of Forgetfulness and Ignorance are not to be ranked under the Title of Sin, because they are not what a Man wills, but what he cannot help* Aug de Gest Pelag cap 18

The Pelagians deny Sins of Ignorance and Infirmity to be Sins

II But this is contrary to the express Doctrine of the holy Scriptures For the Mosaical Law provides an Attonement for Sins of this Nature, which it would not have done, if they had not in them the Nature of Sins *If any Soul sin through Ignorance, he shall bring a She-goat of the first Year for a Sin Offering, and the Priest shall make an Attonement for the Soul that sinneth by Ignorance before the Lord*, Numb xv 27, 28 The Prophet ascribes the Judgment of the Babylonish Captivity in good Measure to Sins of this Nature *Therefore are my People gone into Captivity, because they have no Knowledge*, Isai v 13

This contrary to the Doctrine of Scripture

The

The Persecution which the Jews gave to our Saviour and to the primitive Christians, and which was at last severely revenged on them, is nevertheless ascribed to Ignorance *They shall put you out of the Synagogues, yea, the time cometh, that whosoever killeth you, will think that he doth God Service And these things will they do unto you, because they have not known the Father nor me*, John xvi. 3,4 *And now Brethren I wot, that through Ignorance ye did it, as did also your Rulers*, Acts iii 17 And S *Paul* himself is forced to fly to God's infinite Mercy for the Pardon of his Sins, which he committed out of Ignorance. *I obtained Mercy, because I did it ignorantly, in Unbelief*, 1 Tim i 13

Contrary to the Writings of the ancient Fathers

III Consonantly to this Doctrine, the Catholick Writers, who opposed the Heresie of *Pelagius*, maintained that Human Infirmities, Negligences and Ignorances were Sins For S *Jerom*, in his Dialogue against the *Pelagians*, having shewn by many Instances that God does punish Sins of Ignorance, says, *Pro oblivione errore & ignorantia, quasi pro peccato, offeruntur Sacrificia Deus praecepit, meum est observare quod jussit For Forgetfulness Error, and Ignorance, Sacrifices are offered, as for Sin. God hath commanded, it is my Part to obey what he hath enjoined* Hier. contr Pel Lib i And again, *Tantis Exemplis docere te volui, peccare hominem per ignorantiam, & pro peccato, ut in lege hostiam, ita & in Evangelio offerendam panitudinem I was willing to instruct you by these great Examples, that Man might sin out of Ignorance, and that, as there was a Sacrifice for Sin under the Law, so Repentance was required for it under the Gospel*, ibid. Lib ii To the like Purport S. *Austin*, *Et tamen etiam per ignorantiam facta quaedam improbantur, & corrigenda judicantur, sicut in divinis authoritatibus legimus. There are some Actions which are to be blamed, on the score of Ignorance, and thought worthy of Amendment, as we learn by the Authority of the holy Scriptures*, Aug. de Lib Arb. Lib iii Cap 18. And he confutes the contrary Opinion of *Celestius* the Pelagian, *Quia David dicat, delicta juventutis meae ne memineris & ignorantias, & quod in lege sacrificia pro ignorantia, sicut pro peccato offerantur Because David says, Remember not the Sins of my Youth, and my Ignorances, and because, under the Law, Sacrifices were offered for Ignorances, as for Sin* Aug. contr Pelag Cap 67 But long before that Time, or that the Pelagian Controversy had began, *Lactantius* affirmed the same *Eo accedit, quod nemo esse sine delicto potest, quamdiu carnis indumento oneratus est, cujus infirmitas triplici modo subjacet Dominio peccati, factis, dictis, cogitationibus*, &c. *Add to this, That no one can be without Sin, as long as he is loaded with the cloathing of Flesh whose Infirmity is subject three ways to the Dominion of Sin, by Deeds, Words and Thoughts*, Lact Lib vi. Cap 13.

Obj I But it is objected against this Doctrine, and in Favour of the *Pelagian* Tenet of Impeccability, that otherways God had prescribed Laws, which it is impossible for human Infirmity to fulfil, which as it would argue Injustice in an human Legislator, so it does much more so in a divine one, who is infinitely wise and good And thus *Pelagius* himself argues in his bold Way. *Duplici ignorantia accusamus Deum inscientiae, ut videatur nescire quod fecit, nescire quod jussit quasi oblitus fragilitatis humanae cujus author ipse est, imposuerit homini mandata, quae ferre non possit We accuse God of a twofold Ignorance, as not knowing either what he had made, or what he had commanded as if he had forgotten human Frailty which he himself had created, and had given Man Commands, which it is impossible for him to discharge.* Pelag. Epist ad Demetr. citante Hier adv Pelag

Ans But to this it may be answered, That it is not in general true, that the Commands of God are impossible to be observed (1) For the Ancients very well looked upon this as an impious Assertion Thus S. *Basil* Ἀσεβὲς καὶ τὸ λέγειν ἀδύνατα εἶναι τὰ τοῦ πνεύματος παραγγέλματα *'Tis an impious Assertion to say that the Commands of the Spirit are impossible.* Bas. Hom xix And the like S *Chrysostom*, Μὴ τοίνυν ἀδύνατα εἶναι νομίζωμεν τὰ ἐπιτάγματα· καὶ γὰρ μετὰ τοῦ συμφέροντος πολλὴν καὶ εὔκολον, ἐὰν νήφωμεν *Let us not think that the Commandments are impossible, which are certainly profitable to us, and easy, if we be watchful* Chryf Hom xviii in Mat (2) But tho' no Man can be always so constantly upon his Guard, as to perform every Part of his Duty, during the whole Course of his Life, yet there is no Part of Duty so difficult but that some one or other may perform it, if he sets resolutely upon it, tho' at other times, and in other Parts of Duty, Incogitancy may creep in upon him Which S *Jerom* expresses in these Words *Vides quod Deus possibilia jusserit & tamen id quod possibile est, per naturam nullum posse complere. Dedit itaque praecepta universa, virtutesque varias, quas omnes simul habere non possumus You see therefore, that God has commanded things possible to be done: and yet that which is possible no one by Nature can fulfil He has given universal Precepts, and commanded various Virtues, all of which no one can possess at the same time* Hier Dial i adv. Pelag And again *Possibilia praecepit Deus & ego fateor Sed haec possibilia cuncta singuli habere non possumus, non imbecillitate naturae, ne calumniam facias Deo, sed animi assuetudine, qui cunctas simul & semper non potest habere virtutes God has commanded things possible to be done, and this I own. But all those things that are possible to be done, single Persons cannot perform at the same time, not thro' any Fault of their Nature, for that would be to fix a Reproach upon God, but through the Habit of our Mind, which cannot stand possessed of all Virtues together* ibid (3) The whole Law of God is a Scheme or Platform of exquisite Perfection, which Men are obliged to aim at the Performance of, though human Frailty will not allow them to discharge in every Particular, as long as they continue in this Life, the full Completion thereof being reserved to the more perfect State in the other World This some have compared to the Idea which is laid down by Criticks of a perfect Poet or Orator, the Perfections whereof have been copied some by one, and some by another, but none have been found compleat in all And this seems to have been the Opinion of S *Austin*. *Hoc in illa vita complebimus, cum videbimus facie ad faciem Sed ideo hoc etiam nobis praeceptum est, ut admoneremur, quid fide exposcere, quo spem praemittere, & obliviscendo quae retro sunt, in quae anteriora nos extendere debeamus We shall be compleat in all these Matters, when we shall see Face to Face, but they are commanded us in this Life, that we may be put in Mind of what we ought to wish for by Faith, whither we should extend our Hopes before hand, by forgetting those Things which are behind, we ought to reach out unto things before.* Aug de Spir & Lit Cap. 36.

Object II It is likewise urged in Favour of Impeccability, that the contrary Doctrine of the Sinfulness of all Men does impute a Vice and Corruption to human Nature, which being framed by God, can have no Evil in it, and to say that it has, is downright Manicheism This the Pelagians of old objected against the Orthodox, as is plain by that Passage of S *Jerom* *Reclamabis & dices, Manichaeorum dogma nos sequi, & eorum qui de diversis naturis Ecclesiae bella concinnant, asserentium malam esse Naturam, quae immutari nullo modo possit. But you will cry out against this, and say, that we herein follow the Doctrine of the Manichees, and of those who have raised Storms in the Church by maintaining two contrary Principles, and assert that our Nature is so evil that it cannot be bettered.* Hier Ep ad Ctesiphon.

Answ But to this it is answered, *first*, That there is a great Difference between asserting the Original Evilness of human Nature, and the Fragility or Weakness which it has contracted by the Fall The *Manichees* asserted, That human Nature was at first created evil, but the Orthodox on the contrary asserted with the holy Scriptures, That God made Man *upright*, &c And that the wrong Byass, which it has since contracted, is owing to Sin. And thus S. *Jerom* answers this Objection or Calumny *A me nunquam audies malam esse naturam sed quomodo sit carnis fragilitas differenda, ipso qui scripsit, docente, discamus Interroga eum quare scripserit, Non enim quod volo, hoc operor, sed quod odi malum, illud facio You shall never hear me say, that our Nature is Evil but how the Frailty of the Flesh is to be maintained, you may learn from the Apostle who has taught it in his Writings, Ask him, why he wrote those Words*, for what I would that I do not, but what I hate that do I. *Hier. ad Ctesiph* *Secondly*, This Weakness of human Nature is sufficiently supplied by Grace and the divine Assistance For thus S *Jerom*, *Et sic ingrediendum via regia, nec ad sinistram nec ad dextram declinemus, appetitumque propriae voluntatis Dei semper credamus auxilio gubernari We go a middle Way between the Pelagians and the Manichees, neither diverting to the right Hand or the left, believing the Appetite of our Will to be always guided by the divine Assistance.* Hier in Proem Dial. adv Pel

ARTICLE XVI.

XVI. *Of Sin against the Holy Ghost*	*Of Sin after Baptism.*	XVI De peccato post Baptismum.
Every deadly sin willingly committed after Baptism, is not sin against the holy Ghost, and unpardonable wherefore the place for penitents is not to be denied to such as fall into sin after Baptism After we have received the holy Ghost, we may depart from grace given, and fall into sin, and by the grace of God (we may) rise again, and amend our lives And therefore they are to be condemned, which say they can no more sin as long as they live here, or deny the place for penitents to such as truly repent and amend their lives	a Not every deadly Sin willingly committed after Baptism is the sin against the Holy Ghost, and unpardonable. * Wherefore the grant of Repentance is not to be denied to such, as fall into sin after Baptism After we have received the Holy Ghost, we may depart from grace given, and fall into sin, and by the grace of God we may arise again and amend our lives And therefore they are to be condemned, which say they can no more sin, as long as they live here, or deny the place of forgiveness to such as truly repent	*Non omne peccatum mortale post Baptismum voluntarie perpetratum, est peccatum in Spiritum sanctum, & irremissibile Proinde lapsis a Baptismo in peccata, locus pœnitentiæ non est negandus post acceptum Spiritum sanctum possumus a gratia Dei recedere atque peccare, denuoq; per gratiam Dei resurgere, ac resipiscere Ideoq; illi damnandi sunt, qui se quamdiu hic vivant, amplius non posse peccare affirmant, aut vere resipiscentibus veniæ locum denegant*

* *Wherefore the place for Penitence*, MS CCCC 1571.

a *Not every deadly Sin* &c] This Article is levelled against the Doctrine of the Novatians of old, who held every Sin committed after Baptism to be unpardonable This Doctrine being revived by some of the Anabaptists or other Enthusiasts which sprang up at the beginning of the Reformation, it is not improbable, that the Compilers of the Articles had an eye likewise upon their Heterodoxy For as the Papists were wont maliciously to impute the wild Doctrines of all the several sorts of Enthusiasts to all Protestants, so it was thought here convenient to defend our Church, against the Imputation of any such Opinion But because this Doctrine was first broached by the Novatians, it will not be foreign to our purpose to speak a word or two concerning the Rise and Author of that Heresie

Of the Novatian Heresie

This Heresie was broached by *Novatianus* a Priest of the Roman Church, who before he entered into holy Orders, or at least before he embraced Christianity, professed Philosophy He received Baptism being a Clinick, *i e* upon a dangerous Sickness, his Life being then despaired of, which rendered any one uncapable of Orders by the Canons of the Church This made even his Priest's Orders to be questioned But he got himself to be ordained a Bishop after a most scandalous manner Upon the Death of *Fabianus*, *Novatianus* was a Competitor for the Bishoprick of *Rome*, but however *Cornelius*, having a superior interest and better Qualifications, obtained that Dignity *Novatianus* being nettled at this Disappointment was resolved, as much as in him lay to hinder his quiet Possession of that See Therefore he draws up a Libel against him accusing him of several Crimes, the Principal of which, and which he mostly insisted on, was, That he had admitted to Communion several Christians who had lapsed into Idolatry during the Persecution, he maintaining it as a fundamental Maxim, That none who had fallen into so foul a Sin were ever capable of being received into the Church again whereupon he renounces all Communion with *Cornelius* His Arguments being popular gained him many Adherents, especially among the Confessors in the late Persecutions, who could not easily brook, that those who had so basely betrayed the Cause of Religion, should by an easie Discipline of the Church, be set upon the level with those, who had ventured their Blood in defence of it. *Novatianus* having strengthened his Party by these Arguments and Criminations, next casts about how he might get himself ordained Bishop, which he effects this way. He by some of his Agents prevails upon three ignorant Bishops to come to *Rome*, upon account of accommodating some Difficulties, where having gotten them, he shuts them up in a Room, makes them drunk, (as *Cornelius* says in his Letter) and about ten a Clock at Night causes them to ordain him Bishop. This done he sends into *Africk* to have his Ordination approved of by the Bishops there, who considering of the Scandalousness of his Proceeding, confirmed *Cornelius* his Ordination, and condemned his, and their Example was followed by the Bishops in other Parts. He was afterwards publickly condemned, and thrown out of the Church, by a Synod of Sixty Bishops, convened by *Cornelius*. But however still he continued to avow his Principle, That none who had apostatized should ever be restored to the Church, which afterwards he enlarged to every grievous and wilful Sin, thereby becoming the Head of an Heresie and Schism, which kept up in the Church for several Ages, by a Succession of schismatical Bishops, there being in several Cities, one Bishop of the Orthodox, and another of the Novatians.

CPSIA information can be obtained
at www.ICGtesting.com
Printed in the USA
BVHW070041281120
594336BV00010B/748